KU-579-417

The Daily Telegraph

BOOK OF
MOTORING
ANSWERS

The Daily Telegraph

BOOK OF
MOTORING
ANSWERS

Honest John

ROBINSON
London

Robinson Publishing Ltd
7 Kensington Church Court
London W8 4SP

First published by Robinson Publishing Ltd 1997
This edition published 1998

Copyright © Martonlynn Ltd 1998

Illustrations copyright © John Paley 1998

All rights reserved. This book is sold subject to the condition that it
shall not, by way of trade or otherwise, be lent, re-sold, hired out or
otherwise circulated in any form of binding or cover other than that in
which it is published and without a similar condition including this
condition being imposed on the subsequent purchaser.

A copy of the British Library Cataloguing in Publication Data is
available from the British Library

ISBN 1–85487–585–X

Designed and typeset by Editburo, Lewes, East Sussex

Printed and bound in the EC

10 9 8 7 6 5 4 3 2

CONTENTS

INTRODUCTION

What you need to know about this book before you start reading and using it

This *Daily Telegraph* book gives you the answers to the most-asked questions about cars and motoring. How do I know this? Over the last four years I have replied to more than 16,000 letters. Most sought information. But many also provided it, particularly about older cars. So, whether you're worrying about your next MOT, or you want to know a bit more about a car that grand-dad owned in the 1920s, the chances are you'll find it in these pages.

Condition of Sale

You don't have to be in the motor trade to enjoy this book. You don't need to be an enthusiast, or even a car owner or driver. You don't even have to be remotely interested in cars. All you need to be is someone looking for an answer to a car-related question – past or present. While you're looking, I hope you'll also find plenty to amuse, stimulate and maybe even annoy you enough to write to 'Honest John' at *The Daily Telegraph*.

But, a word of warning. Since all this went to press long before you laid out your money for it, and since I could not know for certain exactly what was going to happen in the future, I can't guarantee that everything in this book can be 100% up to date. So, just like unwarranted cars at auction, you buy this at your own risk. Neither I, nor *The Daily Telegraph*, nor Robinson Publishing, nor anyone else mentioned or involved, will accept any liability whatsoever for any inaccuracies or the dating of any information in this book. Of course, unlike cars at auction, you can sneak a look inside and give it a 'read-test' at the bookshop, so you know exactly what you're getting before you make a bid to the cashier.

About the chapter headings

In editing around 15,000 questions and answers down to 1,000 or so,
I've had to categorise them. So what happened was that the chapter
headings more or less decided themselves. But that doesn't mean to
say a 'Starting and Running Problem' caused by a duff 'Catalytic
Converter' is going to be in both categories. Equally, a list of cars suitable for dog lovers won't appear under both 'Animals in Cars' and
'Horses for Courses'. I'm afraid I'll have to ask you to use your common
sense, a quality you obviously have in abundance because you thought
you'd better read this.

About me

I simply don't have the time to do much car dealing any more. But I still
get down to the auctions around once a week. And I have my own very
comprehensive computer databank of auction prices from the beginning of 1992 – so I always know exactly which way the market is going
compared to the past month, the past year, and up to six years ago.

My first contact with the motor trade was in 1959 when I started cleaning cars for Ron at Sports Motors on Orpington High Street. Ron's stock included a 1926 AC roadster at £225; a 1930 Austin Nippy at £90; a 1932 Lagonda 2 litre two-seat special at £225; a 1938 Jaguar SS100 at £275 (multiply that by somewhere between 100 and 250 to find out just what an investment some of this older stuff has been). Ron also had comparatively modern cars, such as a pair of 1949 Riley three-seat Roadsters, MGAs, TR2s, a Buckler, a Berkeley and a gigantic Buick. Sports Motors folded in 1960, but the murals done by Pete the Painter remain to this day, hidden behind the dry-lined walls of the carpet shop that replaced it.

I bought my first car in 1964, and did my first deal the year after when I sold it. The car was a 1959 BMW Isetta 300, spotted rocking gently on the roof of a fabric-bodied Alvis 12/50 saloon in Shire Ted's scrapyard. 'I can drive that when I'm 16,' I thought. The car was duly delivered on the end of a rope behind a 1938 Oldsmobile and, being the canny man he was, Ted gave me £2 back from my £20. Reconstruction began, and test runs were undertaken around the go-kart track in a neighbour's garden. On my sixteenth birthday the bubble burst forth onto the road. A year later I sold it for £60.

Further gains and losses were made on a 1959 Riley 1.5 bought for £250; a 1942 Ford Jeep bought for £20; a Thames Caravette bought for £175; a modified Minivan bought for £125; a 1949 Rover P3 bought for £40; and plenty of other tackle, including a Wolseley Hornet, a rear-engined Renault and a two-stroke Saab. Then, after writing the ads for a Newcastle-upon-Tyne Rolls Royce dealer, I got into advertising.

Four years of this was spent conveniently close to London's Warren Street where I shared bank, pubs and caffs with the car traders and did a few deals on things like Simcas, Minis, VW Beetles, 2CVs, Fiats and Alfas. Apart from acquiring a pair of 'D&AD' pencils, I have to admit I never really made it in adland. The recession didn't help. Then, deep in the midst of the Gulf War, I had a brainwave: I would launch a completely new type of car magazine about nothing but used cars. The aim was simply to set it going, and then flog it for £10,000 and carry on in the ad game; but instead I became locked into the penury of freelancing features for car magazines. Since this involved reporting on car auctions, watching wasn't enough. Before long, I was back to buying cars and turning them over – retail, trade or on commission – to convert the mag money into enough to live and drive on.

For four months I commuted between London, Amsterdam and Nice, working on pan-European launches for the Mazda Xedos 6 and RX7. Then it was back to buying and selling, writing a column in *Car Week* and an auction column in *The Telegraph* 'Motoring'. Life was moving along quite nicely. Then, at a Christmas party in a room above a pub in Soho, my editor Eric Bailey had an idea.

I'd arrived at the party fresh from an auction where I'd spent £17,250 on three Vauxhalls in the space of twenty minutes, then moved them on to earn a mere £250 each. Eric thought, '£250 a car. He's far too honest for that game', and 'Honest John' was born.

In the ancient tradition of all agony columns the first questions were made up, and they ran on the back cover of *Telegraph* 'Motoring' in the issue of 21 January 1995. The response was phenomenal. Within months, I was answering up to 140 genuine letters a week. By year three, the weekly mailbag sometimes hit 500, and what you'll find in this book is a distillation of the most interesting of these, which by now total more than 16,000.

AIR CONDITIONING

Warming-up time

" *I am in my eighties and use my Citroen BX every day, but I seldom drive more than about five miles at a time. The car has stood up to this punishment remarkably well. Because of the short journeys, it becomes nicely warm in winter just as I am about to leave it. If I buy a car with air conditioning, will I have this problem in reverse? In other words, does a car with a/c take as long to become cool in a heat wave as my BX takes to become warm in an icy spell?* "

No, because the air in an air-conditioning unit is cooled by a compressor in the same way as that in a refrigerator, and the effect of air conditioning will be felt within a minute in the form of an icy blast from the dashboard air vents. It takes a while for a car to become warm because the engine block has first to heat up sufficiently to heat the coolant enough to open the thermostat and allow the hot coolant to circulate through the heater matrix. However, there is a neat answer to this, which is to heat up the engine coolant before you get into the car. A device which does this is the electrical mains-operated Kenlowe 'Hotstart' – a combined immersion heater and circulation pump at around £150 (tel: 01628 823303). This has the added benefit of enabling you to start a warm engine – improving oil circulation, reducing condensation and greatly reducing engine wear.

Air con

" *I wonder if you can assist me in sorting out the air-conditioning system on my car. It is a 1994 Peugeot 405GLXTD which came with standard air conditioning. This recently stopped working, so I took the car to my local Peugeot dealer for repair. The Peugeot dealer, in turn, referred me to a Ford dealer which apparently deals with all types of air-conditioning systems. I was amazed to receive an estimate of some £700 because the condenser and dehydrator needed replacing at a cost of £500 for parts alone. I have been advised that damage to the condenser is a common problem on the 405 because it is located in a vulnerable position between the radiator and the grille. Could it be better protected once re-installed without affecting its performance?* "

Make sure your aircon is maintained as part of the regular servicing of the car, otherwise problems with the system are inevitable.

Speak to the specialists listed in my reply to the next question. The location of the unit behind the grille may have led to premature corrosion from salt spray. The answer is to keep it clean. It worries me that your Peugeot dealer referred you elsewhere. Air-conditioning systems need servicing, with an annual check and a full service every two years. If the dealer has not been doing this as part of the regular servicing of the car, problems with the system are inevitable.

Air pros and air cons

" *As one of the many who bemoan the loss of headroom and the increase in noise due to the silly British obsession with sliding roof vents, I'm interested in having air conditioning retrofitted. Can the compressor be declutched when out of use? Is there a minimum engine size below which air conditioning should not be considered? Is retrofitting aircon a practical, sensible idea? Currently, I drive a VW Vento TDI, bought on your recommendation, which I am very happy with. However, a trip down to southern Spain for the Ryder Cup last year convinced me of the need for improved cabin cooling.* "

In a car with good torque characteristics (like your Vento TDI) you will hardly notice the effect of engaging the aircon pump. I torture-tested an unladen (but still heavy) VW Sharan TDI 110 up-hill in summer, switching the aircon on to see if I could feel the 'parachute effect', and I hardly noticed anything at all. Where you will feel a drag is if the car is relatively weak on torque for the amount of weight it has to pull along, particularly if it is an automatic. W124 Mercedes 230TE autos could be real slugs in this respect, especially when loaded to the roof as so many are. But where a car is adequately endowed with torque the effect of the aircon on economy is likely to be less than that of opening the sunroof fully, and certainly less than opening the windows as well. The pump is clutched or declutched to the pulley when you switch the aircon on or off. Remember, airconditioning systems need to be serviced at least every two years and this will add around £75 a year to a car's service costs. It also needs to be used throughout the winter, but repays you because it is excellent for de-misting. Two retrofitting specialists are Motor Climate (0121 766 5006) and Alpinair (0181 204 9633, who may ask you to take your car along to their premises at 174 Honey Pot Lane, Stanmore, Middlesex so they can investigate to see if they have a system which can be fitted to it). Two other specialists are: Vehicle Air Conditioning Services of Unit 3, The Circuit Centre, Avro Way, Brooklands Industrial Park, Weybridge, Surrey KT13 0YU, tel: 01932 355825, and Vehvac Ltd of Fircroft Way, Edenbridge, Kent TN8 6AJ, tel: 01732 868080. Though the aircons fitted to a Seat Arosa 1.4 automatic and a Ford Ka 1.3 did not feel unduly burdensome, I would think twice about having air conditioning retrofitted to a car with such a small engine.

Not choking

" *I have no realistic alternative but to travel across London by car for up to an hour each day. Seeing cyclists and motorcyclists wearing 'smog masks' I wonder how much in the way of particulates I am breathing in every day. Can smog filters be fitted to the air intakes of any car? Or do I have to sit in my car breathing smog?* "

Lots of recent models, including Alfa Romeos, Citroens, Fiats, Ford Mondeos, Mercedes C Class, all Saabs, most Vauxhalls, and VW Polos, Golfs and Passats, come already fitted with pollen filters. But there may be no need to change your car. George Smart (FS) Ltd, of Bankside Industrial Estate, Falkirk FK2 7XL (Directory Enquiries don't list a phone number) offer kits to install activated carbon air intake 'eco filters' for many makes of car. Vehvac Ltd (tel. 01732 868080) also offer a range of pollen and pollution filters, odour treatments and air-conditioning systems.

Don't get steamed up

" *I have a high-mileage Astra 1.7 estate, bought when it was two years old. Unless I drove it with a partially open window, the amount of condensation generated inside meant that a dangerous amount of misting up occurred. This I cured totally by replacing the pollen filter which had completely clogged up. I wonder how many other models have this problem? I had not realised my car even possessed one.* "

Mondeos do for one. I have mentioned this elsewhere but see no reason not to mention it again. If your car continually steams up, the first thing to do is find out if it has a pollen filter and, if so, change the filter. These can need changing as often as every six months.

ANIMALS IN CARS

Doggy belts

" *Can you recommend a good harness to restrain dogs in cars, one which can be attached easily to the rear seat belts?* "

This was in the first edition, but it's one of the useful lists which are worth repeating. I appealed to dog-loving readers, who recommended either a full harness or, at a pinch, a simple clip by which the dog's collar can be attached to a seat belt. Harness suppliers are: NL Dog Services, 9–11 Peckover Street, Bradford BD1 5BD (tel: 01274 722000), they offer the only BSI-approved product, at £37.50; Harry Irving & Co., Hi Craft House, Sandy Road, Liverpool L21 1AG (tel: 0151 928 2487), which seven readers recommended; and Care Necessities of Rose Hall, Frinton Road, Thorpe-Le-Soken, Essex CO16 0PH (tel: 01255 861324). In most cases, a separate strap is available to harness the dog without using a seat belt, and a lead can be attached when out of the car. The supplier of the simple clip is Hollyjack Products, PO Box 99, Staveley, Chesterfield, Derbyshire S43 2YZ (tel: 01246 450855), price £7.50.

Unguarded moment

" *I recently paid £40 for a dog guard for my Fiat Panda. But within a very short space of time, my dog had chewed his way through the mater-*

ial and was back amongst the children in the back seat. I think this item should have been described as a luggage guard, not a dog guard – unless it was designed for toothless dogs. Can I get my money back? "

Under the Sale and Supply of Goods Act 1994 you should be able to get your money back, as the guard was clearly not 'of satisfactory quality' in that it was not 'reasonably fit for the purpose' it was sold to meet. But you may have a fight on your hands to get your money back. First stop should be the Trading Standards Office which covers the locality of the supplier.

Doggy wagons

" *As a dog exhibitor and the owner of a Peugeot 405 estate I would like to make a few points about the design deficiencies of modern estate cars. First, the slight slope of the rear window of the Peugeot catches the sun and makes the rear compartment intolerably hot in the summer. Since the car comes with standard air conditioning it has no sun roof which could be left partially open to vent the car in these conditions. Second, there are no hooks to tie anything down in the back of the car – extraordinary for an estate model. Third, the pins which hold the rear seat in place protrude dangerously into the load area when the seat is down. They could easily damage a large dog's skull or rib-cage if the dog fell against them. I do hope you can publish this, and perhaps take a look at estate cars in general from the point of view of dog owners, as I am sure many of them read* The Telegraph. "

Thank you for these observations. Peugeot has taken heed of your complaint and the 406 estate has loadspace tie hooks and 'U'-shaped rear seat latching points – as well as three lap and diagonal rear seat belts. I've published this list before, but here is an updated version showing how some other estate cars fare for dog lovers and those carrying children.

- Audi A4 Avant: tie hooks, no pins, 3 × 3-point belts.
- BMW E36 3-Series Touring: tie hooks, small protected pins, 2 × 3-point belts.
- Citroen Xsara: tie hooks, no pins, 2 × 3-point belts.
- Citroen Xantia: tie hooks, no pins, 3 × 3-point belts, suspension lowers which helps older and smaller dogs jump in.
- Citroen Berlingo Multispace: tie hooks, small pins, 2 × 3-point belts.
- Daihatsu Move: no pins, 2 × 3-point belts.
- Daihatsu Grand Move: no pins, 2 × 3-point belts.
- Fiat Marea Weekend: tie hooks, no pins, 2 × 3-point belts.
- Ford Mondeo: tie hooks, exposed pins, 3 × 3-point belts.
- Honda CRV: tie hooks, 2 × 3-point belts.
- Land Rover Freelander 5 door: tie hooks, 3 × 3-point belts.
- Mazda 626: tie hooks, no exposed pins, 2 × 3-point belts.
- Nissan new Primera SLX: tie hooks, no exposed pins, 3 × 3-point belts.
- Mercedes A Class: tie hooks, no exposed pins, 2 × 2-point belts, completely removable rear seats.
- Peugeot 306: tie hooks, semi-exposed latches, 2 × 3-point belts.
- Peugeot 406: tie hooks, no pins, 3 × 3-point belts (option of rear-facing 6th & 7th child seats).
- Renault Megane Scenic: tie hooks, no pins, 3 × 3-point belts, completely removable rear seats.
- Renault Laguna: tie hooks, no pins, 3 × 3-point belts (option of rear-facing 6th and 7th child seats).

- Seat Cordoba Vario: no exposed pins, 2 × 3 pint belts, but deep rear sill.
- Skoda Felicia: tie hooks, exposed pins, 2 × 3-point belts.
- Suzuki Wagon R: tie hooks, no pins, 2 × 3-point belts.
- Suzuki Baleno: tie hooks, no pins, 2 × 3-point belts.
- Toyota Corolla: tie hooks, no pins, 3 × 3-point belts.
- Toyota Avensis: tie hooks, no pins, 3 × 3-point belts.
- Toyota RAV4 5-door: tie hooks, no pins, 2 × 3-point rear belts, low rear loading sill and completely flat floor when the rear seats folded.
- Vauxhall new Astra: tie hooks, no pins, 3 × 3-point belts.
- Vauxhall Vectra: tie hooks, no pins, 3 × 3-point belts.
- Volkswagen Golf Mk III: no hooks, exposed pins, 2 × 3-point belts.
- Volkswagen Passat: tie hooks, exposed pins, 2 × 3-point belts (3 × 3-point belts optional, covers for exposed pins available).
- Volvo V40: tie hooks, no pins, 3 × 3-point belts.
- Volvo V70: tie hooks, no pins, 3 × 3-point belts.

4×4 doggy wagon

" I am a long-time Volvo Estate car owner and presently run a 'K' reg. 240 Torslanda. I am considering changing to some kind of 'off-road' vehicle, such as a Jeep Cherokee or a Land Rover Discovery. I need a general-purpose vehicle to cover 12,000 miles a year, with folding seats as I have to transport two Springer Spaniels. The vehicle will probably be 'M' or 'N' reg. I have no experience of 4×4s, so would appreciate your comments. "

The best compromise for dog lovers who need only limited off-road capability is the Toyota RAV4 five-door.

A Discovery is great if you need to travel long distances on bumpy, rutted, unmade tracks in comfort. Nothing beats it at this. A Jeep Cherokee is better 'on the road', and is powerful with the 4 litre engine, but does not have much space inside. I think the best compromise for dog lovers who need only limited off-road capability is the Toyota RAV4 five-door. The rear sill is low, so dogs can easily jump in. The rear seat double-folds, allowing side access for the dogs if required. And the vehicle drives more like a car than any other off-roader apart from the Honda CRV. The RAV4 is even reasonably abstemious at the pumps. I averaged 27.97 mpg – and that was in the automatic version.

'Cat' and dog situation

" My 'L' registered Ford Escort Estate, not yet 3 years old with 26,412 miles on the clock, has just needed a new catalytic converter, catalyst ASV and gasket. I know from reading your agony column that short journeys are not good for these 'cats', but, although I do a number of high mileage journeys, my first trip every morning has to be one of two and a half miles to exercise my rather large dog. All my previous Ford Escorts ran on Four Star petrol and I had no such trouble. I am considering trading this one in, but for what? I should add that I'm not in the market for an expensive car. "

Fortunately, there is an excellent answer – in the form of the Skoda Felicia 1.9 GLD diesel estate with power-assisted steering and a three-year warranty. The Felicia is based on the VW Polo floorpan, and has a VW 1.9 litre diesel engine, but labour rates in Czechoslovakia are lower than in Spain where the Polo is built and some of the saving gets passed on to buyers. One thing you will need to do is cover up the rear seat locating pins if you drive with the seat

down and the dog in the middle of the car (VAG
has an accessory for this). A harness attached
to the seat belts would also be a good idea (see
above; also available from petshops.)

Dogliner

*" I carry a couple of Jack Russells in the back of my hatchback. Do you
know of any firm that specialises in waterproof and dog-hair-proof covers
for the rear area of a hatchback? "*

Yes, Hatchbag Ltd, which has a 24-hour
brochure hotline on 0151 639 5396. The company makes a range of hatchback boot liners,
waterproof slipover seat covers and fully tailored
waterproof seat covers. Another supplier is UK
Covers on 01869 242224. For heavier carrying,
you need an 'Armadillo' boot or load-area liner
– and these are available through accessory
shops and many franchised dealers.

BODYWORK, APPEARANCE AND INTERIOR

Aggravating alloys

" *Where can I get the corroded BBS alloy wheels on my car restored to their original appearance?* "

Most alloy wheels can be restored by Spit & Polish of Tonbridge, Kent (01732 367771) or Wheelbrite of London (0171 431 9015) for £30–£50 each. Unfortunately, the only way to restore genuine BBS RS101 3-piece alloys is to send them back to BBS in Germany for new rims. But if the wheels are the more common Speedline BBS modular wheel 'copies', fitted to many Audi 80s and 90s, they can be restored, but the studs are an extra 30p each.

Chips and scratchings

" *In the past you have mentioned firms that specialise in removing minor dents, painting in stone chips, and repairing damaged windscreens. Any chance of a quick reprise?* "

For minor dents of the supermarket carpark va-

It's often better to repair a bonded windscreen than to replace it, because removing the old one can damage the car body leading to leaks and rust.

riety, call Dentmaster (0800 433687), who will put you on to their nearest operator. For stone chips and upholstery repairs try Chips Away on 01482 665484. For repairs to cracked or scratched plastic bumpers, call Plastic Technik on 01296 682105. For plastic trim and upholstery repairs call Magic Mend on 0800 901 902. And for chipped windscreens, call Glas Weld Systems on 0800 243 274, or 01372 362362 in the South-East. On modern cars with bonded windscreens this is better than having the entire screen replaced, because removing the old one can damage the car body leading to leaks and rust. (Autoglass, Auto Windscreens and many others offer a similar service.)

Play 'Misty' for me

" *On these cold and miserable winter days my Rover suffers severe misting-up, of the rear window in particular. The heater takes ages to have any effect. Is there such a thing as an internal windscreen wiper to wipe away the condensation? Or do you have a better idea?* "

The rear screen heating element should get rid of normal condensation, but severe condensation is usually caused by an accumulation of moisture inside the car due to a leak. Many car owners fail to realise that car doors contain a waterproof membrane between the door structure and the trim. If this cracks or tears through ageing, water passing through the doors drips through the trim and dampens the carpet. Other sources of dampness inside a car are a leaking heater matrix or hose joint, faulty roof aerial seal, faulty door seal, faulty front or rear screen seal, blocked sunroof drain pipes, and blocked scuttle drain pipes. The coachbuilder

Bauer came up with a novel idea for heating the plastic rear screens of its BMW cabriolets – a small electric fan heater. (A common cause of poor ventilation is a blocked pollen filter, which needs to be checked regularly and may need replacing every six months if the car spends a lot of time in traffic.)

Blow over

" *I have an 8-year-old Golf GTi 8-valve in faded, patchy Tornado red (largely due to neglect). The car has done 70,000 miles and remains a delight to drive, so I thought it was time for some cosmetic treatment. As well as the faded areas, there is blistering on the scuttle and tailgate. How do I choose a good bodyshop to do the work, preferably in Wales where garage charges are in the £15–£20-an-hour bracket, and how much should I expect to spend?* "

According to Barry Ragg of Garage and Engineering Supplies (which supplies Standox paints – tel: 0121 766 7878) you could pay between £400 and £2,000 for the respray alone. Unlike repair garages (until the new EU environmental directives bite), paintshops generally charge £15–£20 an hour, so there's no need to go to Wales. Best save the cost of transport by looking locally, where evidence of workmanship will be parked on the streets. You'll get the finest result from an air-dried base coat topped by a baked lacquer, which means finding a paintshop with a car-sized 'low bake' oven. You should also look for a 'VBRA Approved' sign somewhere on the premises. The blistering on the scuttle and tailgate bothers me, as the metal will almost inevitably be perforated directly under the blister and the only way to repair this properly is with fresh metal. You should wash the car every fortnight in winter, preferably with a jet-wash that allows you to blast the salt off from underneath – otherwise the rust problem will accelerate rapidly.

Self-preservation

A number of readers wrote to me with their recommendations for rust prevention. One of them felt that the best way to preserve his 1984 Renault 4 was to use Waxoyl – re-applied after a jetwash every spring and re-injected into cavities every few years. Four technically-minded readers pointed out that cathodic protection requires a complete circuit, which in turn requires the metal to be immersed in water. (This could be why the recommended place for zinc sacrificial anodes is at the door bottoms – one of the wettest, most rust-prone places on a car.) In providing a very complete explanation, Dr H. McArthur reminded us of his book, *Motor Vehicle Corrosion Prediction and Prevention on Vehicles (1950–Present Day)*, which covers this subject in some detail and is available from Dr McArthur at 18 Rawlins Close, Woodhouse Eaves, Nr Lough-borough, Leicestershire LE12 8SD, tel: 01509 890607, price £10 inc. p & p. What everyone agreed with was that the best way to keep car corrosion at bay was to jetwash winter road salt off, only garage the car when it is perfect-ly dry, and use a dehumidifier or 'Carcoon' (0161 737 9690) to keep the car dry in the garage. (The 'Carcoon' saves energy by keep-ing the car dry rather than the whole garage, barn or warehouse.)

Time for a touch-up

" Do you have any tips for touching-up paint chips? When I have finished, my car normally looks like it has the measles. "

Methods of touching-up paint chips depend on the colour and whether the paint is metallic protected by a lacquer. In general. though, if the car is a solid colour, I just use a well-shaken touch-up bottle and brush, and I'm very careful not to allow too much of a blob to run down the shaft of the brush. Some traders use a technique known as 'blocking'. After allowing the touched-up stone chips to dry, they then go over the panel with the very finest 'wet-and-dry' on a cork block – and follow up with a good resin polish.

Application time

" *I agree with your reader who recommended Waxoyl as a car body preservative. The problem comes in applying it. The various plastic pumps which fit the large-size cans get badly bunged up very quickly – especially if the Waxoyl is not warmed before attempting to apply it. Does anyone make a decent metal Waxoyl sprayer, costing about £20, which can be taken apart and cleaned?* "

Best I could find was a Sealey wax injection kit, from Transpeed Ltd, 213 Portland Road, Hove, East Sussex BN3 5LA, tel: 01273 774578; but the price was £73.95.

'Chamois' or 'Shammy'?

" *Many years ago, at the Ideal Home Exhibition, I purchased a synthetic wash leather. It has proven to be far more effective than any genuine 'chamois' leather, but is now nearing the end of its days, and I have been unable to locate a source of supply for another. Can you help?* "

Two exhibitors at this year's Motor Show had just the thing: the 'Liquid Magic Supershammy' from First Choice Products Ltd, 21 Hospital Road, Pontypridd CF37 4AH, tel: 01443 403531; and the 'Synthashammy' from Bay 6, 22 High Street, Brinsley, Notts NG16 5BN, tel: 01773 765575. However, one reader who bought a 'Synthashammy' found that, while it was very absorbent, 'it leaves water droplets all over the car'. Kent Chamois Company markets a wide variety of car cleaning and polishing products through accessory shops and is very proud of its high-quality genuine chamois. If you want one and can't find one, contact Kent Chamois Company Ltd, PO Box 16, Tunbridge Wells, Kent TN3 0JZ, tel: 01892 837070.

Dirty engine

" I own a 1988 VW Jetta GTi which I purchased new in September 1988 and which now shows a total mileage of 72,000. The bodywork and mechanicals of the car are in very good condition, with the oil changed every 6 months and the cambelt changed at 60,000 miles. In contrast to the gleaming bodywork, the engine compartment looks somewhat grubby due to VW's recommendation that it should never be steam-cleaned as this would remove protective waxes. But is there any form of cleaner I could use? "

You should see the engine compartments of our VWs. Filth and surface corrosion over the tinny bits everywhere. If I was you, I would follow VW's advice and not clean the compartment itself. But you could clean the engine block, gearbox and final drive casing with a proprietary 'brush-on' degreaser as long as you don't use a heavy spray or steam cleaner to get it off and as long as you don't clean any protection from the sump pan. Also possibly worth doing is to remove the cam cover, timing belt cover and radiator fan shroud, wire-brush the rust off, and give them a re-spray. I haven't bothered with ours because I don't have the time, but that's no reason why you shouldn't. If you're keen on the car, why not join the GTi Owners' Club (only £20 a year). Send for a form to Sean Grenyer, Club GTi Membership, PO Box 2747, Brighton BN1 2NP.

Wet-wash

Further to an item on 'dry-washing' a car, a reader from Romford has written to recommend a means of 'wet-washing' a car which involves no hosepipes and is very economical on water. It is the 'Washmatik' brush which he has

After washing your car, it's a good idea to rinse it with rainwater from a water butt, using a watering can with a rose sprinkler.

owned for 25 years and which is still available by mail order from W. E. Selkin of Nottingham (tel: 0115 923 2286) at a price of £22 for the full kit, including post and packing. Two tips are: add Triplewax to the bucket of water you use to wash the car initially; and rinse off with rainwater from a water butt, using a watering can with a rose sprinkler. (A *Telegraph* Reader Offer which may still be available is a 225 litre water butt with lid and 'Rain Saver' drainpipe adapter for £32.95. Credit card orders: 01245 326001.)

Mam knows best

" *My old mam had the answer to David Taylor's tar removal problems. In the good old days, she always removed tar spots with butter. It is an excellent, non-corrosive loosener and solvent for tar. Take a dab of butter on a cloth or piece of kitchen roll, then gently massage the offending patch until the surface is free. A quick wipe over with a good detergent solution removes the fat. It works on any surface, but not leather since this soaks up the butter and leaves a stain.* "

A lot safer than the other suggestions of petrol and methylated spirit – especially for smokers. (If you have any doubt about the effect of petrol on tar take a look at the road surface after a car with a fuel leak has been parked over it.)

Minor blemishes

" *You recently advised me as to the cause of some minor blemishes on the paint of my Honda Civic. I'm pleased to say that my Honda agent has put me on to an excellent cure. It is 'Buffer Fine' creme by Autosmart of Lynn Lane, Shenstone, Staffs WS14 0DH, tel: 01543 481616. Autosmart also offers 'Carnuba Wax' which, to my mind, brings up a shine superior to the resin Autoglym. 'Carnuba Wax' also takes out some of the marks.* "

Thank you for this. Autosmart also does a very pleasant-smelling carpet spray, branded 'Apple Fresh', and Mitsubishi's valeters use this. However, Autosmart is a trade supplier, so private individuals may have to 'do a deal' with a local garage or valet firm to secure supplies. You can also buy a clear plastic product known as 'Armourfend' to coat areas of a car vulnerable to stone chips – and, since it is virtually invisible, it may be preferable to those hideous plastic 'car bras' sold in the USA and Australia. For more information on 'Armourfend', call 01992 642642.

Screen clean

Three readers in a week have asked for a good windscreen cleaner. The best I have found is 'Mer' at some accessory shops or by mail order from Worldwide Marketing and Promotions Ltd, Unit 1, Coulsdon North Industrial Estate, Station Approach Road, Coulsdon, Surrey CR5 2UD, tel: 0181 763 2480. Apply in the dry and use Marigold gloves because this stuff can have a nasty effect on your hands. I also like Mer polish which is particularly good for bringing up oxidised or dirt-ingrained solid colours such as red or white.

BRAKES, CHASSIS AND SUSPENSION

Roll-away Citroens

" Am I right in thinking that some time ago 'Telegraph Motoring' covered a feature on the Citroen car whereby when the car was parked on a slight incline it was liable to move unaided? If so, I would appreciate more information on this matter. "

With early manual-gearbox Xantias, it was possible to park the car and leave the brake only half on. The car would seem to be braked, but as the suspension settled, tension came off the cable and the car could roll away. Though the problem was the result of drivers not applying the handbrake properly, Citroen announced a free recall and simply took some teeth out of the handbrake ratchet so that the lever now flops back down again unless it is properly applied. When parking any car facing downhill, it's always sensible to leave it in first gear (or 'P' with an automatic) and to point the front wheels towards the kerb.

Sticky brakes

" I bought a 'Ford Direct' Mondeo 24v a year ago and it has now covered 15,000 miles. During the recent cold weather and after an overnight cold soak, I found that although the handbrake lever would flop down the brakes

remained firmly locked on. The supplier advises this is a common Mondeo problem, but I have never come across it before. If water can get into the system and freeze up, it seems to me to be a basic design weakness. **"**

Occasional hard braking helps keep rear brake disks clean and dry.

The 24v (also tagged the V6) and the 4×4 were the only Mk 1 Mondeos with rear disc brakes. What probably happened is that you pulled gently to a halt without the rear disc pads actually touching the rear discs and clearing them of moisture. You then applied the handbrake, which clamped the pads onto the rear discs with moisture remaining between them, which then froze. You can't do what I'm about to suggest in icy conditions, for obvious reasons. But otherwise a bit of hard braking will bring the rear pads into play and help keep the rear discs clean and dry.

C-class brakes

" *I own an 'M' reg Mercedes C180 automatic, bought secondhand, but with a full Mercedes agent service history. One day in February I lost all servo assistance to the brakes. A mechanic came out (under the Mercedes Touring warranty) and soon diagnosed that the vacuum pipe had come loose from the servo unit and damaged the throttle cable adjuster underneath. I contacted Mercedes but they would not admit that this amounted to a design defect, suggesting that faulty workmanship by someone had led to the pipe becoming detached. The previous owner denies this. So is there a design defect?* **"**

I think that the pipe coming loose is a 'one off' that could have happened with any car. But there has been a problem with the Mercedes Brake Assist system giving unwanted assistance. Because of this, a recall was issued and the system was temporarily disconnected on 170,000 cars worldwide. It took a lot of 'catching up' for the manufacturer to produce enough modified components, and some owners had to wait a year before this could be fitted and their 'Brake Assist' reactivated.

How to store brakes

" *I recently became concerned when a friend told me of problems with the rear brakes of his C250D automatic. These began when the car had done a mere 25,000 miles and cost around £1,000 to correct. I own an 'M' registered Mercedes Benz C220D automatic, and I expressed my concern to Mercedes Benz in Milton Keynes who wrote back to tell me that rear brake discs are a wearing item and, as a general rule of thumb, would need to be replaced at the same time as every third set of pads. MB also gave me advice as to how to store a car when it would not be used for a few months – as had been the case with my friend's C250D. The advice is to put the car away 'dry' by taking it for a run in dry conditions and applying the brakes several times quite hard in order to ensure that any moisture on the discs themselves evaporates. MB also advised leaving the car in 'P' with the handbrake off, increasing the tyre pressures to 58 psi to prevent 'flat spots', storing the car with a full tank of diesel to leave little room for condensation in the tank and either charging the battery fully, and then again every month, or leaving it on a continuous 'trickle charge'. What do you think of all this?* "

Very sound advice. To see what happens to a disc brake stored in damp conditions you need only look at the discs of a motorbike left parked in the rain. Within a week, the discs will be red with rust. This problem is compounded on the rear discs of cars because the brakes themselves do very little work. On the front, a couple of applications of the brakes cleans the surface rust off the discs. But on the back the pads often don't touch the discs – particularly on a gently driven, lightly-braked car. The result is that the surface oxidation eats into the discs, score marks develop, both the discs and the pads become grooved, and braking efficiency becomes sufficiently impaired for the car to fail its MOT handbrake test. So the advice to do a bit of hard braking and get both front and rear brakes nice and hot before you put your car away is something you should do every time you garage it. All the other advice about storing a diesel car is very sound – but if the car has a petrol engine and a plastic petrol tank, damage from condensation is not a problem. It will be easier on the car's suspension and safer from the point of view of expansion of the fuel tank contents during hot weather to store the car with a nearly empty tank. A trickle charger, such as the Airflow Battery Conditioner, which can be left permanently connected, is a good idea (01635 569569).

Unbrakable Bentley

" Five years ago I purchased a 90,000-mile Bentley T1. Last summer, after 20 miles on the motorway, the pedal went almost to the floor. Next day, at the garage, the brakes worked perfectly. Then two months later, the same problem recurred. A different mechanic diagnosed the problem immediately. What had happened is that the rubber inside the flexible sections of brake pipe has expanded inside the steel braiding. The brake fluid sent to the brakes under pressure is then unable to return, the brakes heat up and the fluid vaporises – leaving the car with little or no brakes. When everything cools down again the brakes once again feel normal. New flexible brake pipes solved the problem. "

Good tip about the brake pipes.

Dodgy discs

" I have a 1990 SEAT Ibiza 1.5. During the last 12 months and 12,000 miles it has gone through no less than four sets of front discs and pads –

each lasting only around 3,000 miles before severe judder is felt. The garage assures me that it does not have any problems like this with other cars fitted with the same make of non-SEAT parts. Can you advise me what the problem might be? A friend says the hubs might not have been machined properly so the discs are not exactly at 90 degrees to the hub centreline. "

Either your friend is right and the discs are very slightly out (a decent machine shop would soon find out and skim them true on a lathe). Or the 'anti-rattle springs' have been lost from the callipers and, with nothing to keep them properly in place, the pads are moving around in the callipers causing uneven wear to the discs.

Skimming the customer

" Further to the question and answer 'Dodgy discs' (see above), what the reader needs is a good Mazda dealer. At Lodge Garage of Aylesbury (01296 770405) we have had a V.B.J. on-or-off-car brake disc skimming lathe for over ten years. It is a wonderful bit of kit and has saved us, our customers and local Rover owners a fortune. Starting at £57 plus VAT per pair, the job represents excellent value for money and complete accuracy. "

There we are. A franchised dealer properly equipped to save his customers money. Though the letter came from the garage boss, it still qualifies Lodge Garage for an entry in the 'Good Garage Guide' starting on p. 321.

Warped minds

" I had a problem of wheel wobble with a Cavalier. The dealer's explanation is that disc warping was caused by heavy braking, then leaving the brakes applied so that the hot pads remained in contact with the disc itself. A lazy driver might, for example, brake heavily for a roundabout, find himself delayed by traffic with priority and, instead of applying the

handbrake, simply hold the car on the footbrake. This is particularly true of drivers of automatics. **"**

Thank you for providing an excellent reason for drivers getting off their footbrakes while stationary.

Running out of brakes

" *Our car is an early 1993 Cavalier 2.0iGLS automatic. On holiday in North Devon, after a short and moderate descent on the A39 near Lynton, the brakes failed on a slow approach to a hairpin bend. My wife, who was driving, managed to bring the car to a halt on the handbrake, after which the engine went dead and all the warning lights came on. My wife thinks that the brake pedal went to the floor. We completed the descent on the handbrake and called the RAC from a place of safety. The patrolman, who arrived with commendable promptitude, regarded this as a common occurrence on this particular hill and blamed excessive use of the brakes vaporising the brake fluid. I could not reconcile this with the gradient in question, which was slight compared to others negotiated during the week, and the car was not being driven 'hard'. The front pads were inspected and considered adequate, so we continued on our way. On our return, a more thorough check was made, no faults were found, but the brake fluid, previously changed six months ago, was replaced again as a precaution. The car has since completed a further 100 miles without trouble, but the incident is slightly worrying and your advice could be very helpful.* **"**

To descend a steep hill in a four-speed automatic, you should lock it in 'D2', or even 'D1' where the gradient is extremely steep.

All the warning lights came on because the engine stalled. At a guess, what may have happened is that during the preceding week you overheated the brakes on numerous occasions and this led to the failure on the comparatively gentle gradient. It was very wise to renew the brake fluid. But to descend a steep hill in a four-speed automatic such as yours, you should lock it in 'D2', or even 'D1' where the gradient is extremely steep. Simply leaving it in 'D' and relying on the brakes alone would overcook them – especially if the car was heavily laden for a holiday. This is explained in Vauxhall owners' manuals.

Discs and pads

" My wife purchased a Fiesta 1.4 16v Zetec S and has been delighted with its power and road-holding. Then, last Sunday, with 18,000 miles on the clock, I decided to check the front brake pads. I was shocked to find that, though the pads were okay, the discs themselves were worn and ridged. My wife took the car to the Ford agent for inspection and was told that the wear was quite normal, the brakes were safe, but the discs would need replacing at around 25,000 miles. This, to me, is absolute rubbish. Can you please give me some advice. "

The best brake pad material for general use and life contains asbestos. But, because asbestos dust is a known carcinogen, the material is no longer used in brake pads. The only generally effective replacement is a harder pad material against a softer brake disc, and the result is that brake discs now wear. Front brake discs wear more quickly when they are comparatively small or non-ventilated and the rear brakes are drums. Soft discs are also more affected by surface corrosion which can lead to the ridging you have noticed. Front discs seem to wear particularly quickly on Kas and post-1995 Fiestas.

Worn brakes

" I own a 1992 Saab 9000 CDXS automatic which has recently completed 55,000 miles. At its last 12,000-mile service I was informed that the ventilated front discs had worn down to 25 mm and should be replaced when they reach the recommended minimum of 24.5 mm. Is this a characteristic peculiar to Saabs in general, or 9000s in particular? My previ-

ous cars – mainly Volvo 240s and 940s – notched up 60,000–90,000 miles without seeming to need new front discs. **"**

See the explanation given under 'Discs and pads' above. A life of 55,000 miles is now slightly better than average for a five-year-old automatic. The other problem that has cropped up is that softer rear discs are less resistant to corrosion than the harder discs were. Rear discs don't do much work on cars weighing less than around 1,250 kg and, unless a car so fitted is braked hard fairly regularly to clear off surface corrosion, the rust will eat into the discs, lumps of it will score the pads and the rear discs may well fail the car's first MOT.

Anti slip-up

" *I have a Volvo 480ES, which is fitted with ABS – a feature which, until very recently, I had no occasion to use. This meant I was not prepared for the loud 'chattering' noise which accompanies its operation. This happened on black ice and caused me to release the brakes momentarily before re-applying them and I ended up stopping just four inches from the car I had been skidding towards. My Volvo dealer agreed that ABS made 'that sort of noise', but surely it is extremely distracting and owners ought to be forewarned.* **"**

A recent report in the USA concluded that owners of cars fitted with ABS were more likely to have accidents than owners of cars not so fitted. Part of the reason was that they were unprepared and consequently unable to use it, and part was driving in the belief it would save them. What ABS does is detect wheel lock-up under braking, releasing the brakes until the tyres can grip normally. What happened in your case, as will often happen on sheet ice, is that the ABS will not find anything to grip on, and the 'chattering' will continue until it does or the car comes to a stop having hit something. I would suggest that owners of all ABS-equipped cars who have not experienced ABS in operation find a quiet lane with an uneven or wet surface, ensure there is nothing behind, and, from about 15 mph, put their brakes on hard so they can experience the effect. Then, on a wet day, find a deserted car park or disused runway, and practise swerving while braking without releasing the brakes. Always remember, while ABS may help save you in the wet, it won't on continuous sheet ice, and often won't on thick snow because it prevents the car bulldozing a wedge of snow in front of the wheels.

Coastal ABS failure

" *Last month I faced a bill of £1,200 to get my five-year-old Peugeot 405 estate through its MOT. This was the cost of purchasing and installing a new ABS brake system. Such systems are intended to last the life of the vehicle. I have taken the matter up with Peugeot in the hope that the company would assist towards this colossal cost as a gesture of goodwill. After discussions with what passes for 'Customer Relations' it swiftly became apparent that Peugeot does not feel inclined to take responsibility for its products after the warranty period has expired. Is it unreasonable to expect a French car company to have a sense of fair play?* "

Your 405 was probably assembled by British workers in Coventry. But what you have not told me is how often you have had the brake fluid replaced during your five-year ownership of the car. Brake fluid is hygroscopic (it absorbs moisture) and Penzance can be a very wet place. Moisture in the brake fluid can lead to premature corrosion inside the ABS master unit. Other readers living in coastal areas have reported the same problem, so, to be on the safe side, I recommend anyone who keeps an ABS-equipped car to have the brake fluid changed every year rather than the recommended every two years.

The problem with ABS

" *I put my 1989 Ford Granada in for its MOT last week and it failed due to a complete lack of braking effort on the rear wheels. The fault was traced to an electronic part of the ABS unit, for which the replacement cost is around £1,000. It is strange that the system is not 'fail safe', providing non-ABS braking to the rear should the ABS fail. In view of the number of Granadas on the road, this must be a matter of concern.* "

All Granada models, from 1985 on, had standard ABS and because of this the brake fluid should be replaced every year or corrosion could result inside the ABS distribution pump. This pump costs between £832 and £1,878, plus VAT, depending on model and year. You're facing the same problem hitting many owners of cars with 'first generation' ABS. The cost of replacement units can be more than the car is worth. Your other option is to find a specialist who can re-build the braking system to work without ABS – but you will need to get insurance approval for this work.

Rock 'n' roll Xantia

" *I have a Citroen Xantia 2.0i 16v VSX, first registered in 1996 and purchased from a Citroen agent at 12,000 miles. As you know, the VSX specification includes 'soft' and 'firm' selections for the self-levelling Hydractive suspension. In the 'firm' position the suspension does appear to give a firmer ride, but generates a high level of roll at speeds up to about*

30 mph – particularly on winding roads and roundabouts. This roll takes the form of an initial lurch, most noticeable when going from one lock to the other, and gives rise to complaints from passengers. I have discussed the problem with the Citroen agent, but get rather huffy comments such as 'you need to get used to a Citroen', or 'your last car [a Renault 21 TXi] was very firm'. How can I properly test the suspension? "

The VSX has an additional sphere to control roll stiffness and you bring this into effect by pressing the button next to the suspension height control. The thing I noticed when I first drove a VSX quickly was that all my bits and pieces on the passenger seat had stopped falling off – so this is a good test as to whether or not the VSX's level of 'active roll control' is working. The Citroen Xantia Activa takes this system a stage further – all but banishing roll entirely. However, it is possible that height sensors can be maladjusted and linkages can seize up on these models [which turned out to be what had happened in this reader's case]. The Xantia also offers 'passive rear-wheel steer' (the rear suspension is bushed to twist slightly as cornering forces build up). This cuts the amount of understeer (which you will have experienced in handfuls in your Renault 21). As a result, the Xantia requires a slightly different driving technique from the Renault – which is to use less steering lock and to straighten up earlier. If you apply the same amount of lock as you did with the Renault, you are, in effect, 'over-steering' the Xantia and it will lurch.

Kept in suspense

" *I have a Vauxhall Astra 1.4i, purchased new in August 1992, and serviced every year by the Vauxhall agent. It has now done 13,000 miles. A* friend told me he had heard of a fault on the control arms of the front suspension, so I raised this query when the car was left for its annual service in August 1997. The reply was that nothing goes wrong with the control arms unless the car has been jacked up by them. I fail to see how I can make sure that this doesn't happen when the vehicle goes into a workshop or a tyre fitter gets his hands on it. Half my mileage is on motorways, so I am very concerned. Should I pay to have new control arms fitted? **"**

A modern car should never be jacked up by its suspension arms or by its engine sump.

You're right to raise this, and it should be a matter of concern for anyone running an Astra or Cavalier built from the mid-1980s. Quentin Willson brought our attention to the potential problem during a BBC 'Top Gear' television broadcast, and it is correct that the control arm can be damaged by incorrect jacking. You should be able to trust the Vauxhall dealer on this point, but if you want a second opinion take the car to an MOT testing station and ask for it to be checked there. Modern garage hoists either raise a car on a pair or ramps or, for suspension repairs, by the car's four jacking points. A modern car should never be jacked up by its suspension arms or by its engine sump as this can completely throw out the suspension geometry.

Ball joint

" In February 1995 I purchased a new BMW 316i Compact, and all necessary services and inspections have been carried out by the BMW agent. In January of this year I arranged for a service and the car's first MOT at a mileage of 14,533. The car failed its MOT for a badly worn tyre on the nearside caused by a defective ball joint in the nearside front suspension. Replacement parts were supplied free of charge, but, in view of the low mileage and the fact that the car has never been kerbed or potholed, I felt that either BMW or the agent should foot the entire repair bill. I welcome your opinion on this. **"**

I think it's disgraceful that, when you put the car in for the pre-MOT service, the agent did not pick up the faults which later led the car to fail the MOT. Any half-competent independent garage would certainly have done so. As for liability for the repair, your car was under BMW's one-year manufacturer warranty followed by a two-year dealer warranty. The terms of the second- and third-year warranty are limited and you received what they provide for. The other factor is that it's very rare for a ball joint to wear to the extent this one has and one of the causes could be putting excessive strain on the joint while the car was stationary, which is all too easy when power steering is fitted.

BUYING AND SELLING

'Ex-management'?

" *When I bought my six-month-old 'ex-management' VW, I was initially a bit surprised that it was not in the condition I expected an 'ex-management' car to be in. I discovered the reason why when I received the V-5 registration document with the first owner listed as 'Hertz'. Many of the faults have now been rectified, but I am still waiting for the second immobiliser transponder keyfob and the original service book. I refuse to regard a duplicate service book as acceptable.* "

You obviously missed my tip published in June 1996 which warned readers to assume any car described as 'ex-management' to be ex-rental unless they were provided with a written assurance it was not. VW has confirmed that your car was sold to the dealer as a 'Hertz Buyback'. The alarm/immobiliser is a 'Logic' aftermarket fitting. If the second transponder cannot be obtained from Hertz, the dealer can order one for you simply by opening the transponder you have and quoting the number inside. If the original service book cannot be found, you get a duplicate and have it stamped up to corroborate whatever services the car has actually had. Whether you are within your rights to reject the car depends on whether you can prove it was mis-described to you in writing (on the order form or in an advertisement) and whether you made obtaining the second transponder and the original service book part of the contract. If you can prove the car was mis-described, then it may be possible to have the dealer prosecuted under the Trade Descriptions Act and you should be able to get redress in a civil court. The mere threat of this usually resolves the matter.

Dealer terminations

A considerable number of readers have written to complain that the franchise of their local Audi, Fiat, Rover, Volkswagen or Volvo dealer has been withdrawn and service facilities either 'consolidated' at a larger dealership further away or transferred to a 'satellite' service facility owned by the larger dealer. There are two main reasons for this. One is an EU Directive aimed at ending 'block exemption' by early next century. This is the means by which manufacturers appoint franchises and only supply new cars through these franchises. The other is rationalisation. The Daewoo chain of wholly-owned car sales centres has opened manufacturer's eyes to the basic inefficiency of selling cars through franchises owned by outsiders. By eliminating middlemen, some of the manufacturers believe they will either make more profit, or have better control of the profit they do make in an increasingly competitive situation. The casualties of this process will be hundreds of known and loved (as well as hundreds of known and unloved) local dealerships. But, if they get their acts together, these should be able to remain in business as independent sales and service specialists, and their continued success will be based on the prices and service they offer rather than any local monopoly they may have once had.

Pricey guides

" *I usually buy and sell my cars privately, using ads in my local press or a regional motoring weekly. In order to establish the correct price I use one of the monthly car price guides sold by newsagents. However, I have noticed that, for identical vehicles, there is considerable disparity in the values suggested by the various guides. How are the values calculated and which is closest to Glass's Guide, the trade 'bible' unavailable to mere mortals.* "

'*Parkers*' used to be the best of the news-stand guides and is now owned by EMAP – which also owns the CAP (Current Auction Prices) *Black Book*. The news-stand guides differ from *Glass's Guide* and the CAP *Black Book* by giving a price for a private sale. *Glass's* merely gives trade and retail for a year, plate and mileage plus mileage adjustment tables. The *Black Book* gives values for 'retail', 'trade clean', 'trade average' and 'trade below average'. *Glass's* tends to work back from the prices dealers think cars should fetch, whereas CAP's *Black Book* tends to work forwards from auction prices achieved. *Glass's Guide* is available to the motor trade on subscription for £200 a year (01932 823823) and the CAP *Black Book* for £195 a year (0870 122 221).

Static Stag

" *When her husband died, an elderly lady friend was left a car which she now wishes to sell. It is a 1971 Triumph Stag automatic, which I presume must be a 'classic'. It was last MOT tested in January 1988, and resprayed at about the same time. My friend is wary of advertising it in case she attracts an unscrupulous buyer. Can you please suggest a reliable method of disposing of the car?* "

I would normally suggest an auction, but this is a non-starter if the car itself is a non-starter.

Standing for eight years is likely to have played havoc with the Stag's very sensitive cylinder heads and there could well be extensive corrosion inside the engine. For this reason, your best source of disposal is likely to be the Stag Owner's Club, c/o John Craddock, The Old Rectory, Aslacton, Norfolk NR15 2JN, tel: 07071 224245, email: stagmemsec@compuserve.com

Ford Direct

" I wonder if you could kindly explain the Ford Direct system and the benefits to be derived therefrom. We hope to purchase a secondhand Mondeo in February next year with reasonably low mileage, but having rung the Ford Direct Helpline I'm still none the wiser. "

'Ford Direct' is the brand name for used Fords, usually less than a year old, which Ford has retained control of. They are basically the pick of ex-rental, ex-company demonstrator, ex-management, ex-press fleet Fords which go through a re-finishing process at a purpose-built factory on the quayside at Tilbury. They are checked over mechanically by RAC-accredited mechanics, then put through a bodyshop which removes every tiny scratch, scuff, ding chip and cigarette burn. When they emerge, they look 'as good as new', carry a 'Ford Direct' hologram badge and a comprehensive 12-month warranty. They are then offered to dealers via an on-line system at a fixed price which depends on supply and demand on the day.

Condition alert!

" Three years ago my wife bought a 'J' reg. VW Golf Driver. A few weeks

later, the police called to tell us the DVLA had advised them that the car had been an insurance write-off. They wanted to check it had not previously been stolen and that it was in sound, roadworthy condition. After we recovered from the shock, we were told that all was well. The car has performed superbly over two years and 20,000 miles, and the bodywork remains in excellent condition. My wife now wants to consider trading it in, so in view of the car's history how might she do this? Is it likely a reputable dealer would accept it, or is her only practicable choice to put it through a car auction and hope for the best? "

If the car was stolen and the insurer settled before the car was recovered there's no problem (this is what I think must have happened). But if the car was an insurance damage write-off, there may be. It will be on what's called the 'VCAR' or 'Condition Alert' register, which anyone can access by phoning HPI on 01722 422422, giving the car's details and paying £28.50 by credit card. If it is on the 'VCAR' register, the thing to do is to have the quality of the rebuild checked by Autolign (01604 859424) or Popplewells Alignment (01992 561571). This costs around £200, and if the car passes, you can then apply to have the car taken off the VCAR register and put onto the 'repaired' register. This is what a responsible dealer would do. If you put the car through an auction you will have to fill in a box stating whether or not the car is on the VCAR register, the auctioneer will read this out at the time of sale and the bidding will allow for it.

P.O.A.

" *Could you please explain the logic behind why so many car dealers advertise a car they have for sale, yet offer it 'P.O.A.' so that any prospective purchaser has to phone for the price?* "

One reason is that the car is at such a low price they don't want their competitors or the manufacturers to know they are undercutting the market. The other is to make you think this and phone them.

Coming clean

" *If a car has a fault which the dealer does not spot when assessing it for part exchange, should the customer point it out to the dealer? We recently part-exchanged a Honda Civic for a BMW convertible. The salesmen inspecting the Civic did not see some minor damage to the fibreglass front valence before making the p/x offer. But when we actually exchanged the car three days later, the sales manager accused us of damaging the Civic between the original assessment and completion of the deal and it has soured our relationship somewhat.* **"**

If you know of a fault, you should point it out. I try to when I sell cars, because not only is it the honest way to do business and the buyer thinks better of you for it, the buyer has no comeback over faults the seller has mentioned. There are also times when I simply have not noticed a fault, the buyer points it out to me before we do the deal, and I am extremely grateful because the deal is then done in full knowledge of the fault.

Leased of your worries

" In May, I will have the opportunity to lease-purchase a company car on a 3-year 36,000-mile full maintenance contract. I am considering a Golf GTi or a BMW 318 Touring. Could you give me your thoughts on the lease suitability of these cars and whether there are any similar alternatives I should consider? Could you also recommend a reputable and competitive leasing company?"

I'm not sure if you mean personal lease-purchase (sometimes available to employees of companies as an alternative to a company car) or a straightforward company lease. GE Capital Fleet Services of Central Park. Ohio Avenue, Salford Quays, Manchester M5 2GT takes the trouble to publish a Company Car Cost Calculator comparison every six months or so (tel: 0161 872 9020). This not only tells you the total annual cost of the car, but also your benefit tax situation. Once you get the Cost Calculator, you can make your own choice. Your alternative to this is a relatively new form of personal leasing. Where an employee is provided with a cash alternative to a company car, taking this route can work out financially advantageous after all tax implications are accounted for. Speak to Nick

Moger at Crown Leasing on 01487 773322; full address: The Green, Abbots Ripton, Huntingdon PE17 2PF.

BMW M635i

" *I need inside information on where and how to sell a reasonably rare right-hand-drive BMW M635 CSI, first registered in 1986, stored 5 years, every indication of a genuine mileage of 50,868, and in excellent condition. One BMW dealer merely referred to Glass's and said it wasn't worth much. But the MD of another BMW dealership said, 'never sell it. It's so rare you could get whatever you want for it.' But what ballpark is that? Is there a market?* "

I hope the first BMW 'dealer' was an independent opportunist rather than a franchise because something very similar happened to another reader last year. He was advised by a dealer in BMWs that his perfect 1986 320i Bauer Cabrio was worth no more than £1,000, but, on my advice, advertised it privately and got nearly £4,000. One way to achieve reasonably close to its true value is to put it up at a classic car auction. Call Robin Lawton or Marcus Ross at BCA on 01252 877317.

Auction buyers

" *I have heard of a service whereby, for a fixed fee, an expert can scan the car auctions of the country for the make and model you require. Do you have any information about this service?* "

You have probably seen an ad for Julian Trim & Co which has been offering this service for years (tel: 01747 838888). If you order a car, their buyers will buy it for you at a fixed fee of the hammer price, plus indemnity fee, plus 6% – and include checking all outstanding liabilities. Another 'buy to order' specialist is Douglas Coker on 0181 340 1868.

Buying the company Saab

" I will retire this year and believe that my company will offer me my final car. It is a three-year-old Saab 9000 CD Eco Power with 48,000 miles on the clock and has only been driven by me. I'd appreciate your suggestions as to whether I should keep it or swap it for something else capable of 10,000 miles a year. Having become accustomed to the power and the comfort of the Saab I do not wish to 'down-size'. "

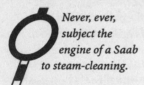

Never, ever, subject the engine of a Saab to steam-cleaning.

Take the car into a Saab franchise, pay around £70 for a thorough mechanical check, and try to purchase an extended used car warranty. If it is a 2.3CD Eco it's a great car, capable of 200,000 miles at high speed and up to 32 mpg as long as the oil is changed frequently. But LEX Reliability Surveys showed up a few problems with Saab ECUs and battery terminal corrosion (easily prevented by a careful owner). You can also expect to have to replace the catalytic converter at some time and readers havè alerted us to a few problems with Saab's direct ignition system. This, and the ECU, are covered by Saab's used car warranty, but not by some other MBI's. Never, ever, have the engine steam-cleaned.

Engineers' reports

" Your readers will find, as I did, that an independent engineer can inspect a car for around half the cost of the motoring organisations. I received a telephone appraisal the next day and a five-page report within 48

hours. The Institute of Automotive Assessors uses a standard 171 point checklist and, if your readers can't find one under 'Assessors' in the Yellow Pages, they can phone 01543 251346 for the number of a member operating locally. "

This is a fair point, but when the RAC or AA inspect a car there is a good chance of reasonable redress if they miss something. However, it is always better to have high-performance cars inspected by a specialist in that vehicle, preferably on his premises, and including individual cylinder compression tests.

Rental review

" *There is a far better way to check out a vehicle you are thinking of buying than to go with a salesman on a test drive. Hire if for a weekend – then any shortcomings would have become apparent.* "

Not a bad idea. Before the rental fleets became dumping grounds for unsold cars, manufacturers used to treat them as a way of introducing cars to prospective customers and they now seem to be coming back to this way of thinking. The variety of cars available for hire is much greater than it used to be.

North/South divide

" *Is it true that prices paid at car auctions are generally higher in the South-East than elsewhere in the country?* "

Only for part-exchanged stuff more than five years old. Some traders fill transporters at auctions in the North and bring the cars down to resell at auctions and out of *Auto Traders* in the

South. But if 'nearly new' and ex-fleet cars
fetched significantly more in the South, that's
where the fleets would sell them. For these cars
there is no general difference in price South to
North. However, a trend can start in one area
and take several weeks to spread to the others.

No sale

" My company Renault 19 16v was stolen while in for a service at my
local Renault agent. After it was finally pronounced unrecovered, I visited the same Renault agent to choose a replacement. But since the replacement car was to be leased and would not be sourced through that agent,
the agent was unwilling even to offer me a test drive. Not the case with a
VW agent who allowed me a helpful, no-conditions test drive even though
the Golf GTi I chose was to be sourced elsewhere. "

You have not pinpointed a difference between
Renault and VW – merely a difference between
a lousy Renault agent and a good VW agent.
The salesman in the Renault agent must have
been on a commission-weighted package, while
the salesman in the VW agent took the view that
even if he didn't land a sale, his garage would
probably get to service the car and earn something from it that way.

Low mileage MGB

" I have a 1978 'T' registered MGB which I have owned from new and
which I now wish to sell. It is yellow, in perfect condition, has been
garaged from new and only used for a couple of months each summer –
hence its mileage of just 13,000. I get The Daily Telegraph regularly, but
don't know how to go about advertising the car in it. "

I could not accurately value the car without seeing it. But, though it is the less desirable 'rubber bumper' model, if it is in perfect condition and has wire wheels and overdrive, it could be worth as much as £10,000. I'd bear that in mind and run a colour photo ad in the next 'Forecourt' on the back of *Daily Telegraph* 'Motoring'. Suggested wording: '1978T MGB Roadster. 13,000 miles only. Dry garaged. Summer use only. Perfect condition. For sale by original and only owner. Offers invited.' Tel: 0171 538 6005 to place the ad. You may or may not get £10,000, but an 81W MGB LE with wire wheels and 12,500 miles once sold for £13,158 including buyer's premium at BCA Blackbushe. The closer to summer you sell, the higher the price is likely to be.

5TDS to MX5

" I have a 1994L reg BMW 525TDS SE with 66,000 miles, full BMW service history and in very good condition. I am looking at a 1990G Mazda MX5 with 42,000 kms (an import), RHD, PAS, aircon, new tyres, new alloys, kick-plates, one UK owner, one year's MOT, rear spoiler and in very good condition. The deal is the Mazda plus £2,800 for my BMW. Is this a good deal? And will there be any problems over the kph speedometer? "

This reminds me of a deal I witnessed while I was polishing cars at Sports Motors on Orpington High Street in 1959. Young punter turns up in a big, solid Standard Vanguard Phase IA Estate Car (very rare nowadays) and part-exchanges it plus cash for a tiny Berkeley sports car. I was only eleven at the time, but I thought he was mad (I kept my mouth shut, of course). You're in the same shoes. You have a big, solid, reliable car which will probably last for ever and you're thinking of swapping it for a personally imported small sports car with a UK-illegal speedo, an ECU which only interrogates in Japanese and no means of checking its history. A final word of warning – older MX5s can suffer rot in the sills and those kick plates are a very convenient way of hiding it. At the very least, get the Mazda inspected and look under those kick plates before you buy.

Minimising selling risks

" My wife wants to sell her beautiful 'British Open Classic' Mini – December 1992K, 10,000 miles, vgc, etc. Please could you give any tips about selling privately. What is the form, for instance, on test runs – should the potential buyer be allowed to drive (obviously not alone)? And what is the best method of payment to avoid bouncing cheques and forged fivers? While no private vendor can be expected to give a guarantee, is it wise to insert a phrase such as 'as seen' in the receipt? "

When selling your car privately, take the number of telephone inquirers and call them back.

I'd try it in the local paper and be prepared to negotiate. If you get no bites, spread the net wider to include a national such as *Top Marques* which has a section for this sort of car. I'll now repeat some advice printed in the column a couple of years ago. You can reduce the security risk to yourself by insisting on taking all callers' telephone numbers and addresses, then calling them back (never give your address or the location of the car to a first-time telephone caller). This helps avoid the car being stolen on the test drive or while parked on the street. Insist on seeing the driver's insurance certificate before letting him or her drive – and remember, the other driver's insurance only provides third party cover to drive your car. Don't go for a test drive with more than one 'buyer' in the car unless they're a couple and, if you drive first, keep hold of the key when changing drivers. As for payment, if it is to be by 'building society cheque', insist on seeing the purchaser's pass-book with the amount of the cheque deducted from their account. If by 'bank draft', only accept this during banking hours when you can telephone the bank which issued it. If by cash, meet the purchaser at a bank, exchange the money for your car's V-5 registration document in front of the cashier, and bank the money straight away. Yes, do insert the phrase 'as seen, inspected and tested' in the receipt and get the purchaser to sign it.

Creative accounting?

" I recently agreed to buy a 'nearly new' current model Rover 416Si and my eight-year-old Rover 216GSi was accepted in part exchange. However, when I received the invoice for the car, though the 'bottom line' had not changed, both the invoice price for the new car and the p/x allowance for the old car were reduced by £750. Have I been the victim of some sort of VAT scam? "

The 'nearly new' car will have been what's know as a 'qualifying car', which means the dealer can reclaim the VAT element of the price he paid for it, but must then pay the VAT element of the full price he sells it for. Your part-exchange is a 'margin car', which means the dealer only pays the VAT element of any profit he makes on reselling it. For stock-keeping reasons, the dealer may have decided to trade the old car out rather than retail it, in which case he may have had to let it go for less than the original part-exchange allowance. Since he can't claim back the VAT element of the loss, it made better sense to reduce the purchase price of the new car by the amount he lost trading out the part-exchange.

- Dealer buys 'nearly new' car in for £9,750 (VAT = £1,452)
- Dealer stickers 'nearly new' car at £10,750 (VAT = £1,601)
- P/X offer for 'G' reg. Rover £2,750
- Trades P/X out to trader at £2,000
- Reduces 'nearly new' car to £10,000 (VAT = £1,489)
- VAT saving £ 112

Customs & Excise don't lose from this because if the trader trades the P/X on for the original £2,750, he is still liable to pay the VAT element of his 'margin' of £750 – which just happens to be £112.

High-miler sought

" I would like to buy a secondhand high-mileage ex-fleet car with a complete, bona fide, cast-iron service history. Could you advise of some reputable dealers who specialise in this type of sale?"

In the South-East, The Great Trade Centre, 44–45 Hythe Road (off Scrubs Lane), White City, London NW10, tel: 0181 960 3366. (Turn North from Western Avenue up Wood Lane past the BBC TV Centre.) Or Venture, at either 333 Western Avenue, London W3, tel: 0181 752 3000 or 80 Ruckholt Road, London E10, tel: 0181 988 5000. The Great Trade Centre is very cheap and stocks 2,000 cars, but requires a deposit for car keys and imposes a £31 sales charge. First find a few cars you may be interested in, then enquire as to whether or not they have full computer print-out service histories before asking for the key. Venture is more like a switched-on franchised dealership with attentive salespeople and free access to 200–300 cars which are usually a bit more expensive. One tip: ex-Vauxhall Masterhire, ex-EVR and ex-Leasecontracts cars leased on full service contracts have comprehensive service histories. Vauxhall even changes the cambelts of petrol-engined Masterhire cars at between 35,000 and 40,000 miles.

One-owner Alpine

" I have owned my 1967 'D' reg. Sunbeam Alpine Mk V since new and it has now covered 51,000 miles. The time has come to offer it for sale and I would appreciate your advice as to the best method of doing so. As you will realise, I don't sell cars very often. "

The Alpine was a very pretty sports tourer based, believe it or not, on the floorpan of the Hillman Husky/Commer Cob van. It's the footwells of this floorpan that go first. But yours looks to be in exceptionally good condition, so is likely to be highly coveted by a member of The Sunbeam Alpine Owners' Club, PO Box 226, Grimsby DN37 0GG. If this proves to be an over-estimate of its collectability, then try a £20 photo ad in Classic Car Weekly (tel: 01733 238855), or in the Telegraph's growing classic car classified section (tel: 0171 538 6005). In your ad, stress heavily that you are the one and only owner, that the car has done just 51,000 miles, and that it comes with full history. Ask £5,000.

Minor matter

" I have inherited my late wife's estate and one of her assets is a 1957 Morris Minor 1000 de-luxe four-door saloon with a genuine 45,661 miles. It has only ever been owned by her and her father before her and I have

*the original invoice for £707 15s 9d. I wonder if you can inform me of what
price to ask for the car and the best method of sale?* **"**

You could offer it to Bob at Morri Spares (01992
524249), to Charles Ware at The Morris Minor
Centre (01225 315449), or to 'wanted' advertisers in *Morris Minor Monthly* magazine (yes,
there really is a Morris Minor magazine). There's
also The Morris Minor Owners' Club, PO Box
1098, Derby DE23 8ZX, tel: 01332 291675. Or, for
a quick result, try the £20 photo ads in *Classic
Car Weekly*. *Practical Classics* magazine (essential reading) values the model at between £1,650
for an average to good car to £2,700 for a Minor
in top condition. If you want to try an auction,
call BCA Blackbushe on 01252 878555, or, more
local to you, H & H on 01925 860471.

Mega-milers in the North

" *Recently you recommended several garages in the South which specialise in relatively young high-mileage cars. Are there any in the North-
East? I am looking for a high-mileage diesel.* **"**

Jack Ford Ltd specialises in ex-police cars, many
of which – such as Vauxhall Astras, Peugeot
306s and Peugeot 405s – are diesel. Even BMW
325TDSs should soon be coming off one of the
forces. Jack Ford is at Unit 5, Brunswick
Industrial Park, Brunswick Village, Newcastle-
upon-Tyne NE13 7DA, tel: 0191 236 6333. If you
fancy combining a visit to the Cotswolds with
buying a car, you could also try one of West
Oxfordshire Motor Auctions ex-police car sales
which are held in the evening twice a month at
Witney, tel: 01993 774413. Remember, though,
police cars do not require MOTs, so if you buy

one at auction more than three years old you will need to get it through an MOT before you can register it to drive away.

Auction 'buyers' premiums'

" *I recently purchased a car at British Car Auctions and my bid of £5,250 was supplemented by an additional fee of £111. I have paid an auction indemnity fee before – warranting good title, that the car has not been an insurance damage write-off and, if the mileage is warranted by the vendor, warranting the mileage for up to four days. This used to be about £50 for a £5,000 car and, since a full HPI check costs just £28.50, I think the £111 is excessive. The mileage of the car I bought was not warranted and this was reflected in the price I paid. But I later discovered it had been clocked by 50,000 miles and I reported the workshop responsible to Trading Standards. Despite all this, I am satisfied with the car as I still saved more than £1,500 on forecourt prices.* "

The time limit to check a car's warranted mileage at auction has been extended to seven days.

Buyers' premiums rather than Indemnities have been applied at BCA auctions since April 1997 and this is clearly indicated on the summary of terms and conditions displayed on the auction hall wall. Leaflets explaining the buyers' premium are also available to both the trade and the public. I'm pleased to note from these that the time limit to check a warranted mileage has been extended to seven rather than the previous four days. The charges are on a sliding scale rather than a direct percentage and are different for private as opposed to trade buyers. However, when you buy your catalogue, you can ask the cashier what the buyers' premium will be for the price range you intend to buy within. The reason why the scales are not displayed on the walls is that, seeing the difference, a private buyer might embarrass everyone by pretending to be a trade buyer. By no means every trader buying from BCA has a BCA account card, so this alone could not be used to define the distinction. You reported the workshop for a non-crime. It is not illegal to alter the mileage reading on a car. It is illegal for a trader to sell a car with an undisclaimed incorrect mileage reading unless he can prove he has shown due diligence in checking it. The disclaimer stickers over odometers of cars on used car lots cover the trader during the period the mileage is being checked with past owners – a process which can take weeks.

Collecting it yourself

" *I would like to recommend the option offered by Mercedes Benz to collect your new car directly from the factory in Germany. This is entirely free of charge (£150 for a partner to accompany you) and includes Business Class flight from London or Manchester, taxis from airport to hotel and hotel to factory, dinner, bed and breakfast in a 5-Star hotel, a superb welcome at the MB reception centre, a film of the history of MB, a factory tour, all documentation and a personal hand-over with thorough briefing by an MB engineer, full tank of fuel, five days' comprehensive insurance, and return to the UK by ferry or Shuttle. I collected my new Mercedes Benz C180 estate car in this way and thoroughly enjoyed the experience.* **"**

This is a good introduction to a new Mercedes and any UK MB dealer can arrange it for you; but it does, of course, involve paying the UK rather than the German price for the car.

Coded messages

" *You might like to warn your readers that when buying a secondhand car they should check that all security codings come with the car. We bought a Honda Concerto some years ago. When the battery went flat, I* *removed it to re-charge it and activated a security device. The selling dealer had no idea of the codes and I had to go back to Honda to get them. The previous owner of the car said he had passed on the codes with the car, and also that his newer car's alloy wheels lacked the special tool to remove the security bolts.* "

Don't buy a late-model Fiat without its 'Red Key' and code card. If these are missing, a new security system could cost you more than £600.

This is sound advice. Ask the salesman for any security codes, and if he says none are needed ask him to record this on the invoice as a condition of sale. Never buy a late-model Fiat without the infamous 'Red Key' and code card because, if these are missing, it can cost you more than £600 for a new security system. If the car is fitted with alloy wheels, make sure the key or a special keyed tool comes with the car. Obviously, you won't even be able to drive a keycoded Citroen or Peugeot away without keying in the correct code, but you can then change this to suit yourself at a later date. Radio codes are a little more difficult because the previous owner may have changed them, the radio might not be able to tell you what they are and, if you disconnect the battery without using a 'slave battery', your only recourse may be to have the radio re-coded by a re-coding specialist (see their advertisements in *Trader* magazines).

UK car price rip-off?

" *I have recently returned from three months' holiday in Australia. Could you please explain why in Australia you can buy a Ford Mondeo (made in Belgium) with air conditioning for only £10,000 while the equivalent model in the UK costs £14,000. Also the Mazda 323, called the 'Festiva' in Oz, is only £5,500 compared to £7,500 in the UK. It seems to me that the UK is literally being taken for a ride with its prices versus Australia, Europe and the USA.* "

The official import system in the UK prevents independent importers bringing in more than 50 of any vehicle which is not European Type Approved in any one year. And it is difficult (but not impossible) for UK private buyers and independent importers to source cheaper, Euro Type Approved RHD cars from continental Europe. The fleets like it this way because they buy more than 60% of new cars sold in the UK, usually at even lower prices than new cars are sold for in Germany, France, Spain and Australia. But they want the private market to think that these cars are much more valuable so that private buyers will pay high prices for them once they end their lives on the fleets. If mass market manufacturers ended fleet discounts, they could probably drop their 'list' prices by 25%. (The joke about company cars is that company drivers pay benefit tax based on the list prices of these cars, not what the cars actually cost.) German manufacturers and importers like the over-hyped UK market because they don't give such big discounts to fleets, and charging £3,000–£6,000 more for a car in the UK brings them £2,500–£5,000 more profit before VAT. That's why VW appealed to the European Court of First Instance against its £70 million fine and block exemption penalty by the European Commission for frustrating cross-border trade.

Into 'the trade'

" I am now retired and am taking up more seriously my love of buying cars at auction. This means eventually selling them on if there is not to be a traffic problem in my driveway. In other words, I will be trading. Can you put me in touch with any trade associations? Also, I need to be able *to get trade insurance cover for the cars and access to* Glass's Guide. *Could you advise me on how I go about doing that?* "

I very much doubt that the Society of Motor Manufactures and Traders would accept someone trading from home as a member. But give them a call on 0171 235 7000. You will need to register for VAT (advice line: 0345 343 343). It will help to obtain account cards for use at the main auction houses such as BCA and CMA. This entails maintaining a balance of at least £10,000 in the relevant bank account, but brings benefits such as lower buyers' premiums. For trade insurance, try ABM on 0181 681 8986, Norton Insurance Brokers on 0121 246 5050, or Road Runner Direct on 0181 660 6666. *Glass's Guide* is £200 a year from Glass's Customer Services on 01932 823823. To take cars away from auctions on the day of purchase you will also need a trade licence from your local VRO (£150) but you will need to show books to prove you have traded some cars first and they will want to come and inspect your premises. Finally I'd better warn you that making an honest living by buying at auction and selling on to the public is far from easy these days.

Midlands high milers

" *In the past you mentioned The Great Trade Centre and Venture as being good places to find a high-mileage ex-fleet car with bona fide service history in the London area. Where can I find them in the Midlands? And why did you so clearly favour Vauxhall cars?* "

Try Arriva Used Vehicle Sales, London Street, Smethwick, Birmingham B66 2SH, tel: 0121 558 5141; Motor Nation, Mackadown Lane, Garretts

Green, Birmingham, tel: 0121 786 1111; Car Supermarkets, A5 Watling Street, Cannock, Staffs (1 mile from M6 J11), tel: 01543 506060 or 0990 289227. Auctions are another good source. I mentioned Vauxhall Masterhire cars because most of these are leased on a full service contract, and when Masterhire disposes of them it supplies a full service print-out with each car.

Montego trade-in

" *I have a May 1992 'J' registered Montego LX, which has electric front windows and sunroof and is in excellent condition with only 33,500 miles. I now wish to change to a smaller car with a reasonable boot and power steering. Can you suggest a suitable two-year-old replacement?* "

A cheap, booted replacement is a Daewoo Espero 1.8CDi. On the basis of auction prices, a two-year-old, complete with air conditioning, should be yours at a dealer for £5,000 and an 18-month-old one for £6,000. Another low-price possibility which is actually quite a good car is a Proton Persona 1.6XLi.

Lease brokers

" *I am the proud owner of what I believe to be a modern classic – a 1992 Saab 900 LPT convertible. A new job entails 30,000 motorway miles a year, for which I need a comfortable mile-eater for up to around £15,000 secondhand. Ideally I would like to let someone else enjoy the Saab for a couple of years on a low-mileage lease deal, without giving ownership, rather than lock it away in a garage. Does anyone broker such arrangements?* "

Yes, then he steals your car. A few years ago a mate of mine nearly lost his Porsche 911 this way. He signed it away on the lease deal and received the first monthly cheque. Then nothing. Because he's a blacksmith's son, whose childhood toys were a club hammer and an anvil, no one with any sense messes with him, and he managed to get his car back before it was resold or broken up for parts. But it was touch and go. The fact is, your car could be in Russia within a week at any time during the 'lease' and you have no control over what happens to it. Forget the idea.

Going for broker

" *I would like to buy a new Toyota Corolla. I understand that 'car brokers' can get you the car cheaper than car dealers. Please kindly give me the names and telephone numbers of a couple of brokers.* "

Steve Tokatlian at Quote to Quote on 0171 603 9999 (6 lines) and Pat Lawless at Carfile on 01335 360763/360022 (9.15-5.45), 0410 081984 (evenings and weekends). Neither ask for a deposit.

Auction caution

" *I don't always read your column – some of the terms used are a little too advanced for me. But I was fascinated to read about the prices quoted at BCA car auctions. Would you be kind enough to advise on the dates and locations of these sales? The only trouble with auctions for the inexperienced OAP is that I might finish up with an expensive lemon.* "

There are so many auctions up and down the country that your best bet is to refer to the lists in *Honest John's How to Buy and Sell Cars, Used Car Buyer* magazine or *Parker's Guide*. The top auction houses are BCA, CMA and NCA. But

The safest car auctions for the public to buy at are manufacturer sales of 'nearly new' ex-rental cars.

there are bargains to be had at smaller evening sales such as West Oxfordshire Motor Auctions, Witney, which specialises in ex-police cars. The safest auctions for the public to buy at are manufacturer sales of 'nearly new' ex-rental cars. But, even then, you will be bidding against the trade, who might take it upon themselves to run you up to the sort of money you would have paid at a 'nearly new' specialist anyway. The next safest are designated fleet sales such as Vauxhall Masterhire or EVR which give full service histories of the cars on a computer printout. By no means all fleet cars are sold with such full histories but ex-fleet cars are usually safer than cars bought at general auctions. Designated part-exchange sales can also be good, but carry rather more risk. At general sales, the cleanest, most polished cars are for sale by auction traders against whom you may find yourself bidding for the trader's own car. Most of these are genuine part-exchanges bought by traders, cleaned up and re-offered, and if a trader has had a car on his hands for too long, he may be prepared to let it go at little or no profit. But you have to be careful.

How to sell a car

" *I have been trying to sell my father's car since he had a stroke. It is a Mitsubishi Galant 2.0GLS, which I know has been regularly serviced and has a true 22,000 miles on the clock. I thought I would have no trouble at all in selling a luxurious car in such good condition, especially since Mitsubishi has such a good reliability record. So I advertised it in the local press and in Auto Trader magazine for around £2,000 but have had no response whatsoever. What am I doing wrong? Or, more pertinently, what should I be doing to sell this car which seems to have all the 'bells and whistles'?* "

You don't give the age of the car, which doesn't help. But the main reason why it's not selling is that most people don't know what it is. Take a whole roll of snapshots of the car, both at three-quarter angles and side-on, against a neutral background such as the sky so that the shape will stand out in a small size on poor-quality newsprint. Pick the best photo and place the ad in the 'Luxury' section of your local *Auto Trader*, headline it '22,000 miles for £1,995', then give the rest of the details.

Pre-delivery briefings

" *In November 1997 you gave credit to Renault for coming up with improvements to its Scenic model. I'd like to give credit to a Renault dealer. Having placed an order for a Scenic, I thought I would like to familiarise myself with a driver's manual before I took delivery. I suggested this as a general pre-sale service in a letter to Paul Davis, MD of Davis of Sevenoaks, and sure enough he responded very graciously – thanking me for taking the trouble to write. So top marks to Davis of Sevenoaks.* "

This was a simple but very sensible idea. Readers subsequently wrote to tell us that Howards Nissan, Peugeot, Citroen and Rover agents of Weston-super-Mare and numerous Renault dealers do this as a matter of course, while Audi dealers supply an introductory video prior to delivery.

The right 'Solution'?

" *My wife has a two-year 'Solutions' personal contract purchase deal with VW on a 1996 Polo 1.4CL. The contract finishes at the end of February 1998 and the terms allowed for up to a total of 30,000 miles. By the end of February the car will have only done 15,000 miles, and though our MGFV final payment is £4,019, the garage estimates it would offer £7,500 in part-exchange for a new Polo on a similar scheme. I am trying to persuade my wife that it would make more sense to loan ourselves the £4,000, pay ourselves back over 18–24 months, then sell and go for a one-year-old secondhand car. Due to changes at work our annual mileage will go up to around 15,000–20,000 miles a year. Do you think my suggestion is the best way forward?* **"**

Tricky one, this. Polos have held their value exceptionally well, so if you p/x in February on the dealer's best estimate your 'equity' in your present Polo is £3,481 against £10,205 for a new 3-door 1.4CL, 'on the road' before any discounts. So the total to finance is £6,724 which means you're looking at a difference of £2,705 to have a brand new car with new tyres, new brakes, new clutch, a year's VED and a new three-year unlimited mileage warranty. I'd be inclined to pin the dealer down to exact figures for a new Polo on 'Solutions' at your increased mileage or a new Polo for cash plus the equity in your current car and compare this with the lower cost but increased risk of continuing to run your present Polo to four years and 45,000 –55,000 miles. The beauty of PCPs on a slow depreciator like the Polo is that they do give you a genuine choice at the end of the contract.

Bits and pieces

I've been reminded of the existence of *Trade Sales Mag*, a weekly trade magazine which is an excellent source of secondhand parts. Other useful sections include towing services, secondhand garage equipment, garage businesses for sale, even jobs in the trade. Readers can obtain a sample copy by sending

£1 in 20p stamps or a postal order (no cheques – they cost 60p to cash) to *Trade Sales Magazine*, PO Box 2509, Rottingdean, East Sussex BN2 8SS, tel: 01273 308292.

How to date a car

" I will shortly be purchasing a new car and, after driving a number of different hire cars recently, I am most impressed by the Peugeot 306 diesel. However, I drive past the Peugeot assembly plant at Coventry fairly regularly and am struck by the thousands of cars stored out in the open. Presumably these are surplus production being stockpiled for later sale as brand new vehicles. For me this raises three questions. First, what effect does the cold, damp winter climate have on the performance and life expectancy of the cars? Second, is it possible to tell when a vehicle was actually manufactured from the VIN number? And, finally, for how long are vehicles stored in this way before being sold as 'new' cars? "

Many years ago, Steve Cropley (now Editor-in-Chief of *Autocar*) wrote a very brave story about this for *Car* magazine entitled 'The New Car Stockpile Scandal'. In 1991 a similar story appeared by Mark Bishop in Cropley's own *Buying Cars* magazine. These stories and the low prices achieved at auction for surplus new cars spurred the mass-market manufacturers into producing fewer cars. Most now claim to build only to order (customer order, dealer stock order, or fleet order). But it can be more expensive to close a production line down than to keep it running, which explains why there can still, occasionally, be surpluses. The cars you saw are more likely to have been awaiting despatch than simply sitting there indefinitely. And even ex-rental cars awaiting reprocessing into 'nearly new' cars are now stored on concrete hard standing rather than the mud

Many plastic components, such as ashtrays, carry circular roundels on their inner sides, from which the date of manufacture can be deciphered..

they used to sink into for up to six months. Exhaust systems and brake discs are the first bits to suffer from prolonged exposure. Shuffling the cars around creates a lot of condensation inside the engines and exhaust systems and kills off the batteries. Manufacturers can be very tight-lipped about the last six digits of a VIN number, but you can usually tell the model year from a VIN. With 'Just in Time' production you can also decipher the year a car was built from the year the glass was made which is etched onto the windows. Plastic components, such as ashtrays, carry circular roundels on their inner sides: the year is shown by two digits in the centre. The figures 1–12 are stamped clockwise round the edge of the roundel and the first of these not punched out denotes the month of manufacture. An alternative plastics marking is an oblong with the year shown at one end and the month shown in two bars of six. The first of these which has not been crossed off is the month of manufacture. In answer to your last question, storage is usually just a few weeks and is unlikely to be more than three months unless the manufacturer has a serious problem.

100-year-old car for sale

" *Please could you advise me how to sell an old 'Benz', the approximate date of manufacture of which was 1898? Also, do you have the names and addresses of any firms in the Reading area who could recondition an old Hillman car built in around 1928?* "

The auction houses Brooks, Christies and Coys seem to have done best with early veteran cars over the past year. Brooks: 0171 228 8000;

Christies: 0171 581 7611; Coys: 0171 548 7444.
Christies achieved some very high prices for
veterans in February 1998: 1901 Barre Type Y
(non-runner) made £15,500; 1899 Clement
Panhard £26,000; 1900 De Dion Bouton
£18,000; 1897 Panhard-Lavassor £130,000 (all
hammer prices before commission). Professional restoration of your Hillman may cost
no more than a few thousand, or may run to
tens of thousands. It is vitally important to establish a proper contract between you and the
restorer before work begins, as a disagreement
could involve protracted litigation. I have had
no dealings with the company, but The Vintage
Coachworks at Hartley Witney in Hampshire
is not too far from Reading; tel: 01252 842589.
The Hillman Owners' Club may also be able to
help; c/o C. Gore, 6 Askham Grove, Upton,
Pontefract WF9 1LT.

Holding the folding

" Why can't one go into any car dealership clutching a carrier bag full of real folding money and drive away in half an hour or so with the car of one's choice? I think I know why, but do you know why? "

> I can, same as at an auction. It's due to the simple fact that I have both trade insurance to drive any car, and licensed 'trade plates'. A member of the public needs to secure first an insurance cover note, then a VED disc for the car, before he or she can drive it away. Fiat and Nissan dealers are now 'on line' to the DVLA and, as long as the new car is insured, can register and tax it for you 12 hours a day, Monday to Saturday.

Negative equity in a car

" I wonder if you have ever come across 'negative equity' in a car? I purchased a brand new FSO Caro in February 1996 for approximately £6,000, putting down a £2,000 deposit and contracting to repay the balance, plus interest, over four years. I am now in the process of changing my job and decided to look at another car, but was advised by the garage (which had sold me the FSO in the first place) that they could not find anyone prepared to underwrite it and as a result could only offer me £500 in part-exchange. The finance company has advised me that to settle at the present time would cost about £2,000, so I now have 'negative equity' in my car to the tune of £1,500. When I asked why, I was told that Daewoo had taken over FSO and had stopped production of the Caro. As a result there was no demand for secondhand models and Glass's Guide no longer quoted values for it. What are your feelings on this? "

> Your FSO was a case of cheap working out to be expensive. The finance sections of motor auctions are full of 'snatchbacks' like this. All too many people bought the cheapest East European and Russian imports on finance of the 'skinnem

and stitchup' variety and have found themselves in the same boat. If you can bear to keep the car until you have paid for it, then that's the best thing to do. If it's dropped from £6,000 to £500 in two years, it's hardly going to continue to depreciate at the same rate. Take £500 for it now and you will still have to settle the finance debt as well as taking on the new debt for its replacement, which is hardly the wise thing to do. Had you bought a mainstream model on a personal contract purchase scheme you would not be in this mess, because these schemes are designed to leave you with enough equity in the car after two or three years to finance the deposit on the next PCP and even guarantee its value.

Mini-mileage Micra

" Don't like cars much, but love your column. Can you help me? My elderly neighbour has an 'H' registered 3-door Micra 1.0LS which has done only 1,881 miles. He wants to sell, I'd like to buy, but I have no wish to underpay him. Any idea of price? "

Ultra-low-mileage on a car suggests problems such as dodgy oils seals and gaskets, sticking brakes and internal engine corrosion.

The public values ultra-low-mileage cars very highly. Someone even paid £74,642, including commission and VAT, for a 650-mile 1975 Jaguar E-Type at a BCA Classic Car sale in February. But to me ultra-low-mileage means problems, such as dodgy oil seals and gaskets, sticking brakes and hidden corrosion inside the engine. So while your neighbour's Micra may be a good buy, I wouldn't over-value the low mileage. A fair price in March 1998 would be £2,500.

CAR DESIGN

Electric windows

" *My Ford Escort has electrically-operated front windows, but manually-operated rear windows. I would much prefer it to have manual front windows and electric rears controlled by the driver.* "

Good point. The only reason I can think of for electrically-operated driver's windows and mirrors is manufacturing economy. But for practical purposes it makes more sense for the driver to get a manual window and mirror, yet have control of an electric nearside window and mirror and at least one electric rear window. I can't think why there is any need for an electric mirror and window on the driver's side. The logical French went part of the way by giving the Citroen ZX Avantage an electric nearside mirror and a manual driver's mirror. The old three-door Peugeot 309GTi had rear windows which could be opened from levers on the console between the front seats.

Colour crazed?

" *Why the craze for colour-coded bumpers? One gentle knock and they need a re-spray. The starting point for my next car will be decent bumpers – if I can find one.* "

We have visited this topic several times before. One answer is the Ford Ka, which has soft grey plastic bumpers which extend to form mud-guards – as one observer said, 'just like them old GPO vans'.

Car or motorcycle?

" *Over the years I have bought a series of VWs – Polos, Jettas and two splendid Ventos. Each winter I drive across the highlands of central France on my way to ski resorts. The autoroutes are often fogbound, and UK-spec VWs have only one rear foglight on the right – the offside. Naturally this becomes the nearside in France, and I am worried about overtaking vehicles assuming, when they see what appears to be a single bright rear light, that my car is a motorcycle. It is virtually impossible to re-wire the empty nearside socket to contain a second rear foglight.* "

Manufacturers stopped fitting rear fog lights in pairs to prevent them being confused with brake lights.

I don't think this is as much of a problem as you make out. The purpose of a rear foglight is to prevent a rear-end shunt. By the time a following vehicle is close enough to overtake, the driver must be able to see the red rear driving lamps as well – unless he is a maniac prepared to overtake in thick fog which renders his view ahead almost completely blind. Manufacturers stopped fitting pairs of rear foglights to prevent them from being confused with brake lights.

Little squirt

" *While otherwise delighted with my Fiat Punto Selecta, which I bought on your recommendation, I think I may have discovered a design fault. Instead of being above the rear screen, the rear washer is below it and only has the power to squirt water two inches up the screen. The Fiat agent has been unable to do anything to improve matters, so could you raise the matter with Fiat?* "

The water has to make a long journey from a

reservoir at the front of the car, through the rear hatch, to the 'V' shaped spray which emerges from the base of the wiper. Fiat says that either the washer pump is not developing enough power or there is a kink in the long pipe from front to back which is restricting the flow. If, armed with this information, your Fiat dealer remains unable to increase the flow to the normal 12 inches up the rear screen, phone Fiat Customer Relations on 01753 511431. Finally, a tip about your Punto Selecta. Be sure to have the transmission oil and filter changed once a year, even if it is not part of the service schedule, and be sure to keep the ATF topped up to the mark.

Let's twist again

" Seven months ago I bought a Rover 100 'Kensington' SE, and to this day have been unable to fill up without petrol splashing onto the car, the road surface and, if I stand too close, my clothes as well. What can be done? "

This is a common problem not restricted to Rover 100s. What happens is that the pump nozzle feeds into the tank pipe at an angle, and the emerging petrol hits a kink on the tank pipe and splashes back. The answer is to experiment by twisting the pump nozzle to different angles until you find one that does not splash back.

Design points

" I recently purchased a 'new shape' Rover 216Sis and, while I am quite pleased with its performance, it has several irritating features. Quite frankly, I wonder if the designers of the car ever drove it. The worst features are: 1. Digital clock/radio display cannot be seen in bright daylight; 2. Lack of rain gullies allows water to pour onto the driver and passenger when the

doors are opened and saturates maps stored in the door pockets; 3. The surrounds of the clock etc. are reflected in the windscreen; 4. The tailgate rattles, despite attention by the supplier; 5. The parcel shelf obstructs loading of the boot and is useless for storage purposes. Why is it that car magazine testers concentrate on performance and fail to notice such things? **"**

The 'new' Rover 200 is a cute, slightly upmarket 'niche car', and, as such, it was never intended to be all things to all people. But in any case, your criticisms could be applied to virtually any modern car. The lack of rain gullies greatly reduces wind noise, improves performance and helps cut the amount of fuel consumed. Tailgate rattles can usually be cured by moving the lock striker to provide a tighter fit. A luggage cover in a hatchback is not intended for storage because this would obstruct vision. The idea is to conceal the contents of the boot. The luggage cover in the raised position does not obstruct loading – it rises with the hatch unless someone has undone the tie strings. Dashboard design often leads to reflections and the best thing to do about this is to try and ignore them. Car magazine testers do point out serious shortcomings, but they can't put themselves in the minds of every driver. Finally, I'd like to mention a 'design plus' of the Rover 200. It is one of the very few cars with door pockets big enough to take a lady's handbag.

No cupholders!

" *I own an 'M' reg. 'old shape' Rover 214SLi and am more than satisfied with it. However, a slightly smaller car would suit us better, so, after three years I would like to change it for a new 200. Snag number one: I want an SLi, but the new 214 is only available as an Si. To obtain the extra features I would need to go to a 216. This doesn't make sense to me as the facility was* *available on the old model. Snag number two: what I have always liked about Rover 200s is the sensible oddments shelf on the top of the dashboard – perfect for putting cups on. A friend of mine recently bought a new 214 and there is no such facility – not even cupholder indentations in the open glove box lid. He has had to buy a piece of moulded plastic to fit into the side pocket and can only use it to hold a cup when the door is open. I wonder if Rover would pay any attention if you brought the fact to their attention.* "

Better add these to the criticisms in the previous letter. Paul Theroux, in his travelogue *The Kingdom by the Sea*, has a bit of a go at the peculiarly British compulsion to drive to a seaside carpark on a grey Sunday, point the car at the briny and read the papers while drinking cups of tea. Americans, like him, use cupholders while on the move: they actually drive while drinking mugs of 'cawfee', which is why they rarely signal at roundabouts first thing in the morning. I actually met my American neighbour, Charles, walking to the papershop, mug of 'cawfee' in hand. Accessory shops offer a variety of cup and can holders for use in cars not so equipped. Rover dropped the SLi-spec 200 because they up-specced the whole range. The new 200 1.4Si is almost up to the specification of the old SLi, while the new 1.6SLi takes the SLi a stage further up-market.

Mirror mirror – scraped off on the wall

" *The protrusion of door mirrors from the sides of a car makes them very vulnerable to damage. They stick out from the widest point of the car. Why don't manufacturers site them at the tops of the doors, where they would give an equally clear field of view, but not protrude so far?* "

Interesting idea. They are sited where you suggest on some supercars, but there may be attachment problems due to this being a weak point on most cars. There may also be severe aerodynamic and wind noise penalties.

Sliding seats

" In the supermini class it should be possible to fit a sliding rear seat to convert the luggage area into a seating area for short trips – so that a five-seater could temporarily become a six- or seven-seater. "

Your five-to-seven-seater suggestion will soon be on the market in the form of the seven-seat Vauxhall Zafira mini MPV, in which all five rear seats can be folded into the floor, while Fiat is about to bring out a six-seater 'Multipla' based on the Brava. The Mercedes 'A' Class, the Renault Twingo and several versions of the Citroen ZX have a sliding rear seat to increase leg room or luggage capacity as required. The Spanish company, Emelba, once built a mini MPV version of the Seat Panda with three rows of seats, there was a 'Multipla' version of the Fiat 600, and the Daihatsu Hi-Jet still offers this arrangement. Motorhoods make fold-away rear-facing seat conversions for most estate cars (01206 796737).

Shatterproof lamps

" Being asked to fork out £100 for a replacement foglamp for my Saab prompts me to write about the vulnerability and replacement costs of such lamps generally. Why must the whole lamp, rather than merely the lens, be replaced? And why are such lamps not made of a material less vulnerable to shattering, such as polycarbonate? "

Good point. In fact, the headlight lenses of a number of new models, such as the new Audi

A6, new BMW 5 Series, Fiat Coupe, Fiat Barchetta, most current Hondas, and the VW Passat, are made of clear polycarbonate. Signam (01926 492685) make polycarbonate lamp protectors for most makes. Armourfend (01992 642642) make self-adhesive clear plastic protectors for both lights and areas of bodywork vulnerable to stone chipping.

Open door policy

" Does the wider door opening of a three-door hatchback make entry and exit more difficult for an elderly person than with a five-door car? I am 6ft, my wife is 5ft 7in., we are both retired and we are looking for a new car in the supermini/small hatchback range. We would appreciate power steering, comfortable ride and low noise levels, good safety features and ease of parking but do not particularly value a sunroof, advanced radio, electric windows and high-performance engine. Apart from local town trips, we have 100–200 mile 'awaydays' and occasional holidays with an Escort-boot-amount of luggage and no other passengers. Any suggestions for a minimum-trouble car? "

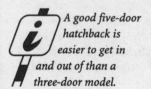

A good five-door hatchback is easier to get in and out of than a three-door model.

I am in no doubt that a good five-door hatchback is easier to get in and out of than a three-door – and it has the added advantage that you don't have to reach back behind you to find the seat belt. The best of these in this respect are the Fiat Punto and the VW Polo. Top marks should have gone to the new Mercedes 'A' Class, but it is not as easy to get in and out of as I expected.

People's cars

" I was impressed by the way the new Mini re-interprets the original Issigonis sketches and design philosophy. Having learned to drive in a Mini, I now own a Cooper which I still think is great fun to drive. You

quote the price of the new Mini as starting at around £13,000. Comparing this with other, much larger, cars in the same price bracket, I expect that the new Mini will be bought only by the select few who can afford this sort of money for a hot hatch, and it will not have the mass appeal and affordability of the original Mini. "

While the new Mini very successfully takes its styling cues from the original, it obviously does not reflect Alec Issigonis' design philosophy any more than the new VW Beetle reflects the idea behind the original Beetle. These cars are being styled as niche products from the outset. The car which comes closest to its inspiration is the Chrysler CCV which echoes all that was good about the Citroen 2CV and Dyane, yet truly innovates with cheap-to-assemble, pre-coloured plastic panels which do away with the high production cost of painting a car. If the CCV can be sold here for less than £4,000, it will most closely reflect the design philosophy of a cheap mass-market car, and I think I'll probably buy one.

Cool face, warm feet

" *My 1984 Astra is needing replacement. I have searched in vain for a car offering similar ventilation, i.e. fresh air at the face at the same time as hot air at the feet. Any suggestions?* "

Square-shape Audi 80 and 90, Audi 100 and 100-shape A6, Austin and Rover Montego, Citroen 2CV, Citroen Dyane, 1975 Datsun 200L, Fiat and Seat Panda, 'old' Ford Fiesta, 'old' Ford Escort/Orion, Ford 'Aeroflow' Cortina Mk 1 and Mk II, Ford 'Aeroflow' Corsair, Ford Sierra, Honda Quintet, Honda Concerto, Honda Civic (including coupe and Swindon-built 5-door), Honda Accord, all Land Rovers, Range Rovers,

Discoverys and Freelanders, Minis (with eye-
ball vents), old Mazda 323, Mazda 626,
Mitsubishi Carisma, Nissan Micra, Nissan
Primera, Peugeot 406 coupe, Renault 4, all
Rover models since the Montego, Saab 95/96,
Saab 99, Saab 900, Seat Marbella, Toyota Carina
E, Vauxhall Nova, Vauxhall Astra Mk 1 and Mk
II, Volkswagen Polo 1983–94, VW Passat to
1987, Volvo 340/360, Volvo 240/260, Volvo
S40/V40, Volvo 850, Volvo 960.

'Most useful features'

I ran a little competition asking readers to nominate the cars with the most useful features. A
reader from Pontfadog won by nominating his
Fiat Panda. Useful features include: cool air to
the face and warm air to the feet; doors can only
be locked with the key, so you can't lock yourself out; all running lights go off with the ignition – if you want parking lights you have to
turn the key through an interlock; the spare
wheel sits on top of the engine where it is easy
to get at; a capacious 'hammock' replaces the
glove box and is far more useful; part galvanized body shell; good economy; low insurance;
low joy-rider appeal; cheap spares; plastic
wheel-arch protectors; and even a clock – all for
just £4,995 on the road when he bought it.

Handbagged

" With the number of 'smash and grab' handbag snatches taking place
at traffic lights I was pleased to see that Renault has addressed the problem with its handbag/briefcase locker in the new Espace. Can other manufacturers please copy this excellent idea? "

Rover 200s have side pockets big enough to take reasonable-sized handbags and keep them where they can't easily be snatched. The Land Rover Freelander has a lockable cubby under the rear load platform. The Honda CRV has a waterproof compartment under the rear floor. The Renault Megane Scenic has at least five under-floor and under-seat storage compartments. The Citroen Berlingo van has an ingenious passenger seat which folds to form a table, then double-folds to reveal a storage compartment. The Berlingo also has cavernous cubbies under the dash. Finally, the Suzuki Wagon R Plus also has a cubby bin under the passenger seat which is removable and can double up as a shopping basket, washbasin, emergency potty or goldfish transporter, as well as a handbag receptacle.

High-level brake lights

" *Can you kindly advise about the desirability of a central high-level brake light, and, if it is desirable, whether it is better sited at the top or the bottom of the rear window, and whether there is any preference for a digital strip lamp or one with a single bulb.* "

Digital strip high-level lights light up faster than bulbs, and the higher they are placed the better, because they then give better warning of trouble ahead, particularly on motorways. But high level brake lights also pose a problem for two reasons. One is that drivers still drive far too close to the vehicle in front and constantly have to brake because they have left no 'control space' in front of them. This creates false warnings and totally unnecessary dazzle. The other problem is lazy drivers of automatics in traffic who sit holding the car on the footbrake, blinding the driver behind with their high-level brake light, technically an offence under the RVLR 1989.

Winter dazzle

" In the summer, when the sun is 'higher' in the sky, sun visors are fairly effective in reducing dazzle. But in the winter they are hopeless, especially when swung to reducing dazzle through the driver's side window. Surely it is within the ingenuity of the motor industry to solve this hazard relatively cheaply. "

Various types of side window blinds are available from car accessory shops. Winter sunlight through the front windscreen can also represent a serious hazard to those of shorter stature. One solution is to buy a deeper visor, such as the type fitted to the Honda CRV. Another is to make a cardboard or plasticard extension for the visor. Yet another is to buy a cantilever extending roller visor blind from a truck accessory shop, such as those at BP Truckstops.

Mudflap

" Why is it that mudflaps are not fitted as standard to cars? Over the past ten years or so I have bought three cars from new and in each case I have paid around £45 for mudflaps as optional extras. The cost could easily be absorbed into the basic price. Surely they would restrict damage to paintwork and wheel arches, reduce road spray in the wet, and thereby improve visibility and safety; and they would reduce the risk of damaging the car behind. Most goods vehicles seem to have them fitted. Are the rules different for private cars? "

Yes, construction and use rules are different. The reason why they are not fitted as standard is that, while you are entirely correct in your list of benefits, mudflaps do have disadvantages: They are ugly. They increase drag, thereby reducing efficiency and increasing fuel consumption. And, if trapped between a rear tyre and a solid object such as a kerb or stone while reversing, a mudflap is very effective at pulling the entire rear valence off a car. Also, every little knick knack added to a car adds to the price. If today's emissions and crash safety regulations were relaxed for economy cars incapable of much more than 70 mph, car prices could start at around the £3,000 mark instead of £4,999.

Beware! Volvo driver approaching

" The irritating and, to me, pointless Volvo 'daytime running lights' are getting brighter and brighter. If they are such an important safety feature, why were they never fitted to the 300 Series models? Originally these lights were just slightly brighter side-lights, but now are dipped headlights which can dazzle on undulating roads. "

I agree. Daytime running lights on S40s and V40s are brighter than on previous Volvos. I also agree that the disadvantages are starting to outweigh the benefit of making approaching Volvos more visible. I get several letters a week voicing the same complaint.

'Multi-purpose' office

" As an ME sufferer re-structuring my lifestyle, I have developed the need for a mobile office and study facility. With this in mind I feel that the full potential of most MPVs has yet to be realised. The two front seats of some can swivel 180 degrees into the cabin, and power points are provided in the back. But the clip-in modular system so far seems to consist of little more than folding seats-cum-tables, fridge units and bike racks. Do

you know of an enterprising manufacturer who sees the potential for converting clip-in seat bases to desks, folding worktops, storage bins, etc.? I should add that I need an automatic capable of transporting teenagers, cellos, and also of towing a caravan. **"**

A conversion specialist is ASGB of Great Bentley, Essex; tel: 01206 250380 and speak to Mr A. Smith. The only vehicles of this type with clip-in systems are the Galaxy/Sharan/Alhambra, the Synergie/Ulysse/806 and the Espace. The new Grande Espace has the best 'clip-in rail' system. To pull a caravan with an automatic MPV you really need a V6 version (Galaxy, Sharan or Espace). Expect to get about 15 mpg in this mode. There is a 110 bhp TDI Sharan automatic, but I wouldn't like to pull a caravan with one.

CAR HIRE

Rough deal

"Many car rental agreements, particularly in the USA, require that the hirer signs an agreement 'not to drive on any unpaved roads'. In reality, this is impossible as many car parks, driveways and back roads are not paved. What is the legal interpretation of this restriction? And is it strictly enforceable by car rental companies?"

The legal interpretation is, if you damage the car by driving on unpaved roads you will be required to pay the repair costs. That's why the clause is there. If you sign it, it forms part of your contract with the car rental company and it is legally enforceable. In practice, you know, and the rental company knows, you will drive on unpaved roads – but it makes you a lot more careful not to damage the car. Remember the rental company's profit depends more on the resale value of its cars than on the rental income from them.

Rent-a-Yank

"Where can I hire an old American car, not necessarily to drive? I just want a ride in one. Is there a club for these?"

Try Carriages Vehicle Agency on 01737 353926. Try Sunshine State of Oxted on 01883 730170. Try David Jones (who runs some very old Oaklands) on 01483 861177. Try the Pre '50

American Auto Club, SAE to Ian Herbert, 17 Great Fox Meadow, Kelvedon Hatch, Brentwood, Essex CM15 0AU. Try the Motorvatin' USA American Car Club on 01376 442478. And try the American Auto Club UK on 01948 74754.

Left-hand hire

" *My American cousin has great difficulty driving a car with right-hand drive. He can't get used to the gear change being on his left instead of his right, and is disorientated in one-way streets and at roundabouts and road junctions. Is there anywhere in the South-East where he can hire a left-hand-drive car?* "

Tricky one, this. If he's going to mainland Europe he can switch from right- to left-hand-drive hire cars in Calais using 'Le Swap', a scheme dreamed up by Hertz and 'Le Shuttle' (0181 679 1799). Or if he's over here for a longer stay he buy a car from 'The Left Hand Drive Place' (01256 461173) on a guaranteed 'buy back' basis, which will probably work out cheaper than hiring, though he will have to arrange his own insurance. Finally, most American motorhomes for hire are left-hand-drive. Try Dudley American Motorhomes on 01993 703774. Or call the Motor Caravan Industry Information service on 01444 453399 for other hirers.

Renting an estate

" *Where in the London area can I possibly hire a Volvo estate for a weekend? I have perused the Yellow Pages, but drawn a blank. Can you assist please?* "

Yes. Hertz, Avis and Woods Car Rentals all have Volvo estates. Car rental companies can't advertise the content of their fleets in Yellow Pages because this is continually changing according to the purchase and disposal deals they can strike.

Rent-a-box

" *In an article in 'Telegraph Motoring' on rooftop carrying boxes, Philip Llewellin suggests that renting would make more sense than outright purchase. My company specialises in the rental of these boxes, together with rooftop bicycle carriers, and we provide a complete fitting service. Our name is Carryscope and our address is West Haddon Road, Guilborough, Northants NN6 8QE, tel: 01604 740735.* "

Tall vehicles such as some 4×4s and MPVs could be made particularly unstable by the use of a roof box.

I'd like to add the warning that anything heavy placed in such boxes will raise the centre of gravity and seriously affect the stability and controllability of the car. Any tall vehicle such as some 4×4s and MPVs could be made particularly unstable by the use of a roof box.

Self-drive Rollers

Several readers (and *Telegraph* staffers) have asked about hiring self-drive Rolls Royces. A bit of digging came up with Hanwells of London, tel: 0171 436 2070. Rates are a reasonable £330 a day all in for a Rolls Royce Silver Spirit II or III and £360 a day for a Bentley Turbo R. Weekends (from mid-day Friday until mid-day Monday are £660 for a Rolls or £720 for a Bentley. The cars are 'J'. 'K' or 'M' registered. There is a £1,000 credit card deposit, out of which will be deducted any scratches or dents on return of the car, but not stone chips. Hanwells' Stephen

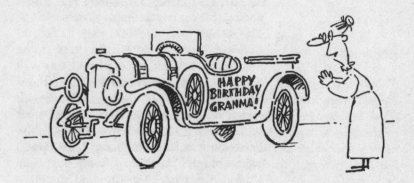

Brown declared 'all cars suffer stone chips, it's a fact of life which we accept'. So no worries about the deposit rip-offs that gave prestige car rental such a bad name a few years ago. The Hanwell Car Centre also deals in used Rolls Royces and Bentleys, and has done so for 14 years.

Hiring something special

" *Next year is my father's 60th birthday. To make it special we wish to send him and my mother away for a night in a hotel. and we would like them to be able to drive there in a classic car. Something like an Austin Healey or an MGA would be appropriate. So far my attempts to locate a classic car hire company have been in vain. Can you help? I also read somewhere of a 'classic car timeshare' club. Do you have any details?* "

The Classic Car Club is a sort of 'classic car timeshare' which costs £500 to join and then £1,750 a year. This gives access to around 40 days use of a pool of 50 classic cars, from Fiats to Ferraris, according to the points per day required for each car. Tel: 0171 713 7313; fax: 0171 713 7316. A good classic car rental company is Bespokes on 0181 421 8686, fax: 0181 421 8588. Its fleet includes E-Types, older Porsche 911s, Aston Martins and Ferraris, prices from £350 a day; it also does long-term contract hire. Carriages Vehicle Agency (01737 353926) offers a wide variety of 'classic' vehicles from a 1920s Dennis bus, through 1930s Rolls Royces, to a 1970s VW Beetle cabriolet. Ray Tomkinson (01204 533447) offers a range of 'classic taxis' from 1930s Austin Landaulettes to late 1970s Checker Cabs.

Rent-a-Wreck

" A friend of mine in France has heard of a car rental firm in England that specialises in hiring out 'old bangers'. He is keen to start a similar business in France. I wondered if you had heard of this and know anything about it, such as an address, what it costs, how it operates, what happens if a car breaks down, etc. "

Back in April 1993, in disguise as the intrepid 'Dan Frazer', I did an investigative story for *Auto Express* on this very subject. When I'm short of a car for a day (not often) I still hire one from 'Rent-A-Cheapie', Church Square Autos, Church Square (by the river), Shepperton, Middlesex, tel: 01932 241843. Current rates are from £13 a day. Why this hasn't taken off more widely, and why Rent-A-Wreck never really got going in the UK, is that daily rental companies launder new cars into 'nearly new' cars for the manufacturers and pay little or nothing for them.

CATALYTIC CONVERTERS

Changes to the 'cat' test

Over the past two years a number of changes have been announced as to which cars must be 'cat' tested to an 'advanced emission control limit' and which need not be.

At first, the rule was to be that every petrol-engined car first registered on or after 1 August 1992 ('K' reg.) had to have a cat and undergo an advanced emission control test at three years old and then every year after that.

Then, allowance was made for non-cat cars still unsold by 31 July 1992 – and again still unsold by 31 December 1992. So even some 93Ks were sold without 'cats' and would not be subject to the 'cat' test.

When the 'cat' test was first introduced, in January 1996, many cars failed because the test data supplied by the manufacturers was either incorrect or simply not available. So further allowances were made to the effect that cars first registered up to 31 July 1995 (end of the 'M' suffix) for which no cat test data had been made available (there are very few such cars) only had to be subject to the non-cat test limits of 3.5% CO and 1,200 ppm HC at standard idle.

All petrol-engined cars first registered on or after 1 August 1995 ('N' onwards) are subject to an advanced emissions control test and, if no test data has been supplied by the manufacturer, they will be tested to the default limits which are: Minimum oil temperature 60 degrees centigrade; fast idle rev range 2,500–3,000 rpm. Limits at these engine speeds: 0.3% CO and 200 ppm HC; Lambda variation 0.97–1.03. At natural idle engine speed 450–1,500 rpm, maximum CO 0.5%.

How to read your cat test print-out

'Lambda' is a constant which represents the stoichiometric air-to-fuel ratio of 14.7:1. At this mixture there is sufficient air to burn all the fuel without excess residue.

If your car fails the catalytic converter test, it will be useful for you to know what the figures on the gas analyser print-out mean.

The requirement is first for a minimum engine oil temperature, which will be shown alongside the oil temperature of your engine when the test took place.

The engine is tested twice at a 'fast idle' of between 2,500 and 3,000 rpm, and the fast idle speed of your engine at the time of the test will be shown (the closer to 3,000 rpm, the better).

The required maximum level of carbon monoxide (CO) will then be shown as a percentage – and alongside it, the measured level for your engine.

Next, the required maximum level of hydrocarbons (HC) in parts per million – and alongside it, the measured level for your engine.

Following that, the acceptable variation from 'Lambda' (the stoichiometric air-to-fuel ratio of 14.7:1) will be shown by two figures – and alongside it, the measured level for your engine. If the figure is BELOW the acceptable variation, it is running too RICH. If it is ABOVE the acceptable level, it is running too LEAN.

Figures for the second 'fast idle' test will be shown.

Finally figures for the 'natural idle' test will be shown. These are:

- A bracket of engine speeds (i.e. 600–900 rpm) against which is shown the measured natural idle speed.
- An acceptable percentage of CO emissions

at natural idle – against which is shown the measured percentage. (Idling at this speed with no 'load' on the engine, the cat will cool down from its operating temperature of 600 degrees centigrade, which is why the percentage CO requirement is lower than during the 'fast idle' test.)

If your car fails, you should first check that the engine speed was between the accepted parameters, which it almost inevitably will have been.

Then you should look at the Lambda figure. If this is below the parameters, the engine is running too rich and the cause of this should be addressed before simply prescribing a new 'cat'. This might be as serious as a malfunctioning Lambda sensor, or as trivial as a duff plug lead, a blocked or dirty air filter or an inlet manifold air leak. A simple replacement of a £5 air filter might, in some circumstances, be enough to get through the test and save the cost of a new 'cat'. If the Lambda figure is above the parameters, the reason also needs to be investigated before fitting a new 'cat'.

To find an independent workshop with the diagnostic equipment and training to check your car and ascertain the most economic means of repair, call the GEA Helpline on 01327 312616.

Finally, when submitting your car for its MOT, the 'cat' must be hot for it to work, and as clean as possible, so give the car a good run before delivering it to the MOT testing station. Merely running a car engine while stationary will not necessarily heat the 'cat' sufficiently, and leaving it running at idling speed can actually damage the 'cat'.

Cutting out

" *My son drives a 1994 Vauxhall Cavalier 2.0 litre. On the motorway a few days ago, travelling at 70 mph in the right hand overtaking lane, the engine suddenly died. Luckily, he managed to freewheel across two busy lanes to the hard shoulder and was able to restart the car from there. The engine cut out several more times in the ensuing days and a friend advised my son to purchase a new fuel pump relay, cost £21 + VAT. This he did and it cured the problem. But the parts manager at the Vauxhall dealership said he sold 'dozens' of fuel pump relays (the original relay had been modified) but that the serial number on my son's broken relay showed it was the modified version. Assuming this is a well-known fault, why is Vauxhall keeping it quiet? I could have lost my only son.* "

A fuel pump relay packing up, or a poor set of contacts to the relay, is one of the most common reasons for an intermittent 'cutting out' or a misfire on most fuel-injected cars – including BMWs. But it's also important to check for other reasons. If there was dirt in the fuel line and the electric fuel pump was struggling, the relay would cut the current to 'save' the pump and the wiring (like a circuit breaker in a domestic ring main) and may have damaged itself in the process. The resulting misfire may also have hot-spotted and damaged the car's catalytic converter, so if your son notices that the car is becoming sluggish it will probably need a new 'cat'.

Second-rate cats?

" *I frequently travel in the US and recently told colleagues there about the high cost of replacing catalytic converters in the UK. They were surprised and had never heard of 'cats' needing to be replaced in the USA due to short journey use or shattering. Is there a fundamental difference between British and American 'cats'? If so, why? If American cats are more robust, why can't we use the same design?* "

The 'cats' are the same, but driving conditions and the quality of petrol are better in the USA. In the USA, 'a short journey to the shops' can be 50 miles – and even if it isn't, any short runs from cold are balanced by much longer runs which give the 'cat' a chance to 'self-clean'. Petrol in the USA is also generally of higher quality with a lower sulphur content – and, with fuel tax so low, less is asked of engines to provide high performance with good economy than in Europe.

Another misfire

" My son's 40,000-mile 'K' reg. Rover 820i has developed a misfire that lasts for up to 30 minutes after cold starts. Apart from this the car is also prone to chug to a halt on hills. The Rover agent has diagnosed sticking valves, which he admits is not uncommon with this engine, and blames unleaded petrol. He has estimated £800 for a repair, using modified valves. But I always thought it was leaded petrol that gummed up combustion chambers. Is there a remedy in a can that might solve the problem without blowing the 'cat' away? And is there a brand of unleaded petrol that would prevent the problem? "

Texaco CleanSystem 3 does. But the fact that the car has been misfiring for some time and 'chugs to a halt on hills' leads me to suspect that the 'cat' has 'hot spotted', disintegrated and blocked the exhaust system – so you'll need to have this looked at anyway. A fuel additive 'injector cleaner', 'fuel system cleaner' or similar may reduce some of the tars and gums on the valve stems. The modified valves the Rover dealer has mentioned are probably inlet valve stems, guides and stem seals altered to allow oil to lubricate the stems in place of the lost lead, but will mean slightly heavier oil consumption.

Scorpio problems

" *My daughter has a Ford Granada Scorpio 2.0i which is suffering from engine surge and cutting out accompanied by a rotten eggs smell from the exhaust. The car has been back to two Ford dealers who have been unable to solve the problem because it is intermittent. My daughter's typical use of the car is school-shuttling three or four miles twice a day, interspersed with perhaps a couple of trips a week of 40–50 miles. What's the answer?* "

The 'bad eggs' smell produced by some catalysers is simply the result of using petrol containing quite a lot of sulphur, which 'catalyses' into hydrogen sulphide when the cat is not fully heated up.

Catalysed Granada 2.0is were notorious for sensor and ECU problems. So, though your daughter's usage of the car should 'light up' its catalytic converter and give the cat a chance to self-clean, a misfire may have 'torched' the cat and destroyed it. If the car lacks power, this is almost certainly the case, as the debris from the torched cat will be partially blocking the exhaust system, creating too much back pressure. Ignore the protestations from the Ford dealers and take the car to an MOT catalytic converter testing station. The results of this will tell you whether or not the 'cat' is damaged. If not, the 'smell' is simply the result of using petrol which contains quite a lot of sulphur, which 'catalyses' into hydrogen sulphide when the cat is not fully heated up to its operating temperature of 400–450 degrees C.

'K' without 'cat'

" *I wonder if you can point me in the right direction. In September 1995 I bought a secondhand 'K' reg. car. It never had a 'cat', and at the last MOT in September I was told it should have one and won't pass its next MOT without one. So where can I get one? And what will it cost me?* "

It would be helpful to know the make and model. But, though 'advanced emissions systems' were obligatory for all new petrol-engined cars first registered from 1 August 1992, an allowance was made for cars built before this date without 'cats' and not sold until afterwards. This allowance ended up stretching into 1993 and a number of 'K' reg. Kias, Saos, Skodas and even a few late-registered Escorts and Sierras were legally sold without cats. The law is that any car sold after 1 August 1992 with an advanced emissions system originally fitted must pass an emissions test programmed for this system. But if such a system was never fitted, all the car has to pass is the standard emissions test for pre-cat cars. You can't simply fit a cat to a car not designed for one. But if the cat has been removed and replaced with a plain section of exhaust, you should be able to get a Timax after-market cat to replace the missing link at a 'fast fit' outlet.

Low mileage cat trouble

" *My wife and I (both pensioners) use an 'L' registered Renault 5 Campus for our limited motor travel. With just 6,000 miles on the clock we were shocked last week when the MOT test centre referred us to a specialised catalyst garage to have the emissions readings reduced. This cost an additional £85 on top of the cost of the MOT. We feel there is something amiss here when the negligible mileage of the car is taken into account.* "

First I'd like to reassure you that I don't think you have been ripped off. When your car failed its MOT for excessive emissions, the lowest cost course of action was taken. In the past, readers had been charged for catalytic converter and Lambda sensor replacements when all that was necessary was adjustment – and this led to the suspension of the 'cat' test for six months in

1996. The low mileage use of your car implies a high proportion of cold starts and short runs which clog up the fuel delivery system, the valves and the catalytic converter and fill the exhaust system with condensation. A Kenlowe 'Hotstart' engine preheater will help (around £150 from Kenlowe Ltd, Maidenhead, Berks SL6 6QU, tel: 01628 823303). More frequent oil changes (at least twice a year) will help, changing your petrol to one with a genuinely high content of a good-quality detergent will help (try Texaco CleanSystem 3), and giving your car an occasional longer run, especially in the winter, will also help.

Cat preserver?

Hold Lloyd has sent me details of its new Redex 'Cat Guard' fuel additive. It costs £9.99 a bottle and contains an ingredient called 'Platinum Plus' which, via the internal combustion process, re-coats the catalytic converter's ceramic matrix with platinum deposits lost through the ageing of the cat. The company claims that 'Cat Guard' also addresses the problem of poisoning the cat, and states that 'use of "Cat Guard" every 6 months or 6,000 miles will ensure that the cat is maintained in peak condition.' The only problem is that one of the greatest killers of cats is an engine misfire. This can create localised hot-spots on the cat's matrix leading it to break up, blocking the exhaust system and leaving nothing much for 'Cat Guard' to re-coat with platinum. Despite my request, I've seen no car manufacturer approvals or endorsements. So, while the product may well offer some benefit to ageing catalytic converters which have suffered no misfires or physical damage, and may help protect cats from 'short trip syndrome', it cannot actually guarantee to extend the life of a catalytic converter in all circumstances. Holt Lloyd tells me that this point is covered in the 'full conditions of guarantee' on the packs, referred to in the small print at the foot of its advertisements.

Impending catastrophe?

" *I own a current-shape Nissan Micra 16v, mileage 13,000, which will be four years old this September. I only drive it locally. The car is running very well, but I am concerned about the catalytic converter in the future. Your advice would be appreciated.* "

As long as the car is running fine, don't be too concerned. Since it is now well out of warranty, you could try dosing the cat with Holt Lloyd's Redex 'Cat Preserver' which costs £9.99 a bottle and which you add to the petrol. However, this can only work if the cat matrix is in good shape and has not been destroyed by a bump or a misfire. An occasional longer trip than your local journeys will also help. The first part of the exhaust likely to 'go' is the rear silencer box, due to the amount of water created in the catalysing process which does not get hot enough to evaporate during short journeys. However, when the 'cat' itself finally expires, at £199+VAT it is relatively inexpensive to replace.

'Cat' test confusion

" *I have a July 1994 'L' reg. Citroen Xantia 1.8iLX. I took it to a Citroen franchise for a service and emissions check at 18,000 miles. Though the*

Citroen franchise is also an MOT 'catalyser' testing station, I took the car to a different MOT station for its MOT test where it failed for having a fast idle Lambda reading of 1.074 in the first test and 1.058 in the second test (against the variation limits of 0.97 to 1.03). I then took the car back to the Citroen franchise where it was emissions tested on the MOT test rig and passed. The car then underwent a full MOT test at the Citroen franchise and again failed the first Lambda test with a reading of 1.13, but passed the second Lambda test with a reading of 1.01. Throughout all the tests, the CO readings were always 0.00% (against a limit of 0.3%) and the HC readings were between zero and 6 ppm (against a limit of 200 ppm). I now discover that the Citroen dealer imposed a high electrical load on the engine in order to register Lambda 1.01, which the Vehicle Inspectorate tells me is illegal, and that I am now illegally using an illegally tested vehicle on the road. I feel that either the VI or the non-Citroen test centre should refund me the £26.50 test fee. "

Though this car was serviced and checked at a Citroen franchise which could have also carried out the MOT, the reader had not realised at the time that an MOT was due. When he did, he had the car tested at a local MOT station 15 miles nearer. The print-out for this test, which shows zero CO and HC readings throughout, casts doubt as to whether the test rig was calibrated correctly (it's unusual to register both no COs and no HCs). Because of this, he may be able to reclaim his test fee under the Sale and Supply of Goods Act 1994. The VI has stated that imposing an electrical load on the engine to replicate a driving 'load' and achieve closer to Lambda 1 is unacceptable because it is not part of the official test data prescribed by the manufacturer.

Mondeo misfire

" *I feel that I would like to bring to your attention what I see as a potentially dangerous situation in relation to catalytic converters. I have a*

Mondeo 24v automatic, which is a great car to drive. Recently while turning from the M6 to the M42 I lost power and came to a halt on the hard shoulder, at which point the engine died. I managed to restart it, but the maximum revs I could achieve were just 2,000 and as soon as I took my foot from the accelerator the engine died again. I had the car taken to a Ford garage where a failed catalytic converter was diagnosed and I was quoted £880 for the damage to be put right. Luckily, even though the car was 30 months old and had done 44,000 miles, Ford Customer Care was good enough to pay 50% of the bill. My point is that the failure could have occurred in a much more dangerous place, such as the outside lane. "

Probably not, as the effect of a disintegrating 'cat' (of which the Mondeo 24v has three) is likely to be gradual. What is likely to have happened is that the car suffered a misfire due to a quite well known failure among the engine management system sensors. This will have melted some of the platinum and rhodium on the catalytic converter ceramic matrix, leading it to fuse together and creating a 'hot spot' (around 800 degrees centigrade, compared to the normal 450-degree operating temperature). In time, more metal melts, creating a bigger hot spot, until eventually the cat matrix disintegrates and partially blocks the exhaust system. This, in turn, creates so much back pressure that the engine dies because it literally can't exhale. (After the December 1997 Mondeo 24v recall to solve this problem, Ford voluntarily refunded the remaining 50% paid by this reader.)

What is Lambda?

" *Our catalysed car recently failed its MOT emissions test on the Lambda reading. A new ECU was installed, which should have cost us £495 but, after a goodwill contribution from the manufacturer, we were asked to pay 'only' £200. But what, exactly, does 'Lambda' mean? Our car passed on COs and HCs, but the Lambda reading was not within the permitted range.* "

Lambda 1 represents the 'stoichiometric' air:fuel ratio of 14.7:1 where there is enough air present in the mixture to burn all the fuel with no excess of either but leaving just enough to set in motion the catalytic process inside a 'three-way' catalytic converter. In effect, the cat depends on 'finishing off' any combustion which did not take place within the engine, forcing the emerging gases to react with each other and convert to a mixture of steam (H_2O) and Carbon Dioxide (CO_2). Where a conventional engine runs too lean, the Lambda reading will be more than 1 and the 'in service' emissions test assumes that this will mean the car is emitting too much Nitrous Oxide (NOx).

Mine's a 'de-cat'

" *I own a 1991 Alfa Romeo 2.0 Twin-Spark. Looking under the car after the winter I noticed that the exhaust pipe in and out of the catalytic converter was becoming very corroded, as were the seams on the 'cat' itself. Since replacing a catalytic converter is very expensive, I have wondered if it is legal to remove the 'cat' and replace it with a length of standard exhaust pipe. I believe this will also liberate a few brake horsepower.* "

You are correct on all counts. Removing the cat will cut down back pressure, increasing power and generally reducing the amount of fuel consumed. It is currently legal to do this to any catalysed car first registered before 1 August 1992 and, when done properly, the increased efficiency of the engine may mean that it actually puts out less harmful emissions than it would do with an ageing cat. But the job is not simply a matter of replacing the cat with exhaust tubing. The exhaust Lambda sensor may need to be re-sited and the engine ECU will need to be re-programmed to expect less exhaust back pressure. Your insurer must be informed of the modification in writing. One de-catting specialist is Brodie Brittain Racing Ltd, Oxford Road, Brackley, Northants NN13 7DY (500 metres back into Brackley from the southernmost roundabout on the Brackley bypass), tel: 01280 702389.

Ten ways to keep cats alive

'Cats' can be fragile, so here are ten ways to help prevent damaging them beyond repair.

1   Don't fill with leaded petrol. (The lead in 4-Star reacts with the precious metals in the 'cat', eventually rendering it useless.) For the same reason, don't use 'mixer' pumps which supply both 4-Star and Unleaded.

2   Don't 'bump-start' the car. Unburned fuel will contaminate the 'cat'. ('Jump-starting' from another car's battery, is, of course, okay.)

3   Don't leave the car idling after starting it, especially on cold days.

4   Don't make too many short journeys from a cold start, or the 'cat' will never reach operating temperature. Instead, balance short trips from cold with longer trips, to give the 'cat' a chance to 'self-clean'.

5   Don't drive the car at all if it misfires.

6   Don't drive the car if it is burning oil.

7   Don't rev the engine before you switch off.

8   Don't ground the 'cat' on 'sleeping policemen', road humps, ridges or bumpy tracks.

9   Don't reverse the exhaust-pipe end into a low wall or kerb.

10 Don't drive through deep water when the 'cat' is hot.

CHERISHED REGISTRATIONS

Inplated prices

" *Is it not hypocritical of the DVLA to sell number plates at astronomical prices (N1 GEL recently sold for £80,000) when a fellow government agency (the police) will stop and fine people like Nigel for re-aligning the digits so they read 'N1GEL'? And why can't we resuscitate our old plates still hanging in the garage? I still have the log books, but MOTs weren't around in those days.* **"**

Yes, it would be hypocritical if it happened to any great extent. But making 'N1 GEL' read 'N1GEL' is not quite the same as creating deliberate confusion like moving a '1' next to a '3' to create a 'B', or making a '7' look like an 'I'. If unsure, check the rules in Hughes Guide to Traffic Law (£15; tel: 01908 676908). You can't resuscitate old plates because you don't 'own' them and never did. The registration remains the property of the DVLA and the keeper is merely the lessee who pays a 'rent' of £150 a year if the plates are on a car or £25 a year if they are on a retention certificate. If this is not paid regularly, keepership of the registration lapses. In any case, registrations can only be transferred from cars which are taxed and tested, or from retention certificates. Ask for leaflet/form V778/1 from your local Vehicle Registration Office.

Better to split?

" My father died just after Christmas and left a 20-year-old Austin Allegro with the registration number 'JSO 11'. The car is taxed and has a current MOT. We wish to sell the car, but expect to gain considerably more for the registration than for the car itself. A registration company has already offered to give us £1,500 on sale of the registration, but does not want the car. Would it be better to sell the registration privately and sell the car to an Allegro enthusiast? "

Since the car is taxed and tested there is no problem in transferring the registration to another car, but it may be worth transferring it to a retention certificate (£80 + £25) before the VED and MOT run out. (You need form V778/1 – which comes with instructions – from your local Vehicle Registration Office.) Elite Registrations (01380 818181) offers to value registrations by post (but not by telephone). For the Allegro, try the Allegro Club International, 20 Stoneleigh Crescent, Stoneleigh, Epsom, Surrey KT19 0RP.

Finding a reg.

Two readers in the same week asked how they could go about finding specific registrations to buy and transfer to their own cars. The answer is to call the DVLA Hotline on 0181 200 6565. This will tell you if the number is available for transfer. If you just want to find out if a registration has been assigned to a vehicle, write to Customer Enquiries (Vehicles), DVLA, Long View Road, Swansea SA6 7JL or fax them on 01792 783657. If it has been, because of the Data Protection Act the DVLA cannot supply the keepership details unless you show 'reasonable cause', such as wishing to check the mileage of a car you want to buy, or to take civil action against a driver who damaged your property. To obtain a list of previous owners under these circumstances, write to: Fee Paying Section, DVLA, Swansea SA99 1AL, enclosing a cheque for £5 made out to 'Department of Transport'. I'd like to see the dispensation of this data freed up for a number of reasons: to help prevent fraud; and to enable organisations such as J.D. Power to compile more accurate random information of customer satisfaction, common faults and recalls. And, when combined with mandatory registration of mileage every time a car visits a garage, it would stop the 'clocking back' of odometers and cast suspicion on odometer disconnection.

Bequeathing a reg.

" I am the 'owner' of a personalised registration mark of some value, but it is currently held on a retention certificate. In the event of my death before this mark is transferred to another vehicle, would those who inherit my estate become 'owners' of the mark or would 'ownership' revert to the DVLA automatically? If the latter is normally the case, is there anything I can do to ensure that my family does not lose the mark and therefore its financial value? "

The rules on the notes which come with form V778/1 are clear on this point. They allow the recorded keeper of a vehicle with a cherished registration to transfer the mark to a retention certificate for 12 months – and for extensions of the period on the retention certificate to be purchased at the rate of £25 a year – otherwise the keeper's right to the mark lapses. The right to keep the mark on a retention certificate is *not transferable*. Your best bet is therefore to use the form 778 Retention Document to assign the mark to a vehicle other than a moped or motorcycle owned by a member of your family. The £80 you paid to transfer the mark to the retention certificate also pays for this.

Keeping a cherished number

" *I have a personalised registration plate, bought from the DVLA, which is on my present car. When I am ready to part-exchange the car I will want to transfer the plate to my new car. Can you tell me how the dealer who buys my car will re-register it, and what registration number he will get bearing in mind that the car will probably be five years old?* "

Now that the number of Vehicle Registration Offices has been reduced there can be a delay of several weeks in transferring a registration from one car to another. To stay on the road with both cars, it may be better to transfer your personal registration to a retention certificate at the time of part exchange, using form V778/1, which comes with full instructions. The transfer costs £80 and the retention certificate, £25. Your old car will then be allocated a registration with a prefix appropriate to its date of first registration. The new car will have to be registered to a standard date plate first, then, after you take delivery, you can use the appropriate form to re-assign the registration on the retention certificate to the new car at no further charge. Don't forget to amend the car's insurance certificate.

PO 1, where are you?

" *How can I find if PO 1, the registration number of my old Rover of which I have fond memories, is still in use?* "

Use the official procedure of writing to Customer Enquiries (Vehicles), DVLA, Long View Road, Swansea SA6 7JL.

The DVLA was able to tell this reader that PO 1 was indeed still in existence, but under the Data Protection Act it could not tell him who is using it; so I asked *Telegraph* readers. One, who lived in Chichester as a boy, remembered the registration on a Chrysler Airflow owned by Mr Eric Smurthwaite, who used to switch the registration to a new car every couple of years. Two others from Chichester wrote to tell me that Mr Smurthwaite, who ran a decorator's merchants on North Street, Chichester, owned the Rover from around 1947. On Mr Smurthwaite's death, thought to be in 1956, his widow sold the Rover and transferred the number to a new Morris Minor (one of the first Minor 1000s – recognisable by its one-piece windscreen). When Mrs Smurthwaite became too old to drive, the car was stored in a warehouse at the rear of the shop, which extended through to Chapel Street. On Mrs Smurthwaite's death, the car and number plate were handed over to Boys Garage at Fishbourne, west of Chichester. A Harrogate reader (a number 'spotter') spotted 'PO 1' on a metallic green Bentley Turbo parked outside the Crown Hotel, Harrogate in 1992.

Age-related

" *In 1980, I laid up my 1960 Morris Minor, reg. 'WDP 383'. A couple of years ago I telephoned one of the cherished number agents advertising in* The Daily Telegraph *and was told that the number could not be transferred unless the car had an MOT certificate and bore a current, free, VED*

disc. It now does, but if I sell the plate what will I get instead? And will the car still be VED exempt? "

You will get an 'age-related plate'. But the replacement plate cannot ever be sold for transfer. Your car will continue to be VED exempt. However, should you decide to take it off the road for any reason, you are now obliged to make a Statutory Off Road Notification (SORN) to the DVLA.

The UK registration system

" *I wish to lament on your shoulder regarding the number of forms and details one needs to fill in and the large fees one needs to pay when one is retaining or transferring a cherished registration. I cannot accept that, after having paid many hundreds or even thousands of pounds for a cherished registration, one does not really own it. It is owned and controlled by the DVLA and only leased to the holder on the DVLA's strict contractual terms. To date it has taken over ten weeks for the retention and V-5 documents to be returned to me. I find the whole process very cumbersome and antiquated. In comparison, the Swiss system is simple, inexpensive and efficient. You own the licence plate, it covers as many cars as you own, and it is transferable from car to car. Everyone is compelled to register all the cars they have and must buy non-transferable road tax badges for each car from the post office. There are no forms to fill in but the fines are very heavy if you fail to register and pay. Mr Blair claims he wants to make Britain 'the leading nation' in Europe by the Millennium. Is it not time to axe our antiquated vehicle registration and taxation system and to bring on line a more efficient one?* "

I agree that the registration system is badly in need of reform and there should be a licensing system, probably by smart card, that continually logs the accumulating mileages of every vehicle on the road and which should be accessible to anyone. The Swiss (and Belgian) system of allocating registrations to car keepers rather than to cars seems like a good one to me and has the added benefit that every registration is immediately traceable back to the owner by means of annual directories and a data bank. In the UK, the Data Protection Act forbids this.

CLASSICS AND NOSTALGIA

First car in England?

" While rummaging through some old photographs, my wife turned up a picture of her great uncle, on the back of which is inscribed, 'Charlie SANTLER – builder of the first car in England'. He lived in Malvern, Worcestershire and, at the time of the picture, taken around 1920, he was more then sixty years old. So, assuming he was about thirty when he built the car, he must have done so between 1880 and 1890. It would be most interesting to know if any of your readers can shed more light on this. "

According to G.N. Georgano's 'Complete Encyclopaedia of Motor Cars', Charlie Santler claimed to have worked with Karl Benz on the Benz 'Velo', launched in 1894, but left because Benz would give him no credit. Santler then built his own very similar car, named the 'Malvernia', at Malvern Link in Worcester in 1898. He went on to build light front-engined cars in 1906 and 1913, and then diversified into manufacturing a motor plough in the 1920s.

Another motoring pioneer

" A friend, now living in Majorca, has supplied information about his father who was a motoring pioneer. His name was Albert Farnell and the specification of the tri-car he built in 1897 was as follows: independent 'sliding pillar' front suspension, 1.25 hp air-cooled motor, tubular chassis, *belt drive via three-step cone pulleys (an early 'CVT'). He later fitted a 'Starley' rear axle, his own patent four-speed non-crash gearbox and worm and sector steering by wheel rather than lever. His address was 75 Manningham Lane, Bradford. Albert Farnell also raced Daimlers in the Isle of Man from 1902 to 1912 and took part in speed trials on the sands of Scarborough and Morecambe. "*

This is one for the motoring historians because it's not in Georgano's *Complete Encyclopaedia of Motor Cars 1885–1968,* Culshaw and Horrobin's *Complete Catalogue of British Cars 1895–1975* nor Hugo Wilson's *Encyclopaedia of the Motorcycle.* The reason for this may be that Albert Farnell only ever built one vehicle, which was quite common among early motoring pioneers.

First Brighton run

" I remember the first commemorative run in 1928, started by the Daily Sketch, *from the Lex Garage. My father, Vernon Balls, took me when I was about ten years of age. There were about 30 to 40 cars, all rusty and un-restored, and when they were started up one could hardly breathe for the smoke. I think the run has been started in the open air ever since. In 1929, father bought a 1903 Oldsmobile (MV 4849) from a little garage at Lympsham near Weston-super-Mare, for £15 (I still have the receipt). This car completed over 30 runs. "*

Thank you for this little gem of motoring history. It's just possible that, as a child or young teen-ager, another reader actually passengered in the first 'London to Brighton' run. If so, the *Telegraph*'s Motoring Desk would be very pleased to hear from you. There's a useful Shire Album on the subject (no. 251), price £2.95, from The Veteran Car Club of Great Britain, c/o Margaret Goding, Jessamine Court, 15 High Street, Ashwell, Herts SG7 5NL, tel: 01462 742818.

Classic car tax

" *My wife owns a Mini, which will be 25 years old this March. We have been told we can obtain road tax exemption, but having read an article in* The Sunday Telegraph *we are completely bemused. We need your expertise to advise us.* "

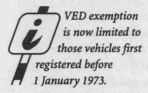

VED exemption is now limited to those vehicles first registered before 1 January 1973.

The old rule was that a car would qualify for VED exemption from 1 January of the year after it became 25 years old. But this all changed in the small print of the March 1998 Budget which has now limited VED exemption to 'Historic Vehicles' first registered before 1 January 1973. This is fixed and there is no longer a 'rolling' 25-year exemption. However, if you can prove that your car or, in the case of a camper, the base vehicle was manufacturerd on or before 31 December 1972 it will qualify for Historic Vehicle VED exemption. The onus is on you to prove its build date either from the VIN number or from features which positively date it as built before the end of 1972.

Classic insurance

" *I agree with the advice in your column about buying an MGB, especially the point that a Heritage re-shell avoids many problems. Anyone who owns a 'B' would do well to check Richard Hosken Classic Car Insurance on 01277 206911 for an agreed value policy. My stunning re-shelled 1973 chrome-bumper MGB roadster is insured for just £88.50 for an agreed value of £9,250.* "

Other 'agreed value' classic car insurers include Firebond on 01223 566020, Classic Direct UK on 01480 484827, ClassicLine on 01455 891330, Jardine Faber on 01604 639001, and Footman James on 0121 561 4196.

Steaming past

" *An article on steam cars brought back memories of a certain Mr Doble who arrived in the UK in the late 1920s. He was the son of Abner Doble, manufacturer of Doble steam cars from 1917 to 1924, and had converted two Lincolns to fully condensing steam propulsion. His favourite weekend pastime was to park in a small lay-by half way up Wenlock Edge, a very steep hill between Much Wenlock and Shrewsbury. Whenever a Rolls Royce or other large car chugged past up the hill, usually in first gear, he would sail out of the lay-by and overtake the other car long before it reached the summit. When it did, they would find Mr Doble parked up once again, this time at the pub in Much Wenlock, and would pull in to find out exactly what it was that had passed them so easily. Doble used his Lincolns to demonstrate the advanced Doble steam propulsion system to the makers of Sentinel Wagons. Two prototype Sentinel wagons were built using the Doble system, but the advent of diesel power and the war inter-rupted development.* "

Having taken steam propulsion a long way in the 'S' type series of trucks, Sentinel did indeed build two very advanced, fully condensing trucks to the Doble design in 1936/37. G.N. Georgano tells us that, though the trucks were highly successful in engineering terms, their high production cost prevented them from being a saleable proposition. However, he writes: 'A fleet of "S" type wagons remained in use by the North Thames Gas Board in London until the early 1950s and a small fleet of tar sprayers on the same type of chassis were used by M.R. Woolley of Bucknell, Salop until the 1960s.'

Lighting up dim old 'classics'

" *I'd like to advise your readers that much brighter halogen bulbs can be obtained for both the front and rear lights of old vehicles. These simply fit as a direct replacement for the old bulbs and can be obtained from me at*

Andrew Brock (Bulb Suppliers), 31A Shawbury Road, East Dulwich, London SE22 9DH, tel: 0181 299 0299. "

I hope the owner of the elderly Morris Minor van which was proceeding Southbound on the M1 at about 25 mph on the evening of 25 January 1998 is reading this. If ever there was a case for all slow old vehicles to lighten up (preferably also with an orange flashing light), this near-invisible dimwit presented it.

Source notes

" *I have a vast collection of old photos, many of which were purchased without any history. What sources do you recommend for identifying obscure old cars?* "

To avoid tedious repetition, I'll give you a list of the sources I have used for this section: Nick Baldwin's *A-Z of Cars of the 1920s* (ISBN 1-870979-53-2); Culshaw and Horrobin's *Complete Catalogue of British Cars 1895–1975* (ISBN 1-874105-93-6); The various *Classic & Sportscar A-Zs* from 1930 until 1980 (three volumes); Nick Walker's *A-Z of British Coachbuilders 1919–1960* (ISBN 1-870979-93-1), Quentin Willson's *Ultimate Classic Car Book* and *Classic American Cars* (Dorling Kindersley); Hugo Wilson's *Encyclopaedia of the Motorcycle* (Dorling Kindersley); Georgano's *Cars 1886–1930* and *Cars 1930–1950*, and his *Complete Encyclopaedia of Motorcars 1885–1968* and *Complete Encyclopaedia of Commercial Vehicles* (these last two are both out of print, but secondhand copies are available from specialist booksellers, priced at around £50); Chris Rees's *British Specialist Cars* (ISBN 1-872004-22-9); Warne's series of books on decades of American cars and trucks; Graham Robson's *Classic Cars*; Ralph Stein's *The Automobile Book* and *The Great Cars* (out of print but available at specialists); *The Vintage Car Pocket Book* by Clutton, Bird and Harding (out of print); *The Vintage Motor Car* by Clutton and Stanford (out of print); Millers Annual Collectors Car Price Guides, plus old Motor Show Reviews going back to the early 1950s; a huge library of magazines and a large number of one-make books. I find Mill House Books best for books still in print or 'remaindered' (tel: 01205 270377).

'Battle of Britain' AC

" *In the summer of 1940 I was at school at Sevenoaks in Kent. From the cricket field we could often see the vapour trails of dog-fights going on over our heads and one of those vapour trails, I knew, could have been my elder brother, Leslie, recently qualified as a sergeant pilot. Every third Sunday we had exeats from school, and on several occasions Leslie, always accompanied by some glamorous girl, took time off to drive me back to my boarding house in a beautiful yellow AC sports car made in about 1936. I believe it would reach 70 mph in third and 100 mph in top.* "

I'd say the car must have been a triple-carb AC 16/80, which Sedgwick and Gillies' *A–Z of Cars of the 1930s* credits as being 'good for over 85 mph'. A restored 1936 prototype of this model sold at a Christie's Classic Car Auction on 6 March 1997 for £67,500, including buyer's premium.

AC Buckland

" *Back in 1948 I crewed as navigator in some club rallies. The driver and owner was my sister's boss, and I was recruited as a recently demobbed RAC navigator. The car was an AC Buckland Sports drophead, finished in cream with red leather upholstery. It was a lovely car with good performance, particularly for those early days after the war when any new car was hard to get. I wonder what happened to the car after the owner died. Although I have been a keen follower of cars and motor sport, I have not seen any reference to this AC model since those days. I know the company went on to produce the Ace and the Aceca, but what happened to the Buckland? And what was its specification?* "

I also remember the Buckland because a friend of my father's owned one from the 1950s to the 1970s and it was the first car in which I was driven at 90 mph on the clock. My most abiding memory was the wind roar tearing through its complex folding top and sounding like a hurricane. The owner was Dr Philip Edmonson who lived at Redcar. The car itself had AC's venerable 1,991 cc ohc six, which dated back to the mid-1920s and sported three SU carburettors to develop 76 bhp. The Buckland tourer had cutaway doors with flaps in the side-screens for hand signals that accounted for some of that wind noise. The model range was built from 1947 to 1956. In the mid-1970s there was a warehouse on Buckingham Palace Road in London, and I remember arranging for the car to be sold on consignment there.

Albert and Belsize?

Two readers asked for information about these extinct models. According to Nick Baldwin the 'Albert' was named after the Albert Embankment in Vauxhall on which it was built by Adam, Grimaldi and Co. before the firm combined with Gwynne and moved to Chiswick. The original 12 hp model was, in Baldwin's words, 'beautifully made but expensive, with relatively high performance for a "twelve" thanks to pushrod overhead valves and a four-speed gearbox.' It also had a 'Parthenon' radiator a bit like a Rolls Royce. Unfortunately, there were a few design weaknesses which led the Official Receiver to axe the model in 1923 in favour of the Gwynne Albert 14/40. Belsize, which was a much bigger operation, was based in Manchester, 'employing 1,200 men and building 50 vehicles a week in 1914.' Once again, Receivers were appointed in 1923.

Alldays and Onions?

" *My late uncle, who lived in Holt, Norfolk, was in the process of restoring an Alldays and Onions car which was little more than a shell. He had just finished making a new radiator shell when he passed away suddenly. Can you tell me anything about Alldays and Onions cars, please? I understand very few were built. "*

Though I had heard of the car, my answer has been gleaned from Georgano's *Complete Encyclopaedia*. He tells us that Alldays cars were built by Alldays and Onions Pneumatic Engineering of Birmingham between 1898 and 1918. The first was a wheel-steered quadricycle dubbed 'The Traveller', and a shaft-driven single-cylinder light car followed. But the company made its name with a 1.6 litre vertical twin side-valve-engined car which it produced from 1905 to 1913. Apparently it was popular with commercial travellers, but also did reasonably well in minor competition events. There was a larger 16 hp four-cylinder car in 1906, then in 1908 the company acquired the Enfield Autocar Company and produced a range of larger cars up to the 30/35 hp limousine. It also soldiered on with cyclecars and it may well be that the model your uncle was restoring was the bull-nose radiator 1100 cc four-cylinder which first appeared in 1914.

Alvis acquisition

" I have just acquired my father's 1928 Alvis TG 12/50. which he bought in about 1950 and which has been stored on blocks in a barn for the last 25 years. I am looking for any information on its value, availability of parts, etc. To this end I have browsed through various classic car publications but found no details of Alvis cars of this era. My father tells me that there used to be a number of clubs, such as the Alvis Owners' Club, The Red Triangle Club and the 12/50 Owners' Club. Do you know whether these or similar clubs are in existence and, if so, please could you assist me? "

Check the wiring of cars which have been stored in bars. Mice are very partial to the insulation.

The magazine that covers cars such as yours (and indeed proper pre-1960 classic cars generally) is *The Automobile*, and its auction correspondent, John Willis, just happens to run The Alvis Register for all pre-war Alvis models. He will be delighted to hear from you and to welcome you to the club; tel: 01483 810308. Auction prices from my own data bank confirm the Miller's Guide estimate of £7,000 for a Condition 3 12/50; £13,000 for a Condition 2; and £20,000 for a Condition 1 (this assumes the car is a 12/50 Sports rather than a saloon or tourer). John Willis will be able to enlighten you further. Please check the wiring of this barn-stored car very carefully. You may find that some of the insulation has been eaten away by mice.

Alvis Silver Eagle

" Between May 1957 and May 1959 I owned a 1936 Alvis Silver Eagle, registration CLT 475, and have often wondered about its history both before and after my ownership. Owing to the Suez Crisis I paid just £107 for it to a garage in Emsworth and sold it to a garage in New Halton, Buckinghamshire for £105. I suppose depreciation of £1 a year is not bad, but I appreciate that the car would be worth very much more now had I kept it. The car was fitted with three SU carburettors, had a four-speed synchromesh gearbox and sported a polished aluminium dashboard with a full complement of instruments. "

The Alvis Owners' Club records kept by David Culshaw (01892 890043) came up trumps on this. The vehicle's all-important chassis number is 13400; engine number 13850; 'car number' 17901; and Cross and Ellis body number 4153. AOC member J. Bolton of Kingswood bought the car in 1954; AOC member E.J. Walter of The Officers' Mess at RAF Halton bought the car in September 1960; and AOC member P.T. Urwin of Tadworth bought it in May 1965. Peter Urwin faxed me from Peterborough, Ontario to confirm that he bought the car with a damaged engine (big end run, broken con rod, oil pump and crankcase damage), rebuilt the engine at a friend's house in Reigate, got it on the road again by the autumn of 1965, then sold it to someone in Sutton, Surrey for £100. History before and after these dates is unknown, so David Culshaw would be glad of any information readers can provide.

Alf and Harry

" *I can't help you with any history of the Alvis Silver Eagle 'CLT 475' [see the previous letter], but the letter did bring back memories of a short period I spent with the builders of its body, Cross and Ellis. I was put in a gang building four-door touring bodies for Alvis. The materials would come from the sawmill formed to shape, and we would have to make the joints and build the body on a trestle, assemble the four doors and hang them, then we would check the outer profile for defects that would interfere with the fit, and for all this the chargehand would be allocated thirty shillings. The company was one of those that still worked on the 'piece boss' system whereby the chargehand would be told by the wages office how much the gang had earned the previous week, and he would tell the office how much to pay each member. Obviously he would have the largest piece of the cake and I felt I had the smallest piece, and when I told him this I was told I was too slow. I therefore told him I learned my trade on high class one-off jobs built to a drawing, and so was moved to the finishing shop and assigned to the final inspector as his rectifications man. I liked this, as one never knew what the next job would be and it was some satisfaction to see the errors corrected. I did not see many Alvises come through this section, mostly Triumphs. But I remember a smart Alvis coupe come through and the customer had supplied two transfers bearing his crest of a mythical bird with a long neck. As this was an unusual request, it fell to Mr Cross's lot to apply them. He was a very brusque man, but after much cursing and groaning he had them in place and stood back with a piece of mutton cloth in his hand to admire his work, then flicked a speck of dust with his cloth and in the process removed the head of the crest. I do not think you would print the comments. The thirty shillings was a very poor price to build a car body, but that was typical of Cross and Ellis. This should be considered with the rate of pay at the time which, for a journeyman, was one shilling and sixpence-halfpenny per hour plus tuppence an hour if one worked within twenty miles of Charing Cross. I hope the memories of an 87-year-old will be of interest to you.* "

Very much so. What you write is confirmed in Nick Walker's *A–Z of British Coachbuilders 1919–1960*: 'No one would pretend that the Coventry firm of Cross & Ellis Ltd. produced coachwork of the highest quality. On the other hand, it survived for nearly 20 years, supplying good looking bodies under contract to the Coventry motor industry at what can only have been cut-throat prices.' The company finally went into liquidation in 1938, but this 'A–Z' provides a good potted history from the time Alf Ellis met Harry Cross in the bodyshop at Daimler.

Ansaldo?

" *My mother-in-law, whose childhood home was in Nenagh, County Tipperary, has often spoken of the first car in town. Owned by the local doctor, it was, to her recollection, an Ansaldo. Despite reading quite a number of books on motor cars I have never come across this particular marque. Is anything known of it? Is there any connection with Juan Antonio Ansaldo, a famous Spanish air ace and monarchist playboy who once organised Falangist terror squads and who piloted the plane which crashed and killed General Sanjujuro?* "

Societa Anonima Italiana Giovanni Ansaldo was Italy's biggest and one of its oldest engineering firms when, in 1920, a subsidiary, SA Automobili

Ansaldo, produced its first car in Turin. The 4C had four-cylinder 1,746 cc overhead cam engines developing 40 bhp at 3,000 rpm. The 4CS was a sporting version with a bored-out 1,891 cc engine which developed 48 bhp. A smaller, 1,325 cc light car was not successful. By 1925 there were two sixes, the 6A and 6B. All Ansaldos were sold with Weymann fabric bodies. By 1929, the company only made sixes and a new low-slung 3.5 litre straight-eight. Fiat took the company over in 1930 and, apart from Ansaldo taxis, the last Ansaldo was a 1931 straight-eight. I can't find any connection with Juan Antonio, but he may have been related.

Going for a burn-up

" *My late father, James Stiven, used to drive a fire engine owned by the Bullionfield Paper Mill in the late 1940s. The machine, bought by the mill from the Dundee Fire Brigade, was a 1910 Argyll 70hp, with solid tyres and a wooden steering wheel. I believe the headlamps were of the carbide type.* "

This is an interesting piece of history. The engine was 13.3 litres and it would certainly have taken some skill with the wooden steering wheel to control the machine on icy winter roads. Argyll is listed in Georgano's *Complete Encyclopaedia of Commercial Vehicles* as having built cars and commercial vehicles at Bridgeton, Glasgow from 1902 to 1906, and at Alexandria-by-Glasgow from 1906 to 1914. Sadly, Argyll's founder, Alex Govan, died in 1907, soon after the move to the new purpose-built factory, and with him went the impetus behind the company. The ornate Alexandria factory never reached the high output it was designed for but was recently restored as a

tasteful shopping mall incorporating a small motor museum.

Armstrong Siddeley

" *Having passed three score and ten I remember buying many wonderful cars for less than £75 from various bomb site dealers, including a Delahaye, a 100 mph Invicta, a Lagonda, etc. Many a blonde 'mechanic' adorned the passenger seats and I always switched my little silver plaque, 'passengers carried at their own risque', from one car to another. But the loves of my life were Armstrong Siddeleys. I had four or five Hurricanes, Lancasters and Whitleys. Do you know of anyone still specialising in these cars? And how can I get in touch with the editor of 'Sphinx', the Armstrong Siddeley Owners' Club magazine?* "

I used to get a lift to school in my dad's mate's Hurricane, the hood of which was patched with more Elastoplast than The Bash Street Kids hockey team. Try Peter Sheppard, Armstrong Siddeley Owners' Club, 57 Berberry Close, Bournville, Birmingham B30 1TB, tel: 0121 459 0742. The main specialist is Sphinx Enterprises Ltd, Hurst Farm House, Hurst, Petersfield, Hants GU31 5RF, tel: 01730 825401, which carries parts for models from 1945 to 1960 and has cars for sale. They also crop up at auction from time to time. Your best source of prices achieved and info on what's coming up is The Collector's Car Auction List, tel: 0181 534 3883 for details of how to subscribe, or faxback 0336 424800 (calls charged at 50p per minute).

Arkley SS

" I own a 1967, 1,275 cc Austin Healey Sprite which has had the Arkley SS conversion and I am trying to find out a little more about the car's history. Its registration is OUY 100E. A change of job and move to London is now forcing the sale of this car. I am keen to know what to ask for it and where to advertise. I would also be grateful for any information about the conversion and how many exist. "

This used to be quite a good way to rescue a Sprite or Midget with iffy bodywork, but it did not replace the cockpit 'tub' or the boot floor which are other areas to look for structural rot. The 1,275 cc engine with Nitrided crank was also the best engine for this car. Unfortunately, the market values them at rather less than a Sprite or Midget of similar age. H&H Auctions of Buxton (0161 747 0561) only took £900 plus commission for one in '1-2' condition in February 1997. But if I was you I'd put yours up for £1,995, hope for the best, then be prepared to negotiate if necessary. The best place to advertise is with a photo ad in *Classic Car Weekly*, which costs £20 a week or £40 for three weeks. The Arkley SS only rates a brief mention in Chris Rees's 1993 book *British Specialist Cars*, where he records production from 1970 to date of a total of around 200 kits. I can't find any reference to a club. Daniel Stapleton mentions the Arkley SS conversion in his book *How to Powertune Midget & Sprite* (Veloce Publishing) and tells me that kits are still being made. The UK contacts are Peter or Chris May, Arkley Sportscars, Midland House, Hayes Lane, Lye, West Midlands DY9 8RD, tel: 01384 422424.

Unusual Auburn

" My grandfather had an Auburn in 1924. Were many of these cars imported into the UK, and are there any examples to be seen nowadays? Do you have any specifications for the model? "

E.L. Cord bought the Auburn company in 1924 and had the entire range re-designed for 1925 by J.M. Crawford, establishing the famous body moulding which came to a point over the bonnet top. If your grandfather's car was a 1924 model, it would be either a 6-43 or 6-63 sedan. The 6-43 had a Continental six-cylinder engine and the 6-63 a Weidely ohv six. Since it has no offside doors, it must have been built for RHD export markets.

Enormous Austin

" Just before WW1, at the age of 18, my father drove a huge Austin. He told me it was one of only four built, and that it was owned by an ex-Army Colonel who became a stockbroker and employed my father as his chauffeur. My father said he had driven it around the Brooklands outer circuit

at 100 mph and that Jack Johnson, the first coloured heavyweight boxing champion, also had one. What can you tell me about the car? Is there one in a museum anywhere? Can the details I have given be substantiated? ''

Stephen Laing of The British Motor Industry Heritage Trust and David Burgess Wise both wrote to tell us that The Heritage Motor Centre has the one remaining 1908 Austin 100 hp in its museum on Banbury Road, Gaydon, Warks (tel: 01962 641188). The car was one of four built for the 1908 French Grand Prix with the 60 hp engine bored out to 9.7 litres and RAC-rated at 100 hp. The engine developed 171 bhp and could take the stripped-down GP cars to 92 mph, so your father's full-bodied car won't quite have managed 100. Two shaft drive cars crashed in practice and were made into one car. Three were brought to the starting line (one with shaft drive and two with chain drive) and driven by Warwick Wright, J.T.C. Moore-Brabazon and Dario Resta. Wright retired with a seized engine, while Moore-Brabazon and Resta finished 18th and 19th. The cars were later re-bodied as large tourers, then sold on (the Gaydon car is shaft drive, has been returned to race trim and now carries the registration 'BE 3'). A reader from Leominster has been able to add that the four 1908 GP Austins were registered AB 983 on 2 May 1908 and AB 1010, AB 1011 and AB 1012 all on 26 May 1908. AB 983 was later sold to G.H. Evans of The Old Manor House, Tettenhall, Wolverhampton.

Austin Greyhound?

'' *You may be interested in a car I rode in sixty years ago described as an Austin 'Greyhound' – beautifully built and a pleasure to drive. I have only ever seen one, and it is not referred to in any car books.* ''

An astonishing number of readers responded to this appeal. I had written that the car depicted looked like an Austin Light 12/6 Sports or an Austin 10/4 Sports, but that those shown in the 'A–Z' had slatted grilles and bumpers. A reader from New Eltham looked up the car in a 1935 Austin catalogue and identified it as either a 13.9 hp (1,496 cc) or 15.9 hp (1,711 cc) 12/6 'Newbury' or a (1,125 cc) 10/4 'Ripley'. The saloon version of the 13.9 and 15.9 was named the 'Kempton'. In another undated Austin catalogue, the name 'Greyhound' was used for the 12/6 sports saloon. Confirming this, the chairman of the Austin Ten Drivers' Club tells us that the car is definitely a 12/6 Newbury because it matches his own. Austin tried to use the name 'Greyhound' for the 12/6 sports saloon in 1933, but found it was registered to AC, so changed the name to 'Kempton' after around 100 were built. The slatted grille of early 12/6s, introduced in 1933, was phased out and replaced by a mesh grille in 1934, but the 10/4 retained the slatted grille. Bumpers were simply an option which many owners chose to not to take up. The first Greyhound/Kempton bodies were actually built by Ambi-Budd in Germany. The Austin 10 Drivers' Club caters for all 10, 12, 14, 16, 18, 20 and 28 hp Austins of the 1930s. Details of the club can be obtained by writing to Ian Dean, PO Box 12, Chichester, West Sussex PO20 7PH.

Austin Swallow

" *Some while ago we exchanged correspondence on special bodied Austin 7s. I'd like to tell you I have found another. I would guess the build date to be around 1930.* "

A reader from Totnes later reported that this Austin Seven Swallow coupe is his car. It is a 1928 model and is the only one known to have survived with its original detachable hard-top. Another unique feature of the car is that it was fitted with twin gearboxes in about 1934 and successfully competed in the Land's End and Exeter trials in 1935. Its present owner kept it in twin gearbox form and hoped to repeat the trials events during 1998.

Swallows back in production

Having spotted a letter in my column about the Austin 7 Swallow coupe, Bernard Cooper of La Riche Automobile Restorers in Jersey wrote to tell me that his company is now reproducing these cars. They take a genuine Austin 7 chassis, completely rebuild and refurbish both it and its running gear, then coach-build on an ash frame a replica Swallow roadster body with either standard 'bee' or optional 'wasp' rear end. This car does not come cheap, but any readers interested should contact Bernard Cooper, La Riche Automobile Restorers (CI) Ltd, Springside, Rue de la Monnaie, Trinity, Jersey JE3 5DG, tel: 01534 864073, website: http://www.leriche.com

Mice munch Hereford

" Our family owns an Austin A70 Hereford pick-up, registration KWO 843. My father bought it in 1953, I think for about £800. I learned to drive in it in 1965 and it was used to go to market until about 1972. It has been kept indoors since then. How many of these were manufactured and is it worth preserving? "

Total production of Hereford pick-ups was 20,434 but, being commercial vehicles which usually get run into the ground, very few have survived. So yours most definitely is worth preserving, even though mice have got at its wiring. Expect a call from David Thornton of The Austin Counties Owners' Club. The new club secretary is Martin Pickard of 10 George Street, Bedworth, Warwickshire CV12 8EB, and advertisements for interesting cars such as this pick-up are free in the club magazine. The best source material on Austin 'County' models is *Austin – The County Years* by Stuart Brown and Dave Wylie (available from the club at £7 plus p&p). Production figures for the A70 Hereford are: saloons: 48,640; countrymen: 1,515; drophead coupes: 266; pick-ups 20,434.

Autovia?

" *In the early 1950s when I lived in Edinburgh my employer acquired a car known as an Autovia which dated, I believe, from the late 1930s and had previously been owned by a cinema proprietor in Edinburgh. As I remember, it was a very large, handsome and luxurious vehicle with 'coffee and cream' two-tone paintwork. I was told it had been Victor Riley's attempt to break into the luxurious car market and came to be known as 'the car that sent Riley bankrupt'. The engine was reputed to be a V8 using two Riley 16 hp four-cylinder blocks mounted on a special crankcase. I did not drive at the time, but recollect sitting in the back seat with my legs fully extended with at least 12 inches still remaining between my feet and the back of the front seat. In the 45 years since then I have never seen any mention of the Autovia in the motoring press, so could it possibly be a figment of my senile imagination?* "

Nothing wrong with your memory, as you have perfect recall. H&H Auctions in Buxton sold a two-seater Autovia sports special for £9,000 net

(£9,523 gross) in July 1997. The engine was a 2,849 cc V8 constructed from two 1.5 litre four-cylinder blocks. Most of the bodies were by Mulliner. And, surprise surprise, there is even a club for this make which will be interested in the snippets of history you are able to provide: Autovia Car Club, c/o A. Williams, Pond Cottage, Bentfield Green, Stanstead, Essex CM24 8HY.

Non-runner Bean

" *In September 1997 I imported a British-built 1927 Bean 18/50 Tourer from Australia. Since then I have been trying to register it, but to no avail. The Vehicle Registration Office at Reading has told me that it will issue an age-related registration, but only after I have insured the car and had it MOT tested, and that registering it goes part and parcel with obtaining a 'tax exempt' VED disc. I need to do some restoration work before the car would pass an MOT, but my insurance agent tells me that he cannot issue an insurance certificate without a registration, so I am stuck in a 'Catch-22' situation. Please advise.* "

Your VRO is correct, but your insurance agent isn't. In the circumstances all you need to obtain insurance is the chassis number, and I'm surprised your insurance agent did not tell you this. ABM on 0181 681 8986 and Rauch and Stallard on 01702 348261 most certainly would have.

Two into one Bentley

" *Recently, I discovered some old photos of two Bentleys that my late grandfather used to own in the 1950s. One was registered MB 4483, the other XMF 547. How can I find out if they still exist? I have some more old photos that I would happily copy and supply to the current owners.* "

Confirmation of *The Daily Telegraph* readership's ability to find lost cars was soon received, as letters began to arrive thick and fast identifying the whereabouts of the lost Bentleys, MB 4483 and XMF 547. A Bentley Drivers' Club member from Grimsby was first to tell me that the Gurney Nutting-bodied standard chassis MB 4483 and the special-bodied short chassis XMF 547 are one and the same car, chassis number 429, engine number 428, first registered in December 1923 to G.F.B. Shand who owned it until 1931. Using the chassis number, Bill Port of the BDC searched the club's records and established that the car was registered to A.E. Carrodus in February 1946, then to C. Baggot in September 1946. G.L. Wills (my correspondent's grandfather) swapped the chassis, fitted a 2/4-seat body, and re-registered it XMF 547 in 1948, but resigned from the BDC in 1951 when the car passed to Barry Smythard. Clive Jones of Oswestry purchased the Bentley in October 1958 and re-registered it GX 3993 (more in keeping with the car) in September 1987. Though Clive Jones's membership of the BDC lapsed in 1982, the club gave me his address enabling me to write to him. The next day Mr Jones called to say all was well with the car. It runs twin 'sloper' carburettors, a 'C Type' gearbox and a 3.5 rear end on a genuine 9ft 9in. 'short chassis'. He has retained the 'V' screen fitted by Leo Wills in 1948, but has fitted blade-type mudguards and modified the body to the rear of the seats to be more appropriate to a Bentley than the Hispano Suiza Mr Wills modelled it on. Apparently, Mr Wills sold the car to finance the purchase of an aircraft, and later offered Mr Jones the original standard chassis. If readers have the chassis and engine numbers as well as the registration, the Bentley Drivers' Club can often tell them what has happened to a car (tel: 01844 208233).

Double bubbles

Two letters seeking information about Isetta bubble cars arrived in the same week. One reader wanted to know the value of a 1959 RHD Isetta 300 found in Cyprus with only one owner from new. The other sought information about the new 'Isetta' kit cars driven by Tony Mason on the 'Top Gear' TV programme.

The Cypriot bubble was rare for being a 1959 model with the tubular front bumpers (most RHDs had a useless 'bumper' which ran across the car under the front door). The convertible top seems to have been sealed up. But, apart from some blistering behind the nearside wheel arch, it looks rust-free, and Isetta 300s in this condition have typically been making £2,000 to £3,000. RHD is bad news for driving because it puts the driver on the same side as the side-mounted engine and the combined weight tends to make right-hand bends a bit worrying. New 'Zetta' replica Isettas are made by Tri Tech Autocraft of Unit 1, The Old Mill Industrial Estate, School Lane, Bamber Bridge, Preston PR5 6SY, tel: 01772 468317. Fully built, with centre mounted Honda 250 cc engine and Bedford Rascal steering gear, they cost around £6,000. The company also makes a replica Messerschmitt, known as the 'Schmitt'. I passed my first driving test in an original LHD 1959 Isetta at the age of 16, back in 1964. After a hair-raising flat-out run down a hill at all of 59 mph, a female companion memorably remarked, 'That was fantastic. I've never been in anything so unsafe.' Alan's Unusual Automobiles specialises in microcars of all kinds (01367 240125). (Three wheelers are exempt from the new Single Vehicle Approval test for grey imports and kit cars.)

Z1

" Does BMW still produce the Z1? If so, how can I obtain details? "

The model ran from June 1989 to June 1991 (UK imports from October 1989) and a total of only 8,093 were built, in LHD-form only. Prices have not fluctuated very much at all over the past five years and you can expect to pay between £18,000 and £22,000 for one. Jeremy Clarkson bought one for his wife. Quite a few Z1s are 'grey' imports from Germany (an 89F certainly is), so make sure that the lights dip left. Also look for old accident damage. I inspected one for a friend last summer and, though the car looked good superficially, the front panel fit was even more iffy than usual, suggesting it had been 'sausaged'. Buy one and you'll need to change the timing belt and tensioner straight away. BMW specifies a maximum 'life' of three years for timing belts on the old 3-Series engines.

Brennabor and Briscoe

" My father owned cars from 1900 until he gave up driving in his 90th year. Two models he owned that I never see mentioned were the Brennabor (where I used to sit high outside in a dickey seat) and the Briscoe, which we called 'Cyclops' because it had one headlight in the centre of the radiator. "

Georgano's *Complete Encyclopaedia* tells us that Brennabor cars were built in Brandenburg from 1908 to 1934. The first was a three-wheeler, but a four-wheeler 10 hp model soon followed. Brennabor cars were robust and reliable and did well in long-distance trials. They were marketed in the UK under the name Brenna, and your father's may well have been the 3-seater 1.5 litre 3/15 ps of around 1914. Briscoe was an American make built between 1914 and 1921 and Georgano presents us with a photograph of the 1915 2.5 litre 'Cyclops' Roadster.

Mystery Bristol

" On holiday in the Dordogne in 1988 I spotted a 2.0 litre Bristol convertible. The two occupants, both wearing straw boaters, told me it was one of only two in existence, the other being in America. Can you confirm this? "

I went straight to the horse's mouth and asked Tony Crook of Bristol Cars. The interesting tubular bumpers help identify the car as a Bristol 400 convertible, of which only two were built. One is in the UK and, though the other was thought to have been broken up, there are reports of it being seen in the USA. Tony Crook did not like the car and withdrew it from the Bristol stand at the 1948 Motor Show before the show opened. A very small number of the later Bristol 401 chassis went to the Italian coachbuilders Touring and Pininfarina, and Pininfarina built one convertible – but not to Bristol standards of workmanship. The model designated '402' was a factory-built convertible version of the 401 based on the Pininfarina design.

A number of readers subsequently confirmed through their ownership that the Bristol

400 convertible remains one of a pair. In summary of these very helpful replies, the car once registered JMR II has now re-acquired its original registration of KHT 203 and is Bristol 400 chassis number 400/1/003, one of four pre-production prototypes, two of which were built as dropheads. It is now owned by a member of The Bristol Owners' Club. Its sister car, also built as a drophead, was chassis number 400/1/004 and is now back in the UK registered SMG 72. This car was shown at the 1947 Geneva Motor Show and its owner has a photograph of it at the Furka Pass on its way to the Geneva Show. (Bristol Cars is still in possession of chassis number 400/1/001, a coupe, reg. JHY 261, and the other prototype, chassis number 400/2/002, reg. NHX 115, was broken up.) A reader from Virginia Water purchased one of the pair of convertibles from Tony Crook in 1956 as a direct swap for his 'nearly new' MG Magnette. At the time it was in a blue 'heather' colour. It frequently travelled to continental Europe, where it was found to be 100% reliable apart from a tendency to overheat at high speed and to swap ends with a full load on. A reader from Whittington tells us that, in 1948/49, he bought what must have been the prototype for the later 402 convertible, built by Pininfarina on a 400 rather than a 401 chassis. His only complaint was that the doors tended to spring open at speed – a deficiency the Bristol factory corrected in the production 402 convertibles.

Swan song

" *My husband leaves* The Daily Telegraph *'Motoring' lying around, and I was particularly impressed with the issue dedicated to Ferrari. By coin-*

cidence, at the time I was also in the process of reading a chapter from My Life and Times *by Jerome K. Jerome. Jerome was born in 1858 and one paragraph from 'The Wheels of Change' caught my imagination. I quote: 'Motors were strange and awful shapes at the beginning. There was one design supposed to resemble a Swan; but owing to the neck being short, it looked more like a duck – that is if it looked like anything. To fill the radiator you unscrewed its head and poured water down its neck; and as you drove, the screw would work loose, and the thing would turn round and look at you out of one eye. Others were shaped like canoes and gondolas. One firm brought out a dragon. It had a red tongue, and you hung the spare wheel on its tail.' I wonder if you, your fellow columnists or any of your readers might have any knowledge of these strange creatures ... and whether any of them survive?* **"**

My first reference for this is *Automania* by Julian Pettifer and Nigel Turner, which accompanied a 1984 TV series of the same name, and can still be found at specialist bookstores. On page 22 is a photo of the very car, 'created in 1912 in Lowestoft, England – to the special order of an English eccentric living in Calcutta, a Mr R.N. Mathewson. It featured a beak that opened, lifelike hisses produced by compressed air and water from the car's radiator, and eight organ pipes linked to a musical keyboard. Though its Suffolk creators are long gone, the "swan song" has not yet played for this remarkable vehicle that lives on in India still terrorising those who dare to cross its path.' Culshaw and Horrobin's *Complete Catalogue of British Cars 1895–1975* goes into a bit more nitty gritty, featuring a picture of the car on page 92 and telling us it was a special body built onto a 1910 Brooke 15/20, a conventional four-cyclinder side-valve car made in Lowestoft. Brooke's main business was marine engines.

Scout's honour

" I bought a 1939 BSA front-wheel-drive car shortly after the war. I drove it satisfactorily for several years, but its weakness was the flexible discs on the front wheel drive. Spare discs became increasingly difficult to find and I sold it in 1952. Can you give any history of this model, and are there any still on the road? "

This model was known as the 'BSA Scout' and a 1,203 cc 1937 Mk 4 example bid to £5,500 at British Car Auctions Classic Car sale on 6 July 1992. I spotted the new owner driving it home afterwards, so it was certainly roadworthy. According to Sedgwick and Gillies's *A–Z of Cars of the 1930s*, the Scout was launched as a 9 hp 1,075 cc model in 1935. The 10 hp 1,203 cc Series 3, 4 and 5 followed from 1936–38, and the Series 6 during 1939 and 1940. Total production was around 2,700 cars. This reader's car, which has wire wheels, seems to be a Series 5, as the Series 6 had pressed steel wheels with hubcaps. A reader from Ferndown very kindly sent me a file of 1938–39 *Autocar* road tests which includes a test of the Series 6 four-seat tourer. The magazine praised its high-geared steering (only one-and-three-quarter turns lock to lock) 'allowing the car to be "placed" to a matter of inches'. The tested top speed was 67.67 mph, 0–30 took 9.2 seconds, and the stopping distance from 30 mph was 28 feet in the dry, which is 18 feet short of the 30 mph stopping distance in the 1997 Highway Code.

Scouting tips

Following these recollections about the BSA Scout, several readers wrote with solutions to the driveshaft problem. One from Surbiton replaced the 'unobtainable' fabric discs with discs cut to size from colliery conveyor belts. Another from Chilworth sorted out the drive hub splines by re-making them to an interference fit forced on with a pressure of about 60 tons. All recalled with affection a car which had excellent steering and roadholding for the day, even at the expense of a 40 foot turning circle. There is, in fact, a BSA Front Wheel Drive Club, chaired by Peter Cook, of Two Chimneys, Pinks Hill, Wood Street, Guildford, Surrey GU3 3BW, tel: 01483 570433; Membership Secretary: Barry Baker, 164 Cottimore Lane, Walton-on-Thames, Surrey KT12 2BL, tel: 01932 225270.

Atalante, not Atlantique

" I'm trying to find out more about a Bugatti I saw in 1937/38 in the South of France. It belonged to one Bill Dobson (his brothers Austin and Arthur raced frequently at Donington and Crystal Palace before the Second World War). Bill Dobson met his death in 1938 or 1939. As far as I am concerned, the car knocks spots off the modern designs. It is utterly beautiful. What I should like to know is, are there any models left in the world today? And can you find out more about the car, such as its engine capacity, performance, current value, etc.? I believe that Earl Howe also owned one of these cars during the late 1930s. "

At first I thought the car was a Bugatti Type 57 'Atlantique', and in a global poll reported in *Classic & Sportscar* magazine of August 1997 this was voted the most beautiful car ever made. Only one prototype, the 'Aerolite', and three 'Atlantiques' were built and, though the prototype was lost, the three 'Atlantiques' all survive – two in the USA and one in France. But this is not an 'Atlantique', it is an 'Atalante' (one-piece flat screen and full-size doors). A type 57 was designated a 57 if it had the standard chassis and a 57S if it had the lowered 'sports' chassis and high compression engine. The latter were distinguished by vee-shaped rather than flat grilles. Supercharged 57s were designated 57C, and a supercharged sports chassis 57 was therefore a 57SC. Power outputs varied from 130 bhp for an early 57 to 220 bhp for a late 57SC. Reg. no. 3188 EH 75 was a 57S with an eight-cylinder, high-compression, six-bearing 3,257 cc 190 bhp dry-sump engine capable of pushing it to 125 mph. The low, faired-in lights suggest that Bill Dobson's car, reg. 4487 BA 6, could have been a later 57SC with the supercharged 220 bhp engine. In July 1990, at the classic car price peak, Sothebys sold a 1937 Type 57 with replica Atalante bodywork for £705,000. In August 1995, at a 'World Classics' auction at Pebble Beach, a 1938 Type 57 Atalante sold for £315,000, and in March 1998 one was sold in Geneva for £264,625 plus commission. This may well have been the same car, as only two genuine Atalantes are thought to remain. A reader from Holt, who corrected the Type 57 nomenclature, tells us that Earl Howe's car was a 57S, later owned by the late Mr J.P. Tingay who converted it to an SC.

'What big teeth you've got'

" *I attended an event last month where the guest of honour arrived in an unusual big black classic car. As it passed, I saw the word 'Dynaflow' on the rear – a make I have never heard of – yet a man in the crowd said it was a Buick. Is it? And does the registration plate, LOI 949 (LO 1949) signify its date of manufacture?* "

The car is a 1949 Buick Series 70 Roadmaster (four portholes – other Buicks had just three). 'Dynaflow' refers to the hydraulic torque-converter automatic transmission, available for the first time on Buicks in 1948. These were magnificent cars – with a very quiet OHV straight-eight engine and, I think, a side-hinged bonnet. The quality of material and construction of 1930s and 1940s Buicks was very high.

More Buicks

" I couldn't agree more with your comment about the high quality of 1930s and 40s Buicks. My father had a 1938 model with encased spare wheels set into the front wings. Then, in 1951, the only way he could replace it with another was to buy the American Ambassador's right-hand-drive 1949 model Special. This car was registered KLW 3, had 13,650 miles under its wheels and cost my father the then enormous sum of £3,250. He drove it for eleven years and sold it for £200 in 1962. "

Another reader sent us an account of how his father purchased a 1947/48 model Buick Eight for £3,000 (reg. JLK 5) and also ran it until 1962, by which time it had covered 300,000 miles. Yet another told us of a 1940 Canadian McLaughlan Buick Viceroy which his uncle bought in 1950. 'The beautiful overhead valve straight eight ... could take all he could give it. I remember the Buick's excellent steering column gear change, the early "cold start" with the Carter carburettor, and the marvellous standards of manufacture (all nuts could be done up with the fingers except for a final nip with a spanner). Spares were easy from Lendrum and Hartman and anything unusual took just seven days from Detroit. I think the only snags were mediocre headlamps, poor windscreen wipers, and, of course, 6–7 mpg in London traffic. Unfortunately, the Buick met its nemesis on the Ridgeway at Enfield when, having stopped in fog because of cars ahead, it was rammed by a lorry. Despite a completely smashed boot and jammed rear doors, the laugh was still with the Buick because it drove home even though the lorry was immobilised. After repairs it was sold.'

Calcott

" Could you tell me anything about an early 1920s car known as the Calcott? "

The Calcott brothers began production of their 10 hp car in Coventry in 1913. Its distinguishing feature was a radiator which bore more than a passing resemblance to the Standard of the time. They were roomy, reliable and modestly priced. The engine was a 1,460 cc side-valve four, which was bored out to 1,645 cc in 1920 to become an 11.9 hp which accompanied the 10 hp to 1925. These were joined by a 2,121 cc 13.9 hp in 1923, a 1,954 cc 12/24 in 1925, and a 2,565 cc 16/50 also in 1925. Production ended in 1927. The Coventry Museum of British Road Transport has a 1921 10 hp, and the National Motor Museum at Beaulieu a 1923 11.9. *The Automobile* magazine carried a letter about these cars in its February 1998 issue. Anthony Wilson of 'Willerby', 61 Ridgewood Drive, RD1, New Plymouth, New Zealand (fax: 00 64 67537461) has been compiling a register of surviving Calcotts (22 so far). But one, RFP 9, disappeared from the VCC records in 1970 and he is very keen to find out what became of it. Past owners included: G. Wilding, J.A.G. Birchall,

C.C. Bowker and C.J. Bendall. Other Calcotts are thought to exist in Holland, India, South Africa and South Australia, and naturally Mr Wilson would be grateful for confirmation of this.

Checkered history

" *Ever since I first saw one I have had a passion for the classic New York taxi. Despite having searched I have found no information on this car whatsoever. If you could tell me of any publication on this car and how to go about buying one I would be very grateful indeed.* "

The classic American-style 'Checker' cabs were manufactured in Kalamazoo, Michigan, from 1923 until 1982.

Brooklands Books offer a compilation of road tests and magazine features on the Checker cab, price £9.95 from Mill House Books, tel: 01205 270377. But your best bet is The Checker Cab Club of Great Britain, c/o Colin Peak, 36 The Avenue, Wraysbury, Staines, Middx TW19 5HA, tel: 01784 483462. Checker Cabs were manufactured in Kalamazoo, Michigan from 1923 until 1982, when they were generally replaced by Chevrolet Caprices. The model you refer to is the A8, which appeared in 1958 and looked a bit like a stretched 1955 Chevrolet. (The earlier model which ran from 1947–1958 was much better looking.) In 1959 the A8 was replaced by the A9, which could also be had as a 'Suburban' estate car or a six- or eight-door 'Aerobus' (at least one of these was used in the UK). Ray Tomkinson (01204 533447) has a few Checkers on his taxi rental fleet and can also supply these cars.

Cheswold?

" *The first car my father bought, in about 1920, was called a 'Cheswold', and I have yet to come across someone who has heard of one. It was made in Doncaster and I understand that only fourteen were made before the factory was taken over for war purposes in 1914. It was an open type with a hood, a bonnet which sloped down at the front with radiator on the scuttle, like contemporary Renaults, big brass headlamps, a gate gearchange, petrol tank at rear with a pump on the steering column to pressurise it and assist petrol flow. The weak point was the back axle which often seemed to break, and when it did so the car had no brakes. Is this one car that time has forgotten?* ""

Not quite, because the very car is pictured on page 377 of Culshaw and Horrobin's *Complete Catalogue of British Cars 1895–1975*. The authors tell us that production lasted six years from 1911 to 1916 but only one model, the 15.9 hp, was ever produced. Details are: 4-cylinder 2,610 cc engine, 9ft 8in. wheelbase, 4ft 6in. track, overall length 13ft 6in., wire wheels, tyres 815 x 105.

Chitty Chitty Bang Bang

"" *May I tell you a story about 'Chitty Chitty Bang Bang'? It was 1948, I had been demobilised and had joined a company in the retail motor trade as a trainee manager. I visited a garage in Brundall, a village a few miles from Norwich, and in the course of conversation with the proprietor, I asked that if he ever had a secondhand car – for example an Austin 7 – would he please let me know. In those days it was almost impossible to buy a car new or secondhand. A few months later I again visited the garage and the proprietor asked if I was still looking for a car, which I was. 'Well,' he said, 'I've just the thing for you.' He then took me to one of the lock-up garages at the rear of his forecourt, opened the doors and the inside was full of car! 'Just the thing for you,' he said. 'What is it?' I said. 'Don't you recognise it?' he said. 'It's Chitty Chitty Bang Bang.' To cut a long story short, he told me it needed a new exhaust manifold and he would accept £25 for it. And yes, you've guessed it, I didn't buy it. Oh, what a fool was I. I wonder how many of your readers know how it got its name? 'Chitty Chitty Bang Bang' is onomatopoeic; it was the noise the engine made when being tow-started at Brooklands.* ""

That's a nice story. But £25? Count Zborowski would turn in his grave.

Any clues about a Cluley?

" In about 1930 my father drove a Cluley, and I wondered if an example of that car still exists. I believe that only a few were made, by a firm which originally manufactured mill machinery in the North of England. My clearest memory is of sitting in the back with my sister, peering through draughty celluloid side screens at the North Yorkshire Moors. On a hot summer's day, we passengers had to get out and walk while father drove up the steep hill out of Whitby. We would find him at the top of the hill sitting in state admiring the view behind the steam from a boiling radiator. "

The Cluley merits half a page in Nick Baldwin's *A to Z of Cars of the 1920s* (ISBN 1-870979-53-2) which tells us that the car was built by bicycle manufacturers Clarke, Cluley and Co. of Wells Street, Coventry between 1921 and 1928. The best-known were the 10.4 hp (1,200 cc) and 11.9 hp (1,300 cc). Georgano's *Complete Encyclopaedia of Motorcars* (from secondhand bookshops, price £25–£75) shows a 10.4 hp tourer which is probably the car your father owned. I have not yet found any Cluley cars in UK museums. A total of nine Cluley 10.5 hp models are known to survive. The Cluley Register is run by Roger Armstrong, 18 The Woodlands, Esher, Surrey KT10 8DB, tel: 0181 398 2711. He would very much like to hear of any more.

Clyno stories

" I wonder if you would be kind enough to help me discover details of a Clyno car which my uncle owned in the 1930s and which we knew as 'Primrose'. "

This turned out to be a Clyno 10.8 hp, in production from 1922 to 1928, with a four-cylinder Coventry Simplex side-valve engine and three-speed gearbox. Coincidentally, two more readers wrote with reminiscences of Clynos. One recalled his father hiring a Clyno two-seater with dickey for a day trip from Bournemouth to Southampton in about 1927. Disaster struck in the New Forest on the way home when, in torrential rain, the car skidded into a ditch. A passenger in the dickey was found unhurt in a hedge which had broken his fall, and luckily all the occupants escaped with no more than bruises. Another reader bought a Clyno two-seater with dickey seat from a friend in Dublin for £12 10s, and two years later sold it for the same amount. He had no trouble with it, but it had been in a crash, so there is a remote possibility it was the very same Clyno described above. Clyno Club and Register, c/o R. Surman, Swallow Cottage, Langton Farm, Burbage Common Road, Elmesthorpe, Leicestershire LE9 7SE, tel: 01455 842178.

Au revoir to an old Ami

" Could you please advise me of the 'kindest' way to sell a Citroen Ami 8 which is 25 years old and has the original 'M' registration? The car is of sentimental value to a lady whose husband died nearly two years ago and who owned and looked after the car from new. "

Get in touch with 2CV GB (Deux Chevaux Club of Great Britain), c/o Barry Bowles, 2CVGB, PO Box 602, Crick, Northants NN6 7UW; also contact the club secretary of The Citroen Car Club c/o Derek Pearson, PO Box 348, Bromley, Kent BR2 8QT, tel: 07000 248258; website:

http://www.ccc-uk.demon.co.uk. Your best chance of selling this car is probably at the GSA and Ami Annual Rally at Reading, Berks.

D Specialists

" Back in 1980 I reluctantly sold – and have since regretted selling – a Citroen D Special. I understood some years later that there was someone in the Avon area who rebuilt these monsters. Have you any knowledge of him or any other DS specialist? "

Retromobile is the main 'Specialist' and is on the Internet at http://www.retromobile.com. Alternatively, phone 0171 498 7111 and arrange to call at Unit 74, Chelsea Bridge Business Centre, 326–340 Queenstown Road, London SW8 4ME. Bring loadsamoney. A bit nearer to you is the Oxford French Car Co. on 01865 316602 (they even do a Chapron cabrio replica). Finally, if you decide to take the plunge, you'd be bonkers not to join the very active Citroen Car Club (for details see previous reply).

Classic camper?

" I have a 1976 Commer camper-van, which I want to sell. I have tried advertising in the local press to no avail. Camper magazines only seem to contain ads for campers priced £10,000-plus (mine is worth perhaps £1,000). How can I sell it without spending a fortune on advertising? "

Your best bet is to get in touch with Steve Cooper of The Classic Camper Club, 40 Audley Drive, Kidderminster, Worcs DY11 5NE, tel: 01562 752432.

Connaughts

" I was P.A. to the General Manager of Continental Cars Ltd, Portsmouth Road, Send, Surrey in 1949/50, and half of the Continental Cars workshop was divided off and designated 'The Racing Dept.' The car that emerged was, of course, the Connaught, designed by Rodney Clarke and Mike Oliver and sponsored by Kenneth McAlpine. I saw the first one rolled out, and saw it return from its first outing at Goodwood. Say no more. But I seldom see any mention of the roadgoing sports version of the Connaught which was assembled in the Continental Cars workshop. They were based on 1.7 litre 14 hp Lea Francis chassis kits. The chassis assembly was much modified and the engine breathed on by the Connaught engineers. The body was full width and the complete bonnet and wing assembly front-hinged, which was very modern for its day. The bodies were built by Leacroft of Egham who underbid Abbots of Farnham. There were also plans and orders for a 1.5 litre version specifically for club racing, but I don't think it was ever finished. "

A friend of mine, then working as an art director for McCann Erickson, the advertising agency, actually owned one of the 1,767 cc Connaught sports cars built between 1949 and 1954, which, with four Amal carburettors, was good for 140 bhp. A Connaught L3, part of the Duncan Rabagliati collection, was sold by Brooks Auctioneers at Olympia for £6,700 plus commission on 8 April 1998.

Coventry Victor?

" In the early 1960s I bought a Coventry Victor three-wheeler. As soon as I saw the huge chromed headlights I was hooked. The owner needed £25 for an engagement ring and the deal was struck. Rather typically of the times, it was towed home and, after many fingernails were broken, was eventually towed away for scrap. The trouble was the aluminium starter bracket had sheared and I couldn't fix it. I've never seen these cars mentioned in any owners' club lists. Can you help? "

The original Coventry Victor 'Midget' of 1928/33 had side-valve, then overhead-valve flat-twin engines of 688 cc, 749 cc or 850 cc and two-speed chain transmission. The later Avon-bodied 'Luxury Sports' model of 1933/38 had 749 cc, 850 cc or 998 cc flat-twins and three speeds. However, it seems that even the 998 was good for no more than 60 mph, so Morgans of the day tended to leave them in the dust. Can't find a specific club, I'm afraid, but the BSA Front Wheel Drive Club, tel: 01483 570433 or 01932 225270, may be able to point you in the right direction.

Cubitt?

" *Many years ago when I was a small boy my father owned a car called a Cubitt which I think he may have taken as part-payment for some transaction in his business as a farmer and cattle trader. Father did not drive, so my elder brother was delegated the task. Father sat in the passenger seat with the door slightly open so he could exit quickly in an emergency and my brother was prompted to hoot at every corner, which he did by punching a bulbous horn. We small children sat in the back, thrilled to bits with excitement. Since those days I have never heard of that make of car. I should be grateful if you could furnish any information.* "

Cubitt's Engineering Co. Ltd of Aylesbury aimed to compete with mass-produced American imports with a rugged, American-style, semi-mass-produced car of its own design. The car had a 2,815 cc side-valve four-cylinder engine and a four-speed gearbox with central gear lever. The model lasted from 1920 to 1925 but never achieved its production target of 5,000 a year due to component supply problems. Only about 3,000 were built.

D.F.P.?

" *Could you tell me anything about the French D.F.P. car? My father had a fine example for about six years from 1920 to 1926. It was a six-cylinder open tourer which, as far as I can remember, gave absolute trouble-free service. Are there any motoring books, preferably in English, that cover the D.F.P.?* "

Doriot et Flandrin started building single-cylinder 'voiturettes' in 1908. When Parant joined them they started building four-cylinder cars with side-valve Chapuis Dornier engines, and in 1912 started making their own engines. Georgano describes the 10/12 as 'being joined by an excellent 2.0 litre 12/15 with pressure lubrication, three bearing crankshaft and 4-speed gearbox capable of 2,500 rpm and 55 mph.' He continues, 'The British concession was acquired by the brothers W.O. and H.M. Bentley, who ran the 12/15 in competition – and by the end of 1913 a specially prepared example had been timed at 89.70 mph.' In 1914 D.F.P. launched a sporting 12/40, with 'V' radiator, and Bentley persuaded the company to fit aluminium pistons, which brought the top speed of the £320 road car to 65 mph. Georgano goes on to tell us that the company never fully recovered from the First World War and, when Bentley set up as a manufacturer in its own right, D.F.P. lost its best export market. I would guess that your father's car was a 12/40 since its successor, the overhead valve, four-speed 13/50, was not launched until 1923. The larger 16/22 2.8 litre and later 3.0 litre models, which had cylinders cast in pairs, were criticised for poor performance.

European Union

" My father owned an unusual car between 1937 and 1938 which had a gravity feed petrol tank. It was a DKW (unkindly referred to within the family as a 'Deutsches Kinder Wagen'), bearing the interlocking circle badge now seen on Audis, and it had a part-steel body with some areas of fabric on an open steel frame. The engine was a transverse two-stroke water-cooled twin which drove the front wheels, the gear lever came straight out of the dash, like a Citroen, and it was right-hand-drive. Can you tell me anything about it?' "

This will have been a DKW Meisterklasse. The model was first seen as the F2 which had a 684 cc two-stroke, double backbone chassis and fabric-covered body. The gearbox was three speed, with freewheel (like later Saabs) and had a 'dynastart' (the starter motor became the dynamo once the engine was running). From 1935 the F5 was introduced with a classier, but still part-fabric, body, the F7 in 1937 and the F8 in 1939. 190,000 F5/F8s were built. After the war, production of the F8 resumed in East Germany and continued from 1948 to 1955. The 1953–58 DKW Sonderklasse grew into the 1958–63 1000 and 1000S. There was also a really super 1000SP cabrio from 1958 to 1965 that looked like a miniature '57 Ford Thunderbird. All had two-stroke, three-cylinder engines. The 1000S then grew into the 1964/66 1,175 cc DKW F102 (still a two-stroke '3') which, when fitted with Mercedes-designed high-compression four-cylinder 1,496 cc, 1,696 cc and 1,770 cc four-stroke engines, became the Audi 60, 70, 75, 80 and 90 of 1965–72. So today's Audi A4 is more or less a direct descendent of the 1000S, and still has the same engine/transmission layout. If any reader wants to join the DKW Owners' Club,

please write to A.S. Cook, 265 Victoria Road, Oulton Broad, Lowestoft, Suffolk NR33 9LR, tel: 0850 634242.

When 'convertible' meant 'convertible'

" *Back in 1923 a ladyfriend of mine, then aged two, went with her father to purchase a 'Dixie' vehicle, designed by Walter Shepherd of Market Bosworth to be truly 'convertible'. In the morning it could be fitted with a 'bus' body to take miners to work at Hinckley colliery, and then the schoolchildren to school. After that, the bus body was lifted off and replaced by a truck back for carrying bricks and coal. Then, in the evening, the bus body was put back on and the schoolchildren and miners were brought home. The vehicle was also used as a wedding coach, and Dixie removable bodies included bus, delivery van, ambulance, hearse, lorry, pig dray and furniture removal car.* "

The idea of a removable body was quite common between 1910 and 1930. Once, when visiting the Cobham bus museum, I remarked on the floor height of a 1925 open-top double-decker and was told that it, too, had a removable body. During the day, it worked as a bus. But in the evening the bus body was removed so the chassis could carry a truck bed to collect fruit and vegetables for Covent Garden market. This is the reason why early double-deckers were open-topped. Had the upper deck also been enclosed the vehicle would have been too tall to go under railway bridges and would also have been in danger of toppling over.

Facel Vega

" As a young man visiting the Motor Show in London, I have lasting memories of being invited to sit in a Facel Vega. I recall the interior finish in particular, and the upholstery of the seats almost reaching my ears when I sat on them. The external styling, with the four headlamps arranged vertically in pairs, also increased my desire to own such a wonderful vehicle. When did the car go out of production, and do examples come up for sale in the UK? Can you give a price guide and advise whether or not spares are obtainable? "

Facel Vegas were imported from France by Hersham and Walton Motors in Walton-on-Thames from the late 1950s to the early 1960s. The company was then run by George Abacaissis and the chief mechanic was Fred Hobbs, who wrote about the experience in his autobiography. The first coupes of 1954/55 were known simply as the Vega and had 4.5 litre, then 4.8 litre, De-Soto V8s. This then became the FVS from 1955 to 1959, with 5.4 litre Chrysler 'Firedome' engines and usually a push-button 'Torqueflite' automatic. Novelist and philosopher Albert Camus died in the passenger seat of a drum-braked Facel FVS in 1960. The HK 500 of 1959–61 followed the FVS, boasting up to 360 bhp, and is more common. The final series Facel II from 1962 to 1964 hid its twin-stacked lights under a single lens and its up to 390 bhp under its bonnet. There was also the Excellence – a huge, Lincoln-like pillarless four-door saloon with 'clap-hand' doors and a propensity to sag in the middle, and the 'Facellia' – a junior, Alfa-like two-seat roadster which started life with a problem-prone Facel-built twin-cam four but ended it with a pushrod Volvo engine. The cars do crop up at auction from time to time. BCA Blackbushe sold a 1959 HK 500 restoration project for £130 in February 1993, a complete 1959 HK 500 for £7,245 in the same sale and a reasonably good one for £19,058 in February 1998. This last car did, however, have a crack in its wraparound windscreen, and it cost a fortune to have a replacement made. Brooks sold a 1960 Excellence for £10,530 in May 1998, and in November 1994 BCA sold a 1961 Facellia with its original engine (but with the 2.0 litre Volvo installed) for £15,034. Facel FVSs are valued at up to £19,000; HK 500s at up to £25,000; and Facel IIs at up to £50,000. Some spares are available through the Facel Vega Owners' Club, c/o Ray Scandrett, 'Windrush', 16 Paddock Gardens, East Grinstead, Sussex RH19 4AE, tel: 01343 26655.

Topolino

" *Back in the 1950s I used to own a 1937 Fiat 500 Topolino. I got great enjoyment out of this little car. Now retired, I am contemplating treating myself to one, as a little toy I suppose. They appear to be quite rare, but when available the asking price seems to be £6,000–£7,000. In view of the potential difficulties with spare parts, are there any clubs that cater for this car? And, when production was resumed in 1948, the 500B and 500C had an overhead valve engine. Did this improve their performance significantly over the pre-war side-valve 500?* "

One of these charming little cars starred in the excellent movie, 'Cinema Paradiso'. A 500A in poor condition sold in Christies' Microcar Auction on 6 March 1997 for £1,659. A quite nice 500A sold at BCA Blackbushe on 12 February 1996 for £4,764 inclusive. The Collector's Car Auction List tells you what's coming up at classic sales generally (Faxback: 0336 424800 – cost 50p a minute, or tel: 0181 534 3883). Miller's Guide shows four 500As at from £1,000 to £5,500 and two 500Cs at £1,800 to £4,000. Sedgwick and Gillies's *A–Z of the 1930s* covers the 500A two-seater and the rather ugly UK-only 500 four-seater, stating: 'Amazing economy and usual viceless handling, but 500s are brutes to work on as everything's so small and cramped. Body tends to rust away at the back.' The *A–Z* covering 1945 to 1970 says of the 500C: 'Much improved over the pre-war model. Delightful to drive and horrible to work on. Watch the sills (for rust).' The Fiat Motor Club caters for these cars and, in 1941, its President, H.A. Collyer, actually owned the 500A auctioned by BCA in 1996. Fiat Motor Club, Barnside, Glastonbury, Somerset BA6 8DB, tel: 01458 831433.

T-taxi

" *My father was in the carriage trade in the early 1920s and I think he drove a Ford. Could you confirm this, and what model might the car have been?* "

All Model T Fords were coloured black because their black Japan enamel was the only paint that would dry quickly enough for the mass-production process by which they were manufactured.

It would be a Model T Ford, the car that put the world on wheels. The first Model Ts from 1908 to 1917 had brass radiators. From 1917 to 1925 they had painted radiators. And from 1925 to 1927 they had nickel-plated radiators. From 1914 until 1926 all Model T Fords were black because black Japan enamel was the only paint which would dry quickly enough for Henry Ford's mass production process. (Each post-1914 Model T took just one-and-a-half man-hours to build.) Self-starters situated on the right of the engine from 1919 left no room for a right-hand steering box and meant that all Model Ts from that date were left-hand-drive. The President of the Ford Model T Register adds: 'Ford T Town Cars, as they were called, were sold from 1910 to 1921. The Model Ts for the UK were assembled at Trafford Park, Manchester from October 1911 with British bodywork on certain models. They were right-hand-drive.' Detachable rims were introduced in 1919. The Model T Ford was and still is the most significant car ever built because it offered cheap independent transport to 15 million people who could previously only dream of such freedom. Ford Model T Register, c/o Julia Amer, 3 Riverside, Strong Close, Keighley, W. Yorks BD21 4JP.

'Chains and dogs'

" *You might be interested in the 1922 GN two-seater sports car owned by my father and mother. It had an air-cooled 9 hp engine with cast iron pistons. Unless the plunger of the oil tank on the running board was pulled up and down about every five miles the engine would seize up, but after it cooled down it was back to normal. The back axle had four chains for forward propulsion and one for reverse. When my parents were away from home, I used to 'borrow' the car to take my pals out for a 'burn-up'.*

We must have hit a top speed of all of 35 mph. I was aged 15 at the time and no one worried about a driving licence or insurance policy. **"**

Your parents' car was indeed an early GN built by H.R. Godfrey and Captain 'Archie' Frazer-Nash. Their transmission philosophy was immortalised by the words of W.H. Charnock:

Nash and Godfrey hated cogs,
Built a car with chains and dogs,
It worked but would it if
They had made it with a diff?

A few years ago I remember being very impressed by a V-twin GN's ascent of the test hill at Brooklands during a Frazer-Nash Owners' Club meeting. Frazer-Nash went on to build the famous series of 'chain gang' Frazer-Nash cars, while Godfrey later built the similar-looking HRG with a conventional transmission and 'diff'. Frazer-Nash cars are often 'handed down' from one generation of a family to the next, and membership of the Frazer-Nash Owners' Club is very close knit. They also continue to innovate and, at the same Brooklands meeting, when a transmission component milled from Duralumin irreparably failed on one chap's car, another member very kindly loaned him his so he could continue competing. Any GN, Frazer-Nash and HRG snippets of information will be welcomed by The Frazer-Nash Archives, Coxon House, Newton Road, Henley-on-Thames, Oxon RG9 1HG, tel: 01491 411491.

Going Goggo

" *Seeing mention of the microcars in your column brought back memories of my 1959 Goggomobil T300 saloon, registration WUF 711, which I* *bought in 1964. This was a delight to drive with a twin-cylinder two-stroke engine and Porsche-designed gearbox. It was the first of my many two-stroke cars and one which I wish I still had. "*

Another reader, from Burton-upon-Trent, wrote to tell us that he acquired WUF 711 in 1967 via an ad in *Exchange & Mart*. He tells us: 'For some time, it faithfully carried me to and from college in Derby. Then, one fateful winter evening, while overtaking a lorry, I overtaxed the poor Goggo's roadholding capabilities and put it backwards through a hedge. Sadly, my father pronounced it beyond economical repair and it was consigned to the breaker's yard. May I convey my apologies to your correspondent, and I hope he is not too upset by this.' At Christies' Microcar auction on 6 March 1997, a 1959 Goggomobil T400 made a remarkable £20,732 inclusive, while a 1959 Goggomobil TL400 van made a staggering £26,260 inclusive. That wasn't the only micro-shock. An Isle of Man-built Peel P50 Trident made an unbelievable £34,552 inclusive. Despite the fact this is unlikely to be repeated, it surely provides some incentive for sheds to be searched for the odd microcar which may be lurking in the gloom. Alan's Unusual Automobiles of Faringdon, Oxfordshire (01367 240125) specialises in microcars, and in the spring of 1998 had a 'rare 1957 RHD Goggomobil TS 300 Coupe', reg. OJG 365, for sale as a restoration project for £995.

Goliath down under

" While living in Australia in the late 1960s/early 1970s I owned a car called a 'Goliath'. It was German, of 1955 vintage, and made I think by Borgward. Under the bonnet was a two-cylinder two-stroke fuel-injected

engine driving the front wheels. The two-door body appeared to be very solid, which perhaps explained its lack-lustre performance. Was this a model known or marketed in the UK? **"**

I thought not until I received this letter: 'I was very interested in Kevin Ash's article on 21 March 1998 on the Bimota bike, and in particular its twin-cylinder direct-injected two-stroke engine. However, this was not the first two-stroke to employ direct injection, as Borgward in the early 1950s developed a similar system for their vertical twin Goliath 700E and 900E saloon cars. The Bosch mechanical fuel injection system injects direct into the cylinders at a pressure of some 40 ATH (560 lbs/sq in). The oiling system uses a separate Bosch pump mounted on the injection pump, feeding oil by drip feed into the air intake as well as lubricating the injection pump. As I own the only RHD Goliath 900E known to survive, I can confirm the need for accurate setting up of this type of injection system. The petrol is injected at BDC and the ignition timing is critical.'

Gordon and Powerdrive

A South-East London reader asked about the 1954–58 Gordon three-wheeler and the later 1956–58 two-stroke Powerdrive which he owned in the 1950s. There is a photo of the 1954–58 Gordon three-wheeler in Georgano's *Complete Encyclopaedia*, where we are told it was built by Vernon Industries, a subsidiary of Vernons Pools, in Bidston, Cheshire from 1954 to 1958, with a side-mounted 197 cc Villiers two-stroke which drove one rear wheel only. Sedgwick and Gillies's *A–Z of Cars 1945–1970* lists the three-seater 322 cc Powerdrive Roadster as a 'David Gottleib-designed three-wheeler with twin tube frame, American style body, motorcycle type 'box and coil spring ifs. Steel and aluminium and too heavy. Villiers and Anzani engines tried. Reappeared in '58 as glassfibre bodied Coronet. Lion mascot about the only collectible element.' As a six-year-old on my way to and from school, I remember passing a Powerdrive every day parked outside a council house in Cheadle Hulme, Cheshire.

Grice, Wood and Keiller?

" My father had a Grice, Wood and Keiller car in the early 1920s. Can you tell me anything about the company and when it went out of business? "

The GWK was built in Datchet, Berks from 1911 to 1914 and in Maidenhead from 1914 to 1931. It had a 'continuously variable' friction transmission and, with their rear-mounted twin-cylinder Coventry Simplex engines, early models sold quite well because they were very economical. The friction discs were made firstly of paper, which wore out regularly, then, from 1919, of cork. Faced with competition from the Austin Seven, the company switched to a much larger four-cylinder 1,368 cc Coventry Simplex engine with self starter. A reader from Nelson had one of these and wrote: 'Although, in theory, the gearing was "continuously variable", there were, in fact, five notches for the gear lever plus one for reverse. When in gear, the two parts of the drive (friction roller and disc) were held in contact by a strong spring, supplemented by pressure from a foot pedal if necessary. Unfortunately, the gear slipped regularly on steep hills causing the friction material to burn rapidly away. The four-cylinder 1,368 cc Coventry Simplex engine was perhaps a little too powerful for the transmission. Nevertheless, the car completed some quite long trips, including a tour of Devon and Cornwall, starting from Padiham in Lancashire.' The company was liquidated in 1922 and Wood and Keiller left, but Grice sprang back with a 1.5 litre front-engined car and the company was named Grice Imperia from 1926. Grice tried yet again in 1931, reviving the original rear-engined layout, but his attempt was doomed.

Reminiscences of an old Guy

" *I was interested to read about Guy in 'Distinguishing Marques', as I still have a Guy 'feathers' lapel badge which was given to me by an uncle in the 1940s. There were two small fleets of Guy lorries in our locality and, as far as I can remember, they were reasonably reliable. The last of these was owned by a one-man milk collection enterprise. There were five farms across the valley from home and on a summer's day we could hear the old Guy toiling from one farm to the next with a distinctive gearbox noise followed by the thump and clatter of the churns being loaded. This old Guy milk lorry kept going for years. I don't think the owner ever drove it faster than about 30 mph. It wouldn't have passed the MOT plating tests, but at the time a driver could more or less make a living with an old lorry driven carefully. My last recollection of it breaking down was in the middle of the village. The owner had to get an acetylene cutter to remove a stubborn bolt and one local wag sidled up and said, 'Good old Fred, so you're getting her cut up at last.' I don't think the poor old Guy went for much longer after that.* "

Chatting with some bus enthusiasts at the Cobham Museum, I heard an embellishment of the story about the 'Red Indian head-dress' mascot. Apparently, whenever Sidney Guy signed a contract in the 1920s, he used a quill pen, which he then added to a collection in an inkwell, saying 'That's another feather in our cap.' It was this, it seems, that inspired one of his more obsequious designers to come up with the famous head-dress mascot with 'Feathers in our cap' headband. There was a series of Dinky Supertoys of the old Guy Vixen with a variety of bodies including van, high-sided truck and flatbed truck, and some of these have become valuable collectors items.

All Hands on deck!

" Reading your various references to cars of the 1920s and earlier reminds me of my first car. It was a 'Hands', purchased at two years old with 22,000 miles on the clock for £100 – plus my AJS motorcycle. I seem to remember that it was designed by the chief engineer of A.C. Cars. "

George Hands originated the Calthorpe car, then, in 1922, left the company to built a light car under his own name. This had a Dorman water-cooled side-valve engine and Wrigley three-speed gearbox and rear axle. Nick Baldwin expands on this to tell us that there were three models in succession – an 1,100 cc '9.8', an 1,100 cc '10/20' and a 1,460 cc '11/22'. Around 150 were built in total. A fourth model – a 15 hp overhead cam six launched in 1924 – later became a new Calthorpe when Hands went back to the company.

H.R.G.

" The husband of a friend of mine inherited an H.R.G. classic car from his father. He takes it out every Sunday for a run around Edgbaston. I am

very interested in classic cars and until I had to give up driving I had a highly modified Morris Minor 1,000 which went like a bomb – much to the annoyance of drivers of posh new cars. But I have never heard of H.R.G. except that they were made in Surrey. Could you tell me more of this car? **”**

H.R.G. (Halford, Robins and Godfrey) built a Singer-powered sports car with the lines of the earlier Frazer-Nash (see 'Chains and Dogs' on page 146). Ron Godfrey left GN in 1922 and, when H.J. Aldington took control of AFN Ltd in 1928, Archie Frazer-Nash also left. Aldington eventually moved on, building around 170 excellent BMW 328-powered cars, and, after the War, set up a deal which enabled the Bristol Aircraft Company to build cars with engines based on that of the 328. AFN then built around 85 Frazer-Nash cars using a tuned version of this Bristol engine, which also found its way into the AC Ace and Aceca. Meanwhile, in 1934, Godfrey, with Halford and Robins, set up H.R.G. to continue the Frazer-Nash tradition, but with the benefit of a conventional transmission. In 1938 an H.R.G. was the highest-placed British entrant at Le Mans. Post-war competition successes included the 1948 Coupes des Alpes, the 1949 Alpine Rally and the 1.5 litre class in the 1949 Belgian 24 Hour Race. The model continued in production until 1956 when Rootes took over Singer and had no interest in continuing the H.R.G.-developed twin-cam engine in the Hunter model. H.R.G. then concentrated on general engineering, but showed a prototype new car using Vauxhall VX 4/90 components in 1966 shortly before it closed down. A total of only 240 H.R.G.s were ever made. (Sources: G.N. Georgano and John Granger of the Brooklands Museum, and Ian

Dussek's book *HRG: The Sportsman's Ideal*, £8.99 plus p&p from Mill House Books on 01205 270377. H.R.G. is also covered in Kevin Atkinson's *The Singer Story*, price £40 from the same source.)

Yup, it's a Hupp

" I am writing to ask if you have any record of a car going by the unlikely name of 'HUPMOBILE'. My memory is of a large and possibly German vehicle, and that memory dates from not long after the Second World War. I say 'large', because we used it to convey an entire cricket team, club bag, players and all. Some car. It reminded me of an advertisement in Motor *magazine many years ago for a 1923 Rolls Royce which stated: 'Seats 8 – room for 10 standing'. "*

Hupmobile was an American marque, manufactured by Robert and Louis Hupp's Hupp Motor Car Corporation of Detroit, Michigan, and latterly of Cleveland, Ohio. The Hupps began with a fairly basic 2.8 litre runabout in 1908, stuck with four-cylinder side-valve engines until 1924, then progressed to straight eights and straight sixes. Hupmobile's biggest year was 1929 when 50,374 cars were sold, and I suspect your car probably dated from around then. The company went 'aerodynamic' for the 1935 model year with a range of well-proportioned cars which incorporated the headlights into the top sides of the bonnet, a style later copied by Opel. Contemporary advertisements listed a 'long-wheelbase 7-passenger Limousine'. Sadly, the aerodynamic model failed and the factory more or less shut up shop in 1936, reviving its name in 1940 for a rakish four-door 'Skylark' sedan which, like the Graham Hollywood of the same period, used the body dies of the discontinued

Cord 810 and 812. (You can get a flavour of this from the 1937 Cord Westchester sedan to be seen at Beaulieu.) 1941 was Hupmobile's last year.

'E-Type' time

" I am soon to come into a small inheritance. Not enough to change the wife, but maybe enough to indulge my long-held fantasy to own an E-Type Jaguar. I will have about £11,000 to £13,000 to spend, so should I buy at auction or from a dealer? My idea is that when the fantasy fades in two to three years time I should be able at least to get my money back. Or am I being a silly old 50-something? "

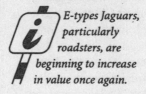

E-types Jaguars, particularly roadsters, are beginning to increase in value once again.

E-Types, particularly roadsters, have been on the up again, with £43,500 paid in August 1996 for a 7,500-mile 1975 Mk III and £75,000 paid for a 650-mile 1975 Mk III roadster in February 1998. A coupe is not out of the question, though, with reasonable 4.2 litre 2+2s still around the £10,000–£15,000 mark. Two things you need to do are: (1) subscribe to The Classic Car Auction List, which tells you what cars are coming up at which auctions and includes a summary of recent prices (Tennyson Publishing, tel: 0181 534 3883, also available by faxback); (2) order *Classic Car Weekly* (from your newsagent) in which Richard Hudson-Evans provides accurate, up-to-date classic car auction reports. *Classic Car Weekly* also contains plenty of private and dealer ads from which to get a 'feel' for the market, and is an excellent medium for advertising a classic car.

Jag in a shed

" I own a Jaguar 240 saloon, first registered in early 1969. Its recorded mileage is just 31,000. The car has been stored in a shed which, due to the

effect of the recent gales, is in danger of collapsing onto the car. Perhaps I should sell the Jaguar. Can you tell me the value and where to advertise? **"**

A 240 is the least valuable 'Mark II'-shape Jaguar, particularly if it has vinyl rather than leather seats, and even worse if it is automatic. The fact that it has been standing for sixteen years does not bode well for the engine, which will have become a very effective corrosion battery, could be badly corroded inside, and will almost certainly be silted up. In other words, even in the unlikely event that the body monocoque, brakes, rear axle and transmission are in good shape, the car is likely to require major work to turn it into a reliable 'runner'. As it stands, it's a condition 4/5, and current auction prices show that it's unlikely to be worth more than £400. If the monocoque shell is structurally very sound, try offering it to a specialist Mk II restorer such as Carpoint on 01909 501532 or Vicarage on 01902 791816. If neither bite, try a photo ad in *Classic Cars*, *Classic Car Weekly* or *Practical Classics* magazines, or a package deal ad in all of them. (If you can't photograph the car, they can supply a library picture.)

Not for Jeepskates

" *I want to buy a Ford or Willys Jeep of WW2 or 1950s era. Would you be good enough to advise me where I can get information to assist?* **"**

A reader in France has sent me details of a useful source of WW2 Ford/Willys Jeep MBs, postwar Hotchkiss Jeep M201s (identical, but with 24v electrics, Solex carb, air filter and French Army-spec tyres rather than 'Trak Grips'). Fully restored Jeeps cost around Ff 35,000 (£3,800) from Garage Ciercoles J.P., 4650 Cazals, France, tel/fax: (0033) 05 65 22 80 31. Garage Ciercoles is honest about its Hotchkiss Jeep 201s, which were built in the French factory up to 1969. Simon Johnson of The Military Vehicle Trust warns that some Hotchkiss Jeeps are being 'passed off' as genuine wartime Ford or Willys Jeep MBs. The Trust offers to help anyone looking for a military vehicle if they write to The Military Vehicle Trust, PO Box 6, Fleet, Hants GU1 9PE. The spares specialist is R & R Services of Bethesden, near Ashford, in Kent (tel: 01233 820219). R & R Services also organises the re-manufacturing of parts no longer available, and reckons to be able to supply everything. (There is a specific Jeep Club, SAE to 65 Grosvenor Crescent, Arksey, Doncaster DN5 0SX, but I'm told it tends to cater more for later Jeep M38s, CJ5s, CJ7s and Renegades.) For Jeep books, try Mill House Books on 01205 270377. Expect to have to pay around £5,000 for a good, genuine WW2 Ford or Willys. An interesting variation is the Willys Jeepster, one of which sold for £5,400 inclusive at BCA's Classic auction at Blackbushe on 11 August 1997. All a far cry from the price of my first 1942 Ford Jeep which cost me just £20 in 1965.

Jowett taxicab

" *Can you or any of your readers shed any light on the Jowett Taxi, manufactured by H. and G. Robinson (Gosforth) Ltd of High Street, Gosforth, Newcastle-on-Tyne? I enclose a page of 'Bargains in Pictures' which appeared in* The Motor *magazine of 11 July 1939.* "

Austria overrun in March 1938. Czechoslovakia

dismembered by March 1939. The British Government on the brink of war, but still dithering. No wonder one of the other advertisers in that issue had panicked and was offering his five-week-old, 1,000-mile Triumph Dolomite Roadster, 'cost £435', for just £280 CASH. Or how about the 1934 Packard 8 Roadster, 'cost £750', offered at £185? (In April 1998 there was a nice one of these for sale at restorers West Hoatley Garage for £55,000, tel: 01342 810402.) This is a preamble to the fact that H. and G. Robinson's taxi building enterprise may not have had much of a future. The company is not listed in Nick Walker's *A–Z of British Coachbuilders* (Bay View Books, ISBN 1-870979-93-1). But there was some merit in taking the twin-cylinder 946 cc Jowett 8 commercial chassis and using it for a 5-seater metropolitan-spec. taxi capable of 50 mph and 35 mpg and of showing a profit of eightpence a mile. A friend of mine in the Newcastle area had an old Jowett chassis rusting in his garden in the 1960s. I hope this wasn't it.

Little Lagonda

" *In the mid-to-late 1950s, my late husband and I bought a car which we were told was a Lagonda Rapier Rapide Eagle, one of only three built in 1936 and of which one was chosen by John Cobb for a land speed record. It had a pre-selector gearbox, and was beautifully and lovingly restored when we bought it with even the exhaust pipe having been chromed. I would be interested to know if there is any truth in the story about the record attempt and what happened to the car after we sold it – to buy, of all things, an Austin A35.* "

The Rapier was a small, 1,104 cc twin-cam four-cylinder model which developed up to 60 bhp in standard form. These cars usually had fairly heavy coupe or drop-head coupe bodywork but, with its slab tank and cycle-type wings, yours is a lightweight version bodied by Eagle coachworks, as you were told. In 1936, Tim Ascroft and colleagues persuaded the Lagonda management to sell them the tooling, and continued building Rapiers underbored to 1,086 cc for racing in the 1,100 cc class. There was an 1,100 cc Land Speed Record, and John Cobb was certainly into record breaking, so that explains how this and the word 'Rapide' crept into the salesman's hyperbole. There is an excellent register specifically for these cars: The Rapier Register, c/o J. Williams, The Smithy, Tregynon, Newton, Powys SY16 3EH, tel: 01686 650396. Mr Williams was able to tell me that your car was first registered in July 1935 and remains in enthusiastic ownership.

Vintage valuation

" I am the proud owner of a 1930 Lagonda 2 litre 4-seater, which I bought in 1957. The chassis was fabricated in 1929, the car sold in 1930 with a vertical Cozette supercharger in front of the 4-cylinder twin-cam engine. However it was not licensed until 1931 – so some purists may consider it not truly vintage. The car was insured on an agreed value basis for £30,000 for a total loss, but local estimates now put it at £35,000. I am a member of the Lagonda Owners' Club, use the car regularly, and it has a current MOT. How much do you think the car is worth? And should I sell it locally, or through auctioneers? "

I used to polish one of these at Sports Motors in Orpington High Street in 1959, and it was up for £225. But I think the current value you have been given is about right for the comparatively rare supercharged version, which

The trick of selling at auction is to enter the car early enough to get into the catalogue and to gain maximum benefit from the hype that surrounds the event.

did not go on sale until 1930 and was good for 90 mph. I would be inclined to reserve the car for £37,500 at auction, and if it doesn't quite make it be prepared to accept a provisional bid slightly lower. Certainly, make yourself available for a quick decision on the day of the sale. Classic car auctioneers include BCA on 01252 877317 and 878555; Brooks on 0171 228 8000; Christies on 0171 839 9060 and 0171 581 7444; Coys on 0171 584 7444, H&H on 01925 730630; Phillips on 0171 629 6602; RTS on 01603 505718; and Sothebys on 0171 493 8080. The trick of selling at auction is to enter the car early enough to get into the catalogue and to gain maximum benefit from the hype that surrounds the event. Yours could even be a 'star car' in the pre-event publicity. Remember, you do of course pay for all this in the form of entry fees and commission.

Augusta appraisal

" *I have a 1934 Lancia Augusta pillarless saloon which I have carefully stored for many years. With a house move due, I will have to sell it soon. Could you advise on how much to ask for it and how best to sell it? Is an auction likely to achieve a better price than a private sale?* "

Since there aren't many Augustas about I don't have much on which to base a valuation. A quite sweet 1935 example, reg. BTT 631, sold at what is now British Car Auctions, Blackbushe on 22 April 1996 for £4,350 net (£4,606 including commission and VAT) and, after 5% plus VAT seller's commission, would have brought the seller £4,094. It had been slightly overestimated at £6,000–£7,000. If I was you, the first things I would do would be to place a photo ad in *Classic*

Car Weekly (01733 238855) and, because it's a pre-war Lancia, also in *The Automobile* (01932 864212). If you get no bites from this, it's worth trying an auction.

Two-stroke Land Rover

" *Many years ago I drove a long-wheelbase Land Rover from London to what was then Salisbury in Southern Rhodesia. You may be interested to know that it had an unusual engine – a three-cylinder two-stroke diesel. So perhaps I made a small mark in motoring history.* "

This was the first I'd heard of a two-stroke three-cylinder Land Rover diesel. But twenty readers came forward with information. One not only identified the engine, but enclosed a copy of an advertisement from *The Autocar* of 29 July 1955, headed 'Operation Enterprise proves Turner–Diesel Reliability'. This described 'a gruelling 10,000 mile journey, over desert and jungle in appalling weather' as 'convincing proof of the stamina and dependability of the Turner–Diesel 2-Stroke Supercharged Engine.' A further article, from *Automobile Engineer* of November 1954, told how these engines were designed by Prof. Hans List of Graz, Austria (where they were called 'Jenbachs') and built under licence by Turners of Wolverhampton in 1.4, 2.1 and 2.8 litre capacities with two, three or four cylinders. Maximum power was 37.5 bhp, 56 bhp and 75 bhp at 2,800 rpm, and maximum torque was 76 lb. ft., 114 lb. ft. and 152 lb. ft. at 1,900 rpm. Rootes also made two-stroke supercharged diesel engines at the time and these were fitted to Commer and Karrier trucks and fire appliances. Other manufacturers of two-stroke diesels were Rolls Royce, Perkins and GMC.

The original Lotus factory

" *I was interested in Giles Chapman's 'Distinguishing Marks' on Lotus because Colin Chapman's first factory was housed in the stables at the rear of my house in Ribblesdale Road, Hornsey. He operated under the brand name 'Progress Chassis', which he used to make up out of square-section tube. A chap by the name of Halliday lived at the house and was one of the welders, while an elderly lady who also lived here made the tea for the workers. The cars they turned out were small, open-top models and they used the Tottenham Lane/Church Lane/Ribblesdale Road triangle as a test-track. When I bought the house in 1970 I found a lot of wooden seats and seat backs in the attic. I still have one but gave the rest away. The pub mentioned by Giles Chapman is a few hundred yards from the stables in Tottenham Lane and is called the Railway, but is no longer trading. Next to the pub was the new factory Colin Chapman moved into in 1953, and a plaque on the wall is still there, stating 'Lotus Engineering Company'.* "

A reader from Norwich disputes the statement that 'A.B.C.C.', incorporated into the original Lotus badge, were actually Chapman's initials. His version of events is that Chapman enlisted the help of two friends, Nigel and Michael Allen, to help him build three Lotus Mk IIIs in 1951, and that the 'A.B.' in the badge is for 'Allen Brothers'. Only one Mk III was built, and Nigel withdrew at the end of 1951; but Michael became the first full-time employee of the Lotus Engineering Company on its formation on 1 January 1952.

Marauder

" *Whilst serving my apprenticeship in the early 1950s, one of the managers had a sports car badged 'Rover Marauder'. We have 41 'classic car' books and not one of them mentions the Marauder. Could I have the name wrong, or was it not such a fantastic car?* "

Only 15 cars were ever built. A reader from Arundel still has the prototype 1950 Marauder, reg. KAC 313, which his family has owned since 1952. The car was the brainchild of Rover engineers George Mackie, Peter Wilks and Spen King. It was based on Rover 75 P4 running gear and a shortened P4 chassis, with some P4 body panels and the rest originally supplied by Richard Mead of Poplar Road, Dorridge, then by Abbey Panels. The company address was Marauder Car Company Ltd, Common Lane, Kenilworth, Warks. The car could be ordered as a two/three-seat roadster or hardtop. Plus points were a P3-type floorshift, the option of overdrive on all four forward speeds in place of the Rover freewheel, quicker steering than the 75, and better handling due to the engine being further back in the frame. The prototype had a twin-carb 2.1 litre ioe 75 engine, but the Type A had a near-standard single-carb 2.1 litre 80 bhp 75 engine, while the Type 100 had a triple-carb 2.4 litre with 105 bhp – but only three of these were built. What killed the Marauder off was the double purchase tax of 67% levied on all cars with a basic price of more than £1,000. At £1,666 for the Type A, rising to £2,002 for the Type 100 coupe compared to £1,538 for a Jaguar XK120 or £1,555 for an Allard K2, it's little wonder that the Marauder found so few takers. Twelve of the fifteen Marauders are known to have survived, and Ian Glass of The Marauder Driver's Club is keen to trace the remaining chassis numbers 11002 (possibly reg. MPC 300), 11012 (reg. FHE 437 – known to have crashed in Sheffield in 1968) and 11013 (possibly reg. FCT 707). His address and phone number are 'Tirionfa', Bodfari Road, Llandyrnog, Denbigh, Clwyd LL16 4HP, tel: 01824 790280.

Marendaz Special

" *In 1950 we owned a Marendaz Special with a 6-cylinder Meadows en-gine (which had plug wells in the top that filled with water). It was a four-seater with soft folding top, two leather straps over the bonnet and three large stainless exhausts snaking from the nearside. In the dark, the radia-tor could be mistaken for a Bentley. We paid £100 for it and, sadly, a few years later paid £5 for it to be taken away. We do not have a photograph of this great machine and would be happy to pay a modest amount for one.* "

Nick Baldwin's *A–Z of Cars of the 1920s* tells us that Captain Marendaz and his wife created the first Marendaz Special on the first floor of The London Cab Company in Brixton in 1926 and subsequently built around 25 cars which looked a bit like scaled-down 3 litre Bentleys. In 1932 they moved to the same site as G.W.K. in Maidenhead. Michael Sedgwick and Mark Gillies's *A–Z of Cars of the 1930s* (£9.95) tells us that free-flow, external tubular exhaust mani-folds were a feature of 1931–36 models, which ranged from the 1,869 cc 13/70 to the 2,469 cc 17/100. The last of the Marendaz models was the 15/90 of 1935–39 which had the same 1,991 cc 6-cylinder Coventry Climax engine block as some mid-1930s Triumphs. Fitted with three carburettors, this model had some success in competition driven by Stirling Moss's moth-er, Aileen. Books available from Mill House Books on 01205 270377.

Metallurgique made for two

" *A Metallurgique car played its part in the escape from her chaperone and the elopement of heiress Madeleine Montgomery, then aged 19, with my uncle, Esdaile Campbell Muir of Inistrynich, Loch Awe, Argyllshire on 15 April 1911. The young lady, then living near Oban, secretly met my* uncle, 15 years her senior, in Munro's Garage where they were 'married in the ancient Scottish manner' by declaring themselves to be man and wife before two witnesses – one of whom was Esdaile's chauffeur and the other the garage proprietor. They then left at speed in Esdaile's 26 hp Metallurgique with Vanden Plas two-seater body, and the marriage was legalised before the Sheriff of Oban two days later. The events caused a sensation in the West Highlands where Esdaile was regarded as a hero and his motoring exploits talked of with bated breath. He later moved to Florida where a libel suit cost the great man $50,000. "

I appealed for more Metallurgique anecdotes and received the following:

Malevolent Metallurgique

" Further to your request for more 'Metallurgique Memories', you might be interested in this story. In 1928 we lived in Letchworth, the first 'garden city'. I was ten years old when a garage owner in nearby Hitchin convinced my father that he should buy a car. Father had no intention of learning to drive, but nevertheless purchased a Metallurgique to be driven by my very much elder brother, Bill. That was only the start of our problems. Before the car was delivered, we had to build a motor house to accommodate it – a substantial affair of brick. The great day arrived, the car was delivered and, horror of horrors, it was too wide to pass between the chimney breast of the house and the neighbouring fence. Father managed to persuade the new neighbour (ironically, a Ford dealer) to sell him a few feet of land in order to get his car to its garage. The car then remained in the garage most of the time. My brother Bill hated driving it. I vividly remember the enormous spanner we had to carry everywhere to unscrew the petrol cap, and also the day Bill drove his wife, dad, mum and me to Clacton for a day out. We had a splendid outward run and parked the car on the front. Unfortunately, by the end of the day, dark clouds had loomed, then the heavens opened. All that could be seen on Clacton promenade was a large, malevolent looking car with its bonnet open and a drenched figure desperately trying to crank some life into it. "

The first 'Quick Six'?

" *I edit the* Year Book *for the Vintage MG Register of the MG Car Club and I am trying to trace part of the history of my own 18/80, a Mk 1 Salonette, registration WL 4440, between the years of 1930 and 1960. The car was originally owned by Cecil Kimber himself, who loaned it to his friend Captain Francis Samuelson (later knighted) to compete in the 1929 Monte Carlo Rally. I have three pictures of the car from those days. The first shows Captain Samuelson and his wife after the rally, which he drove single-handed due to his co-driver becoming ill. The second picture shows the car taking part in the Mont de Mules Hill Climb at the end of the rally. The third shows Captain Samuelson and his co-driver at the MG Works.* "

WL 4440 was one of the two prototype MG 18/80s, nicknamed 'Quick Six'. The car featured in *The Autocar* article on the new model of 17 August 1928, already bearing the registration WL 4440. Though the car was progressively modified, a distinguishing feature is that it carries its spare wheel in the nearside wing, whereas virtually all later 18/80s carried the spare on the driver's side. If any reader can supply information, please get in touch with 'Bev' Hicks, 3 Stickens Lane, East Malling, Kent ME19 6BT, tel: 01732 842930.

A 'B' for me

" *My son, who lives in the London area, is contemplating buying a reconditioned MGB. I understand that these can be purchased with new or reconditioned engines and new or reconditioned bodyshells. What is your view on such a purchase?* "

It's now difficult to find a half-way-decent 'B' for less than £4,000, and a really good restored one with a new 'Heritage' bodyshell could set you back more than £10,000. 'B's always were rot-prone, so

The most sensible MGB to buy as an everyday car is a late, chrome bumper model with Rostyle wheels, overdrive and an oil cooler.

a re-shell or a rust-free California or Arizona import is a good idea. Top values depend on originality, but for a car to use regularly, a modified, updated 'B' is a far better bet. These are high-maintenance cars needing 3,000-mile oil changes, regular greasing of various nipples and regular resetting of tappet clearances. The most sensible as an everyday car is a late, chrome bumper model with Rostyle wheels (not high-maintenance wires), overdrive and an oil cooler. The SU carbs always were prone to go out of sync with monotonous regularity, so replacement with a single Weber DCOE is not a bad idea. There are literally hundreds of MGB restoration, parts and sales specialists. One of the better-known is Brown and Gammons on 01462 490049. For magazines, check out *Classic Cars*, *Classic & Sportscar*, *Practical Classics* and *Classic Car Weekly*. Remember, an MGB is not really the same sort of sports car as, for example, the 1.8 litre Mazda MX5 – it's much more of a pleasant, but long-in-the-tooth, sports tourer, so don't expect too much of it.

Something 'special'

" *I have just acquired for restoration something that was described to me as a 1953 Microplas. I cannot find any information on the model. The car has leaf spring suspension all round and 8-inch drum brakes. The engine is a large side valve unit that looks to be non-original. The car, registered CGK 737, has been in a barn for the past 18 years. I would be grateful for any information.* "

After this appeared in my column, a reader from Oxted picked up the story:

" *Microplas was started by two friends and myself in, I think, 1952. We were keen members of the 750 Club and the original purpose was to make*

*bodyshells for 750 and 1172 specials. The first models were known as
Stilettos. We were then joined at James Estate, Western Road, Mitcham,
Surrey by another friend, who was building a special powered by one of
Archie Butterworth's flat-four engines (not one of the swing-valve ver-
sions). He needed a body, and I designed the shell which became the
Mistral – the side vents were to mate up with ducts from the air-cooled engine. As far as I know, the car was never completed, but the shell also fitted the 7 ft 6 in. Ford chassis and was used as a prototype for the
Fairthorpe Electron Minor. Apart from Fairthorpe, we also sold shells to
AFN and Morgan. In 1956, we sold a mould to a company in New Zealand
which was thinking of building a sports car there. I went out to NZ in late
1956 to help with the project, and we built a prototype based on a simple
twin-tube chassis with swing axle front end and a properly-located live
rear axle. Power was initially a Ford 100E with an Elva overhead inlet
valve conversion. This competed in several local races and was quite successful during 1957. I returned to England in 1958 after we had improved
the shell with proper doors and an optional hardtop. I believe that some
15 or 16 kits were sold and, by sheer chance, I stayed with one of the customers during a return visit to NZ some six years ago. The first TVR (the
Jomar) had bodywork based on two Mistral front ends. Microplas went on
to build boats and other mouldings, including the fairings used on the
Vincent Black Knight motorcycle. In the early days we were also involved
with 'Pathfinder' Bennett, who was trying to produce a microcar – the
Fairthorpe Atom. These were very basic cars with motorcycle engines. I
believe his son carried the name on to more successful cars. I have been
speaking to a friend who was also involved with Microplas, who tells me
that the Mistral-bodied Frazer-Nash was the one driven by Ken Wharton
which crashed and burned out in one of the Ulster TTs.* "

Fans of 1950s specials will get a lot of help and
support by joining the Fairthorpe Sports Car
Club, c/o Richard Disbrow, 16 The Close,
Blandford Forum, Dorset DT11 7HA, tel: 01258
454879. The Climax-powered 1955 TVR Jomar
prototype cropped up at an H&H Classic Car
Auction at Buxton in September 1997, where it
sold for £5,500, plus commission. (H&H
Auctions, tel: 01925 730630.)

Home found for Mini

" I am pleased to tell you that the Friends of Nuffield Place (the former home of Lord Nuffield) have agreed to display on loan your correspondent from Southampton's 'one owner' 1960 Mini, 8472 CR, to join a 1952 Morris Minor, MJK 648, and a 1949 Wolseley Eight, BUD 650. "

Nuffield Place is open to the public ten times a year on the second and fourth Sundays from May to September, entry £3, OAPs £2, children 50p. Built in 1914, the house retains the majority of the furniture and contents acquired by Lord and Lady Nuffield since they took up residence in 1933, and is still decorated in 1930s style. The house is signposted off the road from Henley-on-Thames to Wallingford, between Nettlebed and The Crown public house. Tel: 01491 836654.

'E' Type Morris

" I have a 1938 Morris 8 Tourer which I believe to be a Series E. The car was used as my sole vehicle when I was a student in the 1970s, but has been on blocks under canvas for the past 15 years. The current engine in-situ has a cracked block, but I also happen to own a brand new engine which I believe is the correct one for the model of car. I would be grateful if you could advise me about whom to approach with a view to complete restoration of the car back to its former glory. "

How much do you want to spend? £1,000, £5,000, £10,000, or more? The 1938 Morris 8 Series E was a rebodied Morris 8 Series II with no running boards, lights set into the front wings and a cowelled rather than exposed radiator. This sort of car is best restored by the owner (with a bit of help) rather than consigned to a restoration specialist, because even after a 'concours' restoration costing over £10,000 it's unlikely to be worth more than £5,000. Your best bet is to join the Morris Register (see below), take advice from other members, and find a local man in Yellow Pages to work on your car at Plymouth, rather than South-Eastern, labour rates.

Rare 'Twelve'

" My father would not let us girls drive his car, so in 1936 he bought my sister one of her own, on condition that I could drive it as well when I reached 17. It was a 12 hp limited-edition Morris drophead – and a little beauty. We had some very happy times in it. Sadly, during the War my sister was hard up and sold it for £100. I often wonder what happened to it and if the new owners loved it as much as we did. "

My dad's first car was a 1938 'Twelve' saloon, with batteries under the driver's seat which short circuited and set fire to the seat on one occasion. I also remember that the rear spare wheel proved an excellent crumple zone when a truck ran into the back of us (I was about three at the time). Your earlier '12' drophead was very rare, and if any have survived there is a chance that one of them could be your car. (Wire wheels indicate a three- rather than four-speed car, built before autumn 1936.) If you can remember the registration, get in touch with D.G. Moore of The Morris Register, White Cottage, Jasmine Lane, Lower Claversham, Bristol BS19 4PY, tel: 01934 832340. He may be able to tell you what happened to it.

Record-breaking Napier

" This is to thank all of you at The Daily Telegraph 'Motoring' for the article on John Cobb and the Napier Railton which appeared on 14 June

1997. When I passed my prep school exams (much to my father's surprise), I was rewarded with The Boys' Book of Racing Cars, *which I still have although it has become very dog-eared. In it, Cobb writes about driving the Napier Railton around the Brooklands track. His comments include, 'you get the signal [to start] and the car glides easily away, rapidly climbing to a speed which makes you tingle'. Another was, 'the track seems empty, you are so far behind, but soon catch sight of a car ahead ... it seems rather as though the vehicle is coming back at you.' While at school I used to escape to Silverstone (the only track near enough), and in about 1950 I remember Cobb driving the Railton Special around the circuit. I think they towed it around first to make sure it had enough lock for the corners. I certainly recall the enormous wheels and the high ground clearance which revealed the streamlined underbody. Finally, as a raw and very nervous indentured engineering pupil, shyly staying in a hotel by myself for the first time, I remember the horror of reading about the accident to Crusader.* "

Back in the 1950s I picked up a copy of a September 1938 book, which I still have, entitled *Power and Speed*. It contains the famous photograph of the 23 litre Napier Railton, all four wheels off the ground after the bump on the Home banking, breaking the lap record at 143.44 mph. Another chapter is devoted to 'The Romance of Record Breaking' and is written by none other than our mutual hero, John Cobb. At the end of the chapter is a small announcement. 'STOP PRESS. As we close these pages for press the news has just been received that, on Thursday, Sept. 15, 1938, John Cobb succeeded in breaking Capt. Eyston's record at an average speed of 350.2 m.p.h. *(Editor: On Sept. 16, Eyston replied with a record of 357.5 m.p.h.)*' It's well worth looking out for *Power and Speed* at secondhand book fairs. The Napier Railton is now on exhibit at The Brooklands Museum.

Of Paramount importance

" *In the mid-1950s I owned a Paramount car. It came with a 100E side valve Ford engine which could barely get it to move, and with a replacement 1,508 cc ohv Consul engine it was still pretty poor. The front wheels hopped round corners while the rears slid. I paid £425 for mine, secondhand.* "

Two Paramounts from the Duncan Rabagliati Collection were sold by Brookes for £4,200 and £2,800 on 8 April 1998. There's more about the model on page 426 of Culshaw and Horrobin's *Complete Catalogue of British Cars 1895–1975*, and on page 151 of Sedgwick and Gillies's *A–Z of Cars 1945–1970*. With no less than six separate grilles at the front, the car did look a bit special.

Steam-powered supercar

" *Further to the correspondence about steam cars, there has been a much more modern interpretation of the concept. It is the Pelland steamer designed by Peter Pellandine, with a three-cylinder engine, tubular steel chassis, kit-car body and an all-up weight of just 1,000 lbs. The business itself ran out of steam and the car was eventually sold by Christies in the 1990s.* "

Peter Pellandine was the former owner of Falcon, which built good-looking GRP kit-car bodies in the 1950s and early 60s, best of which was the 515. He left the UK for Australia in 1962 where he designed and built two mid-engined sports car kits under the name 'Pellandini'. He returned to the UK in 1978 and marketed the second of these as the Pelland Sports. Performance and handling were said to be excellent. With its optional hardtop, this formed the basis of the Pelland Mk II Steam Car, a project originally started in Australia and backed by the

Australian government. The intention was to break the world land-speed record for steam cars of 127.66 mph. But the last attempt in 1991 was unsuccessful and the project seems to have died soon after. The car now resides at the Lakeland Motor Museum, Holker Hall, Cark-in-Cartmel, South Lakeland, Cumbria, tel: 015395 58509.

Three-wheeler Raleigh car?

" My aunt had a Raleigh three-wheeler in the mid-1930s. Its simple single front-wheel steering made it capable of turning through 90 degrees, which could be frightening. My father said that my aunt would approach a gate without slackening speed, put the wheel over at the first gate post and in she went. How many Raleighs were made? Do any survive? What was its specification? "

Raleigh tried making cars in 1905, cyclecars a few years later, and a flat-twin-powered car in 1922. But G.N. Georgano's *Encyclopaedia of Motorcars 1885–1968* tells us that the successful Raleigh Safety Seven was produced in volume between 1933 and 1936. This had a 742 cc V-twin engine, three speeds, four seats and sold for £110 5s. It was designed by T.L Williams, who later bought the rights from Raleigh and started the Reliant Motor Company, now revived, in Tamworth, Staffordshire. For friendly help and advice on these cars, get in touch with The Raleigh Safety Seven and Early Reliant Owners' Club, c/o Mick Sleap, 17 Courtland Avenue, Chingford, London E4 4DU, and the Reliant Owners' Club, c/o G. Chappel, 19 Smithey Close, High Green, Sheffield S40 4FQ, tel: 0114 284 8138.

Subsequently, another reader wrote about

the Raleigh cars: 'I actually worked for the company. It was my first job at the age of 14 after leaving school and I was paid the princely sum of ten bob a week. One of my duties was to prepare a "one off" handlebar-steered saloon version of the van for the Motor Manager's daily commute to and from his home in Tamworth. This manager (Mr Williams) and the Assembly Shop foreman (Mr Thompson) later left Raleigh to set up the Reliant factory in Tamworth. Another interesting point is that the company had great difficulty in meeting the 5 cwt limit for the reduced-rate three-wheeler taxation class. They even used magnesium alloys for the crankcase casting and for the differential box, and these could go up in flames if the machinist did not use enough cooling fluid.'

Roadworthy Rhode

" Can you tell me anything about a car owned by my grandfather in the 1920s and 1930s? It was a 'Rhode', reg. HJ 7604. "

The Rhode was a rather good small sporting car built by F.W. Meade and T.W. Deakin in Birmingham between 1921 and 1931. Your uncle's looks to me like a '10.8' – probably the '11/30' version, of which around 1,500 were built between 1924 and 1930. They had 1,232 cc four-cylinder engines – side valve, then overhead valve on later models. A distinguishing feature was that the open side of the channel frame faced outwards rather than inwards.

Riley Stelvio?

" *In the 1930s I purchased a Riley for £25. I believe the model was a 'Stelvio' sports coupe. It was fitted with a fabric two-door wooden-framed body with a large boot and had a six-cylinder engine (with generator at the front driven by the crankshaft), wire wheels and cable brakes adjustable from inside the car by large knurled knobs. Any information would be welcome because my friends do not believe that such a model ever existed. Due to continual big end failure I eventually sold it for £8 and it ended its life as a duck house in the middle of the village pond (shame).* "

The 1,633 cc overhead valve 14/6 Stelvio (with Weymann-type fabric body) was in production from 1928 to 1934 and the name was retained for the 15/6 Stelvio from 1935 to 1938.

Rochdale on wheels?

" *I have a sneaking suspicion that there is, or was, a car called a Rochdale. Do you have any information on such a car, please?* "

In its later form the Rochdale Olympic was one of the best late 50s/early 60s specials. The first Rochdales were mere fibreglass shells for special builders, sold from 1952. Several types of roadster and coupe shells followed, mainly for the Ford E93a chassis. But the Phase 1 Olympic was a proper production model car with Riley 1.5 or Ford side-valve mechanicals. The Riley version was good for over 100 mph and around 150 were built. Then, as Ford's new short stroke engines began to dominate the sports car scene, 997 cc Anglia and 1,498 cc five-bearing Cortina GT engines became available, lifting the top speed of the hatchback Phase 2 to at least 115 mph. Phase 2s were also available with 1,622 cc MGA engines, but, with the right exhaust system, the Ford engine was far freer revving, allowing 7,000 rpm in fourth gear and more than 120 mph.

Freewheeling

" *My first car was a 1938 Rover 14. Do you agree with me that this car had the facility to freewheel whilst in gear to allow the engine to idle when out on the open road for fuel economy?* "

Sort of. I had a post-war Rover 60 P3, reg. HWX 10, which had a freewheel operated by a Bowden cable and a big, knurled knob in the centre of the dashboard (see *Practical Classics*, March 1998, page 37). The freewheel effectively 'clutched in' while accelerating and 'clutched out' when you lifted off, allowing the engine to idle when descending hills. It also meant you could change gear without using the clutch. Saab adopted freewheels in all its models from the 92 to the 96, but with these cars the freewheel was there to prevent engine braking causing a skid on ice. The freewheel effectively did what skid control instructors tell you to do if you get into an uncontrolled slide, which is to dip the clutch until you regain control. I bought a two-stroke Saab 96 for my mum and can vouch for the fact that on ice and snow the freewheel worked brilliantly.

Ruston Hornsby?

" *Can you or your colleagues give me any information about a car by the name of Ruston Hornsby?* "

These were built in the early 1920s by the steamroller manufacturers of the same name. The car had a four-cylinder 3.3 litre engine with a detachable cylinder head but with the inlet manifold actually cast into the cylinder block. The RAC horsepower rating was 15.9 and the engine developed 43 bhp. It had three forward speeds and the tyre size was 820 × 120.

Having seen the above, sixteen readers wrote with anecdotes and additional details of the car and the company. One from Lincoln told us he knows of twelve surviving cars – four in the UK and eight in Australia. Two of the UK cars belong to Ruston and Hornsby itself (now European Gas Turbines Ltd) of Lincoln, and he had the responsibility of restoring a 16 hp Ruston Hornsby in 1967. A second car owned by EGT is also being restored by this reader and his colleagues. A 20 hp Ruston Hornsby is owned by a reader in Compton Pauncefoot, who tells us that the fourth UK survivor is owned by Dormans of Stafford who manufactured some of the 2.6 litre engines for the 16 hp model. A reader from Chilwell sent extracts from a catalogue showing three models of Ruston Hornsby: the 2.6 litre 15.9 hp 'Standard Fifteen' normally fitted with solid disc-type wheels and externally-mounted hood (price £475); a 2.6 litre 15.9 hp Model A-1 'Sixteen De-Luxe' with solid disc wheels and internally-mounted hood; and the 3.3 litre 20/25 hp 'Twenty De-Luxe', normally fitted with steel 'artillery'-type wheels and internally-mounted hood (price £575). Prices were high because the cars were over-engineered. Yet another reader, this time from Cirencester, recounts a visit by R.J. Ruston, then chairman of the company, to Melbourne in 1952 where he witnessed a Ruston car being used as a taxi. When he asked the driver how he managed to obtain spare

parts, he replied that the car never broke down
so he never needed any.

Early tearaway

" *My late father-in-law once owned a Salmson Grand Sport. I have no
idea what year it might be, but he was born in 1901 and started driving
in his late teens. His first car, he used to tell us, was picked up in London.
He had never driven before and all the dealer told him were words to the
effect that 'This is the brake, this is the clutch, these are the gears and this
is the accelerator – now, off you go.' He did, and drove back all the way to
Derby. He also owned a 'Bullnose' Morris, an Austin 7 (in which a family
of four used to go on holiday from Coventry to Cornwall), a Hillman
Minx, a Hillman California coupe, an Austin Cambridge, a Ford Cortina,
a Triumph 1300 and, lastly, a Ford Escort Ghia which we had great difficulty dissuading him from driving in his 89th year.* "

Salmsons were French cars sold from the old
Thornycroft factory in Chiswick. Early models
were handicapped by a three-speed gearbox. But
your uncle's car appears to be a later 'twin cam'
10/20 model and may have been fitted with a
Cozette supercharger. In this form, Salmsons enjoyed a lot of success both at Le Mans and in the
200-mile race at Brooklands. In 1926 one lapped
the Brooklands circuit at 114.5 mph, which is
quite something for a vintage 1,100 cc car.

Another Salmson

" *Seeing the Salmson Grand Sport in your column reminded me of the
Salmson I once owned. It was a 1922 model and, after an impressive test
drive up a 1-in-12 hill in May 1925, I laid down a £3 deposit and stumped
up the remaining £72 the following week. I later realised that the steering
was very stiff and greasing made it no better. Subsequently the cone clutch
started slipping, but I used a blow lamp on the lining and that cured it.*

Then I lost all drive to the rear wheels. On dismantling the rear axle I found it had no differential gear and the two pins which held the crown wheel in place had failed. I replaced them, then swapped the car for a nice BSA motorcycle and sidecar, plus cash. I remember that early Salmsons had an unusual arrangement for the operation of the valves. Could you confirm this? **"**

The engine valves were operated by a single rod for each cylinder that, by means of a rocker mechanism, pushed open the exhaust valve and then sprang back to pull open the inlet valve.

Saxon

" *In the 1920s my parents had a car which they referred to as the 'Saxon'. I don't know if this was a make of vehicle or a pet name. Can you please assist?* **"**

Saxon was an American make, built in Detroit and Ypsilanti, Michigan between 1913 and 1922. They were small for American cars, with 1.4 litre engines, three-speed gearboxes and wire wheels. The UK price was just £105. Total production rose to 27,800 in 1916 – high for the time. Later, artillery wooden spoke wheels became available as an extra, and the range was expanded to include a 2.9 litre 6-cylinder touring car. The last Saxons were known as Saxon-Duplexes.

Seaton-Petter tourer

" *I wonder if you or any of your readers can help me trace information relating to a car my father had in the 1920s. Prior to this, all his cars had been secondhand. But I have a photograph of my family taken in 1926 when I was a 7-year-old schoolboy, sitting in the only new car my father ever bought. It was a Seaton-Petter tourer. I recall that only a few were* *ever made as a 'trial run' and that it could not compete with the Morrises of the day. But, even after referring to numerous motoring history books, I can't find any reference to the Seaton-Petter.* "

The car originated from the Nautilus Works in Yeovil, Somerset, where the Petter family had built up a business mass-producing fire grates, cream separators and engines. They decided to try their hand at mass-producing a £100 car, jointly designed by Percival Petter and Douglas Seaton and to be marketed by the latter. The engine was a 1,319 cc two-cylinder water-cooled two-stroke mated to a three-speed gearbox with central change, but brakes on just the rear wheels and the transmission. Apparently it was one of the first British cars with artificial cellulose paint – and the rear seats of the £150 tourer could be removed for carrying goods. The lowest that prices actually fell to was £110 for the half-ton van version. Over 1926/27 around seventy were produced. Petters went on to produce a two-stroke diesel engine in the 1930s, and the Petter family later started the Westland Aircraft company.

Mine's a Nine

" *In 1938 I owned a Singer Nine Le Mans, reg. ADF 395. It had an overhead cam engine of about 10 hp, a 'fly-off' handbrake, a 17.5 gallon tank and twin spare wheels. Handling was good for its day and top speed was about 80 mph on the optimistic speedometer. Could any of these cars have survived?* "

Many have, and there's an active club. According to Sedgwick and Gillies, 'with the engine capable of 6,000 rpm, 75 mph was on the cards for the Special Speed two seaters, but the car's reputation was ruined by a disastrous crash eliminating three of the 1935 TT cars at Ards – buyers didn't trust a car on which the steering arms broke.' Engine size was 972 cc, and the model was in production between 1933 and 1937. You will get more information from Martin Wray at the Singer Owners' Club, 11 Ermine Rise, Great Casterton, Stamford, Lincs PE9 4AJ, tel: 01780 762740, or from Anne Page at the Association of Singer Car Owners, 39 Oakfield, Rickmansworth, Herts WD3 2LR, tel: 01923 778575.

Where are you now?

" *My first car was a 1935 Singer Nine Le Mans drophead. It seemed to be well ahead of its time with a 9 hp ohc engine, hydraulic brakes, independent front suspension, a freewheel on the gearbox, 12-volt electrics and an aluminium body, the boot lid of which was operated by a cable from inside the car. The engine sported a very simple timing chain adjustment which consisted of a knurled bolt and locknut. My car's registration was AAK 474, and it was the only one of its type I ever saw. I often wonder whether any more were built and what became of this one, which I was forced to sell in 1960 due to the arrival of our first child.* "

Kevin Atkinson of the Singer Owners' Club, and author of *The Singer Story*, has written to tell us that AAK 474 was an Independent Suspension Nine Drophead Coupe. The model was only available from late 1934 until October 1935 at a price of £230, and very few were built. Sadly, no I.S. Nine DHCs are known to survive, though one 11 hp does, and he has a non-original I.S. Nine fitted with a Le Mans engine. He tells us that there was never an official production version of the I.S. Nine Le Mans, but it would have been a simple matter for the factory to drop a Nine Le Mans engine into an I.S. Nine and, because my correspondent's car had the Le Mans mesh grille rather than the I.S. vertical slats, it may well have been a 'one off' I.S. Nine DHC Le Mans. Kevin Atkinson was very keen to be put in touch with my correspondent to swap notes, so I duly obliged. For club contacts see 'Mine's a Nine' above.

'Trunk' roads

" *In the early 1950s I owned a 1930s Singer Nine which had a large black luggage trunk fixed onto a folding rack at the rear of the car. With just three gears, no heater and very little springing, my wife and I frequently drove from London to Inverness to visit family. We carried two babies on the back seat and that luggage trunk was so full the front wheels were nearly off the ground. There were no motorways, of course, only the old A1 and A9 which went through every town and village. It took us three days each way! Interestingly, the old Singer had an electric fuel pump (which was ahead of its time) and no radiator fan. The only spare part I didn't need to carry was a fan belt. I can still remember rounding Hyde Park Corner at about 5 am with the sun shining on a summer morning and no traffic at all. We presently luxuriate in a Renault Clio 1.4 automatic, with all manner of electrical gadgets.* "

Nice piece of nostalgia. You won't be the only *Telegraph* reader to remember the delights of 'trunk' roads such as the A1, A5 and A9 in the early 1950s. Things weren't all that rose-tinted, of course. Being stuck in an underpowered car, unable to overtake a truck limited to 20 mph, was one of the many joys, and helps to explain why your journeys required three days each way. It's a sobering thought, but what I recall most vividly from motoring in the 1950s is the large number of accidents we passed.

Old smoker

" *Can anyone shed any light on the present whereabouts of the 'Soames' steam car? It was apparently made by Sam and Ted Soames of Norfolk and I have a photo of it in use in the 1950s. Those attending are my father, Philip Barrett and, I think, Messrs J. and A. Edwards. I believe it was seen at steam rallies in the 1960s but I have lost track of it and would be interested to know if it is still running.* "

Many readers rallied round with information, and I have been able to piece together some of the vehicle's past as well as its present location. It was built in 1897 by George S. Soames, blacksmith, motor manufacturer, agent and repairer at Marsham, ten miles north of Norwich. A reader from Norwich writes 'the drive, being via flat belts, is at best uncertain and the tiller steering is not exactly precise. All wheels are iron tyred and the drive wheels at the rear are typical of a dog cart in having very narrow bearings which soon wear out.' A reader from Rickmansworth tells us that his grandfather, serving his apprenticeship at G.S. Soames, helped to build the steam cart, and his father remembers it stopping for water at their cottage in the village of Erpingham. It was seen at steam rallies in Norfolk in the 1950s when it was stored at the premises of Edward J. Edwards (Aggregates) Ltd, in Plumstead Road, Norwich (which confirms what my original correspondent told us). The boiler was renewed in 1978, but the remainder of the vehicle is original. It spent some time at the Bressingham Steam Museum near Diss. In the late 1980s it was apparently in Sir William McAlpine's private museum at Fawley. From 1993 it has been owned by Dick Joice of The Bygones Collection at Holkham Hall in Norfolk (open Sunday-

Thursday only, tel: 01328 710806). It has been away for renovation but should be back on display by the time this book is published. Its absence may explain why *The Traction Engine Register*, published by The Southern Counties Historic Vehicles Preservation Trust in 1996, listed its location as Henley-on-Thames.

Eight, or date?

" *I have a 1950 Standard 8 which was given to me by a very senior RAF Officer to whom I was ADC for a short while in 1954. I am shortly to go to live overseas and need to sell the car to someone who will cherish it. Is there a Standard Car Owners' Club I could contact?* "

There certainly is. The Standard Motor Club, c/o T. Pingriff, 57 Main Road, Meriden, Coventry CV7 7LP, tel: 01676 522181, email: homerp@ettwl.agw.bt.co.uk. But this has thrown me into confusion because there wasn't a 1950 Standard 8. Under Sir John Black's 'export or die' single model policy, all pre-war Standard models were dropped by 1948 in order to concentrate production on the Vanguard, and the utilitarian 'new' 8 did not hit the streets until 1953. Your car must be the pre-war design (one of the best little cars of its day), but, unless it first hit the road on MOD plates, why it was not registered until 1950 is a real mystery.

Classic dealings

In mid-February 1998 I received a letter from Bob Stoddart of Hexham, Northumberland, concerning the sale of his 1954 Standard Vanguard Phase II diesel (Britain's first series production diesel car) to the Heritage Motor Centre at Gaydon. The purchase had been delayed because it had first to be approved by trustees, but since I was visiting Hexham the following weekend I paid Bob a call. One thing led to another and it turned out that Bob had been a Ferguson tractor rep and had created a shrine to these wonderful workhorses in the basement of his house. The Ferguson connection led to his purchase of the Vanguard, which had basically the same diesel engine as the tractor, and also to friendship with John Moffitt, who has now amassed the biggest collection of Fergusons, Ford Fergusons and associated equipment in the country. Bob's Vanguard has been garaged at John's place together with a 1903 Ivel, reg. AO 385 (Britain's oldest working tractor – seen working on Channel 4 TV's 'Classic Plant') and a 1928 Morris Cowley van. The van was put together at great expense using an original 11.9 hp Cowley Flatnose chassis and an original Cowley demountable van body once used by Walter Wilson's Grocery Store in Windermere and found stored in a warehouse there. To complete his Ferguson collection, John Moffitt needs a Standard Vanguard Ferguson Tractor Service van, and to get it he's prepared to sell the 1928 Morris Cowley van. Offers of Standard Vanguard vans duly rolled in but no one seemed to want the near-perfect 1928 Morris Cowley van, which John may still have (tel: 01661 843651).

Sir John Black

" I read with interest an item in 'Telegraph Motoring' regarding the Swallow Doretti Sabre which also mentioned Tube Investments and

Swallow as a maker of sidecars. In my many travels as an engineering manager, I was installing some aircraft build jigs on an airfield near Leicester back in the mid-fifties. One lunchtime, when I was taking a walk around the airfield, a motorcycle and sidecar pulled up by the side of me and a rider in leathers and helmet asked if I would mind acting as ballast for the sidecar while he drove around the perimeter track. I might add that it was a most terrifying experience with the offside wheel leaving the surface on cornering and skids that used the maximum of the combination. But when we had finished about three circuits, we stopped and I was thanked profusely by the person who was driving. On returning to work I asked who the person was that had accosted me to partake in this experience, and I was told it was Sir John Black who was chairman or MD of Swallow Side Cars and who took singular interest in testing his new products. Can you confirm his activities and perhaps tell your readers what happened to this obviously great pioneer? "

It's all there in Giles Chapman's *The Daily*

Telegraph 100 Great British Cars. Swallow Coachbuilding Co. Ltd was based at The Airport, Walsall, Staffs (not a huge distance from Leicester) and built both Swallow sidecars and the Swallow Doretti car. How Sir John Black came to be testing Swallow Sidecars makes an interesting story. Sir John had been chief of The Standard Motor Company and was responsible for the 'export or die' Standard Vanguard, the robust four-cylinder engine of which found its way into the Ferguson tractor, the Triumph 2000 Roadster, the Triumph TR2, the Morgan Plus Four, the Peerless and numerous other specialist sports cars, including the Swallow Doretti. Triumph had been bankrupted by wartime bombing raids on its Coventry factory and Standard bought the name in 1945. Sir John spotted that MG TCs and TDs, rather than his more bloated Triumph 1800 and 2000 Roadsters, were selling well in the USA, and he initiated an affordable sports car of his own – the Triumph TR2. American buyers lapped it up and the TR2 soon became Standard/Triumph's top dollar earner. But Black himself was ousted in a bitter boardroom coup in 1954 and went to Swallow. He was badly injured testing the prototype Swallow Doretti and never properly recovered, so my correspondent seems to have had a lucky escape. Sir John Black died in 1965.

'Sunbeamised' Talbot

" Could you give me any information about a car I bought in 1953 for £150 and sold a year later for £130? It was a Talbot with a six-cylinder engine of two litre capacity. Various opinions are that it was a '104' or a 'Talbot Roesch'. In any event, I considered the design and quality of workmanship quite outstanding for the era. It had drawbacks, however. I recall *that the braking was very sluggish. Also, at speed, water from the radiator cap escaped and required the use of wipers whatever the weather. The petrol tank capacity was 20 gallons and therefore it was rarely full.* "

Your car looks to me like a Rootes '75' model built in 1936 or 1937 in the period after Rootes, much to the regret of Talbot fans, took over the company and merged it with another famous marque, Sunbeam. (A 1,000 hp Sunbeam built in Wolverhampton and driven by Major Henry O'Neal De Hane Segrave in 1927 was the first car to exceed 200 mph.) The number plate '775' helps to confirm that your car was a 2,276 cc, 70 bhp '75', which Mark Gillies tells us in the *A–Z of Cars of the 1930s* was emasculated by the fitting of a wide-ratio four-speed gearbox from a Humber in place of its Wilson pre-selector. It also lost its finned brake drums, which partly explains your stopping problems. In 1939 the '75' itself was replaced by the two litre Sunbeam Talbot which, to the horror of Talbot enthusiasts, had a 56 bhp four-cylinder side-valve Hillman engine.

Finding Talbot's Rootes

" *Could you tell me anything about the car I owned in the early 1950s, and in particular how many were built? I sold it in 1955 to someone connected with Sheffield Wednesday Football Club for £250. It was a Talbot, circa 1937, and seemed very advanced for the day with metallic silver paint and aluminium body and dashboard. My wife and I drove it through France to Spain and back at a total cost of £6 return. Those were the days.* "

It's our old friend the Talbot 10, described by Mark Gillies in the *A–Z of Cars of the 1930s* as 'A Hillman Minx in a party frock.' The car was built after the Rootes brothers' 'Sunbeamisation' of Talbot which combined two once-respected marques into badge-engineered Hillmans and Humbers. But, as you say, the cars were attractively presented – a sort of Vauxhall Calibra of the day. Engines were side-valve 1,185 cc Hillman Minx units, modified by Georges Roesch with an aluminium cylinder head to pump out 41 bhp. Top speed was 72 mph and fuel consumption 32 mpg, which will have helped towards that £6 round trip. Total production was 1,748.

A car named Gloria

" *In 1934 my mother had a Triumph Gloria which she still refers to as the best car she ever owned. It was a closed two-door coupe in silver grey with pale-blue leather upholstery, registration BBP 335. The car was stored in Southampton during the war and afterwards was used by my uncle and grandfather for a while. Sadly, no one knows what became of it. Are there any records of this model and can I find out if the car survived?* "

Sedgwick and Gillies's *A–Z of Cars of the 1930s* tells us that the Gloria Four and Six were introduced in 1934 as competitors to the Riley Nine and 12/6. Over the years, the four-cylinder engines grew from 1,087 cc to 1,232 cc, and the sixes from 1,476 cc to 1,991 cc. Vitesse models had twin carburettors, and your mother's car may well have been a Vitesse coupe. The 'BP' plate denotes West Sussex County Council. The Pre-1940 Triumph Owners' Club may be able to help you trace what became of the car. Write to Ian Harper, 155 Winkworth Road, Banstead, Surrey SM7 2JP, tel: 01737 371334.

Triumph of engineering

" *Please could you identify a 1930s car? It was bought secondhand in 1944, a lovely car with leather upholstery and mahogany fascia: a real beauty. I say it is a Triumph Continental, but the knowledgeable men in my life say there never was such a model.* "

The car certainly is a 1937 Triumph Continental. It had a 1,991 cc four-main-bearing six-cylinder engine with twin carburettors, good for over 80 mph. The 1937 14/60 Dolomite was completely re-styled from the earlier Gloria by Walter Bellgrove with a 'Waterfall Grille', but the 'Continental' model retained the more traditional Gloria grille. The spare wheel was transferred to the back for the 1938 model year, which confirms the year of your car as 1937. Ian Harper of The Pre-1940 Triumph Owners' Club (see above) tells us that only one Continental is known to survive and currently resides in Canada.

The Triumph TR7

" *You recently referred to the Triumph TR7 as a 'horror of horrors'. This is throwaway journalism of the worst kind. The TR7 is written off in one sentence without justification. May I suggest you read Steve Cropley's article in the October 1997 issue of* Classic & Sportscar *magazine? To quote: 'A TR7 steers, rides and stops in a far more modern manner than the MGB.' And: 'The TR7 is one of the emerging classic car bargains of the 1990s.' It may be ugly to some, but for affordable open-air touring, how can you beat it? I know you can't. I have one. Come for a test drive once I bring it out again in April.* "

The trouble is, one of these monstrosities was foisted upon me as a 'company car' in 1978. It was a five-speed coupe with a Webasto roof, and I speak from a year of the most miserable motoring I have ever experienced. The only good thing about it was it spent so much time in the garage I got to drive many far better 'pool cars' such as a Lancia Beta 2000 coupe and a Citroen GS 1220 Estate. Good grief, even a Fiesta 1.3S was a better car than that TR7. Its legion of faults included overheating at 80 mph on the Autobahn, leaking poisonous carbon monoxide into the passenger compartment, dashboard rheostat fires, 15 mpg on a good day, a pair of loony 'emissions' carburettors that, when I lifted off for an ice-covered bend, *increased* my speed from 70 mph to 90 mph. When a car keeps trying to kill you, I reckon its fair comment to describe it as a horror. Because Roverhire, the Triumph West London agents, could never get parts and could never fix the damn thing, they resorted to cheering up disgruntled customers by handing them a motoring joke book (no kidding). Not only that, the car rusted almost as badly as my previous Alfa Romeo 105 coupe. You can forgive rust on an Alfa, but not on the appalling piece of junk the TR7 was. Steve's right about the suspension. It was twenty years ahead of that of the MGB, but still rubbish compared to an Alfa's. He's also right that the TR7 is a 'classic car bargain'. They go for buttons at auction (coupes: £300; roadsters: £850). I accept that, over the years, a painstaking owner such as yourself, using aftermarket mods, may well have solved many of the car's design and build deficiencies, but this was impossible when I had mine and the TR7 remains the worst car I have ever had to live with.

Trojan

" *I well remember, in 1926, my father taking delivery from May and*

Jacobs in Guildford High Street of a three-door open Trojan Tourer, registration PF 2070, fitted with optional pneumatic tyres. The four-cylinder two-stroke engine was housed under the front seats and the rear wheels were chain-driven. There were two forward gears and reverse, and the windscreen wiper was manual. In 1929 the open tourer was replaced, again from May and Jacobs, by a Trojan four-door Achilles fabric saloon (official description). Same engine, same drive, same gears, but an electric windscreen wiper. The registration was AN 9327. I would be interested to know who built the fabric-covered body. Brooke Bond ran a fleet of Trojan vans for many years – I believe up until the 1960s. Trojan also made a rear-engined saloon in 1930/31, but it did not enjoy popularity. **"**

The Trojan was a simple, strong utility car originally designed by Leslie Hounsfield and first shown in prototype form in 1910. It was finally put into production by Leyland Motors Ltd of Kingston-on-Thames in 1922 and sold an impressive 17,000 by the time the rights reverted to Hounsfield in 1927 and he re-commenced production at Croydon. 'PF' was an old Surrey County Council registration, but 'AN' was West Ham Borough Council. The only coachbuilder mentioned in connection with Trojan in the *A–Z of British Coachbuilders* is Alban Crofts of Croydon, who seems to have continued the association building van bodies. A 1924 Trojan PB Chummy cropped up at a BCA Classic sale in April 1996 and sold for £3,650, plus commission. There's one on display at the Heritage Centre in Gaydon and one at Beaulieu.

Vixen valuation

" For the past 23 years I have been the proud owner of a 1972K TVR Vixen SIV. The car has a 1.6 litre 'crossflow' Ford Cortina GT engine, has covered 65,000 miles, and was in constant use until last year. Now my daughter has bought a plot of land in Brazil and wants to build on it, so *the TVR may have to go to provide the necessary funds. Apparently only 28 SIVs were ever built. Can you give me any idea of what the car is worth and how best to sell it?* **"**

I remember these well as I helped a neighbour finish an SI from a half-assembled 'kit'. They were about 10 mph quicker than the Cortina GTs their engines came from, and a lot flatter round corners. The classic guides estimate Vixen SIs to SIVs at £2,500–£6,000. A nice, restored Vixen SII (one of 438 built) sold for £5,717 (including 5.875% buyer's premium) at a recent BCA auction, which suggests that £4,995 would be a good price to advertise. It's worth contacting the TVR Club, PO Box 36, Telford TF6 6WF, tel: 01952 770635, and specialist in older TVRs Steve Reid, on 01928 719267 (mobile: 0831 389500). If you are a member of 'Telegraph Motoring Plus', you can put a colour photo ad in our own Forecourt Section for £150 (tel: 0171 538 6005). Or you could try a photo ad in three issues of *Classic Car Weekly*, one issue of *Classic Car* and one issue of *Practical Classics* for a combined £90 (buy one of the magazines for a form).

Vale Special

" *I had an uncle called James Vale who built a small sports car by the name of the 'Vale Special', which he used to race at Brooklands. Family records show that a total of 103 Vales were built, but only around six are thought to survive. My grandsons are very interested in motor racing and all have go-karts. Now they are asking about their long lost relative and his cars. Can I order copies of car magazines of the period? And can you give me any more information about the car?* **"**

The Vale Special was quite a pretty, very low-slung sports car with Rubery Owen chassis, powered by a modified 832 cc Triumph Super Seven engine and built by Vale Engineering of (coincidentally) Maida Vale, London, between 1932 and 1936. G.N. Georgano's *Complete Encyclopaedia of Motor Cars* tells us it did not exactly take off because it was too low-slung for trials and not quick enough for the track. This was put right by a 1934 decision to replace the Triumph engines with Coventry Climax 1,098 cc fours or 1,476 cc sixes. In 1935, a supercharged Vale Six was built for the racing driver Ian Connell, and replicas were priced at £625.

Found – after 66 years

" *I should like to know whether a 1923 Vauxhall 30/98, reg. ND 818, is still on the road. In 1932 we took it on a six-day rally to Scotland. It was garaged in Thatcham, Berkshire, and was known to have done over 100 mph at Brooklands a few days before we went on the rally.* "

I'm pleased to say it is. Ray Cooper at The Vauxhall Heritage Centre confirmed that the car was still in good health and put me on to the owner, who was delighted to receive news of his car's early days. The side-valve 'E Type' Vauxhall 30/98 was indeed the 'E Type' of its day, and all were guaranteed to exceed 100 mph with the right body and the correct axle ratio. ND 818 is a very early overhead-valve 'OE' model, which gave an extra 15–20 bhp from its 4,224 cc. When it was built, chassis number OE 28/28 did not have front brakes, and the front axle from OE 98, together with its 'brake kidney box', was fitted at a later stage. Other modifications include removal of running boards, side exit exhaust, cycle-type mudguards and two very large horns. We know for certain the car came up for sale in *The Autocar* in 1934 because, unusually, the ad gave its chassis number.

Those were the days

" *I wonder if you may be interested in my reminiscences of my father's Vinot car. It was French and he bought it in about 1912. As a baby I used to be put on the floor in the back in a laundry basket, while my father drove us from Oxford to Cheltenham via Witney, Burford, Northleach and Andoversford. Later, as a seven-year-old, I vividly remember passing endless stone walls, and also the cold, as the side curtains were not a very good fit. The car had no spare wheel. Instead it carried a 'Stepney', which was a tyre mounted on a rim to be bound with leather straps to the rim of the punctured tyre and the car driven very slowly to the nearest garage. The main object of those journeys was the fact that brandy snaps were sold in Cheltenham but could not be obtained in Oxford. What bliss.* "

I suspect your father liked driving and your mother liked brandy snaps. I had not heard of the Vinot, but G.N. Georgano devotes a page to it in *The Complete Encyclopaedia of Motor Cars 1885–1968*. The full name for the marque was Vinot et Deguingand, and your father's looks like either a 12/16 or a 16/20.

Voisin taxi?

" *In the early 1930s when I was at school our local taxi man was using a rather stylish limousine which had 'Avions Voisin' in a decorative motif on the front of the bonnet. Can you furnish any details of this marque?* "

Your taxi driver certainly had taste. Voisin cars were built between 1919 and 1939 by SA des Aeroplanes Gabriel Voisin in Issy-les Moulineaux, Seine. Voisin was a renowned aircraft pioneer and beat the Wright brothers by making the first powered take-off followed by a powered flight. (The Wright brothers used a catapult.) His cars all used sleeve-valve engines and your taxi driver's was probably a four litre 18CV limousine or coupe de ville. Some Voisins, such as the 4.8 litre V12 of the early 1930s, carried spectacular and unusual bodywork. Voisins also had 'Lalique' glass mascots on their radiator caps and these have become highly prized collectors' pieces.

Des res with bay window

" *In 1976 we bought a one-year-old N-registered Volkswagen Devon Camper. It has now done 56,000 miles and, having been kept in our garage, shows little sign of rust. Even the elevating roof is in good working order. The only replacements have been the alternator, battery and, of course, tyres. I have used it locally for shopping and it has been regularly serviced and MOT tested. It is comfortable to drive, with excellent vision, and I am loth to sell it, but have to accept that I have come to the point when I really need something smaller. I have no idea what to ask or where to advertise. Can you help?* "

I know these quite well, because my parents had a Type 2 in the seventies as a second vehicle. Because of the shape of the front, VW Camper aficionados dub it the 'bay window' version. There is a very strong demand for good ones and I think you could be very pleasantly surprised at what it's worth: possibly as much as £3,000–£4,000. If I were you, I'd contact the clubs: The Classic Camper Club, c/o Steve Cooper, 40 Audley Drive, Kidderminster, Worcs DY11 5NE, tel: 01562 752432, and The VW Type 2 Owners' Club, c/o P. Shaw, 57 Humphrey Drive, Charford, Bromsgrove, Worcs B60 3JD,

tel: 01527 872194. A quick chronology: VW fans describe all VW vans as Type 2s because the original VW Beetle was described by the factory as the Type 1. They then split the vans down into various 'T' numbers, which are as follows: the T1 (split window) ran from 1950 to 1967; the T2 from 1968 to 1972; the T2.5 (an improved Type 2) from 1973 to 1979; the square-fronted T3 from 1980 to 1990; and the current front-wheel-drive T4 from 1991 on.

Biggest VW

" *During the 1970s I worked in Kenya for the VW main agents in East Africa. Obviously I drove a number of VW vehicles in that time and for the last couple of years had use of a 412 Variant. It proved to be a very reliable load-carrying vehicle capable of dealing with some very rugged ter-*

rain, especially when on safari. With the front bonnet luggage space as well as the load area above the engine an enormous amount could be fitted in. Now that I have reached the age of nostalgia I would like to buy a 412 Variant. Is a price of £1,000 realistic for a Condition 1/2 vehicle? Are spares available and, if so, how expensive are they? Finally, how can I actually get hold of one? If necessary, I would settle for a 411 instead. "

UK imports of the 1,679 cc 411 ran from 1968 to 1973, and of the 412 from 1973 to 1975. They were fuel-injected from October 1969 giving 80 bhp. Twin carburettors then replaced fuel injection in October 1974, when the swept capacity of the engine grew to 1,795 cc. Total production of 411s was 264,549 (I don't have a figure for 412s). I am led to believe they were very good for snogging in winter because they had an independent petrol-fired heater. In VW nomenclature, 411s and 412s were designated Type 4s and your best bet for information, help and even a car is to join the VW Type 3 and 4 Club, c/o J. Terry, Exted Farm, Exted, Eltham, Canterbury, Kent CT4 4YG, tel: 01303 840241. Two specialist magazines will also be useful: *VW Motoring* and *Volksworld*. £1,000 looks a bit optimistic for a condition 1/2 412. *Practical Classics* magazine reckons £2,250 for a C1; £900 for a C2 or £200 for a C3, and the Variant is bound to be the most valuable model. Mechanical parts should not be too difficult, as many were shared by the Transporter vans, but body parts could be scarce – which explains the very low price estimate for a Condition 3 car. I should add that I have never ever seen one at a classic car auction.

Waverley

" *My father bought a car called a 'Waverley', for which he paid £550 in 1924. It was produced in small numbers in a small factory in Willesden and had very good performance for those days. I'm afraid I have no figures for its specification.* **"**

Nick Baldwin's *A–Z of Cars of the 1920s* devotes more than a page to Waverley cars. Production began in 1910 using French components, and culminated in the late 1920s with the 'All British Six'. Most bodywork was by E.B. Hall & Co., which later became The Carlton Carriage Co. Nick thinks car production probably stopped after the Wall Street Crash, but Waverleys continued to be listed until 1935 and the company remained in business as general engineers long after WW2. Your father's car appears to be a Waverley Fifteen, current from 1919 to 1924. Later models had a 2,304 cc Tylor side-valve four-cylinder engine, electric self-starter and four-speed gearbox with cone clutch and right-hand change. An unusual feature was two sets of quarter-elliptic springs at the rear. Both hand and foot brakes were in the rear drums, rather than the handbrake being on the transmission. Records show that 100 gearboxes were ordered from Meadows in 1923, but only seven appear to have been delivered. I hope this helps to stir some memories for you.

Windsor by name

" *In the mid-twenties my great uncle owned a car he descrbed as a 'Windsor', perhaps a 14 hp tourer. He was an engineer and the car was possibly purchased because of its better-than-usual quality. The radiator badge was rectangular, with 'WINDSOR' in capital letters.* **"**

The Windsor was a light car of 10.4 hp (1,353 cc) and was indeed characterised by a very high standard of construction. The cars were built in

Notting Hill, London, by James Bartle and Co., a company controlled since 1910 by C.S. Windsor. The prototype had an 1,870 cc engine, but production models used the 1,353 cc side-valver. The car was launched at the 1923 Olympia Motor Show, but Windsor died in 1925 and the company went into liquidation in 1927. Dealers Watkins and Doncaster of Stamford Hill bought the jigs, tools, spares and drawings, and continued to produce a few cars into the 1930s. E. Farebrother, the designer of the car, then went to Clarke Cluley to design the Cluley 14/40 and 14/50.

Compressed-air Wolseley

" *I was interested in the air starter which you mentioned in your column. Our old family Wolseley, owned between 1918 and 1920, also had an air starter, but a simpler system that supplied compressed air to the engine cylinders themselves. The air was contained in a bottle on the chassis, kept at pressure by an engine-run pump and also by a lever in the cockpit, and carried to each of the six cylinders by copper pipes. When the driver pressed a pedal, air was supplied to the cylinders which spun the crankshaft until the engine started. This massive engine, comprising three blocks of two cylinders apiece, was almost impossible to start on the crank handle in cold weather unless two people worked at it (at considerable risk), but the air starter was completely efficient.* "

Wolseley built some big engines before the First World War – a 7,096 cc 40 hp and an 8,928 cc 50 hp, and after the war the company continued to offer five- and seven-litre sixes. Georgano's *Complete Encyclopaedia of Motorcars* confirms that the big sixes had compressed-air starters up to 1919, when they were supplanted by conventional electric starters. The compressed-air starter is fully described in an interesting book entitled *Wolseley Cars in Canada* by Charles G. Neville, which tells the tale of seven 1912–14 Wolseleys unearthed in a barn in Canada and subsequently restored to their former glory. Price £14.95 plus £1.50 p&p from Thelma Waddilove, Regalia Secretary, The Wolseley Register, 45 Larkfield Lane, Southport PR9 8NN.

Wartime Hornet

" *In the early months of 1939 I purchased a 1932 Wolseley Hornet Special for £32 17s 6d and ran it until September of that year, when I was called up into the Navy. After the war was over I ran it for a few months before selling it and leaving the country to work abroad. Although the standard Wolseley Hornet was seen in large numbers, I never saw another Hornet Special. Was mine unique? If not, how many were produced? It gave me great fun and if it still exists I would love to see it again. The registration number was GY 3279.* "

Sedgwick and Gillies's *A–Z of Cars of the 1930s* tells us that 2,397 Hornet Special 12s were produced between 1932 and 1934 with 45 bhp engines that gave them a top speed of up to 75 mph. They were bodied by specialists such as Swallow and Eustace Watkins, but the model illustrated in the *A–Z* has exactly the same pointed rear-end treatment as your car. There is a Wolseley Hornet Special Club which may be able to tell you what happened to yours from the registration number, but they might require a chassis number. The club's address is: c/o Ms Chris Hyde, 'Kylemor', Crown Gardens, Fleet, Hants GU13 9PD, tel: 01252 622411. You could also try The Wolseley Register, c/o Mike Schilling, 31 Malin Close, Hale Village, Liverpool L24 5RU.

R. Serjeantson, Chairman of The Wolseley Hornet Special Club, subsequently wrote to tell us that GY 3279 is alive and well in Cheshire. He would be pleased to hear from my correspondent, and anyone else who owned one of these cars, because he is planning to write a book about pre-war Hornets and Hornet Specials. (Tel/fax: 0181 789 8385, email: R.M.Serjeantson @btinternet.com), or write to 25 Roehampton High Street, London SW15 4HL. He believes that production figures were much higher than those quoted in the *A–Z*.

COOLING SYSTEM AND LEAKS*

Overflow

" *Despite his best efforts, my local Honda dealer has been unable to help with a problem that started 18 months ago on my E-reg. Honda Accord automatic with 53,000 recorded miles. When the engine is switched off after a long run, particularly in hot weather, the coolant overflows, even though the correct coolant levels were present at the start of the journey. So far this does not seem to be having an adverse effect on the engine, but as well as being of concern it is also very embarrassing to leave puddles!* "

Could be an airlock. With an airlock in the system, levels will appear to be correct, but only because the airlock is displacing coolant. From cold, run the engine for a minute or two with the heater control set to maximum heat, which will make sure the valve into the heater matrix is open. Then stop the engine, open the filler, and top up the coolant. A second possible cause is that the electric engine fan is not working. At speed, air is forced through the radiator, but when you stop it needs help, which is why the electric fan on cars fitted with one often continues to run even after the car is stationary and locked up. Without the fan, coolant in a hot engine will boil and overflow through the pressure cap even after the engine is switched off.

---

* This section includes information about oil leaks.

I later heard that the cause of this leak was discovered to be a worn-out spring and seal in the radiator cap which allowed water to escape at a lower pressure than it was designed to. The reverse of this problem has happened with BMW E30 3-Series models, which were recalled in 1998 because a corroded cap could over-pressurise the cooling system.

For the sake of a clip

" A couple of days ago, on a lonely country road in the midst of a gale, the engine of my Rover 420 Tourer expired. I opened the bonnet to be confronted by a cloud of steam and soon saw that the short length of pipe from the radiator to the header tank had come adrift. One end was clipped, but the end that had come adrift was not. After a long trudge I found a kindly householder who called the local Rover dealer. Rover was also kind enough to supply a replacement engine free of charge. But I am left with the cost of the recovery and of having the new engine fitted – all for the sake of one little clip. May I use your column to ask all 420 owners to ensure there is a clip at both ends of the pipe from header tank to radiator? "

It goes without saying that, if a warning light on the car's dashboard comes on, you should stop the car immediately.

You certainly can. It's worth all readers popping their bonnets from time to time to look for leaks such as this (it takes no mechanical knowledge to spot one). Also, make sure the coolant is up to the mark in the header tank itself. And, of course, if a warning light comes on, stop the car immediately.

Corrosive anti-freeze

" The Rolls Royce Owners' Club magazine contains an article which effectively states that ethylene glycol is very toxic and we must be careful not to get it onto a vehicle's paintwork; that in time ethylene glycol's anti-corrosion properties deteriorate and it breaks down into corrosive ele-

ments, so should therefore be changed every two years; and finally, that if it gets into contact with oil it will gel and the resultant mixture will not flow. Is this correct? I would be most interested in your view. **"**

Many cooling systems contain coolant in which the corrosion inhibitors have degraded, allowing severe corrosion inside the engine.

The Rolls Royce magazine is correct. Coolant is highly corrosive, and an engine built from at least two different metals forms a very effective corrosion battery. Because of this, good coolant contains corrosion inhibitors. These last for two to three years in MEG coolants and 4 years in the new Trigard-based MPG coolants. Unfortunately, far too many owners and garages simply test the coolant's antifreeze strength, entirely forgetting that this is no test of the corrosion inhibitors. The result is that many cooling systems contain coolant in which the corrosion inhibitors have degraded, allowing severe corrosion inside the engine. First to go is usually the cylinder head gasket, which contains different metals from the block and the head and which effectively becomes the sacrificial anode in a 'corrosion battery'. (See *Motor Vehicle Corrosion Prediction and Prevention* by H. McArthur, ISBN 0-9515787-0-7.) Where the compression ratio is higher, as in a diesel engine, a partially corroded gasket will give way earlier than in a low compression engine. The answer is a pre-mixed Trigard-based, non-toxic, bio-degradable Mono Propylene Glycol coolant such as Comma Coldstream, Esso Ready Mixed, Quantum (VW/Audi) Ready Mixed Coolant, Bluecol Protex Anti Freeze, Unipart Super Plus Anti Freeze, Batoyle Masterfrost and Silkolene Iceguard. These all last about four years – double the 'safe' life of ethylene glycol antifreeze.

Keeping your cool

" As an owner/driver who does more than 25,000 miles a year, I take special notice when friends tell me about sticking thermostats leading to expensively blown engines. Surely there is a way of making thermostats fail-safe? "

Glad you asked, because by coincidence the answer is staring me in the face from page 87 of the May 1997 issue of *Diesel Car & 4×4* magazine. It's the Failsafe thermostat by Truport Ltd (tel: 01707 377123), which fails in the open rather than the closed position and allows coolant to circulate freely rather than overheat locally and blow a gasket.

Pipeworks

" I own an L-registered Rover 418 which is fitted with the PSA 1,769 cc XUD diesel engine. Some weeks ago, after returning from an outing, a large pool of oil suddenly appeared on my driveway at the front of the car. Investigation showed that the sheath of the bonnet release cable had chafed through one of the steel oil pipes connecting the oil cooler to the oil filter head. After going to some expense to get it repaired at a local garage, I discovered that a modification bulletin has been issued to Rover agents to fit a rubber spacer between the oil pipe and the bonnet release cable. Since then, I have visited three Rover agents and none had heard about this modification. Why could the defect not have been notified direct to the car's owner via the recall system? "

It can't have been deemed serious enough. But let me take this opportunity to warn all owners of old-shape PSA diesel Rover 200s and 400s (and VM diesel 800s for that matter) to check for chafing of this oil pipe – and all the other hoses. It's not unknown for the clip to fall off the hose which connects to the coolant header tank.

DISABLED DRIVERS*

Back-up

" I would like to offer some advice for drivers who suffer from slipped discs and resulting nerve and muscle damage. First, make sure the driving seat is long enough to give support under the thighs. Second, make sure that the rear of the seat squab is not low so that the base of your spine is below your knees. Third, avoid a low-slung seat which can jar your spine as you drop down into it. Fourth, make sure your legs are not stretched out straight in front of you. The best seats I have found are in 'K' and 'L' reg. Suzuki Vitara 5-door models and in customised models, the leather seats of which have reverted back to the old shape. Of course, no two back problems are the same and this will not provide the answer for everyone. "

Other readers have recommended older model 'K' and 'L' reg. Vitaras. I think the best alternative is the five-door Fiat Punto SX or ELX which have both a height-adjustable seat and a height-adjustable steering wheel. This car is extremely easy to get in and out of and the seat is fairly high. Lower-spec. Puntos are also good, but not as good. It should be added that the seating in both the Punto and the Bravo/Brava were researched and designed by the Ergonomics Unit at Loughborough University, headed by Professor Mark Porter, so might be expected to have been designed with the British in mind. As

---

* Includes tips for the elderly and drivers with back problems.

a general tip Professor Porter recommends changing your seat position slightly from time to time, and doing some 'stretching exercises' after a long drive. Instructions for this are in *Stretching* by Bob Anderson.

Lumbared

" *My physio recommended me to buy a product known as the McKenzie Lumbar Roll which comes in two densities (standard and heavy) from Medipost Ltd, Oldham, Lancs OL1 4AY, tel: 0161 678 0233. The cost is about £9 and I think it's great for small people or people needing more lumbar support than is provided by the car seat.* "

I hope this will provide some relief for back sufferers. A frequent 'Telegraph Reader Offer' is the 'Ortho Cushion', which suspends the coccyx over a hole and tips the pelvis forward to re-create the spine's natural lumbar curve. In 1997 it was priced at £10.95 including p&p (check price before ordering) from The Daily Telegraph Ortho Cushion Offer (V1595), Belton Road West, Loughborough, Leics LE11 5XL, tel: 01509 638625. Another good product is the 'BackFriend', which I'm sitting on as I write, from MEDesign Ltd, Clock Tower Works, Railway Street, Southport, Merseyside PR8 5BB, tel: 01704 542373.

A 'drive-in' car

" *I have an elderly parent who needs wheelchair assistance but is not confined to her wheelchair (she can travel in a normal car seat). We recently purchased a motorised chair which is too big to lug over the sill at the back of my 'M' reg. Citroen ZX Elation 1.9D. So I would like change the car for an estate car with no loading lip. I don't want anything too*

large or too highly powered, or, for that matter, too expensive. And I certainly don't want one of the 'Popemobile'-style vehicles. "

At the 1996 Motor Show I had a word with Rod Brotherwood of Brotherwood Mobility (01935 872603) about adapting a Citroen Berlingo Multispace for 'drive-in' wheelchair use. He did a deal with Citroen and had the vehicle ready to go on sale in the UK the day the Berlingo Multispace officially arrived in Spring 1998. This vehicle is much better than any previously offered in the lower price range.

...and another

" *Last year you recommended us to look at the new Citroen Despatch/ Fiat Scudo/Peugeot Expert as the basis for a conversion suitable for the disabled. Your reasoning was that, with a lower floor and higher roof than the Citroen Synergie/Fiat Ulysse/Peugeot 806 on which they are based, these vehicles would offer enough height inside for a wheelchair and passenger without the need for a raised roof. I'm pleased to tell you that we are now offering just such a conversion at prices from £16,705, with a self-contained rear loading ramp at an extra £1,100. We also offer conversions of the new Chrysler Voyager at prices from £26,800, and prices of our more basic converted vehicles start at £12,140 for the Fiat Fiorino.* "

This came from Linda Ling of Gowrings Mobility at 3 Arnhem Road, Newbury, Berks RG14 5RU, tel: 01635 529500. Gowrings is the largest converter of vehicles for the needs of the disabled in the UK. These and virtually every other mobility aid available in the UK will be on show at the 'Mobility Roadshow' at the Transport Research Laboratory, Crowthorne, Berks. The Peugeot Partner TD is now available as a 'Combi' (windows in the sides and a removable rear seat) for £16,625.

Handy hand controls

" *A friend of mine who is disabled will be changing her car from a Mini automatic to a Rover 100CVT in July, under the Motability scheme. She cannot transfer the hand controls from the Mini to the Rover 100, and the firm which made them seems to have disappeared. Can you help?* "

A good and inexpensive hand control adaptation was developed by Lynx Hand Controls, Mansion House, St Helen's Road, Ormskirk, Lancs L39 4QJ, tel: 01695 573816, and featured in *The Daily Telegraph* in December 1996. It costs £225, plus £10 for next-day delivery (check price before ordering). If this proves unsuitable, try the National Mobility Centre helpline on 01743 761181.

Scooter carrier needed

" *I recently became disabled and qualify for the full Disability Living Allowance. However, I want to be able to accompany my able-bodied husband and another couple on country walks, and for this purpose have been advised that the best 'scooter' is the Sterling Classic, which is 38.5 in. high and 24 in. wide. I need to get an automatic car with power steering and hand controls which will accommodate up to four people and the scooter and into which I can load the scooter single-handed when I am out shopping by myself – possibly by means of an electric hoist which can be removed from the car at the end of the three-year Motability Contract. An Astra estate seems to offer the best loadspace.* "

You need specialist advice from The Disabled Drivers Motor Club (01832 734724), which you will need to join, or The Federation of Independent Disabled Motorist Clubs National Mobility Centre (01743 761718). Brotherwood (01935 872603), Gowrings Mobility (0800 220878), Universal Mobility (01293 871019) and The Widnes Car Centre (0151 420 2000) all make suitable vehicles with electric drop-down ramps at the rear which would allow you to drive the scooter straight in, and all are in the Motability catalogue, but all require a substantial advance payment.

Fully mobile again

" *I wrote to you asking for advice about getting a disabled person's scooter into the back of a Vauxhall Astra estate car. You gave me some very useful addresses, including that of the Disabled Drivers Motor Club, which I joined, and pointed me at the Mobility Roadshow, which I attended. Now I'm pleased to report that my problems are solved. K.C. Mobility Services of Batley not only installed a hoist which I can operate to lift my Sunrise Medical scooter into the load area of the Astra, they also lowered the scooter seat so that it does not need to be removed beforehand. I have now been on my holidays and was able to 'scoot along' the country lanes, taking part in the family walks I had so missed. I hope this is of interest to disabled readers.* **"**

The Astra estate of 1991–1998 vintage has the largest, most accessible load area of any estate car of the same age and external size.

Others have pointed out the merits of the 1991–98 Astra estate for this purpose. It seems to have the largest, most accessible load area of any estate car of the same age and external size, and, of course, power steering has been standard since autumn 1994 (all 1995 model year 'V' grille models). The Citroen Xsara estate and the new Vauxhall Astra estate should be just as good, with the Citroen offering particularly good ride quality. All that remains are the names and addresses: The Disabled Drivers Motor Club, Cottingham Way, Thrapston, Northants NN14 4PL, tel: 01832 734724; Royal Association for Disability and Rehabilitation (RADAR), 12 City Forum, 250 City Road, London EC1V 8AF, tel: 0171 250 3222; K.C. Mobility Services, 501 Bradford Road, Batley, W. Yorks WF17 8LN, tel: 01924 442386; Sunrise Medical Ltd, Fens Pool Avenue, Brierley Hill, West Midlands DY5 1QA, tel: 01384 480480.

Disabled Drivers Association

Janet Johnson of The Disabled Drivers Association has written to offer copies of the Association's booklet, *The Road to Mobility*, free to readers in the hope that on the strength of this they will join the Association. This covers the subject of car adaptations in some detail and lists suppliers throughout the UK. A self-addressed A4 envelope stamped to the value of 80p will cover postage costs and the booklet is available from The Information Officer, The

Disabled Drivers Association, Ashwellthorpe, Norwich NR16 1EX, tel: 01508 489449.

Getting Motability

" *Our local Hyundai garage is advertising the invalidity scheme whereby I forfeit my disability allowance and rent a car. Could you please let me have full details of the scheme so that I will be knowledgeable before I contact them? A 'must' is that it should be a small car with automatic gears and power steering. Could you therefore list all makers who incorporate these essentials? My preference would be a well-looked-after two-year-old Punto.* "

Motability has a helpline (01279 635666), which I have used to order an information pack for you. This lists all makes and models available on Motability, together with additional contributions for those cars not available solely for the Higher Rate Mobility Component of the Disability Living Allowance. Motability cars are new, of course, but the sheer size of the Motability fleet allows Motability Finance to buy the cars at considerable discounts, much of which it passes on to its lessees. On the list you were sent, there were four automatics with PAS which you could have for no deposit and no additional payment. The Renault Clio RL Phase III 1.4 three-door would bring you a weekly refund of £4.10. Or, for the full allowance, you could have a Hyundai Accent 1.3i three-door coupe; a Nissan Micra 1.0 three- or five-door; or a Vauxhall Corsa 1.4i Merit three-door.

Simple disabled aids

" *May I suggest some simple ideas to help those with back, hip or knee problems to get in and out of cars? When emerging from the front seat, push it back as far as possible. When emerging from the back seat, get the driver to move the front seat as far forward as possible. Put a supermarket plastic bag on the seat to enable you to swivel more easily while still seated. Open the window and use the door frame and window sill to hold onto while getting in or out. Try to have someone at hand to lift your leg over the door sill.* **"**

Thank you for these suggestions. They are all very helpful, particularly the plastic bag trick.

Pedal extensions

" *I am soon to take delivery of a new Jaguar XJ8 and it will be my first new car for ten years. Airbags are therefore a new innovation to me, and since my wife will also drive the car I am concerned about her sitting too close to the wheel. What Car? magazine recently suggested pedal extenders. Where can I get these fitted?* **"**

Adaptacar had fitted removable pedal extensions to a new XJ the week your letter arrived. These are custom-built to the customer's exact requirements, so will involve a trip to 55 Cooks Cross, South Moulton, North Devon EX36 4AW (tel: 01769 572785). Since this is exactly what a new car needs as part of the running-in process you might consider turning the trip into a short holiday.

Wheelchair-adapted Prairie

" *When my father died in September, he left a 1983Y, 70,000-mile, 1,488 cc Nissan Prairie which has been modified by having the front passenger seat removed and replaced by an electric wheelchair with electric hoist. I would be grateful if you would indicate how much I could sell this combination for.* **"**

To the average trader this vehicle is worth very little. But to a person who needs such a vehicle it is worth considerably more than the average 83Y Nissan Prairie – possibly as much as £2,000 depending on the condition of the structure. (With no central 'B' pillar, this model of Prairie is extremely vulnerable to rot in the floorpan.) The modifications may, of course, be transferable to another vehicle. If I were you I would first make enquiries at your local centre for disabled people and also your local GP, who might allow you to put a postcard ad in his waiting room. Finally, a reader from Stevenage suggests contacting The Disability Equipment Register of 4 Chatterton Road, Yate, Bristol BS37 4BJ, tel: 01454 318818. This organisation publishes a monthly magazine for buyers and sellers of all mobility equipment, including a ten-page section of adapted vehicles.

Parking places for the disabled

Dr Adrian Stokes, chairman of The Disabled Drivers Motor Club (01832 734724), has written to alert us of the problem of able-bodied people stealing spaces allocated to the disabled. His point is, 'For an able-bodied person not to be able to park their car close or near to their destination is no great hardship; for a disabled person it is essential to be able to park as close as possible.' A meeting was held to agree an Action Plan, encouraging stricter enforcement of both on- and off-street Orange Badge parking spaces, to reduce abuse of the Orange Badge scheme, and generally to promote greater awareness of the needs of disabled drivers. I hope that publishing this helps. Shame on any able-bodied, non-Orange Badge driver who parks in a space allocated to the disabled.

Automatic wheelchair transporter

" My wife is now wheelchair bound, and I seek to part exchange my 1989F Mercedes 190 for an automatic car capable of accommodating the wheelchair. I'd like the car to be as small as possible, obtainable with metallic paint, and with electric front windows. "

I'd check out the new Vauxhall Astra 2.0 DI automatic estate car. The old Astra estate was generally reckoned to be one of the best small estates for carrying wheelchairs, and the new one can be ordered with the benefit of an economical direct-injected diesel engine allied to a four-speed automatic transmission. Even with the autobox, performance as tested by *Autocar* (1 April 1998) seems to be better than the manual Vectra DI estate, and now that this chain-cam engine is de-bugged it should be good for a very long life.

DRIVING ABROAD

Joining the AAA

" *Kindly advise me where/how to join the American Automobile Association – in the UK, in Europe or in the USA?* "

Phone 001 407 444 7700 (they're in Orlando, Florida).

Coast-to-coast car

" *Four of us intend to spend our summer vacation driving coast-to-coast from New York to California, taking in all the sights. We would be grateful if you could advise us what would be the best car to buy, taking account of accommodation, reliability, fuel costs and resale. We will have a budget of £3,000–£4,000.* "

Looking at the reliability of six-year-old cars in the American 'Consumer Reports Annual Auto Issue', the following should be good bets: Acura Legend, Honda Accord, Mazda 626 manual, Nissan Maxima auto, Toyota Camry, Toyota Corolla, Volvo 940. Nothing too exciting there, but excitement from the car isn't what you want, is it?

Continental cover for an older car

" *I have a 1977 Volvo 245 Estate and plan on driving it to France this summer for our annual holiday. I would much appreciate it if you could*

advise me where I can get European Recovery and Roadside Assistance for a car of this age. The AA and National Breakdown will only cover cars up to ten years old. "

The RAC offers cover up to a total value of £2,000 (excluding the cost of spare parts and UK car hire while awaiting repatriation of your car) for £50.75 for 17 days, plus £3.75 each extra day, plus £37 for vehicles 11 years old or more. Annual cover is £143.96 for members, £155 for non-members. For more information call 0800 550 055. Before you go, make sure you have the car serviced – with particular attention to the cooling system and the tyres. Also take great care not to overload the car. No loading up to the roof inside or you will create a combined danger of instability, a blind spot, and shifting luggage that could kill you.

Left and right dip

" *I frequently travel to France and fit bits of sticky black plastic to my head-lights to prevent them dipping to the left. Back in the UK, I have been told by the police to remove them. Is there a better remedy? What do truck drivers do? Do they have a different set of lights for each side of the channel?* "

Truck lights can be switched from left to right dip either by using special lights or by switching over to a different set of lights. Some dip down rather than to the left or right. Depending on the make and model of car, there may be a simple switch allowing you to go from left to right dip, as on the new BMW 3, 5 and 7 Series. Alternatively, if the headlights are a relatively simple 'slot fit' (as on some Citroens and Peugeots), buy a pair of right dipping headlights and swap them over in the ferry queue or while on Le Shuttle.

Continental kit

" *I am shortly going on a motoring holiday to France. I have been given various lists of equipment which I need to take with me, ranging from fire extinguishers to a first-aid kit. I would be very grateful if you could give me the correct information.* "

It is illegal to transport petrol, other than in the car's tank, across or under the Channel and across some borders.

First-aid kit, spare bulb kit, warning triangle, headlamp dip deflectors, fire extinguisher, GB plate, empty fuel can, vehicle's V-5 registration document, insurance certificate, if the car has a manual gearchange a spare RHD clutch cable, and £250 in francs for on-the-spot fines. It is illegal to transport petrol other than in the car's tank across or under the Channel and across some borders – and while legal requirements will vary slightly from year to year and from one

European country to another, this list should keep you on the safe side.

What the oil light tells you

" *Following the hire of an Opel Astra in Malaga, my credit card has been hit for the enormous sum of over £2,000 as a result of engine damage I am alleged to have caused. This is despite taking out all the insurances and indemnities I was offered at the time I arranged the hire of the car in the UK. On the fourth day of my holiday, the oil light flashed. I checked the oil level, which was adequate, and continued to Ronda where I intended having the car checked over. But, half a mile short of the town, the car came to a halt and I was unable to restart it. I later discovered that, at some time, the sump had been struck causing damage to the oil pump and leading to the failure of the engine. The UK offices of the rental company back up their Spanish counterparts and AA Legal Services have also been unable to help.* "

This can be a bit of a time bomb following any holiday involving the hire of a car. Whether you arrange car hire in the UK or not, the rental company will not let you have the car without taking a credit card number – for obvious reasons. But this does raise another very important point for every driver. If the oil light comes on, it signifies a lack of oil pressure (in your case due to the damaged oil pump), which in turn means that oil is not circulating around the engine and lubricating it. Checking the oil level does not tell you all is well. If the oil light comes on, you should stop the car, switch off the engine immediately, then seek help. Also, before taking delivery of the hire car, check it for any damage, including the sump and exhaust system, and make sure this is marked on the rental contract. There was a problem with 1.4 litre Astras because even the slightest tap on the

sump could damage the oil pump. If this occurred with a car less than three years old in the
UK, Vauxhall replaced the oil pumps and fitted
the cars with modified, deeper sump pans.

DRIVING CONDITIONS*

Rail-roaded

" *I'm not surprised that readers are forsaking the joys of rail travel and purchasing cars instead. I live in St Albans and work in Horley, near Gatwick. Since there is a railway line that runs from St Albans through Horley to Gatwick, I thought at first this would be ideal. Although the train did not stop at Horley, I had only to travel to Gatwick, then make a short hop back to Horley. Unfortunately, the short hop was nightmarish – late, dirty, unreliable, infrequent if missed, frequently cancelled, and so on. The connection time shortened with every timetable revision until I had only a 50/50 chance of getting to work on time. Added to that I was paying over £3,000 a year for a season ticket and £420 a year to use the unpatrolled station carpark. So I did some calculations and worked out that by using the car I would be £1,000 a year better off. I now find, to my surprise, that I am arriving at work between 30 and 60 minutes earlier and getting home 30 to 40 minutes earlier, so driving round the M25 is also saving me about 260 hours travel time a year.* "

Good point. Instead of making driving less attractive, legislators should concentrate on making public transport more attractive. Many people will still have no alternative but to drive, but at least those who can use public transport will be more inclined to do so.

---

* With appropriate reference to the Government's Integrated Transport Policy.

Anti-car planning

" *I am a retailer in Tunbridge Wells and I read with great interest your article on the death of the traditional town centre. Recently, Tunbridge Wells produced its own transportation strategy which, together with the anti-car bills currently passing through the Commons, has forced me to look very hard at the future. If all these measures are brought into force, they will see the end of both my business and those of many other independent retailers. This anti-car steamroller needs to be stopped and pointed questions asked, but I suspect that the organisation I have in mind would only respond to someone with the backing of a national newspaper.* "

The car is the goose that lays the golden tax egg, and any government that ignores this simple fact will have to raise revenue by heavier taxes on other things. Just think of all the ways cars earn tax revenue: VAT, fuel tax, VAT on fuel tax (a tax on a tax), VED, registration tax, company car benefit tax, insurance tax, warranty tax, parking tax. Legislate cars totally out of existence and not only will alternative employment need to be found for many millions of people, tax in general will need to be raised to make up for the lost tax revenue earned by cars. It seems more logical that governments will simply continue to increase taxes on motoring, but only by as much as the motoring public will bear without deciding to give up their cars en masse. The June 1996 story 'Death of the traditional town centre' was intended to point out the folly of pedestrianising town centres and totally excluding cars. All this has ever done is shift trade to parkable 'out-of-town centres' and ruin many of the shopkeepers in the pedestrianised town centres. If the use of cars were subsequently to be restricted, great hardship would be imposed on the elderly, forcing them to take the bus to buy essentials from out-of-town centres because the town-centre shopkeepers have all gone bust. After traffic calming measures killed off trade in the village centre of Southwater, West Sussex, many villagers campaigned to bring the traffic back.

Too many cars?

" *We currently own a three-year-old Nissan Primera 2.0SLX 5-door which has done 42,000 miles. We have three children aged 11, 9 and 4, and we need space for our twice-yearly camping trips to France when we tow a small trailer. For ferrying the children to and from school and for shopping we use a battered Fiesta. I'm thinking of changing cars, but is spending around £15,000 sensible when the car stays on the drive 47 weeks of the year? Should I carry on running the Primera (I've been offered £6,000 for it) or change cars? Bearing in mind depreciation and the fact that we can afford about £200 a month in repayments, what's the best option in your opinion, and what's the best value on the market for our needs?* "

As I write, transport policy and environmental planning aimed at forcing us to use cars less is still being debated. But yours is a clear case of simply not needing two cars. All the time your Primera just sits there it is deteriorating in hidden ways (corrosion inside the engine, gearbox and exhaust system, for instance). So my advice is to take the £6,000 and bank it, sell the trailer, and hire something like a Galaxy or a Previa for your camping trips. (Using just five seats, there is as much luggage space inside as in your Primera and trailer combined.) Then, when the Fiesta looks like it's on its last legs, use some of the £6,000 to replace it with a new small car such as a Perodua Nippa that qualifies for reduced VED.

Parking adjudication

" Last August you advised me of the London Parking Appeals Service to mediate on a parking ticket I had received from Camden Council. I am delighted to report that the adjudicator referred to his 'Parking Attendant's Handbook', decided the ticket was completely unjustified, and cancelled the penalty. "

Good. Other readers parking in areas controlled by Camden Council should be aware of this service, which should, in fact, be offered as soon as they dispute any parking penalty in London other than on a 'Red Route'. The address of the London Parking Appeals Service is PO Box 3333, London SW1Y 4XP, tel: 0171 747 4700. If your car is towed away or clamped in London, call Vehicle Trace on 0171 747 4747 (24 hours).

Signs of the times

" Perhaps you would like to comment on what I regard as the three silliest road signs in Britain. These are the black stripe across a white circle which denotes 'National speed limit applies', the 'Slow' sign and the 'Reduce speed now' sign. The latter two invariably precede or accompany a hazard sign of some description. I wrote to the DETR about this, recommending my own solution, and I received a fatuous reply. "

Strange that you should be writing from the Isle of Man where a black slash across a white circle still means 'unrestricted'. To find excellent solutions to all the problems you outline, we need look no further than Spain. There, the end of a speed limit is logically marked by a diagonal line through the limit which has ended. The approach to a town or to most serious hazards is marked by decreasing speed signs, such as '80', '70' and '60' when approaching a 50 kph town limit. All vehicle speeds are then automatically measured and, if you fail to slow down to the precise limit, an illuminated '50' sign switches on. Still fail to slow down and a red traffic light comes on over the carriageway in front of you. As you slow for the red light, orange flashing lights are substituted and you are allowed to proceed so as not to interfere with the traffic flow. I first saw this truly brilliant system in action in, I think, Benisa on the N332 fifteen years ago. It was adopted on the Denia Playa road around twelve years ago, and it is now used all over Spain and the Balearics, removing any need for speed traps on the approaches to towns. In an age of increasing restrictions it makes far more sense to adopt good ideas already in use in other EU countries than to try and invent new ones just for the UK.

Motorist's representative

" *Does anyone really represent the poor, downtrodden motorist these days? Here we are, subsidising education, the health service and the House of Commons canteen with the 380% tax we pay on petrol, yet all the government seems to want to do is crush us.* "

Contact the Association of British Drivers, PO Box 19608, London SE19 2ZW, tel: 07000 781544, website: http://www.deltacom.co.uk/abd

Temporary speed limits

" *I should like to query the operation by the police of the motorway matrix warning signs. A few days ago I was on the M27 and passed a long queue on the other carriageway caused by an accident. The warning signs on that side were flashing 40 mph. Two hours later I returned on that side and, though the accident was completely cleared away, the 40 mph warning signs were still flashing. No one was taking any notice of them, which was not surprising on an obviously clear road. This seems to me to be very dangerous because, the more often these signs unnecessarily cry 'wolf', the more often people will ignore them and the more likely they are to be caught out when there is a real problem. I also saw a related problem on the M25 where the variable speed limits were posting 60 mph. A quarter of a mile further on, traffic was stationary in all four lanes. Anyone not used to the system might think they only had to slow down to 60 mph and would crash if not keeping a proper lookout. Now that there are speed sensors and video cameras on many motorways, surely the police should check the temporary limit signs more often and ensure they are switched off as soon as it is safe to do so?* "

You're half right about the temporary speed limit signs. Drivers will exceed limits if they can't see any reason for them – no matter how much the 'law and order' brigade jumps up and down insisting that we should always obey the law whether it makes any sense or not. But these limits are sometimes imposed to slow down a body of traffic because of a problem far ahead that becomes cleared by the time the traffic reaches it. You're not right about the variable speed limits on the M25. These are actually controlled by sensors which gauge traffic flow and impose traffic calming disciplines when traffic exceeds pre-set levels. In general, it seems to help prevent jams (I live right next to this section of the M25). That said, all these systems are fallible and do go wrong from time to time. Of course drivers can crash if 'not keeping a proper lookout'. They can also run over a child if 'not keeping a proper lookout' in a 30 mph zone. Drivers should *always* keep 'a proper lookout' and they commit a far more dangerous offence than exceeding a seemingly pointless temporary speed limit if they don't. (Road Traffic Act 1991, part 1, section 2.)

Warning! Slow vehicles ahead!

" *I wonder if you could put out a warning to younger drivers. I run a 1937 Austin 7 Ruby and a 1956 Austin A30 and my problem is the lack of allowance made for the performance of these cars by drivers of modern machinery. Most seem to regard them as a slow-moving nuisance to be overtaken at the earliest and sometimes most dangerous opportunity. And this is why (as Paul Ripley always advises) we try to keep a gap between ourselves and the vehicle in front. Semaphore trafficators are not very noticeable and not understood, it seems, while hand signals are useless at night. Flashing indicators can be fitted, of course, but are not a legal requirement if not original equipment. We use our cars quite extensively, covering 3,000 miles in 14 days this year on a charity run in aid of 'Fight for Sight'. Please urge other drivers to make allowances for slower vehicles.* "

Some owners of elderly cars already adopt 'trailer board' systems to bring their vehicle lights and indicators up to modern expectations. Since these are easily removed, they do not affect the originality or 'correctness' of the car and seem to me to be a good idea. I'd also like to see flashing amber warning lights displayed by all vehicles normally travelling at less than 40 mph on dual carriageways and motorways. For example, a showman's road tractor towing two trailers is restricted to 20 mph on motorways and is a serious hazard at this speed without flashing amber lights.

New road markings

" *During the past year, there has been an increasing number of road markings in our area. The width, spacing, colours and textures are varied and inconsistent. Their appearance gives rise to caution, but is there a document setting out their use and meaning? I cannot find any mention in the current issue of The Highway Code.* "

The reason for the many and varied types of 'traffic calming' measures is experimentation to find out which are the most effective in real, as opposed to 'off-road' experimental, situations. The DETR has published so many Traffic Advisory Leaflets on the subject that it has even had to publish an index to them (TAL 10/96 *Traffic Calming Bibliography*). These are available free from the Traffic Advisory Unit, Zone 3/23, Great Minster House, 76 Marsham Street, London SW1P 4DR, tel: 0171 271 5169. You might also want to obtain Leaflet 2/93 *The Highways (Traffic Calming) Regulations 1993* from NGM3, Highways Agency, Room 12/3, St Christopher House, Southwark Street, London SE1 0TE.

Helpful truck drivers

" To facilitate overtaking of slow-moving vehicles I seem to remember that, in the days when trucks were slow and lumbering, in France they used to be fitted with green overtaking lights which the driver used to indicate it was safe to overtake. "

I remember these too. Once, in Spain, I was very pleasantly surprised when the truck driver in front pulled right off the minor road we had only just turned onto to let us past. But, as with the use of headlights to 'flash' other drivers out, a question of liability arises if a driver responds to the signal and has an accident as a result. It is always the responsibility of the overtaking driver to make sure the road ahead is sufficiently clear to complete the manoeuvre safely.

Don't get 'drowned'

" I am writing to ask that you use your column to warn readers of the

danger to their engines of driving through standing water so common at this time of year. With well-sealed electrics, many owners of petrol-engined cars might get away with this, but the air intake of most diesels is just 10–12 in. from the ground, and if this picks up a quantity of water, the engine will 'hydraulic', resulting in bent con rods, smashed cylinder head, etc. ''

Well said. Old-shape Renault Espace TDs, Astra and Cavalier diesels and Citroen Xantia diesels are particularly vulnerable. However, the Xantia has a trick up its sleeve in that it can be raised on its suspension, often enough to lift the air inlet clear above the surface of the water.

DRIVING COURSES

Earlydrive?

" *A caption to one of the pictures in your column mentioned 'Earlydrive', a scheme at Brands Hatch by which children under the age of 17 can legally learn to drive with proper tuition. I can't find any such course in my area, where the local circuit is Snetterton. Could you supply some names and telephone numbers?* "

'Earlydrive' courses are available at Brands Hatch circuit in Kent and Oulton Park circuit in Cheshire. The combined enquiry/booking number is 0990 125 250. The Silverstone Driving Centre at Silverstone circuit, Northants, also offers young driver courses. For information, tel: 01327 857177, and for bookings, tel: 01327 857788. There are no age restrictions, but to be able to reach the controls the young driver must be over 4ft 10in (1.48 m).

Unqualified instructors

" *Several times you have mentioned the 'Pass Plus' scheme designed to acquaint newly-qualified drivers with aspects of driving outside the scope of the test. The trouble with this is that instructors can vary enormously in quality. Every instructor is checked and graded regularly. Grades 1 to 3 are unacceptable and must improve their performance in the next check in order to keep their instructor's licence. Grades 4, 5 and 6 are of increas-*

ing merit. But the problem with 'Pass Plus' is that an instructor about to lose his or her licence could conduct the course, and there are even allegations floating about that 'Pass Plus' certificates have simply been sold to the pupil to help get discounted insurance. "

> Good point. Learners should ask their 'qualified' instructors to what grade they are 'qualified'.

'Beginners'

" *A teenager, having passed his or her driving test, will obviously be delighted and, understandably, will be tempted to 'have a go'. Quite a number of accidents are caused by such novice drivers, and it might be an idea, when the 'L' plate is no longer required, to have an obligatory period of, say, two years when youngsters have to indicate their inexperience by displaying a 'B' plate, for 'Beginner'. To avoid discrimination, this might be applied to all newly-qualified drivers.* "

It's a good idea for newly-qualified drivers to take an IAM course and test, before 'bad habits' have a chance to develop.

New drivers already have to re-take their tests if they accumulate more than six penalty points on their licence in their first two years, and the parents of many of them already make them display green 'L' plates to signify their inexperience. That said, the low uptake and general abuse of the 'Pass Plus' scheme is a scandal. The idea was to train new drivers in areas not covered by the driving test without the threat of a test hanging over their heads. Night driving, motorway driving, etc. were all included. But some crooked instructors simply 'sold' 'Pass Plus' certificates to enable young drivers to get insurance discounts, and take-up of a proper course of lessons as run by BSM has been abysmal. An Institute of Advanced Motorists (IAM) course and test is also a good idea before 'bad' habits have a chance to develop (tel: 0181 994 4403). For just £85, a youngster can take a novice course on a race track. This teaches discipline (a 4,000 rpm limit, for example), braking, steering control and other forms of good driving practice that are of great benefit and are likely to teach a hot-headed youngster how much skill he or she needs to gain before even attempting to drive quickly. See the list below for telephone numbers.

Driving courses, skid training and circuit courses*

NOTE: 'Pass Plus' is a course of six post-test lessons aimed to familiarise a new driver with aspects such as night and motorway driving not covered in the driving test. Courses are available with BSM and other approved driving instructors, and the cost is usually offset by a discount offered by most insurers on the new driver's first year cover.

● Driving Development, 61 Holly Bank, Ackworth, Yorks WF7 7PE. Tel: 01977 612094.

● Ecole de Pilotage Winfield, c/o Winfield Motorsport, PO Box 839, Ascot, Berks SL6 7SB. Tel/fax: 01344 876169. (Advanced Racing Driving Techniques, including 'trail-braking'. Possibly the best racing driving school in the world. Techniques taught in Formula Renault cars at the Paul Ricard Circuit, South of France. First two days £700; next two days £660.)

● Defensive Driving Consultants, Litton House, 52/56 Buckingham Street, Aylesbury, Bucks HP20 2LL. Tel: 01296 398783.

● AA Driving School Head Office, Basingstoke. Tel: 01256 20123 (press office).

---

* Listed in alphabetical order of office address.

- Road Safety Services Ltd, 162 Eversley Road, Bexley Heath, Kent DA7 6SW. Tel: 01322 337523.

- RoSPA, Edgbaston Park, 353 Bristol Road, Birmingham B5 7ST. Tel: 0121 248 2000. (Defensive Driving Courses. RoSPA 'Advanced Drivers' are re-tested every three years.)

- Lancs County Council Road Safety Office. Tel: 01772 264472. Lancs CC Road Safety Office runs £10 Skid Control Courses at its Road Safety Training Centre, Ewood, Blackburn. Tel: 01722 254868.

- Bill Gwynn Rally School, Turweston Aerodrome, Westbury, Brackley, Northants NN13 5YD. Tel: 01280 705570; fax: 01280 701691.

- Brands Hatch 'Earlydrive' and all circuit courses. Tel: 0990 125 250. (Circuit itself, tel: 01474 872331.) Basic track course in BMW 318i and single-seater £85 (highly recommended for learning braking and gear-changing disciplines). Skid control courses £59.

- Defensive Driver Training Ltd, Business & Technology Centre, Pound Road, Old Bury, W. Midlands B68 8NA. Tel: 0121 552 8844.

- Club 89 Trackdays. An excellent club providing on-track instruction, rides with British Touring Car Championship drivers and the chance to drive your own car on racing circuits throughout the UK. Club 89, PO Box 89, Attleborough, Norfolk NR17 2QS. Tel: 07000 89 89 89, fax: 01953 457 989.

- Motor Safari, Milestone Inn, Milestone Trail Park, Ruthin Road, Bwlchgwyn, Wrexham LL11 5UT (half-day off-road courses from £89). Tel: 01978 754533.

- Cadwell Park, Lincolnshire. All circuit courses, tel: 0990 125 250. (Circuit itself, tel: 01507 343248.)

- System Advanced Driver Training, 62/66 Lowther Street, Carlisle, Cumbria CA3 8DP. Tel: 01228 515914.

- Forest Experience Rally School: Tony and Christina Higgins, Carno,

Montgomeryshire SY17 5LU. Tel: 01686 420201.

- Castle Coombe Circuit, Chippenham, Wilts SN14 7EX. Tel: 01249 782101. (Skid pan courses from £49.50.)

- Peak Performance Management, The Stables, Walton Lodge, Chesterfield, Derbyshire S42 7LG. Tel: 01246 568953.

- Institute of Advanced Motorists, IAM House, 259/365 Chiswick High Road, London W4 4HS. Tel: 0181 994 4403.

- Croft Circuit, near Darlington, North Yorkshire. Silverstone Driving Centre courses in single seaters from £85. Tel: 01327 320326.

- 'Drive and Survive' skid control courses, Crowthorne, Berks. Tel: 01344 751117.

- Jim Russell Racing School, Donington Circuit, Donington Park, Derby. Tel: 01332 811430.

- Jonathan Tait Skid Control, Donington Circuit, Donington Park, Derby. Tel: 01332 811430.

- The Cardrome, Upper Rainham Road, Hornchurch, Essex. Tel: 01708 471340. (Off-road 'real road' system where youngsters under driving age can learn to drive safely in safety, from £9.)

- Road Sense Ltd, Royal Highland Centre, Ingliston, Edinburgh EH28 8NB. Tel: 0131 333 3000.

- Driving Services, Portside House, Lower Mersey Street, Ellesmere Port, Cheshire L65 2AL. Tel: 0151 355 2873.

- Driving Management Ltd, Midlands Skid Pan, Fradley near Lichfield, Staffs. Tel: 01264 771074.

- Peter Gethin Driving Courses, Goodwood Motor Circuit, Goodwood, Chichester, PO18 0PH. Tel: 01243 778118. (Single seaters; also rides in

Ferrari F40 at three laps for £50.) Goodwood Skid Control courses. Tel: 01903 691810.

- Harrow Driving, Cycling and Road Safety Centre, Christchurch Avenue, Harrow, Middx HA3 5BD. Tel: 0181 424 1993. (Eight-session driving course for 16-year-olds: three theory, five in-car; £80.)

- Drive & Survive UK Ltd, The Maltings, Bridge Street, Hitchin, Herts SG3 2DE. Tel: 01462 441844.

- Under Seventeens Car Club, 59 Coleridge Close, Hitchin, Herts SG4 0QX. Tel: 01462 457813. (Sponsored by BP Oil.) Membership Secretary: Eileen Simpkin, 51 Deerhurst Chase, Bicknacre, Chelmsford, Essex CM3 4XG.

- Autodriva Driving Instructor Training Courses by Margaret Stacey in preparation for the ADI Parts 1, 2 and 3. Margaret Stacey, The Mount, 53 Heanor Road, Ilkeston, Derbyshire DE7 8DY. Freephone: 0500 55 57 57.

- AA Training Services, AA College, Widmerpool Hall, Keyworth, Notts NG12 5QB. Tel: 0121 501 7389.

- Phill Price Rally School (RAC MSA approved), Coed Harbour, Llangunllo, Knighton, Powys LD7 1TD. Tel: 01547 550300.

- Road Skills, Hill Rise, Canada Crescent, Rawdon, Leeds LS19 6LT. Tel: 0113 250 1756.

- Paul Ripley Driving Courses, Paul Ripley Promosport, PO Box 2, Horsforth, Leeds LS18 5UE. Tel: 0113 258 5194.

- British School of Motoring Head Office, London. Tel: 0181 540 8262 (press officer Leslie Miles). BSM 'Masterdrive' two-hour course at £49 to check and brush up observation skills.

- Everyman Driving Centre, Mallory Park Circuit, Leicestershire LE9 7QE. Tel: 01455 841670.

- City of Manchester Road Safety Unit. Tel: 0161 234 4480.

- DriveTech, 32 Beechingstoke, Marlow, Bucks SL7 1JH. Tel: 01628 473537.

- Fusion Centre, Millbrook Proving Ground, Bedfordshire. Tel: 01525 404918.

- Drive Alive UK, Rowan House, 26/28 Queen's Road, Hethersett, Norwich NR9 3DP. Tel: 01603 259989.

- Aintree Racing Drivers School, 1 Fairoak Court, Whitehouse, Runcorn, Cheshire WA7 3DX. Tel: 01928 712877. Prices: £95–£155; courses at the Three Sisters Circuit, Wigan.

- Chris Birbeck International Rally School, Manx Lodge, Low Farm, Brottom, Saltburn, Cleveland. Tel: 01287 677512. Half day: £99; full day: £160; weekend course: £300.

- Snetterton, Norwich. All circuit courses, tel: 0990 125 250. (Circuit itself, tel: 01953 887303.)

- James Pritchard Associates, 3 Bolts Close, Old Marston, Oxford OX3 0PP. Tel: 01865 241854.

- London Rally School (Oxford area). Tel: 01869 278199. Half days £95; full days £180.

- Drive-It-All Rally Driving Courses, The Rally & Off Road Driving Centre, Church Enstone, Oxfordshire OX7 4NP. Tel: 01608 678339.

- PGL Adventure Holidays, Alto Court, Penyard Lane, Ross-on-Wye, Herefordshire HR9 5NR. Tel: 01989 764211. 'Grand Prix' children's holidays in which they learn to handle go-karts, trials bikes and ATV Quads at Borreatton Hall, Shropshire and Myerscough College, Lancs from £259; 'Motocross' children's holidays on trials bikes and Quads at Beam House, Devon, Dalguise, Perthshire and Tan Troed in the Brecon Beacons, from £249. Driver Awareness Courses of six half-day sessions of theoretical and practical instruction in dual control cars at Court Farm, Herefordshire, The Bluecoat School, West Sussex, Moreton Hall, Shropshire and Myerscough in Lancashire, from £289.

- Rally Drive International Rally School, Kings Street, Sancton, Yorkshire YO4 3QP. Tel: 01430 827430.

- Scottish Forest Rally School. Tel: 01467 267311. Courses from £99.

- Silverstone Driving Centre, near Towcester, Northants NN12 8TN. Tel: (info) 01327 320326; (bookings) 01327 857788.

- Silverstone Rally School. Tel: 01327 857413.

- Driver Education Centre, Canute Road, Southampton SO14 3FJ. Tel: 01703 333058.

- Oulton Park, Tarporley, Cheshire. All circuit courses, including Earlydrive, tel: 0990 125 250. (Circuit itself, tel: 01829 760301.)

- Driving Dynamics, 19 Town Street, Thaxted, Essex CM6 2LD. Tel: 01371 830496.

- Driving Management Ltd, Thruxton Circuit, near Andover, Hants SP11 8PW. Tel: 01264 771074. Skid control courses.

- Ian Taylor Motor Racing School, Thruxton Circuit, near Andover, Hants SP11 8PW. Tel: 01264 773511.

- SAGA Group Car Confidence Courses, Centrex Centre, Telford, Shropshire. Tel: 0800 300 500. Seven-night basic residential course: £399; Advanced course £499. Reduced-price rail or coach travel to and from Telford can be arranged.

- AGS Formula 1 driving, Circuit du Luc, Hyeres/Toulon, Var, France. Agents in the UK: Wildside Adrenalin Sports, tel: 0181 366 1766. Cost: at least £1,000.

- Tunbridge Wells 4×4 Driving School, 23 Pennine Walk, Tunbridge Wells, Kent TN2 3NW. Tel: 01892 514389. Courses £69 and £99.

- Advanced Tuition and Skid Training, Hanger 1, Hurricane Way, North Weald, Essex CM16 6AA. Tel: 01992 522287.

- High Performance Course (John Lyon), HPC Ltd, 21 Church Street, Wellesbourne, Warks CV35 9LS. Tel: 01789 841229. Prices from £125.

- Brooklands Auto Project (pre-driver training for 15/16-year-olds over four Sunday mornings at Brooklands, price £20) c/o Paul Jobson, Elmbridge Area Youth Office, Public Library Building, Church Street, Weybridge, Surrey KT13 8DE. Tel: 01932 840986.

- BSM Qualified Driver Training, 81/87 Hartfield Road, Wimbledon, London SW19 3TJ. Tel: 0181 545 1350.

- Corporate Driver Training Ltd, Elnup House, 6 Sherington Avenue, Wigan, Lancs WN6 8AT. Tel: 01257 422331.

- High Wycombe: Day course for 16-year-olds on Bovingdon aerodrome, organised by Professional Driving Instructors Group, High Wycombe. Tel: 01494 813064.

- T.I. Rally School, The Airfield, Seaton Ross, York YO4 4NF. Tel: 01759 318820. Half-day courses from £95, full-day from £129.25, inc. VAT.

Local driving schools and instructors recommended by readers

- Birmingham: Graham Birchall, tel: 0121 456 4244.
- Kenilworth: Brian Snook, tel: 01926 852206.
- Wembley, London: Neil Wallace, tel: 0181 902 9498.
- Hampshire: Adrian Dobson (disabled-driving instructor), tel: 01264 736262

Advanced motorcycle road riding

- BMF Rider Training: 01825 712896.
- Cooper Bike Training: 01633 374782.
- Institute of Advanced Motorists: 0181 994 4403.
- Highway Rider Training: 0121 742 2936.
- Newcastle Rider Training: 0191 276 1972.
- Open Road Advanced: 01375 382124.
- Roadcraft: 01489 896041.
- Road Runner: 0114 278 9943.
- Shire Training Services: 01480 464689.

Motorcycle track days

- Circuit Breakers: 0181 330 3351 and 09733 61858.
- Honda Britain Performance Riding School: 01455 251800.
- Kawasaki Riders Club: 01652 680060.
- No Limits: 01952 606777.
- Redline: 01244 680000.
- Ron Haslam Racing Academy: 01332 883323.
- Speed Freak and James Witham: 0161 487 2222.
- Track Attack: 01332 810048.
- Track Time Promotions: 01384 278387.
- Yamaha Race Schools: 01507 343555.

DRIVING TIPS AND DRIVING LAW

Please note that this section was compiled before the new Highway Code was published. Any reference to the new Code is to the draft document which went out for consultation prior to publication and to which changes may have been made.

Brakes or gears?

" *What are the pros and cons of controlling a car's speed with the gearbox and accelerator and only using the brakes for final halting or slight speed adjustment? For the record, our 1984 MG Metro bought new and driven in the manner described has had one set of pads and linings, one replacement rear brake compensator and one clutch in 90,000 miles. The gearbox is now noisy.* **"**

Driving in the manner you describe is pointless and dangerous if it becomes obsessive. It promotes wear on the gearbox and clutch, which are expensive to replace, instead of on the brake discs, pads and linings, which are comparatively cheap to replace. If a car has rear disc brakes and the driver does not brake heavily enough from time to time for the rear brakes to operate, the discs will not 'self clean', will rust rapidly and will probably need replacing every two

In a modern car the gearbox should only be used to retard progress by 'engine braking' when descending a steep hill.

years rather than every four or five. Brake lights also tell other drivers what you're doing. Of course, it's 'good driving' to leave enough space in front not to have to brake frequently. But the gearbox should only be used to retard a car's progress by 'engine braking' when descending a steep hill. In normal road use you can also use it to help shed some speed into a corner, but a racing driver would use the brakes. Things were a bit different in the old days when cars had just two rear-wheel brakes, and even in the 1960s when four-wheel drum brakes could still be fairly poor. Now that every car has discs on the front at the very least, and often four-wheel discs backed up by ABS or 'brake assist', brakes are a lot more trustworthy. That said, you should never touch the brakes when descending a slippery incline.

Slippery slime

" I'd just like to point out that while the leaked oil on the road might be dangerous if a car ventured onto it, the consequences for a motorcyclist could be fatal. One of the worst offenders is transmission oil, which seems to slop out past dodgy oil seals on dangerous bends. It's high time greater attention was paid to oil leaks as part of the MOT test. "

Good point.

'Move over'

" Is it possible to start a campaign that encourages drivers to drive in the nearside lane on motorways? I have noticed in the 25,000 miles I travel each year that lane discipline is getting much worse – with commercial vehicle drivers occupying the third overtaking lane, which by law they are excluded from. There are far fewer vehicles in the centre lane and near-

side lane, and if everyone moved over one lane to the left wherever possi-
ble it would create an extra lane on the motorway – far cheaper than
building another lane. As far as I am aware, it is also an offence to drive
alone in a lane when you could easily drive in the empty one next to you.
Making overtaking both sides legal would soon fix this problem. **"**

In a poll conducted from my column in 1996 and published in the previous *Daily Telegraph Book of Motoring Answers*, *Telegraph* readers came out against lane hogs 15:2 (pity about the two). The new Highway Code rule 238 is clear about middle lane hogging on motorways. It states, 'You should drive in the left-hand lane, even at 70 mph, if the road ahead is clear. If you are not in the left-hand lane and your speed is such that you are delaying traffic behind you, move into a lane to your left when it is safe to do so. Slow moving or speed restricted vehicles should always remain in the left-hand lane of the carriageway unless overtaking. You MUST NOT drive on the hard shoulder except in an emergency or if directed to by signs.' You aren't quite right about the third overtaking lane and commercials. The only vehicles which may not use this lane are: any vehicle drawing a trailer (weekend drivers, please note), any goods vehicle with a maximum laden weight exceeding 7.5 tonnes, and any bus or coach longer than 12 metres. A 7.5 tonne GVW Ford Cargo box van, for example, can legally use the third lane for overtaking.

Inside story

" *Your comments about drivers hogging overtaking lanes are most welcome, and many motorists in a similar situation would advocate 'undertaking'. However, the interpretation by some drivers of Rule 167 of The Highway Code is increasingly becoming one of the more dangerous prac-*

tices in motorway driving. This occurs when several vehicles are in the outside overtaking lane waiting to overtake slower traffic in the centre overtaking lane and a fast travelling car 'dives' into the centre lane, overtakes on the left and then 'cuts in' further up the queue. To prevent this, drivers inevitably, and wrongly, reduce the gap between vehicles and leave insufficient space for safe braking. Your comments on this form of 'undertaking' would be appreciated. "

It's already there in black and white in Rule 242 of the 1998 Code (which replaces the Rule 167 of the previous Code): 'Do not overtake on the left or move to a lane to your left to overtake. Under congested conditions, where adjacent lanes of traffic are moving at similar speeds, traffic in left-hand lanes may sometimes be moving faster than traffic in lanes to the right. In these conditions, you may keep up with traffic in your lane even if this means passing traffic in the lanes to your right. Do not weave in and out of lanes to overtake.'

HGVs overtaking

" *I know from driving along motorways and dual carriageways that HGV drivers usually pull in as soon as they have overtaken, but there should be a change in the law to stop them overtaking on an upward incline. Some pull out into the second or third lane if there are four lanes on a hill and have not got the power to overtake in reasonable time, causing car drivers to pull out into faster-moving traffic. There should also be a ban on using the third lane of a four-lane motorway.* "

Sorry, but I can't possibly agree with this. The real problem on motorways is car drivers who will not pull over to the inside lane when they are not overtaking anything. Trucks carry a great weight with a limited amount of power and are mostly governed to a speed of no more than

60 mph. A truck driver must use all the momentum he can generate to keep as close as possible either to the maximum speed he is allowed to drive or, if less than that, to the maximum speed the truck will do in order to meet his schedules. Remember, truck drivers are delivering goods on which the economy depends. Since, as you rightly acknowledge, they pull over as soon as they can, car drivers should help them as much as possible rather than seek to impose extra restrictions for their own selfish benefit.

Car park signs

" *Do signs in supermarket car parks have the force of law? My local supermarket has sensibly tried to ensure safety by indicating traffic flow with painted arrows which encourage a clockwise direction of traffic. Unfortunately, many drivers ignore these signs and drive against them to shorten their approach to a parking space. I seem to remember that some years ago it was ruled that, despite being private property, these road markings had some force of law. I would value your opinion on this and on to what extent, in the event of an accident, the driver who ignored the arrows would be held responsible.* "

While I would never dream of parking in a space reserved for the disabled, I have to confess I abhor any petty restriction which forces drivers to drive further than is absolutely necessary. Any car park which makes drivers take an unnecessarily circuitous route to empty parking spaces creates an unnecessary nuisance and causes avoidable pollution from exhaust emissions. The drivers who take short cuts are not antisocial. They are merely showing the planners how they should have designed the car park traffic flow in the first place. But if a driver taking a short cut did have an accident, he or she could be held responsible. Inconsiderate driving is a prosecutable offence in any 'public place'.

Two left feet?

" I would be grateful if you could settle an argument for me. I have been driving since 1946 and my first car had a crash gearbox. However, since 1970 I have always owned an automatic, although I have also frequently driven cars with manual boxes. When I got my first automatic I made the decision to use one foot on each pedal. It seemed logical: two feet – two pedals. This enables me to take full advantage of the automatic, in that I can, when the occasion demands – such as a rapid take-off from traffic lights – rev the engine and hold it on the foot brake for a short period. Also I can have my left foot over the brake if conditions suggest I might have to brake suddenly. I have never had any difficulty adjusting back to a manual. I frequently drive both types on the same day. My friends are unanimous in saying one should drive an automatic with the right foot only, so am I the only one out of step? I am sure I have seen reference to two-footed driving somewhere – possibly in your column. My friends will accept your word as the official answer. "

There is no rule. Drive 'two-footed' if you can. Drive 'one-footed' if you can't.

Out of control

" Some time ago I read several reports of cars with automatic transmissions suddenly surging forwards or backwards and out of control. Now it has happened to me. My car is a six-month-old Mitsubishi Galant, and whilst turning in the drive of my house it suddenly shot backwards and struck the car of a visitor. The agent could find no fault with the car, but said he would refer the matter to the Colt Car Company. Is the cause of this surging known, and are you able to help me get a reply from Mitsubishi? I am sufficiently worried about this to consider changing the car. "

The new Galant automatic is a very good car, so

The intense dazzle of high-level brake lights from automatics held in traffic on the footbrake can cause temporary blindness to the driver behind, and is technically an offence under the RVLR 1989.

please, first, consider changing your driving. To protect the catalytic converter after a cold start in winter conditions, engine management systems of modern cars may increase engine revs from a normal idle to up to as much as 1,500–2,000 rpm. Clearly, if the car is left to its own devices, this will be enough for the car to move if 'Drive' is engaged. One way to combat such movement is by judicious use of the handbrake. But the method I prefer is to hold the car on the footbrake with the left foot when engaging 'Drive'. You can then balance engine power to braking and remain in full control of the car. This may not be the way you have been taught to drive an automatic, but I know of at least one death directly attributable to the 'one foot rule' where, using only his right foot, the driver mistook the accelerator for the brake. (It's known as 'Unintentional Acceleration Syndrome'.) If your mind and body can take left-foot braking on board, you might consider using your left foot for the brakes and your right foot for the accelerator all the time. Two-feet–two-pedals is entirely logical. However, in stationary traffic, apply the handbrake, put the autobox into neutral and *please* get off the footbrake. The intense dazzle of high-level brake lights from automatics held in traffic on the footbrake can cause temporary blindness to the driver behind and is technically an offence under the RVLR 1989. (The Colt Car Company confirmed there was no fault with the car.)

Not automatically

" *I refer to an item in which you rebuked 'inconsiderate drivers using the footbrake to hold their cars stationary in traffic'. Drivers of automatic ve-*

hicles have no choice but to hold their vehicles in this way. I trust you can see your way to withdrawing the words 'dipsticks' and 'prosecuted' to drivers of automatic vehicles. "

Certainly not. Automatic drivers have two options. They can either fit a switch to the high-intensity high-level brake light so it can be switched off in slow-moving traffic jams. Or they can drive their cars properly. Whenever they come to a halt, they should apply the handbrake, release the footbrake, and move the gear selector from 'D' to 'N'. I appreciate that this may not be possible for a disabled person, but any able-bodied driver who sits on the brakes in traffic is a 'dipstick' who ought to be 'prosecuted' for the existing offence of 'using any lamp so as to cause undue dazzle or discomfort to other persons' under the RVLR 1989.

Foggy thinking

" *Now autumn is here, many of us are being confronted by the latest craze of drivers with their 'yuppie' fog lights blazing into oncoming traffic. Would you please advise me if the use of these lights is legal other than in fog and other low visibility conditions?* "

I shouldn't have to, because it's all there in black and white in rules 94 and 95 of the new Highway Code. These state, 'Use fog lights when visibility is seriously reduced, generally to less than 100 metres (328 feet). You MUST NOT use fog front or rear lights unless visibility is seriously reduced.' Under the Road Vehicle Lighting Regulations 1989, RVLR No. 27 (also in the Highway Code), it is an offence to use front or rear fog lights unless visibility is seriously reduced. Fog lights must be fitted with their centres 24 in. above from the ground or lower, and may work independently of the headlights, in which case they must be fitted with a warning light. Fog lamps must be a maximum distance of 16 in. from the sides of the car and a minimum distance of 14 in. apart. Driving lights (not fog lights) may be fitted with their centres 24 in. to 48 in. from the ground and must be wired through the headlights so that they extinguish on dipped main beam. No light on a car may be used in such a way that it causes undue dazzle or discomfort to other drivers and this, of course, includes high-level brake lights. In 1995 there were a total of 37,324 prosecutions for vehicle lighting offences.

Dippy dazzlers

" *I agree with your comments about 'dipsticks' who dazzle. My other pet hate is drivers who park on the wrong side of the road at night, usually on the pavement, while their partner picks something up from a shop. Don't they realise that their dipped headlights dip to the left, straight into the eyes of oncoming motorists?* "

If they don't, they're stupid, and anyway they are committing an offence under the 1989 RVLR. But there's another way dipped headlights can blind other drivers, especially on motorways. If you drive in the correct lane, you will soon find yourself dazzled by 'hoverers' who drive at a steady speed in the overtaking lanes at precisely the point from which their dipped beams shine straight into your mirrors.

Joining in

" Driving 50,000 miles a year, I find it incredible that the police turn a blind eye to queue jumping where the road narrows at roadworks. At least five miles from each lane closure, there should be a sign indicating which lane is to be closed. At four miles a sign should instruct drivers that they have two miles to merge into the lanes that will remain open. Then for the two remaining miles before the roadworks, anyone caught driving in the lane to be closed should be prosecuted for the offence of 'driving without reasonable consideration for other persons using the road'. "

The new 1998 edition of the Highway Code was going to change the rules about this. New Rule 263 was going to state, 'At lane restrictions or closures, traffic, when queuing, should fill all approach lanes and merge alternately at the lane restriction.' But since this would have forced British people to break the habit of a lifetime to form an orderly queue, the new rule was abandoned.

Ignorance isn't bliss

" As a driving instructor for 16 years I find ignorance of the Highway Code to be almost total. Since last year, learners have had to pass a Theory Test in which they must answer correctly 30 out of 35 questions. If any of your readers have children who are undertaking the Theory Test, they should try a mock test themselves. I believe they will be unpleasantly surprised. Two of my favourite gripes regarding ignorance of the Code are motorists not giving way to pedestrians who are crossing the road at a junction into which they are turning, and not signalling at roundabouts. Ask a motorist which lane he or she should be in and what signal they should give for an exit that is after 12 o'clock? You will have a good laugh at all the different answers you get. I once remember a motorist saying, 'Why should I signal at roundabouts? I know where I am going.' "

Rule 8 (aimed at pedestrians) states: 'At a junction. When crossing the road, look out for traffic turning into the road, especially from behind you.' Part of Rule 145 (aimed at drivers) states: 'Give way to pedestrians crossing a road into which you are turning; they have the right of way if they have started to cross so watch out for them before you turn.' This is not quite the same as the rule for Zebra crossings, where the Code warns drivers to look for pedestrians and 'Be ready to slow down or stop to let them cross.' Common sense and cooperation is required from both drivers and pedestrians at road junctions, but where the pedestrian is about to cross and the driver, signalling to turn into the side road, is about to get wiped out by a lunatic behind who is driving too close, everyone is in danger. I find it helps to start signalling some distance before the turn. The new Code is more specific about signalling rules at roundabouts (Rule 161). In summary it asks drivers to avoid unnecessary lane changes (so, if going straight on, use lane 1, not lane 2), to only signal left when you have passed the exit before the one you want to take and, if taking the third or fourth exit, to signal right on entering the roundabout, then left immediately before the exit.

Slip road slip up?

" I wrote to you some time ago on the subject of motorists joining a motorway from a slip road and expecting traffic already on the motorway to move over and let them on. Your answer, confirmed by Paul Ripley, was that drivers already on the motorway should move over to let slip road traffic on when it is safe for them to do so. The same question was recently asked of the AA, and answered by Mike Watkins in the Summer 1997 issue of the AA magazine. His reply read, 'Just to clarify, the Highway Code states that traffic joining the motorway must give way to traffic al-

ready on it. The advice is given to adjust speed on the slip road so as to join the left hand lane when there is a safe gap and at the same speed as the traffic already in that lane.' Who is right? "

We both are. Mike Watkins is correct in his summation of the advice given by Rule 158 of the old Highway Code. But he missed the following from the inside front cover, which states, 'The rules in The Highway Code do not give you the right of way in any circumstance – but they do tell you when you should give way to others. *Always* give way if it can help to avoid an accident.' Any driver who asserts his or her position on a motorway when traffic seeks to join from a slip road, and by doing so causes an avoidable accident, poses as much of a danger as a driver who bullies his or her way onto the motorway. When there are dead bodies all over the carriageway, a defence of 'I had the right of way' sounds a bit hollow.

Immobile phones

" *I have been following the controversy over the use of mobile phones in cars. But, with twenty representatives on the road, all of whom need to make fifteen to twenty visits a day, travel a possible 200 miles between visits, and are now faced with a maximum 48-hour week, please tell me what alternative our company has? Are we simply to shut up shop?* "

I'd like to ask the enforcers how using a mobile phone on the move is any more dangerous than smoking on the move. Smoking involves first removing a paper tube of tobacco from a packet (usually a two-handed operation), inserting the tube into one's mouth,

setting fire to it by accurately bringing a naked flame or car lighter to a point less than four inches from one's lips, creating acrid smoke which causes temporary blindness, then safely controlling the burning end and the disposal of ash produced. Surely 'a reasonable man' would find this far more distracting while driving than speaking into a mobile phone? However, there is also a difference between *making* calls on a mobile and *taking* calls. *Making* calls involves the distraction of keying in the number, or at least a three- or four-digit number code, then often the frustration of going through a switchboard and the inevitable waiting. However, *taking* a call can be accomplished by pressing one button, speaking briefly to the caller, and then pressing another button. This can be no more distracting than changing channels on the radio.

Fair weather flashers

" Are there any reported problems with the operation of Gatso speed cameras, particularly during wet and windy weather? The first traffic light camera in London was installed 300 metres from my house and the first speed camera on the A316 at Twickenham a couple of miles away. I have seen several of these cameras flashing whilst driving in a group of cars, all travelling at well below the speed limit (traffic density and the tail-back from a roundabout often dictates this on the A316). On one occasion I was nearing a camera from the opposite direction to which it was pointed, with no traffic approaching the camera, when it flashed. The common factor was heavy rain or strong winds. "

Assuming a film has been installed, the speed camera takes two pictures of whatever triggers it. If it's a leaf or heavy rain blowing towards it at more than the trigger speed, then obviously the leaf or rain will not be prosecuted. Where two or more vehicles are pictured because one of them is speeding, the relative positions of the speeding vehicle will show up against the roadside markings – which confirm its speed at the time. Innocent motorists have nothing to fear from these cameras except in two situations: when they are situated on a road where the speed limit keeps changing, such as the North Circular (we really need more 'reminder' signs to show us what the limit is on each stretch); and when they are situated at the only safe overtaking points on a two-lane 'A' road.

White van disease

" I have seen in the press some concern expressed at the reckless driving of anonymous 'white vans'. Before the war, all commercial vehicles had to carry the owner's name and address, printed in small letters, together

with the weight limit for the vehicle. Re-adopting this procedure would make the vans more readily identifiable. **"**

All road vehicles are supposed to carry a registration mark and it is through these that drivers are eventually identified from speed camera photographs. There is a move afoot to emblazon all commercial vehicles with a phone number which, in conjunction with the registration, can be used by other motorists to criticise or praise the drivers. However, by the standards of driving I see every day, I'm not too sure that all of Britain's motorists are competent to pass judgement on white van drivers. A great many white vans are driven by couriers keeping the wheels of commerce turning by delivering packages under tight schedules. The best advice I can give is to drive considerately and, if they want to overtake, to help them do so.

Invisible cars

" *Here is a notice I saw on the back of a juggernaut: 'IF YOU CAN'T SEE MY MIRRORS I CAN'T SEE YOU'. Would you say that's good advice?"*

Every truck should have one. Far more sensible than a 'How's my driving?' phone number.

Bike rack warning

I can confirm that police patrols have been instructed to get tough on drivers of cars carrying bikes on the back which obscure the car's number plate and lights. The relevant legislation being enforced is Section 43 of the Vehicle Excise and Registration Act 1994, and the maximum fine for such offences is £1,000. Several readers have reported being stopped by the police and advised they are committing an offence; others have been issued with an 'on-the-spot' £20 fine. The answer is a 'trailer board' which repeats the car's number plate and lights to the rear of the load. Interestingly, the Cyclists' Touring Club advised its 50,000 members not to use rear-mounted cycle carriers more than three years ago. A survey by the club revealed that most of the bikes carried on the backs of cars are owned by lazy people who merely want a means of transport on footpaths at the end of their journey and who are not committed cyclists. The CTC recommends its members to transport their bikes inside their vehicles and to select vehicles capable of this.

'Block changing'

" My daughter is currently taking driving lessons, supplemented by driving experience out in the car with me as passenger. One aspect of current teaching methods that disturbs me is 'block changing'. When changing down, pupils are taught to shift from fourth to second. If the speed it too high, as it often is when learning, this puts a terrific strain on the transmission components. Should the road be slippery, it increases the risk of a skid. In crossing the gate, a nervous pupil is often unable to find second and ends up 'coasting', which is illegal. Instructors tell me that block changing is taught to reduce the number of gear changes a pupil needs to be concerned with. But I find this all most alarming. "

Years ago I had the good fortune to go on a 'brushing-up' lesson with Class 1 police driving instructor Margaret Stacey (0500 55 57 57). After picking me up on cornering positions and driving too close to vehicles I intended to overtake, she introduced me to 'block changing', and for the rest of the lesson I practised doing this smoothly. Now I do it as a matter of course (usually from fifth gear to third while slowing down). The point is, it requires a degree of mechanical sympathy, coordinating engine speed with road speed, to accomplish this smoothly. A new driver taught this technique from day one should become a better driver, even if father's car's synchromesh has to suffer the trauma of the technique being learned.

'Pelican crossing' detector

" Amongst the morning's junk mail I found an envelope with a speed camera symbol on the outside. Inside were leaflets for speed trap detectors. What do you think of these devices? "

I bought one a couple of years ago and soon found out it was more effective at detecting Pelican crossings than anything else. A radar detector can only detect radar in use. So if a policeman points a speed 'gun' at a car and squeezes the trigger, the radar detector will beep. Similarly, if a Gatso speed camera bounces a radar wave off a passing car, the radar detector will also beep. But if yours is the only car on the road, the only thing the detector can warn you of is your own speed being detected, by which time it would be too late. Also, with most 'combined' devices, the range at which they can detect a police laser is shorter than the range at which the laser can detect speeding cars. Finally, you will have seen large white squares at fixed distances apart on motorways, dual carriageways and fast, open stretches of main road. These enable the police using VASCAR to time your speed over a fixed distance from a car, from a van or simply from behind a bush. No radar detector can detect VASCAR. It could even be argued that the sort of person who speeds dangerously because he thinks his detector makes him immortal is more likely to be caught speeding. (In a Judicial Review case brought before the Queen's Bench Divisional Court in January 1998, Lord Justice Simon Brown ruled that the use of radar detectors is and always was legal. The Wireless and Telegraphy Act 1949 only forbids intercepting radar 'messages', but since there is no information in police radar, no offence is committed in detecting its presence. But, by the time you read this, a new law forbidding the use of radar detectors may have been passed.)

Guide to traffic law

" A few weeks ago you mentioned a book written by an ex-police traffic officer detailing the points that decided prosecutions and the arguments considered. Could you give me the author, title, etc.? "

The Book is *Guide to Traffic Law for the Enforcement Officer* by K. Mark Hughes, priced £15 (including p&p), ISBN 1-899691-01-4, available from Motorvation Consultants, PO Box 3250, Milton Keynes MK6 3ZT, tel/fax: 01908 676008. Six-monthly updates cost £8 a year. I highly recommend it.

Motorway breakdowns

" I am a member of the Guild of Experienced Motorists and subscribe to the Guild's low-cost recovery scheme. I also tow a caravan with my 1989F Honda Accord. The clutch of this car was replaced 15 months ago by a 'Mr Clutch' franchise, but failed suddenly on the M6. GEM's rescue service got

us off the motorway and also returned the car to a Manchester 'Mr Clutch' franchise which replaced the clutch free of charge under its two-year warranty without quibbling. I did, however, have to pay the recovery charges and claim them back from GEM. The total charges were £266.82. **"**

A salutary lesson for those who dare to venture onto the UK motorway system without some form of recovery insurance.

Night driving glasses

" *My wife and I are both senior citizens and use varifocal plastic lenses to correct our vision. These are much better than bifocals. Recently we began to find night-time glare an increasing problem until we had replacement lenses to correct small changes in our vision after our regular two-year checks. The new lenses apparently cured the problem, and on inspection the old plastic lenses were found to be covered with a myriad of scratches due to cleaning and wear. These must have caused diffraction of oncoming headlamps, making the glare much worse. We will not use coated plastic lenses and will change back to more durable glass for future spectacles.* **"**

Interesting point, because minor scratching of plastic lenses is not a big problem with ordinary glasses. Plastic is not only lighter and puts less pressure on the bridge of the nose, it is stronger (the lenses don't break if you drop them) and safer (no risk of shards of glass in your eyes after an accident). However, it is more expensive. My last pair cost me £210, including the frame, at Boots. While there I learned that in continental Europe it is now illegal to drive with even mildly tinted glasses at night.

How fast is 'speeding'?

" *For many years our local constabulary operated a 12 mph tolerance* *when enforcing the 30 mph speed limit, and prosecution was unlikely un-less 42 mph was exceeded. Recently a police officer friend told me that under the government's 'kill your speed' campaign the tolerance was now 'ten percent plus two' and that prosecution for exceeding 36 mph was like-ly. Since I wish to retain the clean licence I have held for the past 25 years, I now spend more time with my eyes on the speedometer and less with my eyes on the road. Does this make me a safer driver?* **"**

Of course not. First, remember that 30 mph is the upper limit and that your eyes should tell you if conditions warrant an even lower speed. Second, if the road seems to be completely clear and you allow your speed to creep up slightly, you should see the policeman with the radar gun before you are in range, giving you plenty of opportunity to reduce your speed to an indicated 30 mph (probably a true 28 mph) in good time. If you don't see the policeman, then you are driving too fast for your eyesight and too fast to miss any dog, cat or child which might suddenly leap out in front of your car.

Dual carriageway dangers

" *I would like to issue a word of warning to those using the A1. Much of this road is still not motorway. There remain numerous dangerous cross-ing points which drivers can arrive at unawares. Also, because of the many stopping places for trucks, car drivers need to be very aware that a truck in the nearside lane may either be slowing down to a near standstill or slowly accelerating to its governed top speed, rather than travelling at a normal motorway speed of 55–60 mph.* **"**

You are right to issue warnings about the A1. There are truck stops, crossings and lay-bys all over the place and drivers should treat signs for these as warnings of a possible obstruction ahead. Finally, if you are in a high-performance car, remember that the cars or trucks behind you may not be able to stop anything like as quickly as you can. Keep an eye on your mirror when braking and, if necessary, get off the brakes and give the vehicles behind a bit more room to stop.

Extra endorsements

" *My daughter was recently fined for speeding. She did not pay within the specified time so, of course, the court increased the fine. But on top of this the court added a further three penalty points to her licence, so she received six in all. Is this correct?* "

Yes. If the police give you the option of a 'fixed penalty' of £40 and three penalty points, it is usually better to take this on the chin. If you refuse the fixed penalty, or fail to pay within the stipulated 28 days, your case will be tried in court, the fine will probably be greater, and the magistrate will be empowered to award up to six penalty points.

Why? Why? Why?

" *May I through your column ask people why they drive at 50 mph along roads subject to a 60 mph limit, even when traffic is light and conditions are good? Even when I travel between midnight and 3 am, the same thing happens. Two or three cars in a short convoy doing 50 mph! When I try to overtake, the drivers seem astonished to see my car there, as if they are in a trance. When I spoke to such a driver, who pulled out in front of me, he said he thought the limit was 50 mph. When I said I was doing 60 mph, he thought I was travelling too fast. Where do these people get their ideas from? What are they doing on the road if they don't know the laws and the Highway Code? Why do they travel at 50 mph instead of 60 mph? Why do they still travel at 50 mph when driving through a village with 40 mph or even 30 mph signs? Why do drivers today seem oblivious to other traffic? As for lane discipline at roundabouts, don't even ask.* "

It's probably because they or someone else in the car are scared of higher speeds. I have to say, drivers are allowed to drive at speeds below the speed limit if they don't feel comfortable driving faster. They only commit the offence of 'Inconsiderate Driving' by pootling along in those little bumper-to-bumper convoys you refer to. They should always leave enough space for an overtaking car between themselves and the car in front, and should expect to be overtaken.

Smash but not grab

" *To foil 'smash and grab' handbag snatchers, simply hook the handles of the handbag through the passenger seatbelt and fasten the belt.* "

An excellent idea: as good as a *Viz* 'Top Tip'.

'The hazard of the third dog'

" *On reading Paul Ripley's article 'Mad dogs and school children', I was reminded of an experience some years ago, which I call 'The hazard of the third dog'. I was driving on the outskirts of Liverpool when two dogs ran across the road. It was springtime and the leading animal, a bitch, was on heat. I braked, but a lady behind my car overtook me and killed the third dog which followed the first two. Often, when a bitch is on heat, more than one dog is trying to catch her, and you should always be ready for the third dog.* "

This reads like an ancient Chinese aphorism, but it's sound advice and easily remembered. From now on, *Telegraph* readers will be on the alert for 'The hazard of the third dog'.

Does one drink kill?

" *On average in the UK, ten people die and eight hundred are injured every day as a result of road accidents. These are mostly caused by the 80% of drivers who are sober at the time of the accidents. The Government's message is 'Drink Driving Kills'. Do you not think this is the wrong message? Some terrible drivers must think, 'I am sober, therefore I am safe'.* "

Your point was covered on the leader page of *The Daily Telegraph* on 3 February 1998. It is the Editor's view that 'a tighter drink-driving limit would make at best a marginal difference to overall road safety, and that a far more appropriate target for ministerial attention is simply bad driving, particularly among the irresponsible young who are often the most dangerous offenders.' The Government Consultation Document states, 'It has been estimated that about 80 road users a year are killed in accidents where at least one driver had blood alcohol over 50 mg but no driver had blood alcohol over 80 mg (the current limit).' My problem with these figures is that the estimate does not state whether the driver with between 50 mg and 80 mg blood alcohol caused the accident, could have avoided the accident or was the innocent victim of circumstances beyond his control. It may well be that no more than 25% of these deaths were caused by the action of the apparently impaired driver, and that this percentage would have occurred anyway had that driver been drinking or not. A new system of reporting of accidents in much greater detail than hitherto should be in force by the time you read this, and should enable accurate statistics to be compiled in the future.

EPHEMERA

Bookworms

Though this information was in the last book, readers continue to ask how they might dispose of old motoring literature. The answer is to try the following, all of whom take stalls at various events and 'autojumbles' throughout the year. (Remember, most have day jobs, so it's better to call them in the evenings.) Eoin Young, tel: 01483 283311; Anton Spencer, tel: 0181 337 7452; Peter Davidson, tel: 01295 810853; Graham White, tel: 01243 771961; Alan and David Burden, tel: 01923 246668; and Alan Riley, tel: 01327 351203. Don't expect magazines from later than the 1960s to be worth much, though. The dealers who attend 'automobilia' events are not very interested in them because of the sheer weight they would have to carry around. Three shops which deal in collectible motoring literature are Chaters Motoring Booksellers of South Street, Isleworth, tel: 0181 569 8273, The Vintage Motorshop in Batley, tel: 01924 470733, and Pooks Motor Bookshop on 0116 237 6222; but don't expect them to come and collect. To advertise, try *Practical Classics* magazine which has a Motoring Literature classified section.

Petrol coupons

" *I have in my possession an unused petrol ration book which was issued to me during the Suez Crisis. Someone informed me that it could be quite valuable. Is it?* "

No, because during the 1970s every car owner was re-issued with reprints of these same ration books which were never actually required. Another reason is that, marked on the book is the printed statement 'This book is the property of Her Majesty's Government'.

Birthday issues

" *I take absolutely no interest whatsoever in cars or motoring, but my husband does. Some time ago I think I remember reading that it was possible to purchase old issues of* Autotrader *magazine that coincided with birthdays. I thought it would be quite a nice idea for a birthday present for him. Can you help?* "

Yes. This is a service offered by fellow freelance columnist Giles Chapman. The magazine is not *Autotrader* but *Autocar*. Giles can source 'Birthday *Autocars*' back to 1940 and charges £14.95 an issue (or more for particularly rare issues). He can be contacted at 9 Ledbury Mews North, London W11 2AF, tel: 0171 727 6461.

Old magazines

" *I have in my attic 756 copies of old car magazines dating from 1959 to 1978. My copies of* Autosport *are almost complete from 1959 to 1968. Do these have any value or interest? Who best should I contact regarding disposal?* "

See the list of dealers above under 'Bookworms'. But, because of the great weight involved, dealers are not usually prepared to

collect magazines dating from later than
the 1950s.

Prescott cup

" *I recently retrieved from my loft a 6 in. silver cup, given to my wife by*
Mrs Mays (the mother of Raymond Mays) many years ago. It is inscribed:

Prescott National Hill Climb
[Bugatti Radiator Motif]
Bugatti Owners Club
September 10th 1950
Class 7
R. Mays
46.67 Secs

If you are aware of any reputable club or organisation which might be in-
terested in this item, I would be pleased to pass it on to them to add to
their memorabilia or trophy cupboard. "

The Bugatti Owners' Club would be delighted to
have this. The Club bought the 64-acre Prescott
estate in 1936 for £3,500, and immediately set
about surfacing the drive to the house and installing a bridge just below Orchard Corner. The
first Bugatti Owners' Club hillclimb was held in
1938. Raymond Mays was, of course, a very famous Bugatti campaigner who scored many of
his early successes driving a Bugatti Type 13
'Brescia'. I have a photo of him apparently driving the car flat out while dressed in a dinner
suit. A director of E.R.A. and E.R.A. team driver, Mays earned 68 Road Star marks in the 1937
BRDC list, making him second only to 'B. Bira'
(Prince Birabongse of Siam), and he later went
on to develop the post-war BRM. Club Secretary
of The Bugatti Owners' Club is Mrs Susan Ward,

Prescott Hill, Gotherington, nr Cheltenham, Gloucs GL52 4RD, tel: 01242 673136.

Model auction estimates

" *I was fascinated when I eventually read your article on Dinky Toys ('From Kids Stuff to Collectors Items', 15 November 1997) as I have a collection of some 300 Dinky and Corgi Toys of my own. The majority of these are mint and boxed and, not having seen your invitation at first, I independently sent lists to all the main auction houses for valuation. These estimates varied between £5,000 and £17,000, leaving me more than a little suspicious of the wide margin. I should add that I am not exactly a novice in the field of values. The company quoted in your article gave one of the lower valuations, and since you write under the title 'Honest John' I feel you should know what goes on behind the scenes.* "

If a sale is not particularly well attended, then the items offered will probably be knocked down for at most 'trade price' which, in the case of collectors' models, tends to be around half the retail price. This is why auctioneers estimate on the low side.

The article stated very clearly both that Christies had achieved some of the highest prices ever paid at auction for Dinky Toys and that the estimates for Colin Snell's collection were 'conservative'. Had the collection been valued against the estimates in John Ramsay's catalogues, which show retail prices, the valuation would have been far higher. I think you have misunderstood, first what sort of free valuation is possible from a mere list and second the nature of collectors' auctions themselves. If a sale is not particularly well attended, then the items offered will probably be knocked down for at most 'trade price' which, in the case of collectors' models, tends to be around half the retail price. This is why auctioneers estimate on the low side. If, on the other hand, the sale is attended by several rich and avid collectors who 'must have' an individual item, then, by bidding against each other, they can send the price realised into the stratosphere. This not only happens with models, it also happens with real cars, as was the case at Christies' auction of the Bruce Wiener collection of microcars in March when a 1964 Peel P50 microcar sold for an astonishing £34,553 inclusive. No one in their wildest dreams had estimated this price beforehand. Nor had anyone expected two bidders at a BCA sale in February 1998 to fight the price of a 650-mile 1976 E-Type all the way up to a crazy £74,600.

Global question

" A few years ago I came into possession of the illuminated pump globes for a Shell Dieseline pump (the shell-shaped type) and a Pink Parrafin pump. I would like to know who would value these and where I could realise their value. "

Miller's Guides show that undamaged pump globes tend to fetch between about £100 and £500 depending on scarcity and desirability. There are also plenty of reproduction Shell globes around, which tends to depress prices. You could try an auction house such as Christies (0171 321 3274) or Sothebys (0171 493 8080), or tote them along to an autojumble event in Spring or Summer.

Old road tests

" I drive a 1975 Rolls Royce Silver Shadow I. Could you please tell me where I can obtain a copy of any road tests of that model? I tried Haymarket Reprints (tel: 01235 534323) as you frequently recommend for newer models, but they were unable to oblige. "

There are two main sources of collected Road

Test Reprints: Brooklands Books and Transport Source Books. For your purposes, these are: *Rolls Royce Silver Shadow I & II and Wraith*, Transport Source Book 298, price £9.95; *Road & Track Rolls Royce and Bentley Road Test Reprints (American spec models) 1966–1984*, Brooklands Books, price £8.95; and *Rolls Royce Silver Shadow Gold Portfolio 1965–1981*, Brooklands Books, price £12.95. All are available mail order, plus p&p, from Mill House Books on 01205 270377.

Autojumble

" *I have two pre-war two-gallon petrol cans, one stamped 'Shell' and the other 'Pratts'. They are both in good condition, though not in their original paint. I also have a 1930s vintage 'Autovac'. Could you tell me what they are worth and the best method of disposing of them?* "

Take them along to a big 'Autojumble'. The biggest and the best are the Spring and Autumn Beaulieu Autojumbles at Beaulieu, Brockenhurst, Hants (tel: 01590 612345). Though these items will have some value (£10–£20 apiece), the cost of advertising and carriage won't leave much change, so an autojumble is the best disposal route.

FUEL AND EMISSIONS

'Cleaning up' on the MOT

" *My 1993L Citroen Xantia failed its first MOT 'cat test' and the reason was diagnosed as a faulty Lambda sensor. This, and the spark plugs, were replaced, but it still failed. The garage then offered to 'carbon clean' the engine using a special machine, and after this had been done the car passed. It struck me that, had the carbon cleaning been done first, it might have saved me the cost of the new Lambda sensor.* "

You are almost certainly correct. Even Lambda sensors themselves can sometimes be cleaned. But it would be better to do all you can to prevent the engine coking up in the first place by judicious use of a fuel system cleaning additive or petrol which itself contains a significant amount of detergent.

Consumptive?

" *I have a 1995 Vauxhall Cavalier 1.8iLS which has now done 17,000 miles. Since April I have been keeping careful records of the fuel consumption. Between April and September the car was averaging 40 mpg. But since September, the average has dropped to 35 mpg. Use of the car has remained consistent throughout. Is this solely due to the change in ambient temperature and weather conditions? And, if so, how do manufacturers arrive at fuel consumption figures?* "

It's a typical Summer to Winter drop. Basically,

the engine runs richer for longer in the cold. Manufacturers' 'Government Figures' are achieved at constant ambient temperatures over stipulated speeds and cycles. The rules recently changed and the urban cycle now includes cold starts, with the result that consumption on the urban cycle has risen by a few mpg. But the constant 56 mph and 75 mph (80 kph and 120 kph) led manufacturers to 'chip' cars so they consume less fuel at these speeds – and this is not necessarily ideal for achieving the best balance between overall performance and fuel consumption.

Short-Run Syndrome yet again

" *I want to get rid of my old 1.2 Nova for a newer used car of similar size. I only do short journeys and you have often stated that this ruins a catalytic exhaust. Any suggestions, please?* "

I get so many letters on this subject, it's time to cover the issue again. Most of the first generation of catalytic converters fitted to cars in the UK, and compulsory from August 1992 (with some latitude for late registrations), take three to five minutes of driving the car at a reasonable speed to reach full operating temperature of 400–450 degrees centigrade and to fully catalyse the engine's emissions. But while the engine is warming up from cold, cats also have to cope with a massive amount of condensation from hot gases containing hydrogen and oxygen passing through cold steel. In winter, the inside of the engine, gearbox and exhaust system will not get hot enough to evaporate that condensation until the car has done around ten miles at a reasonable speed. So it's not just a catalysed exhaust which suffers from a life of short journeys from cold starts; the engine and gearbox do too. One answer is an engine pre-heater, such as the Kenlowe Hotstart, which is a combined immersion heater and pump for the engine coolant run on mains electricity (cost is around £150, tel: 01628 823303). Whatever car you buy, fit one of these. You could opt for a pre-August 1992 petrol-engined car (J-plate or earlier) or a post-August 1992 diesel (K-plate or later). Small diesels with oxidising 'cats' (such as Corsas) are not as problematic as small petrol cars with 'three way' cats, and the remaining condensation problems will be greatly reduced by a Hotstart.

P versus D

" I wonder if you could list the pros and cons of petrol as against diesel cars. A garage local to us has a good supply of used turbo-diesels – Rover 418SLDTs, Mondeo TDs, Cavalier TDs, Xantia TDs and Peugeot 405TDs – all 'L' reg., all in excellent condition bodily, but all with 70,000–90,000 miles. We are a retired couple and drive only 3,000 miles a year, so would such a purchase be suitable for us? "

Diesel pros: On average 30% more fuel-efficient and therefore more environmentally friendly; less pollution on start-up than a first generation catalysed petrol car; no catalytic converter to worry about replacing (even when a diesel has an oxidising cat it's cheaper than a petrol car's cat); better mid-range 'pull' – especially on motorways; higher gearing, so more relaxing to drive; sometimes no engine electronics to go wrong; simpler, cheaper routine maintenance.

Diesel cons: The 'anti-diesel' lobby and the way this is used to increase taxes on diesel; many turbodiesels feel flat at low revs; more likely to blow cylinder head gaskets when corrosion inhibitors in the coolant degrade; the fuel itself does not evaporate if you get it on your hands; more frequent oil changes needed (though not in the case of TDIs); DERV tends to be more expensive than unleaded – especially in the winter; a heavier engine sometimes compromises handling; poor quality 'low sulphur' DERV with no lubricity enhancer damages diesel injector pumps.

Generally I recommend young, high-mileage cars over old, low-mileage cars because any car that clocks up 30,000 miles a year or more must do most of it at the proper running temperature rather than on short runs from cold starts. Your extremely low mileage of 3,000 miles a year could actually be worse for the new car than the 30,000 miles a year it has done to date – but you'll be getting a much younger car for the money than you would otherwise, and gradually the years will catch up with the miles. The first jobs to do are to change the timing belt, the coolant, the brake fluid, the engine oil and the filter. Then, even though you are only doing 3,000 miles a year, it would benefit the car to change the oil and filter every six months. Of the secondhand models you list, I'd say the Xantia TD is the best bet because its suspension does not 'bag out' in the same way as the others, but avoid Xantias with ABS because the computers go and cost £700 to replace.

Rocket fuel

" *I decided to purchase some VAG Injector Cleaner, part G001 700 03, for my 1989 VW Jetta GTi. But the instructions make no reference to injectors, only to carburettors, so can you confirm that I have the correct product? Second, the directions state it should be added in the ratio of 10 ml of additive to 10 litres of fuel. Therefore, how much of the additive should I use in my 55 litre tank?* **"**

Nice, easy, Jetta questions, for a change. Yes, this is the right additive (the fuel-system-cleaning ingredients are basically the same whether the car has carburettors or fuel injection). Use a third of the tube to a tankful of petrol – first fill, down to the '100 ml' mark; second fill, down to the '50 ml' mark; etc.; but put the additive in to an empty tank at the filling station, then fill with petrol to ensure it mixes. (DON'T GET ANY ON YOUR HANDS OR THE CAR'S PAINT.) Your car will almost immediately feel smoother and quicker because the product also contains an octane enhancer. You may find that, because the bottles do not have child-proof lids, you are not able to buy this additive off the shelf and will need to get your VW specialist to dose the car for you.

'Blei Ersatz'

" *Living close to the German border, now that Germany has banned leaded petrol, I'm tempted to buy a product sold there which is known as 'Blei Ersatz' (lead substitute). It costs no more than £40 for enough to treat 250 litres of petrol, and apparently it's also good for spark plugs.* **"**

Such products were developed in the USA donkeys' years ago. Something similar is added to the 'unleaded 4-star' sold at Save and Total filling stations. But how much protection it is able to offer the valve seats of older cars with cast iron heads depends on the type of lead substitute, the concentration of it in the petrol, and the engine speeds at which the car is driven.

Unleaded heads

Several readers wrote concerning the use of un-leaded petrol in older Rover V8s and Jaguar sixes. One from Belper pointed out that in the 1960s and 1970s Jaguar multi-sourced its valve seats, and a 1970s UK-market Jaguar could be fitted with 'American' valve seats that can take unleaded. But he pointed out that when con-verting a non-unleaded Jaguar head, rifled valve guides also need to be fitted and the valve stems honed to suit them – so that oil is allowed to replace the lead in providing lubrication for the guides and stems. Another reader, from Taunton, sent copies of old Rover Technical Services Bulletins pointing out which Rover en-gines can take unleaded without damage and which require modification. One from Frome, who has considerable experience of the alloy block Buick/Rover V8s, says all are tolerant of unleaded providing the timing is retarded. Problems arise with the high-compression V8 fitted to P5B saloons and coupes which had a 10.5:1 compression ratio and which run too hot when retarded the necessary six degrees to ac-commodate 95Ron unleaded. The solution to this is to switch to Range Rover pistons giving lower 8.13:1 or 9.35:1 compression ratios and accept the reduced performance.

Unleaded Jaguars

There has been some disagreement about whether a reader may not be able to run his 1984 XJ 3.4 on Superunleaded without replac-ing the valve seats. The question arises because unleaded petrol burns hotter than leaded petrol and is more likely to lead to valve seat recession and burned-out valves.

However, Jaguar specialist David Marks of Nottingham (01159 405370) tells me that there is a multiplicity of other reasons for valve seat recession on XK engines. These include wrong timing, wrong carburettor settings, manifold air leaks, coked up oilways and incorrect valve clearances. But by far the most likely cause is localised engine overheating.

If the coolant has not been changed religiously every two years, the corrosion inhibitors in it degrade and, because the steel and alloy construction makes the engine a 'corrosion battery', internal corrosion is rapid. This creates a sludge which tends to collect around the rear of the engine and block the waterways.

The engine's coolant temperature sensor is situated at the front of the engine, which may be cooling correctly, so gives no indication of the severe overheating taking place at the back of the engine.

Add to this heat the extra heat caused by running on unleaded petrol, and either a valve or cylinder head gasket disaster is inevitable. Localised overheating can be checked for by external thermometers, but by far the best way is to have a specialist remove the appropriate core plugs and look for sludge inside the block. At the same time, the thermostat should be checked because many Jaguar engines have been found to be running the wrong one.

As far as we can glean, up to 1967, Jaguar XK cylinder heads were fitted with plain cast-iron valve seats. From May 1967, sintered iron valve seats were fitted and Jaguar says that on a healthy, properly cooled engine, these are safe with Superunleaded, as long as prolonged high engine revs are avoided. This means keeping a 4.2 automatic below 65 mph on a motorway, because at 70 mph the engine will be turning over at 3,000 rpm.

The cylinder heads of American-specification fuel-injected and catalysed Series III XJ6 4.2s from 1979 were designed to run on unleaded with a greatly reduced power output. All AJ6s fitted to XJ40 models were also designed to run on unleaded. Series III 3.4s, early XJS 3.6s, and early AJ6 2.9s were designed for leaded petrol, but, as is the case with earlier engines, can tolerate Superunleaded for 20,000 to 40,000 miles.

The latest AE 6000 aftermarket Jaguar valve seats are manufactured from a wrought steel alloy with 13% chrome and molybdenum content, making them suitable for Superunleaded and also for LPG. (The fitted cost is roughly £300–£400, depending on the labour rate.)

Some Jaguar specialists recommend the Broquet fuel catalyst as a means of running an older Jaguar on unleaded, because Broquet claims to catalyse the fuel in such a way that combustion is cooler. However, neither the Jaguar Enthusiasts Club nor David Marks have put this to the test. And obviously it can't work if the real cause of the problem is a blocked radiator or a sludged-up cooling system.

No choking

" I have a 'P' reg. Nissan Micra automatic. Twice I have had to call out Nissan Assist because it would not even attempt to start in the garage. The first chap said it was 'flooding', not my fault, and it happened once in a blue moon. The second chap was much more helpful. After some detective work, we narrowed it down to the fact that the previous time I had started up the car it was only to move it out of the garage, wash it and put it back. Apparently, with the fuel injection automatic enrichment system, after you first switch on the engine you should drive the car for about ten minutes before you switch it off. Seems wrong, but nobody warns you. Also, he showed me how to remove a fuse, turn the ignition once or twice, replace the fuse and Bingo!! **"**

Q *Starting an engine and switching it off again almost immediately is extremely bad for a car. For a cold engine to fire, it needs a rich fuel:air mixture, the residue from which will tend to wash any lubricant from the cylinder bores immediately after switch-off.*

Oh, dear. There's a much bigger issue here than you and a lot of other readers may realise. Starting a car engine and switching it off again almost immediately was always extremely bad for a car. For a cold engine to fire, it needs a rich fuel:air mixture, the residue from which will tend to wash out the cylinder bores immediately after switch-off. Starting from cold also creates a massive amount of condensation both inside the engine and inside the exhaust system, which does not dry out if the car is not then driven 7–10 miles. An engine suffers its greatest wear immediately after a cold start (far more wear than from being driven 200 miles down the motorway at 70 mph). And, to compound all this, modern catalysed fuel injection cars are set up to run through a two-, three-, sometimes four-stage cold-start cycle. If this is not completed, the car can massively over-fuel. So, if you want to clean your car and your garage and drive are level, it's far better to push the car out of the garage and to push it back in again when the sun has thoroughly dried it. Don't make any really short trips. And, if forced to do so, try to balance them with frequent longer trips of ten miles or so. You should also change the oil and filter of a little-used car at least every six months because by the end of that six months the oil will be badly contaminated by unburned petrol.

Advice taken – test passed

" *Further to the various letters about emissions test failures, you may be interested in my own experience. I run a 1,300 cc Mk 1 Cavalier, one of the last made, which I bought new in 1981. Last year, at 31,894 miles, it barely passed the test with a CO level of 4%. Following your tips, I changed the air filter element and began filling up with Shell petrol in the hope of benefiting from its detergent content. I also made sure I had driven the car ten miles and got the engine and exhaust hot before submitting it, at 34,162 miles, for this year's test where CO was a mere 2.58%. I have been filling up with unleaded and leaded in a 4:1 ratio to help protect the valve seats, but in view of the reduced lead content of Shell 'low lead' 4-star is this sufficient?* "

A 4:1 ratio using Shell 'low lead' will not provide enough dry lubrication to protect the valve seats at speed or over a long distance. If the ignition timing suits Shell's 97Ron 'low lead' 4-star, run the car on that exclusively. However, if you rarely exceed 3,000 rpm, don't travel further than a few miles a time on motorways and use the car mainly for local journeys, the evidence suggests that your valve seats will suffer very little damage on their existing diet.

Stop that knocking

" *Having benefited over the past year from your good advice about using fuels only from the big brands, recent experience leads me to ask if the unleaded petrol being sold by the big brands has been reduced to the same lower quality as that sold at supermarkets. In other words their 95 octane petrol is, in fact, of a lower octane. Last summer I switched from supermarket petrol to big brands. The problems of pinking, poor starting and gummed up injectors which I had been experiencing with my Volvo 760 V6 promptly vanished. However, over the last five months, the pinking has returned, almost continuously. This was addressed at the last service. The garage noted increased incidences of pinking on other older cars and their belief is that even big brand unleaded is now lower in rating than the 95 or 98 it is supposed to be according to BS 7070. I therefore changed to big brand four star leaded (98 octane), pinking stopped immediately and engine performance is much improved and cleaner. Could there be any truth in what the garage told me?* **"**

Unless you are using Total or Save brand 'unleaded 4-star', the 4-star you are using only has to be 97Ron, not 98. We actually had the opposite experience to you. When the first tax went up on Super, we switched our oldest car first to Shell 'low lead' 4-star. It was fine for a while, then it started to pink, so we switched it to Texaco CleanSystem 3 4-star which is guaranteed to keep the fuel system clean but on which it still pinked a bit at high revs, despite having retarded the ignition three degrees from the setting for Super. So we switched it to Texaco CleanSystem 3 Super which had the effect of reducing HCs to a mere 79 parts per million (it's allowed 1,200 ppm). Running our other car on a constant diet of Shell Superunleaded, this also passed the test, but with just over 200 ppm of HCs, which seems to suggest that the dertergents in Cleansystem 3 do the job. I should add that, on Super, both cars give two to four miles per gallon more than they do on 4-star. New high-performance cars, such as Golf VR6s, Volvo T5s, Rover 200 Vis, Peugeot 306 GTi-6s and Alfa 156 24vs all go better and take you several miles a gallon further on Super than they do on premium unleaded.

Idle moments

" *I have a mildly modified 1979 Mini Clubman Estate. Last week, it failed its MOT emissions test with an HC emission level of 1,600 ppm. Carburettor adjustments only made things worse, so I took the car back to* *the tuning firm which modified it. There I was told that a high lift camshaft had been fitted which gave better power at high engine speeds but less efficient combustion at idling. I was also showed Section 6.4 of the MOT Inspection Manual, which states, 'If a vehicle meets the CO requirement at its normal idling speed, but fails the HC check, re-check the HC level at a high idle speed of around 2,000 rpm. If the HC reading is then 1,200 ppm or less, the vehicle should be considered to have met both the CO and HC requirement.' When this procedure was followed, the car passed easily with an HC reading of 300 ppm at 2,000 rpm. Moral: know your engine and make sure the MOT emissions check is done by the book.* "

Good tip. In fact, the catalytic converter test of CO and HC emissions is conducted at a 'fast idle' speed of between 2,500 and 3,000 rpm (depending on manufacturer's test data). For the 'natural idle' test at 600–900 rpm, only a CO reading is taken.

Colour-coded pumps

" *Would it be possible for forecourt diesel pumps to be painted a different colour from petrol pumps? I was on a crowded forecourt the other day, reached the only free pump, and found out it was for diesel only. I badly dented a door reversing away from it trying to find the right pump.* "

The tubes from diesel pumps are usually coloured black, tubes from 4-star petrol pumps red and tubes from unleaded and super, green. It's not going as far as painting the pumps themselves, but it should help you find the right one.

More fuel for thought

" *I recently drew up at a petrol pump in Eastbourne and put £5 of unleaded into my tank. I then went to pay for it by credit card and was asked to pay £25.45. It turned out that the previous customer at the pump had filled with £20.45 of four-star, then, as they say, 'done a runner'. The different fuel proved I was not to blame, but please warn your readers that this could happen to them.* "

Said and done.

For richer, for poorer

" *I have an Audi 80 with the 1.9 litre TDI. The car is a 1994L, now at 60,000 miles. What concerns me is that, despite regular servicing by Audi agents, the car has failed its first MOT emissions test twice over the last two years, necessitating extra work to get it through on both occasions. The last service was in March and the car failed its MOT in July. When I telephoned the Audi agent, the service manager immediately diagnosed a faulty oxidising cat. Another local VAG garage pronounced itself unable to inspect the car for two weeks. So finally I turned to my local one-man garage who cleaned the injectors and got it through the test. I feel that, after having been charged top rates for Audi servicing, which cannot have been properly performed, I am at least due some compensation and estimate this at £105. I would be interested in your views.* "

The MOT diesel emissions test involves revving the car's engine to its maximum governed speed several times and measuring the opacity of the smoke produced. If a diesel car has been driven slowly at low engine revs for some time, a considerable amount of soot will have gathered in the exhaust system and will be blown out during this test. An oxidising cat will reduce the amount of smoke, but will not eliminate it, so a diesel car needs to be prepared for the diesel emissions test. The standard way is to pour in a bottle of diesel injector cleaner fuel additive, take the car for 'an Italian tune-up' (a long hard blast down a motorway), replace the air filter with a new, clean one and, if available, fill up with 'City Diesel' from Sainsburys or Tesco. All that said, TDIs can be still be tricky to get through the smoke test, so your best policy is to combine the MOT with a service at a decent VAG specialist. The specialist will then pre-check the car, preferably with the latest VAG 1552 electronic interrogator. If necessary, the operator can re-set the car's ECU to run leaner (underfuel slightly), thus reducing the un-burned fuel emitted as uncombusted hydro-carbon particulates. I should add that even without the VAG 1552, any competent VAG garage, be it Audi, Seat, Skoda or VW, should be able to re-set the fuelling. In your case, the car may have been fine in March when it was serviced but, since then, soot accumulated in the exhaust system and the injectors got a bit clogged up which resulted in the smoke test fail-ure. Not necessarily the fault of the Audi agent, but I agree it is disgraceful that no local agent could help you in your hour of need.

Oil imports

" *I have a diesel car and, during a recent visit to France, noticed that diesel can be purchased there very much more cheaply than in the UK – from 42p a litre at current exchange rates. I wonder if you can tell me if I can import diesel to the UK in reasonable quantities if, like wines and spirits, it is clearly for one's own use. If so, does diesel 'go off' in the same way as premium unleaded? Finally, do you know of anyone who rents out small road tankers?* "

Only in the fuel tank of the vehicle.

Sick of travelling

" *Recently I have done a lot of travelling as a passenger in a large Rover*

800. On longer journeys I have found myself becoming increasingly dizzy, then headachy and sometimes nauseous. This I assume to be car sickness. I am wondering if I have suddenly developed a motion sickness problem or whether my troubles are associated with the car? **"**

These are the classic symptoms of carbon monoxide poisoning. I suspect that fumes from a very slight leak from the exhaust manifold are finding their way into the car where they are held relatively captive. If it isn't CO, it is car sickness, and you may be able to prevent it with some tablets called 'Joy Rides'.

Unleaded Volvo

" *I have just bought my first car, a 1984 Volvo 360GLE injection in near perfect condition. I'm very pleased with it, but for one problem. It's strictly four star only, and I'd like to run it unleaded. I've been told that it is near-impossible to convert because the engine is very high compression. Can it be converted? How much will this cost? Are there any brands of unleaded which are safe to use in my car?* **"**

A guide published by Shell in New Zealand when that country went unleaded tells me that the B19 and B200 engines from 1982 are safe for use with unleaded petrol of 96Ron or more without the need for any other additive. So you can run your car on any Superunleaded or the Unleaded 4-star sold by 'Save' and 'Total' filling stations.

LPG for classics?

" *Could you tell me the state of affairs regarding the promotion of LPG (Liquified Petroleum Gas) for private car users in the UK? I wrote to Calor Gas some time ago and they assured me they were lobbying the government to get the duty lowered and the availability increased. The duty has* *been lowered, but a list of outlets I obtained from Calor recently still shows only 42 in the whole of the UK, with only two in London. Here in the Netherlands, around 10% of cars run on this cleaner fuel which is currently 23p per litre. The road tax is, however, much higher for LPG powered cars and it only works out cheaper to run on LPG if you drive more than about 15,000 miles a year (hard to say exactly because road tax also depends on the weight of the vehicle). Cars fitted with the new generation of LPG systems pay less road tax. I think more private car users in the UK should consider switching to LPG and help reduce pollution, as this is a much cleaner fuel than either petrol or diesel. Perhaps then it would become more widely available. In Britain, LPG is currently around 40p a litre and a conversion costs in the region of £1,100. I drive a road-tax-exempt 1969 Rover 3.5 litre P5B powered by LPG.* ''

LPG is our current government's favoured fuel and the whole issue is on the agenda for the UK's 'Integrated Transport Policy'. Chris Wise of vehicle gas converters Autogas 2000 (01845 523213) tells me that, though LPG is 100 octane, the lack of lead and the fact it burns hotter can still result in exhaust valve and exhaust valve seat recession in 'classics' with cast-iron cylinder heads. Alloy-headed classics, which already have sintered valve seat inserts, may be okay but really need high-chrome-content exhaust valve seat inserts and valves. CNG (Compressed Natural Gas), on the other hand, requires a far heavier tank than LPG so is better suited to commercial vehicles such as Vauxhall's new 'dual fuel' Combo van. The biggest UK converter of cars and vans to LPG and CNG is Gentrac Systems Ltd, Victory Close, Chandler's Ford, Hants SO53 4BU, tel: 01703 254744. Another firm specialising in CNG/LPG conversions for cars and boats is Marine Ecopower Ltd, 7 Lymington Yacht Haven, Kings Saltern Road, Lymington, Hants SO41 3QD, tel: 01590 688444.

Just gassing

Two readers wrote in response to the previous reply. One, from Falmouth, tells of a 1978 Austin Maxi he still owns which was converted to run on LPG when new but for which he has not been able to get LPG since 1988. Another, from Exeter, tells of visits from his son who lives in Holland and runs an LPG-converted Fiat for which he cannot buy fuel in the UK and which, incidentally, is banned from travelling on 'Le Shuttle'. The answers to all but the 'Shuttle' problem are that Autogas 2000 of Thirsk, tel: 01845 523213, supplies a list of all UK LPG 'Gas Stations'. The Natural Gas Vehicle Association, tel: 0171 388 7598, can supply a list of CNG 'Gas Stations'. British Gas, tel: 01784 646030, already operates twelve at Bournemouth, Bristol, Dudley, Old Kent Road (London), Merton (London), Loughborough, Northampton, Slough, Britannia Road

(Southampton), Portswood (Southampton), Walsall and Warrington. Gentrac Systems Ltd, of Chandler's Ford, tel: 01703 254744, is currently engaged in converting quite large numbers of Ford vans and cars for fleet use. It was by concentrating on the private market that the UK got it wrong first time round. Only by pushing LPG into the fleets will enough LPG and CNG get used to encourage wider availability of the appropriate 'Gas Stations'.

Unleaded and Broquet

" A Dr A. Lawson of Alresford has proclaimed via the Saab Owners' Club magazine that his 1972 Saab 96V4 has been successfully converted to unleaded fuel by fitting the 'Broquet Fuel Catalyst'. As an added bonus, he writes that he has seen his fuel consumption lift from 37.5 mpg to 43 mpg, an improvement of 14%. This has been achieved over 3,500 miles on a daily round trip of 113 miles. He has not changed oil, timing, dwell angles or plugs during the trial. Having myself just purchased a Saab 96V4 I may well take the plunge myself. Some time ago you wrote that a Broquet distributor, D. Lock & Associates, had sent you a Broquet. I am quite prepared to carry out a detailed trial on my V4 using your freebie. "

Having confirmed the benefits of Texaco CleanSystem 3 for a year, I tried to install the Broquet in the fuel tank of a 12-year-old VW Jetta GT. It wouldn't fit, so I sent it to this reader on the following conditions: that he installs it straight away – it's hopeless comparing winter fuel consumption figures with those achieved in Spring because they improve by at least 10% anyway; that he uses only 'premium unleaded' petrol; that he keeps detailed records; and that he regularly exceeds 4,000 rpm. Obviously I take no responsibility whatsoever for any damage to his car or any consequences of this, but we will be very interested in how his exhaust valves and seats stand up to running on premium unleaded with the Broquet installed, especially after 200 miles of motorway cruising at 4,000 rpm. He may have little to worry about. We recently heard from Julian Barrett that he races a 128 bhp 1,380 cc Mini Cooper S to 8,400 rpm on premium unleaded with two V8s worth of Broquet discs in the fuel tank. Richard Lane races a Triumph Stag fitted with a 585 bhp 383 ci Chevy V8 to 8,200 rpm on 95Ron unleaded with Broquet in the tank. More information on Broquet from D. Lock and Associates of Horsham, tel: 01403 823507.

Unleaded 205

" *I am recently retired and own a 1988 Peugeot 205GTi with the 1.9 litre high-compression engine and only 36,000 miles on the clock. It was supposed to see me through the rest of my driving days. Can its cylinder head be treated to replacement parts to run on 98Ron Superunleaded? If so, will the compression ratio of 9.6:1 also need reducing? I have a hydraulic press to fit new valve seats and a lifetime of engineering experience.* "

Rest easy. According to Peugeot, all 205GTi 1.9s can be run on 98Ron Superunleaded, or 98Ron 'unleaded 4-star', without any modification. In fact, the engine should produce slightly more power and be slightly more economical on Super than it has been on 97Ron leaded 4-star. What you do need to do without fail is have the timing belt and camshaft end-seal changed ASAP. They are now at the age and mileage when the end seal starts to leak oil onto the belt, which could be about to fail anyway, and I won't need to remind you of the consequences of timing belt failure.

Super petrol, amazing price

" *Recently I inadvertently filled my 'N' registered Ford Escort 1.6 Automatic with Superunleaded and was shocked to find it cost 79.9p a litre, while the same filling station charged 63.9p for premium unleaded. Can you explain this huge difference in price?* "

Superunleaded fuel costs a lot more to refine than 'premium' unleaded, so it is a basically more expensive fuel. It's also more heavily taxed.

I can't explain all of it, but I can explain some of it. Super costs a lot more to refine than 'premium' unleaded so it is a basically more expensive fuel. It's also more heavily taxed. Several years ago, the Total and Save chains of filling stations introduced 'unleaded 4-star', which is 98Ron superunleaded base with a valve seat recession preventative added to it. Fearful that millions of motorists would switch to this instead of the more heavily taxed 4-star leaded, and thus cause a revenue shortfall, the then Chancellor of the Exchequer hiked the tax on superunleaded by an extra 4p, effective from May 1996. This same tax hike, of course, also hit unleaded 4-star and discouraged millions of motorists from switching from leaded to unleaded. In the 1998 budget the tax hike on super was increased by a further 1p.

British economy champ

" *Further to your various reports on fuel consumption, could I remind you that there is a British-built large family estate car which compares more than favourably with your test vehicles? In mixed daily motoring measured over 4,500 miles, my 1993 Montego Countryman DI 7-seater estate car returned an overall figure of 53.4 mpg, and that figure even includes a few hundred miles pulling a trailer. I accept that it is hardly a stylish vehicle, but when the time comes to replace it can anyone suggest another vehicle offering such incredible practicality and fuel economy at anything like the price? I doubt it.* "

I think you're going to have to wait until the rest of the new crop of common rail direct injected turbodiesels arrive before you finally make your choice. In the meantime, take a look at the 2.0 litre Vauxhall Astra DI Estate.

Running on

" *I have owned a Ford Sierra 1.6LX since new in 1987. During the first five years it did 50,000 miles using supermarket 4-star petrol driving 25-mile round trips four days a week plus four 50-mile round trips per month. My garage then adjusted the timing so the car could take ordinary 'premium' unleaded petrol and my mileage reduced to 6,000 a year, half being trips of 50 miles or more. The engine ran well until last year, then started running rough. The HT leads and distributor cap were replaced. Then, after a full service in mid-1997, the engine started to run-on after switching off. I tried an off-the-shelf 'liquid decoke' and also regularly added upper cylinder lubricant, but the running-on still occurs. Do you recommend a proper in-situ liquid de-coke and, if so, who can do it? Alternatively, should I have the head removed and reconditioned? What else should I do?* "

Your experience is fairly typical of a car which has been retarded to run on 'premium' unleaded and has then been run on cheap petrol with no significant detergent additive in it. Retarding the engine makes it run richer and cooler and will tend to leave more carbon deposits in the combustion chambers. These remain red hot when you switch off the engine and provide the spark which makes it run on. Misfires from the duff HT leads will have exacerbated this. First, have the timing re-set back to the original setting (for 97–98Ron petrol) and either use an additive such as STP fuel system cleaner or switch to a petrol that is guaranteed to contain a high proportion of detergent (such as Texaco CleanSystem 3). This might solve the problem by itself. If it doesn't, there is a company that does a mobile cylinder head 'dialysis' which has been recommended by readers. Its old name was 'Mobile Carbon Clean', it's new name is 'Decoke Master UK', and you can locate its nearest operative by phoning 01484 683300 (day) or 01484 682601 (evening). Another little problem about to manifest itself is that your Sierra has basically the same 1,597 cc CVH engine as that fitted to millions of Escorts and Orions. Besides being very prone to sludging up with old contaminated oil, they tend to need replacement valve stem seals at about the age yours has reached. Stem seals can be replaced with the head in situ, but the cost of a full head overhaul, including new stem seals, may be less than the dialysis decoke plus stem seal replacement. It will also show up any more serious damage to the valves.

Will Rover take to unleaded?

" Further to the articles about the withdrawal of Four Star from year 2000, I have a 1986 Rover 213SE which is still in excellent condition with a very low mileage. At the moment I am using four star leaded petrol. I have been told it would be all right to use unleaded petrol in this model. Could you please advise on this?"

In your case, yes – and the answer should prove helpful generally. Your Rover has a 12-valve Honda engine and all Japanese engines have been designed to run on unleaded petrol since around 1980. However, the car has an 8.7:1 compression ratio which is a bit high for running on 95Ron Premium Unleaded. I'd try it on half a tank of Premium Unleaded, and if you hear a 'tinkling' sound from the engine when driving uphill, fill the rest of the tank with Super-unleaded or 4-star Unleaded.

Super consumption

" *I bought a 'K' reg. Sierra XR 4×4 2.0 litre DOHC six months ago. I was not happy, but not surprised, to find that the fuel consumption was considerably worse than my 'H' reg. 1.8 Sapphire. However, I recently filled with 98Ron Super Plus unleaded and enjoyed fuel consumption comparable to the 1.8 Sapphire. Is this due to the grade of petrol? I normally fill with 95Ron premium unleaded.* "

Yes. If a car has a compression ration of 9:1 or more it is likely to benefit from running on Super.

Biodiesel

" *I have just purchased a VW Golf 1.9TDI and in the owner's manual it states that this car can also run on RME (Rapeseed Methyl Ester). The manual elaborates that RME is almost totally sulphur free, that the combustion of RME emits practically no sulphur dioxide, that the exhaust gas contains less carbon monoxide, hydrocarbons and particulates than fossil diesel fuel, that RME is biodegradable, that it can be used in temperatures down to minus fifteen degrees centigrade and that it can be mixed in any ratio with fossil diesel fuel. This is obviously a wonderful 'green' fuel, so where can I get it?* "

There are two further advantages of Biodiesel: Since it is grown, it is not a diminishing resource. And burning it does not add extra carbon dioxide to the earth's atmosphere. The reason for this is that, in growing, the crop itself absorbs as much carbon as vehicle engines emit while running on Biodiesel. Converting the oilseed rape to RME is a relatively simple

The main constituent of Biodiesel is derived from oilseed rape, which can be grown on set-aside farmland, and which consumes as much carbon dioxide in growing as it emits when burnt as a fuel.

process which also yields glycerine and cattle cake as residues. It is widely used in Austria and blended with fossil diesel in France and Germany. Not only that, the crop can be grown on the 5% of farmland allowed to be 'set-aside' without affecting the set-aside subsidy. But, despite its considerable advantages, Biodiesel is subject to the same rate of fuel duty of 44.99p a litre plus VAT as 'conventional diesel' and does not qualify for the slightly lower rate of 42.99p + VAT on ultra low sulphur 'City Diesel'. Tests in 1997 at Millbrook showed that, compared to conventional diesel, emission levels from burning Biodiesel were 46% down in hydrocarbons, but slightly up in carbon monoxide, nitrogen oxides and particulates. If the amount of set-aside land were increased and the tax on Biodiesel reduced you'd soon see Biodiesel pumps on the forecourt.

Stop-starter

" *During all the debate on traffic pollution I have never seen it suggested that vehicles should be fitted with a device whereby the engine automatically stops when the vehicle comes to a halt, then starts again when the accelerator pedal is pressed.* "

The VW Golf Mk III diesel 'Ecomatic' had this feature and Citroen have come up with an improved system branded 'Dynalto'. Citroen's system is sited between the engine and the gearbox and combines the function of starter motor, alternator and electric motor. The Xsara Dynalto automatically switches off the engine when the car is stationary for more than two seconds, then re-starts it when the accelerator is pressed in less than a tenth of a second. The 'Dynalto' also serves as a power booster, providing extra power for extra acceleration. So far the Xsara Dynalto is a prototype only, but is expected to be in production by year 2000.

Reduced tax diesel

" *I recently read in a newspaper that 'duty on ordinary diesel rises to reduce the price differential with cleaner but more expensive "low sulphur" diesel. Further increases are signalled.' For a long time, Shell, BP, Sainsbury, Tesco and other large suppliers have led us to believe that the diesel they were supplying contained the requisite additives and was sufficiently refined to make it environmentally safe. Some have called it 'City Diesel', some called it 'Super Diesel'. The price has been about one penny a litre less than unleaded petrol. I have not been aware of any higher grade diesel being sold anywhere. So why has this 'improved' fuel had 5.5 pence per litre added to the price, in many cases putting it above the price of unleaded petrol?* "

Only one type of diesel meets the special refining criteria to qualify for what is now a 2p per litre cut in fuel tax, and that is Greenergy's 'City Diesel' sold by Sainsbury (and Tesco within the M25). All diesel is now required by law to contain less sulphur, but is still not quite as 'clean' as City Diesel and therefore attracts the tax rate of 44.99p a litre rather than 42.99p. Remember that this isn't all the tax you pay. VAT is also levied as 14.89% of the pump price inclusive of fuel tax, so when you buy 50 litres of diesel at 69.9p a litre you pay £27.70 in tax and just £7.25 for the fuel itself. In fact, many oil companies have now cut the price of ordinary diesel to 67.9p a litre, so you pay £27.55 in tax and £6.40 for the fuel.

GEARBOX AND CLUTCH

Discovery gearboxes

" *The manual gearbox of my 35,000 mile 'M' reg. Land Rover Discovery TDI failed for a second time in June. The first failure was covered by warranty, but this subsequent failure resulted in a bill of £997.82. The car has always been regularly and professionally serviced. Is this a common problem with Discoverys? And can I expect any help from Land Rover towards the cost of the repairs?* "

In my view there is no vehicle more capable of transporting five to seven people across rough ground or tracks in comfort than the Land Rover Discovery or Range Rover. But problems with the smoother-changing manual box fitted from 'L' reg. onwards are, shall we say, 'not unknown'. These have been covered in this column, in *Diesel Car and 4×4* magazine and on BBC's 'Watchdog'. Negotiate wisely, calmly and carefully by telephone, first through your Land Rover agent and, if unsuccessful, direct with Land Rover, then follow your telephone conversations with confirming letters, and you should be able to obtain some compensation. Land Rover is extremely keen to keep its owners in the 'Land Rover family' for obvious reasons, so I am confident it will provide at least some help towards this bill. A special gearbox oil with molybdenum additives from Land Rover dealers may prevent further failures.

Land Rover gets it right

❛ *'Bad news,' consoled Jane of Dutton Forshaw, Maidstone. 'Your two-and-a-half-year-old, 40,000-mile Discovery has a gearbox oil leak and we need it for two days. Good news,' she continued brightly, 'Land Rover is going to pay for it and we'll lend you a car in the meantime for nothing.'* ❜❜

That's what I like to hear. It will also help keep a new Discovery top of your list when the time comes to change. All new Land Rovers are now covered by a three-year 60,000-mile warranty.

Open the box

❛❛ *My wife has a cherished 'T' reg. Mazda 323 automatic which has only done 25,000 miles. I am told that the Borg Warner gearbox will be okay without an oil change. Is this true?* ❜❜

Trevor King of King Automatics could halve his workload of transmission rebuilds with his answer to this one. He recommends changing the autobox ATF oil and filter every 12 months regardless of mileage, and anyone with one of the old Metro AP automatics should change the combined engine and gearbox oil and filter every six months. To check the oil level in the JATCO box in your Mazda, the gearbox dipstick is located on the right hand side. Draining involves removing the sump pan. Refill through the dipstick aperture. (Trevor King, King Automatics, 'The Chalk Pit', College Road, Epsom, Surrey KT17 4JA, tel: 01372 728769.)

Well clutched

❛❛ *I recently read in your column about a Rover car which had needed a new clutch at 35,000 miles. I use a 1973 Morris Marina for local journeys and this car has travelled over 130,000 miles on its original clutch. Are modern clutches made of softer material than those of the 1970s?* "

Clutch wear is often caused by the habit of many drivers of sitting with the clutch pedal depressed for long periods at traffic lights and junctions.

Like any wearing part of a car, the life of a clutch depends on what's asked of it. The clutch of a high-performance car driven hard obviously won't last as long as the clutch of a low-performance car driven gently. Another factor is that many drivers ride their clutches while driving, and sit with the clutch disengaged for long periods at traffic lights and junctions, all of which causes unnecessary wear. And yet another is that 'self-adjusting' clutch cables often don't, leading to clutch slip and premature wear. (Two more readers reported clutch failure on 'old' Rover 200s and 400s at around the 40,000 mile mark, and yet another at 29,000 miles.)

Weirdly geared

" *The computer governing the 3-speed automatic gearbox of my Renault Clio is programmed so that, after dropping into 2nd, 3rd cannot be regained until the car is doing more than 40 mph. As this would be illegal within the 30 mph speed limit, I have followed my Renault dealer's advice and changed manually. Last year, you described an automatic gearbox on a Honda that 'did all that could be expected of it', but was fitted to the large, expensive Shuttle model. I am now ready to change my Clio and wonder if you could recommend a similar-sized car with an automatic gearbox programmed for UK urban conditions.* "

Second gear in a three-speed gearbox has to bridge a large gap – particularly if 'top' is a high cruising gear. A car that uses the same gearbox as the Clio, but with different gearing and programming, is the Citroen Saxo 1.6 automatic. This can do more than 60 mph in first and more than 90 mph in second, so the second gear is a bit like the fourth of many five-speed manuals and is as high as you need in town. The alternative is to go CVT, and the best of these are the Honda Civic 1.6i ES automatic and the Rover 200 1.6 CVT. The CVT in the Honda, unusually, has a 'Sport' setting, and works very smoothly indeed. With the Rover, on the other hand, takeup is very abrupt and there is no hesitation when entering a stream of traffic. It's also a well sorted, very pleasant car to drive and, as far as I know, there are no obvious production compromises with either the Honda or Rover CVT. Any CVT does, however, require a sympathetic right foot. If you simply stamp on the accelerator they all wail and scream, but if you let the road speed increase with the engine speed your progress will be smooth and plenty quick enough. One thing is for sure with any CVT. Around town you will never find yourself stuck in the wrong gear or hunting between two inappropriate ratios.

Any bearing on the matter?

" *After a clutch replacement at just 29,200 miles, the gearbox of my Rover 200 started making a noise which has been diagnosed as worn bearings. Rover has refused any 'goodwill' help over this. Can you throw any light on the reasons for these problems?* "

I bought a VW Jetta GTi 16v with a noisy gearbox mainshaft or final drive bearing in June 1996, poured some STP gearbox treatment in through the speedo drive hole and it's stayed together ever since. Any similar 'superlube' product such as Slick 50, XZX1, or Molybdenum Disulphide, just might do the same job for you.

It's worth trying, and a lot cheaper than a re-conditioned gearbox. (If you do this, be very careful – see 'Famous Five' below.)

Famous 5

" *I recently purchased an old Renault 5 for my daughter to use at university. I removed the speedo cable from the gearbox and cannot get it back in. Is there a simple solution, or does the gearbox need to be dismantled?* "

Speedo cables are usually driven by a nylon cog on the end of the cable which may have slipped off into the gearbox when you removed the cable. If this is the case, try draining the gearbox oil, and the cog – or the chewed up remains of it – may emerge with the oil. Have a look at a replacement speedo cable at a Renault dealer to check if I'm right. At least the gearbox of an early Five is right at the front and is easy to get at.

Slippery clutch

" *I have today had to fork out £398.91 for a new clutch for my 1994L VW Passat TDI estate which has covered 44,000 miles. Neither I nor my wife drive with a foot on the pedal. We only do family motoring and have never towed. My only previous clutch replacement in 30 years of motoring was on a nine-year-old, 96,000-mile Peugeot 305 – and that cost a fraction of the £400 I had to pay for the VW clutch. Do you think that the clutch wear and cost are unreasonable?* "

VW is always approachable over matters such as this. The company recently agreed to replace a clutch which had lasted a mere 5,000 miles on a London-driven Golf GTi, but drew the line at paying for a new clutch for a Passat estate in a similar case to yours. On that occasion, the car had been very heavily laden when the clutch failed, but the clutch itself was found to have failed due to wear rather than to any manufacturing defect. I'm afraid that checks led to the same finding with your clutch. £400 is not unreasonable for a clutch replacement on this car. It can work out a great deal more on a Mondeo diesel, for example, due to the level of dismantling involved. On VWs fitted with self-adjusting clutch cables it is important to feel for any sign of slippage because, if the self-adjuster fails, the level of clutch wear can accelerate rapidly. If you experience any sign of this, have the cable replaced. It only costs around £20, compared to around £350 for a clutch.

One too many

" I see that the new BMW 540 V8 can be had with a six-speed gearbox. What is the point of this? Surely you only need six gears in a car with a very narrow power band. When you consider that electric and steam locomotives can go from a standstill to over 125 mph with no gears, does BMW really think it is necessary to give their most powerful engine the most gears? Audi also fits six gears to its A6 TDI, I believe. Why? Surely the Germans can design an engine management system which gives enough spread of power and torque to match five gears? "

With a big, torquey V8 or V10, 'sixth' is usually an extremely 'high' ratio, giving 35–40 mph per 1,000 rpm for fuel economy at high speed. The same is true with the Audi A6 TDI 6-speed, which pulls 33.8 mph per 1,000 rpm in sixth, allowing a fuel-efficient 100 mph cruise on German autobahns – and an even more fuel-efficient cruise on the UK's speed-restricted motorways. The other five gears, in both cases, enable the driver to accelerate either more quickly or more fuel efficiently or both (think how long a locomotive takes to get to 125 mph). Two more 'economy' six-speeders are the 1.3 litre Toyota Corolla G6 and, surprisingly, the manual Chevrolet Corvette. Six speeders geared for performance rather than economy include the Fiat Punto 55EL, Peugeot 306 GTi-6, Alfa 156 2.5 24v, BMW M3, Vauxhall Lotus Carlton and Honda NSX. You don't have to use all the gears, of course. When the time is right, you can 'block change' from fifth to third or fourth to second, just as in any other car.

Automatic recommendation

" *May I ask, is Trevor King of King Automatics perhaps a relative, or a personal friend of yours? He is extremely lucky to get so much free advertising in the national press. Hardly a month passes without a mention of his expertise and phone number. It may interest you to know that there are a few hundred Automatic Transmission Specialists in this country, many of whom could pass on the same advice as Mr King. It would be more prudent (and may I venture more 'Honest') to refer your readers to the Federation of Automatic Transmission Engineers – tel: 0585 228595. This organisation could put your readers in touch with their nearest approved specialist and thereby share out the pie more evenly.* "

When I have an autobox query I call Trevor King, for four reasons. (1) The other automatic transmission engineers I had tried before were unable to advise on some transmissions, yet Trevor King has never failed me. (2) Mr King was recommended by a senior police officer who had travelled 300 miles to get the AP box of his cherished Fiat repaired by the only specialist he could find willing to repair rather than replace it. (3) Manufacturers and importers with CVTs in their range have turned to Mr King when the production engineering of their boxes led to problems they and their agents were unable to solve. (4) Mr King is always there when I need him and my queries are answered without any delay – though readers should not expect their own general queries to be answered so readily, as this would be unreasonable. But if they have a real problem they now have a choice – call the Federation on 0585 228595, or call King Automatics on 01372 728769.

Exploding gearboxes

" *We would like to issue a warning to all owners of Ford Sierra and Escort Cosworth 4×4s. A customer's gearbox had seized, and when we examined it we found it had virtually exploded. We re-built the box using secondhand parts, but on test the car still displayed chronic 'shunting'. The customer told us, yes, the car had been jerky when cold. So driving it in this state must have initiated the failure of the weakest point of the transmission – the small transfer prop shaft universal joint, which, when it failed at high speed, thrashed around and caused extensive damage. We then found that the water temperature sensor was failing and sending the wrong messages to the ECU. Once this was changed, the problem was cured. So the warning is, any jerky running, have this sensor replaced or you could end up with a very expensive exploding gearbox.* "

A helpful warning from our old friend Dave Brodie of BBR (tel: 01280 702389 for Cosworth problems, 'de-catting', and chipping of ECs for better performance and fuel consumption). Colleague Andrew English was a witness when the box of the Escort Cosworth 4×4 being driven by Gerard Sauer on a banked test track curve did exactly the same thing, catapulting the car into the trees. Gerard was very lucky to emerge with little more than a bloody nose.

Transmission torment

" *I have a 1988 Carina II automatic and, after 72,000 miles, I recently changed the ATF. The handbook states that the capacity for drain and refill is 2.5 litres, but nearly 4 litres came out. I replaced it with 2.5 litres and, on checking, the level was correct. But then, once the box was up to temperature, the level had dropped so far it required an extra litre to raise the level to the bottom of the dipstick. My dilemma is compounded by the fact that the manual expressly states on no account to over-fill the box. The car has never given me any trouble, but I have never been happy with its acceleration. It winds up very slowly, but, once up to speed, is quite responsive, even with the overdrive switched on. I have approached my local Toyota dealer and have been told to keep the level within the hot range in spite of being over-full when cold. What advice can you give?* "

You have a car which is naturally a bit slow when left to its own devices. Have you tried holding it in 'L' to 6,000 rpm when accelerating? This will show you if it is capable of being a bit quicker off the mark, and may indicate that the kickdown cable is slack. As for the oil levels, I presume you removed the oil pan and replaced the filter (something you should do every year rather than after nine years and 72,000 miles). Trevor King of King Automatics tells me that what usually happens is that the torque converter retains 3–4 pints of ATF even with the pan off. In your case, this seems to have drained out, but it's why the drain and refill is stated as 2.5 litres rather than the true capacity of the box. The procedure for refilling is to fill to the mark, start the engine and warm the box up in 'Park'. Switch off, top up, then re-start and move the lever between P and D a few times with your left foot firmly on the footbrake. Switch off, top up to the mark, drive the car round the block a few times, then top up again to the mark. What your Toyota dealer told you was correct.

Tiptronic *versus* manual

" *I was considering purchasing a VW Passat 20v Turbo Tiptronic rather than a manual, but have been put off by the quoted performance figures. The Tiptronic seems to be slower and thirstier than the manual version. I thought that a Tiptronic was supposed to mimic Grand Prix gear changes, yet it appears to perform worse than an ordinary automatic. Could you shed some light on this?* "

A good autobox can sometimes seem quicker than a manual because what the driver loses on the straights he may gain in the corners.

A torque converter will always absorb some power and, for this reason (plus the fact that an automatic usually has fewer ratios), an auto is usually slower and thirstier than a manual. In real life a good autobox can sometimes seem quicker than a manual because what the driver loses on the straights he may gain in the corners. (F1 cars and British Touring Car Championship cars have sequential boxes, but no torque converters.) When I finally got my hands on a Passat Turbo Tiptronic, I was very impressed. The torque converter allows high ratios (120 mph in fourth; fifth geared to give 30 mph per 1,000 rpm). Over 768 miles I averaged nearly 28 mpg. My only criticism is the way the lever works – forward to change up and back to change down. This goes against the laws of physics because, when you are braking and want to change down, your body if forced forwards, so it would be much more natural for the change pattern to be forward to change down and back to change up.

Granulated gearbox

" *Last year I wrote to ask your advice as to whether or not I should change the gearbox oil of my ten-month-old Ford Mondeo. You wrote back to say that changing it could do nothing but good, so, at 16,000 miles I did change it. I was amazed at the quantity of metal dust suspended in the oil I removed. It was opaque with whorls of shiny metal accompanied by some granule-sized pieces which had obviously been produced as the transmission bedded in. It may be my imagination, but the gear change now feels a little smoother – or could that be due to the 'Slick 50' I put in at the same time?* ??

It will be due to a combination of both. I put some STP into the box of my old Jetta 16v which has noisy bearings two years ago, and it's still holding up. We always recommend a change of automatic transmission fluid and filter every year, but you have certainly confirmed that a change of manual gearbox oil after the first year could eventually repay an owner handsomely.

Boxing clever

" A friend of mine has a Vauxhall Senator 2.5 litre which now needs a refurbished gearbox. I seem to remember there was someone in Gloucestershire who dealt in these cars and also refurbished them. Do you have their name and address? ??

The main source of sensibly priced Senators is West Oxfordshire Motor Auctions at Witney (01993 774413), which continues to sell ex-police Senators held back and first registered on 'M' plates. A specialist in reselling these cars, tidied up and fully sorted, is Portaploy on 01256 322240. And the best source for parts is the Vauxhall Spares Centre of Romford on 01708 384720. Rather than have your Getrag 5-speed manual gearbox rebuilt, which requires specialist tools and costs a fortune, a used box at £200–£300 makes better sense.

Disposable gearbox

" *At 79,000 miles my 1991 Granada Scorpio 2.0i automatic recently required a new speedometer sensor unit, the failure of which had caused the gearbox to refuse to engage fourth. After fitting, the gearbox specialist informed me he'd be seeing me again very soon for a replacement gearbox costing £600 – as all Granada automatics failed at around 80,000 miles. The first sign of trouble is a time lag when selecting reverse (mine has that), followed by slipping from second to fourth, missing third. I have checked around, and this does seem to be the case even with new models. Surely Ford must have been aware of this problem for many years, so can this failure be justified at a mere 80,000 miles? The specialist told me the fluid was fine and that changing it or any other remedial work would be a waste of time.* "

This is generally correct but has confirmed to me the wisdom of consulting Trevor King of King Automatics. The reason for the problem is that the mass-production of the A4LD box can leave the centre carrier capable of movement. What King Automatics do when rebuilding these boxes is to 'thrust them up', preventing the movement and giving the rebuilt box a longer life than the original. Autoboxes on later Scorpios have bearings which help to prevent the movement. King Automatics frequently develop modifications to overcome common problems and can be contacted on 01372 728769.

Continuously troublesome transmission?

" *You referred to problems with the CTX autobox on Fiestas. As I have recently purchased a 1991 Escort 1.6 Ghia CTX auto, could you please tell me if the problems also apply to this model, what the problems are, and what is the remedy?* "

The production engineering of the CTX box in

Once the fluid gets low in the CTX autoboxes of some Fiestas and Escorts, disaster is virtually inevitable, so it is vital to check the transmission fluid level at least once a week and replenish with the correct fluid whenever necessary.

Escorts and Fiestas led to a possibility of fluid loss via the inhibitor switch. Once the fluid gets low in these boxes, disaster is virtually inevitable, so it is vital that all owners check the transmission fluid level at least once a week and replenish with the correct fluid (from their Ford dealer) whenever necessary. The fluid and filter should also be replaced every year. There is another problem with this box which manifests itself in juddering. Independent automatic gearbox specialist King Automatics has identified the cause of this and is in the process of developing a replacement part which eliminates the tendency to judder. More details from King Automatics on 01372 728769.

Not automatically

" *The automatic transmission of my wife's 1990G Renault Five broke at just 18,000 miles, due to the failure of the oil cooler which allowed engine coolant and automatic transmission fluid to mix. This is despite the car having been serviced at the stipulated intervals at Renault specialists and despite an improved oil cooler having been fitted. Renault admits that the original oil coolers had a problem, which is why they were routinely replaced 'in service' free of charge by Renault agents. But the company has refused any assistance towards the £1,280.75 we were charged for a new oil cooler, new multifunction switch and transmission rebuild by an independent Renault garage. The garage informed us that a warning sign of the trouble to come was that the gearbox fluid had turned pink.* "

While I am sorry you have suffered this trouble and the distress of having to fork out £1,280.75 for a repair, I'm afraid that the car is far too old for you to expect the manufacturer to bear any financial responsibility. A change of automatic transmission fluid and filter every year is recommended as routine preventative maintenance anyway. It also makes sense for automatic owners to check the transmission fluid as part of their normal weekly inspection. This should include: tyres (pressure and condition); engine oil (level and colour); brake fluid level; coolant level; power steering fluid (level and colour); automatic transmission fluid (level and colour where dipstick is fitted); screenwash level.

Busted box

" It is possibly a rather special kind of situation when your 1986, 100,000-mile Mitsubishi Shogun, a wonder for hard work and the preferred kennel of my working sheep dogs, starts to complain vociferously from its gearbox. What do I do when the repair to the box or a replacement looks a bit like the value of the vehicle? The dogs want it kept, of course, at all costs. "

Get in touch with API on 0500 830530. This company specialises in importing engines and transmissions from low-mileage Japanese cars, prematurely scrapped due to Japan's 'Shaken' roadworthiness test regime. (I can't vouch for any of the other replacement engine and gearbox companies advertising in *Exchange & Mart*. The cowboy operators have made this too much of a lottery.) If you can't source a good gearbox at a sensible enough price, you are at least very close to an excellent source of a replacement vehicle. Russell Baldwin and Bright hold the biggest auctions of 4×4 vehicles in the country at Leominster every fortnight (tel: 01568 611166).

Sumped!

" My grandson bought a 'Y' reg. Metro about 12 months ago and now a

*big end has gone. I seem to remember that the first car I owned, a 1938
Morris 8, had this problem, which I cured by dropping the sump and
putting in new shell bearings. Is the Metro as easy as this to do?* "

No, because its gearbox is in its sump. Metros
of this age tend to have developed a fairly serious rust problem. If your grandson's is sound,
then your best bet is to pick up a combined engine and gearbox from a body-rot MOT failure
at a breakers (preferably one still in a car that
you can hear running, or one the breaker guarantees to be a runner). Now, here's the hard
part. If your grandson's car has a rust problem
as well as a big end problem the most sensible
thing to do is to sell it for spares or scrap it.

Laborious clutches

" *I had a number of problems with a new Renault Megane 1.6. At 6 months
old and 5,000 miles the crankshaft thrust bearing went and it needed a new
engine. After re-assembly, gear selection was not as sweet as it had been and
the gearbox, too, was replaced at 11,000 miles. Now, having learned that the
gearbox and engine cannot be separated without hoisting them in unit out
of the car (which takes seven hours) I am dreading the thought of clutch replacement. How does this fit in with trade intelligence?* "

It seems that Renault must have followed
Vauxhall, which in turn followed Ford.
Replacing the clutch on a Mondeo is a major operation which involves removing parts of the
front subframe and can take from five to seven
hours of labour. Replacing Cavalier clutches is
a doddle because the gearbox input shaft can
be pulled right out and the clutch removed with
the engine and box *in situ*. But replacing the
clutch of a Vectra is again an 'engine out' job.
Once the public cottons on, private buyers will

become very wary of buying ex-fleet examples with 75,000–90,000 miles and the prospect of an imminent £500–£600 clutch replacement.

Squirrel method

" I have a Mondeo automatic and when I first start off there is a thump when selecting 'drive'. After that, it is fine. The thump is only after a cold start, first thing in the morning. Is this normal? "

Yes. On start-up all Mondeo four-cylinder models go through a cold-start cycle which commences with idling at higher than normal revs to protect the catalytic converter. I have only driven a Mondeo 1.8 automatic once. The occasion was when my American neighbour had parked hers on a steep uphill drive and caught a squirrel by the tail under the offside rear tyre.

The squirrel was none too happy about this and it fell to me to remove the Mondeo from the squirrel. I did what I always do when driving an automatic in a confined space. Started it up. Put my left foot on the footbrake. Put the lever in D. Gave it some revs. Then, holding the car on the footbrake, gradually eased off the handbrake and pulled the car forward a couple of inches. The squirrel didn't stop to say thanks and disappeared up the nearest tree. The point of this little story is, if you ease the car into D by holding the footbrake against the accelerator you will make a smooth, safe and fully controlled getaway from cold. If you merely put it in drive and accelerate you may get a 'clonk'.

CVT warranties

" In December 1996 I purchased a six-month-old Fiat Punto 60 Selecta from The Great Trade Centre at White City, London. The car had done only 7,800 miles and was a former Hertz rental vehicle. I have been very pleased with it since and it is used mainly by my wife. However, the week before last, the car developed a major transmission fault at 14,500 miles. Fortunately, when I purchased it, I took out a two-year mechanical breakdown insurance with Motorway Direct plc dating from June 1997 when the Fiat warranty expired. I am pleased to advise that they took care of transferring the car to an approved repairer and fitting a new electro-mechanical clutch and gearbox without any quibbling at a total cost (to them) of £1,801.28. This was excellent news to us as the two-year MBI premium had only been £300. My question concerns the failure of the transmission at such a low mileage. Is the type of transmission fitted to the Punto Selecta unreliable? "

Good to read that The Great Trade Centre's warranty looked after you properly. Yes there have been a few problems with both Ford and Fiat CVT transmissions (though not with Rover,

Volvo 440 Nissan Micra and Honda CVTs). The Fiat has a quite sophisticated electromagnetic clutch which successfully eliminates 'creep' but can prove to be a bit delicate. If the lever ever feels reluctant to move into gear, forcing it almost inevitably smashes the gearbox. Another problem common to both Fiat and Ford is an ATF leak. If a CVT transmission ever gets low on fluid it usually destroys itself. These boxes are not maintenance-free either. Both the ATF and filter need changing once a year.

GIZMOS AND TOOLS

Static

" *My daughter's new car is a Renault Megane Scenic, and yes it does take the three children, two cellos, etc. The only drawback is the static electricity. Unfortunately, one granddaughter receives electric shocks when she steps out of the car. What is the cause, and what is the cure?* "

Though my editor, Peter Hall, covered triboelectrics in some detail in 1995 it is a question that keeps coming back. What happens is that static electricity is developed when two different materials come into contact and are then separated. They could, for example, be a shirt containing nylon and a wool jacket, or wool trousers and a nylon car seat. So it is you that becomes charged, not the car. Any static charge in the car itself constantly trickles to earth through the tyres which, because they contain carbon black, are conductive. If you get a shock touching part of the metal of the car with a finger it is caused by the static in your clothes discharging into the car body. But if you 'wipe' the car body with the fleshy side of your fist the discharge is spread and you probably won't notice it. Mazda fits a special button on the door through which you can discharge static, and a company called Statpad makes a key-fob that serves the same purpose, an example of which

I enclose. (Since I have no more left, other readers will have to order these at £4.95 each inc. p&p from Statpad Ltd, AMTRI House, Hurdsfield Industrial Estate, Hulley Road, Macclesfield, Cheshire SK10 2NE, tel: 01625 615524.)

Reading lamps and dashboard dials

" A small torch plugged by cable into the cigar lighter socket would help your correspondent read in the dark while waiting to pick up his children from evening activities. It will also be very useful for peering under the bonnet and under the seats. He can buy one from most accessory shops. Now here's a grouch. Why do modern cars have such large rev counters and such small clocks? Ears are a good judge of engine speed, but none of our senses can accurately tell us the time. "

Good point about the reading light. A rally navigator's light does a similar job. But the answer to the rev counter *versus* clock question is to buy a base-model car. They almost all have a huge analogue clock where the rev counter would sit in more upmarket versions.

Under pressure

" You recently showed a picture of a dial-faced tyre pressure gauge being applied to the valve of a Discovery. What is the make and price of this gauge? I am in my mid-seventies and would find such a gauge much easier to use than the usual 'pencil' type. "

That was my hand in the picture, since I was the only one who had turned up with a foot pump and gauge, so I got the job of sorting out the soft tyre. The gauge is an 'Accu-Gage' which I bought last year following a favourable review in *Auto Express*. It still comes out top in tests as the most accurate gauge at a reasonable price, and costs £13.50 (check price before ordering) from the International Tool Co., 82 Wrenbury Road, Duston, Northants NN5 6YG, tel: 01604 591200. (Website hhtp//www.itc.u.net.com) The 4×4 version at £21 does not come out so well in tests and is not worth the extra outlay, unless you really need a gauge with a longer arm.

Rat-proof cars

" *I run an Audi A4 1.8 which I regularly drive to Germany. While touring there last September, a creature known as a Marder (of the Marten-Weasel-Stoat family) twice chewed through the gearbox and cruise control cables. The damage was repaired free of charge the first time, but on the second occasion I was asked to pay DM 95.00. I then ascertained that Audi is aware of this problem and actually offers an 'anti-rodent kit' for the car at the not inconsiderable cost of £250. Since their cars are vulnerable to attack by these creatures, which occur not only in Germany but also in Cumbria, Northumbria and Scotland, I do not feel I should be compelled to pay for this essential modification. I enclose a file of correspondence with Audi UK.* "

The solution (supplied by a reader from Portchester) is an electronic deterrent which emits a signal with a frequency between 17 kHz and 19.5 kHz, with a sound pressure of between 90 dB and 110 dB at a distance of 30 cms. In an issue of the 'Weekend Telegraph' magazine, Bodywell Ltd had taken a full page to advertise its mail order 'Ultrasonic Pest Raider', a device costing £58.50, to protect barn, garage or home from these creatures. It is claimed to be far more effective than poisons that might, accidentally, do away with the family cat or dog. The telephone number is 0990 673546 (24 hours). The company's address is Bodywell Ltd, Freepost, PO Box 30, Blacknest Road, Alton, Hants GU34 4BR, and the company is MOPS registered. Another mail order supplier is Good Ideas, 7 Station Approach, Blackwater, Camberley, Surrey GU17 9PD, tel: 0990 502 054, which offers two devices, one at £39.95 and another at £19.95.

Acoustic parking

" *I am trying to locate an electronic car reversing aid which warns a driver of unseen obstacles in the path of a reversing car. I am told such products exist, but no motoring store appears to stock them. How reliable are these devices and where can they be obtained?* "

One product, which uses coloured lights as well as bleeps, was originally designed for reversing caravans. It is made by Brigade Electronics, is called the 'Backscan RI-OS', costs around £200 including fitting, and worked well fitted as an optional extra to a Ford Scorpio I tried. Brigade Electronics can be contacted on 0181 852 3261. Another device, known as the 'Proximeter', uses infra-red rather then ultrasonics, can detect small children and posts as well as bicycles, and emits bleeps which intensify as the object is approached. This costs £164.50 inc. VAT from The Proximeter Company Ltd, 16 Tiller Road, London E14 8PX, tel: 0171 345 5050. Two more are 'Smart Eye' from Ball Ltd (0181 574 0003) at £69.99 plus £5 p&p, and 'Ultrapark 2000' from Laver Technology (01279 436080) at £340 plus £6 p&p or £399 fitted. (Prices may change, so check before ordering.)

Cruising speed

" I recently purchased a Citroen Xsara automatic and would like to have cruise control fitted. Being elderly, it is a great relief to have this feature on long journeys. "

The longest-established supplier is Easycruise, of Unit 23A, Arthur Drive, Hoo Farm Industrial Estate, Kidderminster, Worcs DY11 7RA, tel: 01562 827730. Another is Cruise Control Services of 66–102 Cherrywood Road, Bordesley Green, Birmingham B9 4UD, tel:0121 771 3004. I know you are going to be sensible in its use, but please remember that if you set the cruise control to 70 mph, then fall asleep, 70 mph is the speed at which you will crash. You will not gradually lose speed before crashing as would be the case if you were controlling your speed with the accelerator. I should also warn you that some electronic speed control devices can be irritatingly jerky in their action. Nice comfortable car, the Xsara.

GOOD GARAGE GUIDE

In Summer 1996 we ran a reader's story about the difference between big garages in Britain and small garages in France. I felt that the contrast was more likely to be between bad garages and good garages generally, so I asked for readers' recommendations. The first 100 or so came in thick and fast, and suggestions have continued to arrive through 1997 and 1998. The result is this updated list which now reaches into the far corners of the land.

I'd like to set the scene with a quotation from an old and yellowed magazine story kindly sent in by a reader from Kinghorn. 'His garage is a murky wooden den lit up only by George's dazzling smile for a customer.'

Remember, the list is based purely on readers' recommendations (plus four from me). Inclusion is not a guarantee of quality, competence or good value, and neither The Daily Telegraph *nor me can accept any responsibility for the consequences of taking a car to any of the garages listed. Nevertheless, many of the testimonials I have received were fulsome in their praise, so if you are looking for good service, this list may be a good start. This is the original. Do not confuse it with any other 'Good Garage Guide'.*

- ABBERLEY: Alan Hole, P. Owen & Sons Ltd, Motor & Agricultural Engineers, The Abberley Garage, Abberley, Worcestershire, tel: 01299 896209.

- ABERDEEN: Harpers of Aberdeen. Main workshop, tel: 01224 697772. Rapid Fit (open 7 days), tel: 01224 663232. (Good, helpful, Ford franchise.)

- ALDEBURGH: Chris Copeman, Copeman & Son Engineering, Hazelwood Farm, Aldringham, nr Aldeburgh, Suffolk, tel: 01728 830640 (mobile: 0860 614518).

- ALTON: Neil Carpenter, Farringdon Industrial Centre, Alton, Hants, tel: 01420 587 403.

- AMERSHAM: T and F Motors, White Lion Road, Amersham, Bucks, tel: 01494 765286.

- ANDOVER: Chris Monaghan and Martin Dix, Intech GB Ltd, Unit 12B, Thruxton Industrial Estate, Thruxton Circuit, nr Andover, Hants, tel: 01264 773888. (Service and repair specialists for Japanese 'grey' imports from Honda Beat to Lexus Soarer Coupe.)

- ASHBOURNE: Hulland Ward Garage, Main Street, Hulland Ward, nr Ashbourne, Derbyshire, tel: 01335 370209.

- AYLESBURY: Ivor Miles, Churchway Garage, Churchway, Haddenham, Aylesbury, Bucks HP17 8HA, tel: 01844 291263.

- AYLESBURY: Lodge Garage (Aylesbury Mazda) Ltd, Bicester Road, Kingswood, Aylesbury, Bucks HP18 0QJ, tel: 01296 770405.

- BALLATER: J. Pringle, Victoria Garage, Ballater, Grampian AB35 5QQ, tel: 013397 55525.

- BEDALE: John Gill Ltd, Bedale, N. Yorks, tel: 01677 423124. (Daihatsu dealer and general repairs.)

- BEXHILL-ON-SEA: Peter Johnson, Motor Engineer, Unit 3, de la Warr Mews, Station Road, Bexhill-on-Sea, East Sussex TN40 1RD, tel: 01424 224169.

- BEXLEYHEATH: Paul at PDQ Car Services, Bexleyheath, Kent, tel: 0181 303 1618, mobile: 0831 138463. (Best to phone first for directions.)

- BILLINGSHURST: Geoffrey Sizzy (Automobiles), Wisborough Green (nr Billingshurst), West Sussex, tel: 01403 700661. (Independent Peugeot specialist – sales, service, very good after-sales service.)

- BIRMINGHAM: R. Newman, Motor Engineers, rear of J.H. Hancox

Ltd) Alcester Road, Portway, Birmingham B48 7JA, tel: 01564 824996.

- BIRMINGHAM: G. & B. Clements, Baldwins Lane Service Station, Baldwins Lane, Hall Green, Birmingham B28 0XB, tel: 0121 744 5453.

- BOGNOR REGIS: Middleton Garage, 169 Middleton Road, Middleton-on-Sea, Bognor Regis, tel: 01243 58276. (Very helpful Fiat franchise.)

- BOSTON: Mick Barsley, Barsley Motor Engineers, 78 High Street, Boston, Lincs, tel: 01205 355396.

- BRACKLEY: BBR (Brodie Brittain Racing Ltd), Oxford Road, Brackley, Northants (300 metres from Southernmost roundabout on A43 into Brackley), tel: 01280 702389. (Tuning, turbocharging, engine management and diagnostics specialists. Motor fault-finding helpline: 0897 161123, 9.00–5.30, calls cost a maximum of £1.47 a minute.)

- BRIDGWATER: Tim Stiles Racing, Units 5 & 6 Transform Estate, Wylds Road, Bridgwater, Somerset TA6 4DH, tel: 01278 453036. (VW/Audi performance modifications at reasonable prices and labour rates.)

- BRIDGWATER: Stogursey Motors, High Street, Stogursey (8 miles from Bridgwater near Hinkley Point power station), tel: 01278 732237. (Car, van and motorcycle repairs and MOTs.)

- BROADWAY: Alan Aston Motor Engineers, Childswickham, nr Broadway, Worcs, tel: 01386 852311.

- BROMLEY: Ted and Neil Craker, The Vehicle Test Centre, 107 Southlands Road, Bromley, Kent BR2 9QT, tel: 0181 460 6666. (Very well equipped and sensibly priced servicing workshop/MOT test centre, with two 'rolling road' brake testers and full diagnostic equipment.)

- BURTON-ON-TRENT: Peter Sharp, European Car Specialists, Parker Street, Burton-on-Trent, tel: 01283 540414.

- BUSHMILLS, CO. ANTRIM: James Wylie Auto Repairs, 40A Ballyclough Road, Bushmills, Co. Antrim BT57 8UZ, tel: 01265732096. (Citroen specialist, as well as other makes.)

- CANTERBURY: Ashford Road Service Station, Chilham, Canterbury, Kent CT4 8EE, tel: 01227 730223.

- CANTERBURY: Hewitt Motors Ltd, Rhodans Town, Canterbury, Kent, tel: 01227 464386.

- CARDIFF: Continental Cars (Cardiff) Ltd, tel: 01222 542400. (Mercedes franchise; treat elderly drivers with extra consideration.)

- CARNFORTH: The Mountain Family, Lune View Garage, Melling, Carnforth, Lancs LA6 2RB, tel: 015 242 21457.

- CARNFORTH: Mill Brow Garage, Kirkby Lonsdale, Carnforth, Lancs, tel: 015 242 71248.

- CASTLEFORD: Castleford VW Spares, Methley Road, Castleford, W. Yorks, tel: 01977 518254. (VW/Audi servicing and parts.)

- CHELMSFORD: Mr & Mrs John Plumb and son Steve, Central Garage, Latchingdon, nr Chelmsford, Essex, tel: 01621 740284.

- CHERTSEY: Speedtest, Unit A, Gogmore Lane, Chertsey, Surrey, tel: 01932 568921. (Honest, straight servicing and MOT centre. Good with Citroens and Renaults.)

- CHESSINGTON: Mole Valley TVR, Chessington, Surrey, tel: 0181 394 1114. (Good TVR dealer – two recommendations.)

- CHIPPENHAM: David Giddings, 14 Brook Street, Chippenham, Wilts SN14 0HN. (Specialist cars including Alfas and Jensens.)

- CHISLEHURST: Paul and Tony at PDQ, 1a Albany Road, Chislehurst, Kent, tel: 0181 295 0121. (BMW and Jaguar specialists.)

- CREWKERNE: Misterton Garage, Misterton, Crewkerne, Somerset, tel: 01460 72997. (Ford retail dealer – good for servicing and repairs at reasonable prices.)

- CWMCARN: Bijou Motor Services, rear of 99–101 Newport Road, Cwmcarn, Gwent NP1 7LZ, tel: 01495 271033. (Citroen specialists.)

- CROWBOROUGH: John Cottenham, Care's Garage, School Lane, St Johns, Crowborough, East Sussex TN6 1SE, tel: 01892 653519. (VW.)

- DAVENTRY: Dave Carvell Cars, Staverton, nr Daventry, Northants, tel: 01327 300739.

- DERBY: Citrognome, Great Northern Road, Derby, tel: 01332 345869. (Citroen specialists.)

- DORCHESTER: Loders, Dorchester, Dorset, tel: 01305 267881. (Good franchised dealer, Audi service.)

- DORKING: Steve Bradstock, The Coach House, Beare Green, Dorking, Surrey, tel: 01306 713424.

- DRUMNDROCHIT: J.E. Menzies and Son Ltd, Lewiston Garage, Drumndrochit, Inverness, tel: 01456 450212.

- DURHAM: Volksparts, Langley Moor, near Durham, tel: 0191 378 0284. (German car specialists – Audi, BMW, Mercedes, VW.)

- EAST HORSLEY: Philip Stonely, The Body Workshop, Forest Road Garage, Forest Road, Effingham Junction, Surrey KT24 5HE, tel: 01483 284805.

- EASTBOURNE: Visick Cars Ltd, Birch Close, Lottbridge Drove, Eastbourne BN23 6PE, tel: 01323 722244.

- ELVANFOOT: South of Scotland Coachworks, Elvanfoot, Lanarkshire (adjacent to A74M), tel: 01864 502236. (General repairs and service.)

- EMSWORTH: Lillywhite Bros Ltd, 40 Queen Street, Emsworth, Hants PO10 7BL, tel: 01243 372336.

- ENFIELD: Stephen James, London Road, Enfield EN2 6JJ, tel: 0181 367 2626. (Friendly BMW agent with sensibly priced servicing.)

- EPSOM: King Automatics, 'The Chalk Pit', College Road, Epsom, Surrey KT17 4JA, tel: 01372 728769. (Automatic transmissions of all types, including CVTs.)

- EPSOM: Kwik-Fit, 166 East Street, Epsom, Surrey, tel: 01372 739955. (Replaced a reader's tyre valve free of charge.)

- EPSOM: Drift Bridge Garage, Epsom, Surrey. (VW.)

- EXETER: Volkswagen Services, 11 Coombe Street, Exeter, Devon EX1 1DB, tel: 01392 493737. (VW servicing.)

- EXETER: Carrs of Exeter, tel: 01392 823988. (Good Mercedes and Porsche service.)

- EXETER: Snow and Stephens, King Edward Street, Exeter, tel: 01392 256552. (General car repairs.)

- EXETER: Rockbeare Motor Services, Rockbeare, Exeter EX5 2DZ, tel: 01404 822410. (General car repairs.)

- EXMOUTH: Karl Brigham, KB Auto Services and Repairs, Victoria Way, Exmouth, Devon, tel: 01395 223330.

- EXMOUTH: Bentleys Garage, Chapel Hill (High Street), Exmouth, Devon, tel: 01395 272048.

- FAREHAM: Peter Cooper, Fareham, Hants, tel: 01329 288233. (Good, helpful VW franchise.)

- FERRING: John Cooper Garages, Ferring, West Sussex, tel: 01903 504455. (Very helpful Honda franchise.)

- FINCHAMPSTEAD: Cresswells, California Crossroads, Finchampstead, Berks, tel: 01734 732201.

- FORRES: Pedigree Cars, Forres, Morayshire, tel: 01309 672555. (Citroen garage.)

- FRENCHAY: Frenchay Garage, Frenchay Common, Frenchay, Bristol BS16 1NB, tel: 0117 956 7303.

- GARSTANG: H. and J. Kitching, Hornby's Garage, Lydiate Lane, Claughton on Brock, Garstang, Lancs, tel: 01995 640229.

- GRAVENHURST: Chris Case, Town Farm Garage, Campton Road, Gravenhurst, Beds, tel: 01462 711017.

- GUILDFORD: A.H. Autos, Unit 11, Foundation Units, Westfield Road, Slyfield Green, Guildford, tel: 01483 303942. (VW/Audi specialists.)

- HARROGATE: Mr Greenwood, Western Garage, Valley Mount, Harrogate, N. Yorks H62 0JG, tel: 01423 502902.

- HEMEL HEMPSTEAD: V.P. Autos, Hemel Hempstead, Herts, tel: 01442 68163.

- HENLOW: Alan Turner, Henlow Car Centre, Henlow, Beds, tel: 01462 814668.

- HERSHAM: Colin Marshall or Keith Rhoods, Wheelbase Garage, 43 Queen's Road, Hersham, Surrey, tel: 01932 252515 or 01932 252881. (VW/Audi specialists.)

- HEXHAM: Almond and Scott, Haugh Lane Garage, Haugh Lane, Hexham, Northumberland, tel: 01434 60 4163 or 0836 532999.

- HOLMFIRTH: M and M Engineering Services, Clarence Mills, Holmbridge, Holmfirth HD7 1NE, tel: 01484 687706. (Citroen.)

- HOLT: Eddy Lynton, Academy Garage, Castle Street, Holt, Clwyd LL13

9YL, tel: 01829 270781.

- HOUNSLOW: Franco Motors, 29 Vine Place, Hounslow TW3 3UE, tel: 0181 570 3798.

- HYTHE: Auto Pat, 3 Hardley Industrial Estate, Hardley, nr Hythe, Hants, tel: 01703 804163.

- ILFORD: Whichford Rover, 404 Eastern Avenue, Gants Hill, Ilford, Essex IG2 6NW, tel: 0181 554 8888. (Rover dealer, fixed faults on recently purchased used cars at no charge and without question.)

- ILKESTON: Dave's Motors, West Street, Ilkeston, Derbyshire, tel: 0115 9441 886.

- JARROW: David Ellis, Jarrow Coachworks, Curlew Road, Jarrow, Tyne and Wear, tel. 0191 4892715, mobile: 0860 424813.

- LANGPORT: J.A. Scott, Langport Motor Co., Westover Trading Estate, Langport, Somerset, tel: 01458 251100. (Citroen specialist.)

- LEAMINGTON SPA: Brian Ricketts, tel: 01926 451545 (VW/Audi.)

- LEAMINGTON SPA: Midland Autocar Co., Russell Street, Leamington Spa, Warks CV32 5QB, tel. 01926 421171. (General repairs and service.)

- LEAMINGTON SPA: Bull Ring Garage, The Bull Ring, Harbury, Leamington Spa, Warks CN33 9HR, tel: 01926 61275. (Excellent local garage.)

- LEDBURY: R. and J. Mathews, Blacklands Garage, Canon Frome, nr Ledbury, Hereford and Worcester, tel: 01531 640374.

- LEEDS: David Wood, Whinbrook Service Station, Whinbrook Crescent (off Scott Hall Road), Leeds LS17 5PN, tel: 0113 268 9983. (VW/Audi.)

- LEEDS: IVC (Independent VW/Audi Centre), Globe Road, off Water Lane, Leeds LS11 5QS, tel: 0113 242 0875. (VW/Audi.)

- LEEK: Andy Jackson of A&C Vehicle Services, Ball Haye Road, Leek, Staffs, tel: 01538 398227. (VW/Audi. Bends over backwards to help – have received many reader endorsements.)

- LEIGHTON BUZZARD: Tom Goodman Motors, Comptons Yard, Grovebury Road, Leighton Buzzard LU7 8TS, tel: 01525 375972.

- LEWES: Morris Road Garage, Western Road, Lewes, East Sussex, tel: 01273 472434. (Independent. Bosch fuel injection specialists.)

- LICHFIELD: Central Garage (Lichfield) Ltd, Queen Street, Lichfield, Staffs WS13 6QD, tel: 01543 262826. (BMW and Mercedes.)

- LISKEARD: Ken Rowe, Rowe's Garage Ltd, Dobwalls, Liskeard, Cornwall PL14 6JA, tel: 01579 320218. (Citroen franchise.)

- LITTLEBOROUGH: J. Stanton, Stanton's Motor Garage, Brookfield Mill, Canal Street, Littleborough, nr Rochdale, Lancs, tel: 01706 370166.

- LIVERPOOL: Orlando Heeson, Landers Autos, 19–22a Cathedral Road, Liverpool L6 0AT, tel: 0151 263 4913.

- LOANHEAD: Stewart McLennan Garage, 44 Lawrie Terrace, Loanhead, Midlothian EH20 9ET, tel: 0131 440 0597.

- LONDON E5: Tony, D.A.M. Car Repairs, 1–8 Broadway Mews, Clapton Common, London E5 9AF, tel: 0181 800 7121.

- LONDON N4: G. Horscraft, Supertune Motor Engineers, 2A Beatrice Road, Stroud Green, London N4 4PD, tel: 0171 272 7678.

- LONDON N4: Nick Sandamas, G. and N. Garages Ltd, 54–58 Wightman Road, Harringay, London N4 1RU, tel: 0181 340 331. (Independent Saab specialist.)

- LONDON SE6: Gonella Brothers, 9–13 Catford Hill, Catford, London SE6, tel: 0181 690 0060. (Alfa, Fiat and Lancia specialists.)

- LONDON SW2: Hearn Bros Ltd, The Hill Garage, 94 Brixton Hill, London SW2, tel: 0181 674 2888. (Twenty-four recommendations.)

- LONDON W8: ACE Cars of Kensington, tel: 0171 938 4333. (Specialises in older Saabs – 900, 99, 96.)

- LONDON W12: AC Automotive, 247–251 Goldhawk Road, London W12, tel: 0181 741 9993. (American car parts and servicing.)

- LOWER BASILDON: Les Allum, Allum Auto Services, Reading Road, Lower Basildon, Berks RG8 9NL, tel: 01491 671726.

- LYMINGTON: Dory's Garage Ltd, Sway Park, Station Road, Sway, Hants, tel: 01590 683432. (Citroen specialists.)

- MANCHESTER: Derek Boardman, Units 12–25, Morton Street Industrial Estate, Failsworth, Manchester, tel: 0161 681 0456. (VW/Audi.)

- MANCHESTER: Westron, 7 Nell Lane, Manchester M21 8UE, tel: 0161 881 1061. (Citroen suspension specialists.)

- MALVERN: Denver Davis, The Station Garage, Thorngrove Road, Malvern, Worcs, tel: 01684 574088.

- MERSTHAM, John Witty, Witmun Engineering, 67 Nutfield Road, Merstham, Surrey RH1 3ER, tel: 01737 644828. (Citroen specialists.)

- MIDDLESBROUGH: Dave Stott Motors, Charlotte Street, Middlesbrough, tel: 01642 224805. (Independent Citroen specialists.)

- MORETON-IN-MARSH: N.E. Repairs, Hospital Road, Moreton-in-Marsh, Gloucs, tel: 01608 650405.

- NEEDHAM MARKET: Richard Robinson, Robinson's Motor Engineers, Debtrac Centre, Needham Market, Suffolk, tel: 01449 722240.

- NEWTON ABBOT: K. Tapper, Decoy Motors, Unit 10 Silverhills Road,

Decoy Trading Estate, Newton Abbot TQ12 5LZ, tel: 01626 68701.

- NORTH SHIELDS: John Gallagher, Collingwood Garage, North Shields, tel: 0191 296 2888.

- NORWICH: Peter Whitley Motor Services, 7 Low Road, Drayton, Norwich NR8 6AA, tel: 01603 860154.

- NOTTINGHAM: David Marks Garages, tel: 01159 405370). (Jaguar specialists.)

- ORPINGTON: Chelsfield Motor Works, Court Lodge Farm, Warren Road, Orpington, Kent BR6 6ER, tel: 01689 823200.

- OULTON BROAD: John Pope, Pope Brothers, Station Garage, Bridge End, Oulton Broad, Lowestoft, tel: 01502 573797.

- OXFORD: North Oxford Garage Ltd, 280 Banbury Road, Oxford OX2 7EB, tel: 01865 319000. (Helpful BMW franchise.)

- PENRHYNDEUDRAETH: Dafydd Williams, Garreg Lwyd, Penrhyndeudraeth, Gwynedd LL48 6AW, tel: 01766 770203. (secondhand Twingos, servicing, advice and 'hard to get' parts.)

- PENZANCE: Autostop Service Centre, Longrock, nr Penzance, Cornwall, tel: 01736 330300. (Excellent, non-franchised service and repair garage.)

- PERIVALE: AC Delco, 19 Wadsworth Road, Unit 14, Perivale, Middx., tel: 0181 810 4595. (American car parts and servicing.)

- PETERBOROUGH: Brian Pitts, 'The Complete Automobilist', 35–37 Main Street, Baston, Peterborough PE6 9NX, tel: 01778 560444.

- PETERHEAD: Harpers of Aberdeen, Rapid Fit (open 7 days), tel: 01779 474849. (Good, helpful, Ford Rapid Fit centre.)

- PEWSEY: Stevens Cars, Nicol's Yard (rear of Post Office), Pewsey, tel: 01672 563330.

- PLYMOUTH: Simon Rouse, Peverell Garage, Weston Park Road, Peverell, Plymouth, Devon PL3 4NS, tel: 01752 266099.

- POOLE: Connellys, Ashley Road, Upper Parkstone, Poole, Dorset, tel: 01202 738700.

- PORTHCAWL: John Rogers, Station Hill Garage, Porthcawl, Mid Glam., tel: 01656 786705.

- PORTMADOC: The Glanaber Garage, Borth-y-Gest, Portmadoc, Gwynedd, tel: 01766 512364.

- PRESTON: J.C. and M. Davis, Garstang Road Garage, Garstang Road, Pilling, Preston PR3 6AQ, tel: 01253 790322. (General repairs, but good with diesels and Citroens.)

- READING: Clever Cars Ltd, Prospect Mews, Prospect Street, Reading, tel: 01734 576405. (Citroen specialists.)

- SADDLEWORTH: Greenfield Service Station, Chew Valley Road, Greenfield, Saddleworth, nr Oldham, Lancs, tel: 01457 873700.

- ST ALBANS: Godfrey Davis St Albans, 105 Ashley Road, St Albans, Herts AL1 5GD, tel: 01727 859155. (Good Ford servicing facility capable of correctly diagnosing problems.)

- SANDERSTEAD: Steven Pengelly, Vorne Motorsport, 145 Limpsfield Road, Sanderstead, Surrey, tel: 0181 651 5344.

- SEVENOAKS: Antwis Engineering, Rye Lane, Dunton Green, Sevenoaks, Kent, tel: 01732 450386. (Very good with BMWs.)

- SHEFFIELD: Bridgco Garage, 160 Broad Oaks, Sheffield 9, tel: 0114 2441775.

- SIDCUP: Steve King, King's Auto Services, 313–315 Blackfen Road, Blackfen, Sidcup, Kent SA15 9NG, tel: 0181 298 9225.

- SOUTHAMPTON: E. and J. Jarvis, Motor Engineers, Onslow Road, Southampton, tel: 01703 229297.

- SOUTHAMPTON: Hilton Motors, Bond Road Garage, Bitterne Park, Southampton SO18 1LH, tel: 01703 555600. (General service, repair, sales garage and automatic transmission specialist.)

- SOUTH MOLTON: Andrew Geen, Geen's Garage, South Molton, North Devon, tel: 01769 572395.

- SOUTHSEA: John Skerratt, Owl Motor Services, Richmond Road, Southsea, Hants, tel: 01705 736393.

- STEBBING: Bob Rains, Drakeswell Garage, Bran End, Stebbing, Essex, tel: 01371 856391.

- STOCKPORT: Chris or Stewart, Tenby Garage, Lavenders Brow, Churchgate, Stockport, Cheshire SK1 1YW, tel: 0161 480 5075.

- STOCKPORT: The Dave Arnitt Citroen Repair Centre, Arthur Street, Reddish, Stockport, tel: 0161 432 0636. (Citroen specialist.)

- STOCKTON: Shearborne Engineering, Preston Farm, Stockton-on-Tees, tel: 01642 677744. (Independent Jaguar specialists.)

- SUTTON COLDFIELD: G. Chamberlain and Sons, Four Oaks Garage, Lichfield Road, Four Oaks, Sutton Coldfield, W. Midlands B74 2UH, tel: 0121 308 0309. Dave Buckland, D.J. Buckland (Motor Engineer), rear of 162 Birmingham Road, Wylde Green, Sutton Coldfield, tel: 0121 355 7634 (out of hours tel: 0121 350 6881.)

- SWINDON: Fish Bros, Elgin Drive, Swindon, Wilts SM2 6DU, tel: 01793 512685. (Fiat, Alfa Romeo and Mitsubishi franchise – good at diagnosing unsolved faults on Alfas.)

- TAUNTON: Paul Lyall, Fairwater Garage, Staplegrove Road, Taunton TA1 1DF, tel: 01823 277268.

- WADEBRIDGE: John Smith, Old Forge Garage, St Miniver, Wadebridge, Cornwall, tel: 01208 863323.

- WANTAGE: Paul Rivers, Hillcrest Garage, Reading Road, West Hendred, nr Wantage, Oxon OX12 8RH, tel: 01235 833363. T.A. Collins Motor Engineers, Denchworth Road, Wantage, Oxon, tel: 01235 768321. (Volvo specialist.)

- WARRINGTON: Dave Roundell Services, Milner Street, Warrington, Cheshire, tel: 01925 635958.

- WEOBLEY: John Simpson, Whitehill Garage, Weobley, Hereford HR4 8QZ, tel: 01544 318268.

- WEST BROMWICH: The Sun Garage Company, Sandwell Road, West Bromwich, West Midlands B70 8TG, tel: 0121 553 0296.

- WEST MALLING: B. Butler, The Saab Sanctuary, 'Almandene', Woodgate Road, Ryarsh, West Malling, Kent ME19 5LH, tel: 01732 872722.

- WESTON-SUPER-MARE: Howards Citroen (tel: 01934 644644) and Howards Rover (tel: 01934 643434), both of Hildersheim Bridge, Weston-Super-Mare BS23 3PT.

- WESTON-SUPER-MARE: Howards Peugeot (tel: 01934 636049), Searle Crescent, Weston-Super-Mare BS23 3YX.

- WESTON-SUPER-MARE: Howards Nissan (tel: 01934 416454), Herluin Way, Weston-Super-Mare BS23 3YN. (Howards are franchised agents for Citroen, Rover, Peugeot and Nissan – all, very unusually, in the same town.)

- WEYBRIDGE: S.S. Motors, 16c Hanwell Lane, Weybridge Business Park, Weybridge, Surrey KT15 2SD, tel: 01932 821555. (Mercedes specialist run by Mercedes-trained ex-franchise service manager.)

- WINDERMERE: Keith Donnelly, Oldfield Road Garage, Oldfield Road,

Windermere, Cumbria LA23 2BY, tel: 015 394 46710.

- WINDSOR: New and Son, West End Service Station, Dadworth Road, Windsor, Berks, tel: 01753 862078/851685.

- WOLVERHAMPTON: Roger Williams, Oxley Service Station, Fordhouse Road, Wolverhampton, tel: 01902 787386.

- WORTHING: Rod Denton, Denton Motors, 1–3 Park Road, Worthing, W. Sussex, tel: 01903 233790.

- WRAYSBURY: George Williams, Lakeside Garage, 48 Welley Road, Wraysbury, Middx TW19 5JD, tel: 01784 482158.

- YEOVIL: Eastside Garage, Lufton Trading Estate, Yeovil, Somerset, tel: 01935 31412. (Citroen specialist.)

- YEOVIL: Auto Wizard, Penhill Trading Estate, Yeovil, Somerset, tel: 01935 410532.

- YORK: John Galley Motors, Pocklington Industrial Estate, Pocklington, York, tel: 01759 303716. (VW/Audi.)

European garages

- FRANCE (CHERBOURG): Garage Pichard, 124 Rue du Val de Saire, Cherbourg 51000. (Rover agent.)

- SPAIN (VALENCIA): Imperauto, Valencia, tel: 342 06 22. (Land Rover.)

HORSES FOR COURSES

Diesel automatics

" *I have a 'G' reg. Jaguar Sovereign with 83,000 miles which I love dearly, even though it's only the underpowered 2.9 litre version. Now I'm retired I want to sell it and buy a lower-mileage automatic diesel for which I have £15,000–£18,000 earmarked. I particularly want a diesel because of the huge price differential between petrol and diesel in France. What choice is there of diesel automatics?* "

I'm going to try and list them all in alphabetical order. Audi 80TDI, Audi A4TDI, Audi A6TDI, BMW new 320TD, BMW 325TD, BMW 325TDS, BMW 525TD, BMW 525TDS, Citroen ZX Avantage and Aura D to 1996, Citroen Xantia LXD and SXD to 1996 (Xantia 1.9TD auto from Spring '98), Citroen XM 2.1TD (but not 2.5TD), Ford Granada TD, Ford Scorpio TD, Land Rover Discovery TDi, Range Rover TDi and TD six, Mercedes Benz 190 2.0D and 2.5D, Mercedes C Class 220D, 250D and 250TD, Mercedes E Class 300D and new E Class 300TD, Mitsubishi Shogun 2.8TD, Old Nissan Primera D (not turbo); Peugeot 605 2.1TD, Suzuki Vitara TD, Vauxhall new Astra DI, Vauxhall Omega TD, VW Golf Mk III Ecomatic (very rare), VW Golf Mk IV TDI 90 (from mid-1998), VW New Passat TDI, VW Sharan TDI 110, VW Caravelle Multivan 2.4SD, Volvo

S70TDi. Though relatively expensive, a Mercedes is likely to be the longest lasting. My personal choice would be a VW new Passat TDI 110.

Driven back to the car

" I presently commute to work by rail but, faced with another increase in fares in January, I have decided to buy a new car and put two fingers up at Great Eastern Railway. This will mean driving a total of 300 miles a week in fairly heavy traffic and, while comfort will be a big consideration (I am just over six feet tall), fuel economy will be of primary concern. I am expecting to spend up to £11,500 and quite like the new Escort and Polo, but would welcome your recommendations. "

It's going to have to be a diesel, and your budget buys you a Seat Ibiza TDI which, besides having bags of poke and being fun to drive, will give you 55–60 mpg. 'Friends of the Earth' may be furious that you have been driven back to a car, but the villain of the piece is the price of your season ticket.

S-Cargo?

" I am trying to find a vehicle I have only ever seen once while I was working in London. It is a Nissan (van-type) S-Cargo – so named due to its resemblance to the spiral-shelled gastropod. It looks like a 'fun' car and I was hoping to import one to Ireland. What is it based on? Is it available with rear seats? How much can I expect to pay for a reasonable secondhand version? And will I face any particular problems bringing one over here? "

I have only ever seen one at auction, a 17,000-mile 92K which fetched £5,400 in March 1993. But that was a one-off and I think you'll have to pay a fair bit more than this. Thoroughbred

Cars on 0181 501 2727 had a 36,000-mile 89F S-Cargo for £6,995. Melvyn Rutter at The Morgan Garage, Little Hallingbury, near Bishop's Stortford, Herts (01279 725725) wanted £6,995 plus VAT for a 30,000-km 90G. Unlike the other Nissan retro-specials, the S-Cargo was Sunny rather than Micra based and had a 1.5 litre engine with automatic transmission. I think they all had a folding rear bench seat (but no rear seatbelts) and a full length canvas sunroof. Weird is the word. Your best bet is to talk to an import specialist such as Julie Knight on 01635 867694. But from May 1998, all trade imports less than ten years old which are not EC Type-Approved have faced a Single Vehicle Type Approval test and quotas on the numbers which can be commercially imported in any one year. Intech at Thruxton circuit specialise in servicing these cars, and any other 'grey' Japanese imports (tel: 01264 773888).

Automatic 4×4

" *My weekend cottage is on an icy hill and I should be glad if you could recommend a 4×4 vehicle with automatic gears and power steering. At present I drive a 'J' reg. Honda Shuttle, so I don't want a big chunky 4×4.* "

Your best bet is a Subaru Impreza 2.0GL five-door automatic.

Astra to Nexia?

" *I am thinking of changing my Astra GLS automatic, due for its first MOT in January, for a Daewoo. On mentioning this to two car salesmen, they said the Daewoo is really just an old-model Astra and that its depreciation is enormous. But it can hardly be worse than that of the Astra,* " *which had dropped £7,000 in less than three years. The package that Daewoo offers looks very attractive. What is your opinion?* "

The fact is, all an awful lot of motorists want is a three- or four-year-old automatic car with power steering for between £3,000 and £5,000 – and this means a ready market for a Nexia automatic, however dated its looks, ride and fuel consumption. Open-market Daewoo values dropped faster than trousers after a curry, but soon bounced back to a level where the cars look great value for money.

Proton praised

" *After reading of the dubious 'after sales service' provided by some manufacturers I thought you might like to hear of one who takes it seriously. I have owned a Proton Persona for three years and have enjoyed 42,000 miles of trouble-free motoring. On a recent trip to the Dales, the nearside indicator glass fell off. Cost of plastic 5p. Replacement cost of whole unit £49. I wrote to Proton and the company agreed to re-imburse the cost of the unit. The car is easy to drive and hard to fault. So here's a good product backed by good service. It may not be considered a 'prestige car' by some of the snobby motoring correspondents, but at least it spends most of its life on the road rather than off the road in yet another failed attempt to put it right.* "

I agree. The Persona is quite a good car – the 1.6 is much livelier than a 1.6 Escort. The Persona I drove three years ago was spoiled only by a curious gear-change and more than a few rattles – yet it handled and drove very well. You're right that Protons do have an image problem – largely caused by the hideous body kits and laughable wheel trims fitted to some of the older 'MPI' models. But in the 1998 BBC *Top Gear*/J.D. Power Customer Satisfaction Survey,

Proton Personas scored 90% and came twelfth out of 120 cars.

Zetec-S Fiesta

" *I am thinking of buying a Fiesta as a retirement car. The salesman has recommended the 1.25 litre engine, as opposed to the 1.3 litre engine. The 1.25 is a 'Zetec-S'. Can you give any reason for paying £750 extra to have this engine rather than the 1.3?* "

Yes. The Zetec-S 1.25 litre engine is brilliant, but the old 1.3 litre pushrod engine is no more than mediocre. With the 1.25 and power steering, the Fiesta LX (or its Mazda 121 counterpart) drives like a little GTi – it's spirited and fun and handles very well indeed. However, they do seem to suffer from early brake disc wear.

Fiesta footnote

" *I was interested to read your comments on the Fiesta 1.25 16v. I bought one of these cars a month ago and am delighted with it. I used to run much larger cars until I retired, then downsized from Sierras and Cavaliers to a Peugeot 306 1.6XT and finally to the Fiesta. I can assure you it's been no hardship at all. It does, however, tend to get hit by the insurance companies who put it in Group 5 – the same as my previous 306 1.6XT. Maybe that's another reason why Ford do not fit the 1.25 engine to the new Ka.* "

The 1.3 litre Ka is in the extremely low Group 2, compared to Group 4 for a 'new' Fiesta with the 1.3 engine and Group 6 for a Fiesta 'Classic' with the 1.3 engine. The reasons for this are the great strides Ford has recently made in what insurers call the 'damageablilty and repairability' of its cars. The 'new' Fiesta is very much

better than the 'old' Fiesta in this respect. But the Ka goes one further by having soft plastic bumpers and mudguards capable of withstanding minor carpark knocks without damage. This is the sort of feature which *Telegraph* readers have been crying out for over the past few years.

Non-sporty automatic required

" My wife and I are retired and drive a 2 litre Cavalier automatic which we bought new eight years ago. Though the car is garaged and covers no more than 5,000 miles a year, we have experienced some mechanical troubles including the need for a £1,450 reconditioned gearbox eighteen months ago. I am struck by the price and specification of the 2 litre Chrysler Neon, for which the dealer is local to us. Though this car has been available for 18 months, I have not seen many about. Why is this? And what other 'non-sporty' automatics should we consider? "

Yes, the Neon is fairly good value and has a good warranty. Though the autobox is only a three-speeder, I prefer it to the manual because it masks the coarseness of the engine much more effectively. The Neon also has good features such as standard air conditioning (also now standard on the Citroen Xantia, Ford Mondeo, Peugeot 406 and Vauxhall Vectra) and electrically folding door mirrors. You have not seen many Neons because not many have been imported – and so far this has helped Neons retain their value. To my mind, the best automatics in the price range you're looking at are made by Honda, Mitsubishi and Toyota. The big news here is the forthcoming Nissan Primera 2.0 litre CVT – the first CVT with a 2 litre engine. Incidentally, your Cavalier gearbox would have lasted better with an annual ATF and filter change. Once again, following fleet-based skimped servicing recommendations has resulted in premature gearbox failure.

Happy Neon owner

" Last July I wrote to you asking for information on the then new Chrysler Neon. I weighed up the pros and cons you provided, then ordered the car for August delivery. A couple of minor faults were rectified immediately, and in compensation we were offered 12 months free servicing. Since then we have covered 8,000 miles in a car with which both myself and my wife are completely satisfied in every way. There's just one problem. In 35 years of motoring, having owned twelve cars and driven eight company cars, I have never driven a car which attracted so much attention. One poor pedestrian was so enraptured by the vehicle he managed to walk straight into a lamp post. "

Thanks for letting me know. Information on customer satisfaction with this rare car is hard to come by and this will be helpful to other readers considering a Neon.

Sitting up

" *I am an eighty-year-old man, six feet tall with long legs. I have bad arthritis of the knees. My present car is a Honda Accord 2.3SRi which I am quite satisfied with. But it sits rather low on the road, making it hard to get in and out of. Could you please suggest a car that sits a bit higher, price not above £20,000?* "

Your Honda dealer may be able to help you here, with a Honda Shuttle. From your point of view, this five- to seven-seater, fully automatic, air-conditioned car is ideal. It's higher than a saloon, but not as high as some other MPVs. The front seats are fully adjustable and extremely comfortable. The rearmost bench very cleverly folds into the floor when not in use. And it actually drives extremely well – second only to the manual Galaxy/Sharan VR6. The four-speed automatic gearbox in the Shuttle is one of the very best you can buy.

Saab replacement

" *We run an ageing and well-worn 1986 Saab 900 saloon, but the time has come to look for a replacement. Our main priorities are space for family camping holidays, reliability in an area prone to flash floods, safety for our two young children, economy, and better 'response' than our present car gives. We have thought of a 16v or a 9000, or should we look for an estate car? Our budget is £5,000.* "

The hatchback versions of your present car have a low sill and huge luggage capacity which makes them ideal for camping. Old 900s also enjoy a growing classic status. Moving up slightly, I have always liked the 9000CD 2.3 which has bags of space and usually comes with leather, sunroof, alloys and maybe aircon. But they also all come with a 'cat' and direct ignition problems are not unknown, so whenever one popped up at auction in the £5,000 bracket I kept my hands in my pockets. The 'bargain' big estate car is a Citroen XM, and you may even get the 40 mpg 2.1TD with a few miles under its wheels within your budget, but you will have to be prepared for the odd electrical glitch. £5,000 also gets you into Mondeo estate territory. These are very strong, quite heavy, fairly spacious cars and, apart from the clutch, reasonably cheap to fix when things go wrong. Even the cats are only about £200. Finally, don't dismiss an older Renault Espace with around 100,000 miles. I know one which has done well over 200,000 miles of extremely hard work with very few problems.

£3,000 car

" My son is 17 years of age and is learning to drive. Once he has passed his test, what cars costing around £3,000 should I consider buying him? My main considerations are, of course, safety and insurance costs. "

First put him through a BSM 'Pass Plus' course which covers types of driving not included in the driving test (motorways, night-time, fast A roads, etc.). I think that the current best 'starter' car is a pre-cat Fiat Uno Mk II with the 999 cc 'Fire' engine, introduced in January 1990 on a 'G' plate. The bodies of Mk II Unos (not Mk Is) are electro-galvanized, the previously rust-prone rear hatch is plastic and, properly maintained, a 999 cc 'Fire' engine is good for 200,000 miles. Insurance is Group 3. Whatever you do, don't go for the old 903 cc 'Formula' pushrod engine, despite its Group 2 insurance category. Another car in the £3,000 region which isn't bad is the newer-shape 1.0 litre 16v Nissan Micra, but don't buy if the timing chain rattles. Basic 1.0 litre and 1.1 litre Fiestas are the best Fiestas. Nicest looking (but not very strong) is the Peugeot 205.

£5,000 car

" My son has just been accepted by the RAF as a trainee pilot. He currently runs a rusting 5-door Metro. He will be making regular 300-mile round trips from Cranwell to Tynemouth. What would you suggest in keeping with his new image, costing below say £5,000, and not too expensive to insure? "

The best bargains on the supersites are Daewoo Esperos. Allowing a typically low supersite profit margin, he should be able to pick up a two-year-old 20,000-mile Espero 1.8CDi (with air conditioning) for £5,000–£5,500.

£50,000 car

" I will be attaining the big Five-Zero next May and, to ease the pain, have set aside around 50 grand to invest in a sports car or coupe. The car doesn't necessarily need to be brand-new (value for money has always been important to me), but as I am six feet tall and sixteen stone in weight I obviously need something fairly substantial. The car must have the 'Three A's mentioned by Steven Norris in the Telegraph, as my wife will also drive it and will not contemplate a manual gearbox. I know about tractors and combines, but I don't know about cars, so would much appreciate your help on this. "

If we're talking 'auto, air and alloys', we're not really talking sports cars. I'd say your choice lies between a new Jaguar XK8 or the evergreen Mercedes SL. If you prefer something a bit more 'racy', but still automatic, you could consider a secondhand Porsche 911 Tiptronic or a second-hand Honda NSX automatic.

Best buy

" *Given the option of importing from Europe, likely increases in fuel prices, reliability and warranty, what do you consider to be the best new car buy on the UK market?* "

The Seat Ibiza 1.9 TDI Salsa. Prices are 'on the road' and include a three-year unlimited mileage warranty, good power steering, Pirelli P6000 tyres, electric front windows, sliding sunroof, driver's airbag and really cheerful Spanish patterned trim. The car has sports car performance (0–60 in 10.5 seconds, 110 mph) yet will average over 50 mpg at 90 mph. It handles well enough, but the joy of it is having better-than-GTi 'oomph' under your right foot for emergencies without any fuel consumption penalty. Drive it within the UK 70 mph limit and you should have no trouble at all averaging over 60 mpg. The only downside is it's just a bit noisy. The trouble is, in Holland, in Spring 1998 the pre-tax price was just £6,638, and even with UK VAT it only added up to £7,800, admittedly with LHD and without the three-year warranty.

Mother's ruin

" *I have a problem with mother, who is in her seventies. She has a*

Wolseley 1300 MkII automatic on a 'J' suffix that is showing its age. It gives her and the family a lot of grief and dominates our lives whenever she visits. The engine has to be protected from rain and frost, which means parking it in a position that blocks our drive. She starts it every day, and if it won't start she calls the AA. Her arrivals and departures are timed, to the hour, between likely rain, wind, frost, etc. Wherever we have lived the car has had to go to a local garage for repairs. Mother insists that a 'Wolseley' is the only car she could drive and that she could not get used to having to think about the controls of another car. She says it is well built, safer than a modern car, that lots of them are still running around in London and that hers really isn't much trouble. But the fact is it is costing her a fortune which she hasn't got. Can you suggest a sensible modern alternative that she might be prepared to consider? **"**

Most Japanese models still have their indicator stalks on the right of the column.

The Seat Arosa 1.4 automatic which has power steering as standard and a three-year warranty included. The 'Comfort Pack' of height-adjustable seats, pollen filter, carpeted boot, parcel shelf and nicer trim is a very worthwhile extra. If she thinks it's a bit too stumpy, you could shop around for a VW Polo 1.4 or 1.6 automatic, but even secondhand this is likely to be more expensive. If you go for a slightly older automatic, with the exception of the Subaru Justy CVT, a Japanese one is likely to be the most reliable. Also most Japanese models still have their indicator stalks on the right of the column, like mother's old Wolseley, and this may be less likely to confuse her.

BM to Guernsey

" *I have moved to Guernsey and aim to be here for 3–5 years. I had intended on bringing my old style BMW 518i over in the next couple of months. I have owned it since new on 1 August 1987, and it has a full service history with only 84,000 miles on the clock. My concern is how it will cope with the narrow lanes and a speed limit of 35 mph. Would you rec-*

ommend selling the car or trading it in? It's years since I have driven a smaller car. **"**

Your car will be better suited to Guernsey than any other model in the 5-Series range. In fact, many drivers prefer four-cylinder 3- and 5-series BMWs for city driving because the engines feel more lively than the heavier sixes around town. Your car also has no catalytic converter to worry about and a fairly straightforward Bosch L-Jetronic fuel injection system. I'd invest in a Kenlowe Hotstart (01628 823303) to 'pre-heat' the engine before driving on cold mornings. And, if possible, try to get it over to France or to the UK occasionally to blow the cobwebs out.

Carlton or Mondeo?

" *I am retired and am running my ex-company Carlton 2.0CDX, which has now done 87,000 miles. I live in Central London and all my travel in town is by tube, bus or taxi. My question is, should I keep the Carlton until it has done, say, 120,000 miles? Should I buy a new Mondeo 2.0 automatic at a 20% discount through relatives who work at Ford? Or should I buy a low-mileage ex-factory Mondeo or similar at a 'closed' auction?* **"**

You can't buy at a 'closed' auction. (Even I can't.) 'Closed' means open only to franchised dealers and other dealers with reasonably large premises who the manufacturer allows to buy at its auctions. A 20% discount pulls a £15,660 Mondeo back to £12,528 (assuming the deal is permitted). Your Carlton is worth about £4,000. But any car which sits around for most of the time in a city square will deteriorate, so if I was you I'd rather see my £4,000-worth deteriorate than my £12,500-worth.

W123 for me

" *In March 1986 I purchased a 1986C Mercedes 230E automatic – one of the last of the 'old-shape' W123 models. It has central locking and an electric sliding sunroof, and had done 66,000 miles at the time of purchase. I paid £5,000. The car gives me a lot of pleasure, but I would like to know what it cost when new and whether I paid too much for it.* "

An old 'Glass's Guide' listed the new price as £16,141, and £5,000 was a fair price to pay a dealer for yours. One quirk of the four-cylinder W123 engine (and the same engine in early versions of the succeeding W124 'E' Class) was the propensity for the Simplex timing chain to give trouble at 60,000–80,000 miles. You would be well advised to have this, its tensioner and the oil feed to it, changed at the earliest opportunity, because if it breaks the resulting engine damage could cost £2,000 to put right. Once the job is done, keep the oil clean by changing it and the filter regularly – every six months or every 3,000 miles, whichever comes first. That's the down side. I once found a 3,000-mile-serviced W123 230E that had done 350,000 miles with no trouble, and my local minicab firm still relies on the model.

Chrysler Lamina?

" *Many similar-looking MPVs have been reviewed in the* Telegraph's *motoring pages, but I have never seen mention of the very elegant Chrysler range that came out in the USA in the early 1990s. These were sold as the Pontiac Trans Sport, Chrysler Lamina and Oldsmobile Silhouette. These vehicles were daintier and less bulky looking than their European cousins. What a pity a RHD version was never made available in the UK.* "

I think you must mean the Chevrolet Lumina (it's quite easy to confuse Chrysler and GM products). The GM range of Chevrolet, Pontiac and Oldsmobile 'mini vans' was launched in the late 1980s to compete with the immensely successful Chrysler Voyager and its variants. They were sold in Europe and a few made it over here as 'personal imports'. I have noticed a bit of a problem in the bonding between the upper edge of the deep front screen and the roof. The American 'Consumer Report' on 1996-model cars rated the Chrysler Town & Country, Dodge Grand Caravan and Plymouth Grand Voyager as the best American 'minivans' overall, and the Chevrolet Lumina, Oldsmobile Silhouette and Pontiac Trans Sport SE as the worst. But the excellent Honda Odyssey (Honda Shuttle over here) was head and shoulders above all of them. A pair of Oldsmobile Silhouettes starred in the John Travolta movie 'Get Shorty'.

318i or 190E?

" Which would you consider to be the best used buy? A 'K' or 'L' reg. BMW 318i or a 'K' or 'L' reg. Mercedes 190E? "

Apart from the catalytic converters (which never do last for ever), these are both long-lasting cars. In March 1997 I spotted a 'K' reg. BMW 318iS coupe with 214,000 miles at auction and the engine was still quiet. (You can't dose these with heavy oil to quieten them down because the lifters for the 16 valves will gum up.) Make sure you find a post-September 1993 'L' reg. 318i, which has a timing chain rather than a timing belt. The 190E 2.0 is also a good, long-lasting car (it had a Duplex timing chain long before 'K' reg.), but an automatic is a much better choice than a manual. At the end of the day, it boils down to whether you prefer the slightly sportier way the BMW drives and handles to the solidity of the Mercedes. Unless you're tall and need the headroom, don't buy either without a sunroof or air conditioning, preferably both.

480

" I have a Volvo 480 Turbo automatic with which I am enormously pleased. I read in one of your replies that the 480 had a lot of troubles in its early years, so perhaps they had been ironed out by 1990. Is there anything to which I should pay particular attention? And is there a 480 owners' club? According to Volvo, only 22,000 480s were produced in ten years, so perhaps a well-maintained example will hold its value. "

Early 480s suffered a lot of niggling problems, usually electrical, that led one magazine to dub them 'the coupe fron hell'. They had become a lot better by 1990 and I receive a lot of praise for the car from owners of later models. The part-galvanized body lasts well, but the clips that hold the rubber side-window rain shields tend to rust under the rubber. By 1990 catalytic converters were optional but not legally required, so they can be the cause of considerable unnecessary expense. The 1,721 cc Renault engine is reasonably reliable and it may be possible to source Renault parts such as gaskets more cheaply than from a Volvo franchise. The 440/460 could develop a fuel sender pump problem – nothing more than an electrical contact in the pump 'drying out'. Change the engine oil to a fully synthetic oil such as Mobil 1 or Esso Ultron and change that and the filter every six months. Since your car is an automatic, you should also have the transmission oil and filter changed every year. You may be right that a well-kept example will become a minor classic. I know of two Volvo Clubs – The Volvo Enthusiasts' Club, tel: 01872 553740, and The Volvo Owners' Club, tel: 01705 381494.

Max headroom

" *My husband is 6ft 5in., and has a chronic back condition. I have Parkinson's Disease and an arthritic knee. We are both approaching retirement and need one car which can fulfil all our needs. It must have good headroom but not be too big for me to drive, it must be easy to get in and out of, and it must have automatic transmission and power steering. What do you suggest?* "

During summer 1995 I spent a week in the ideal car for you. This is the Mitsubishi Space Runner (an abbreviated Space Wagon) with an excellent automatic transmission, power steering and air conditioning. It surprised me by its ability to cruise all day at 80 mph with the aircon on, yet still return an excellent 33.58 mpg. It's also tall with plenty of headroom, and is easy to get in and out of. A 1997 addition to the range of such cars was the versatile Renault Megane Scenic, from around £14,000; and a 1998 addition, with headroom of the chef's hat variety, is the Citroen Berlingo Multispace, from £12,000. Other readers with a similar problem have praised the Suzuki Vitara five-door automatic, the Toyota RAV 4 five-door automatic, and the Honda CRV automatic. Also on the small automatic front is the Seat Arosa mini-hatch, which arrived in June 1997 with 1.4 engine, four-speed autobox, power steering, three-year warranty and bags of headroom.

Buying a well-used Lexus

" *My Honda Accord has given me 148,000 trouble-free miles. When I finally replace it I am considering purchasing an early-model Lexus LS400, which will have covered at least 100,000 miles. In view of the model's outstanding reliability, the high mileage does not bother me apart from the manufacturer-recommended oil change intervals of 9,000 miles. Even using fully synthetic oil, several mechanics to whom I have spoken state categorically that this is too long and will result in premature wear. Do you agree? Is it possible to ask Toyota if they have experienced any problems with high-mileage Lexuses as a result of the extended oil changes? And has the company stripped down any engines which have done in excess of 150,000 miles?* "

I agree with the mechanics. David O'Brien, who runs secondhand Japanese engine suppliers API (tel: 01295 226300) changes the oil of all his company's vehicles, and his own Lexus coupe, every 3,000–6,000 miles. Quentin Willson bought a 150,000-mile Lexus LS400, which appeared on the BBC 'Top Gear' TV show and which gave him a year's trouble-free motoring before he sold it at a profit and bought another. Toyota GB has not stripped down a 150,000 mile engine, but says 'make sure the car has a full Lexus service history, that the automatic transmission fluid and filter have been changed every year, that the shockers and suspension are okay, that the timing belts have been changed at 60,000 mile intervals, and that there is no excess wear on the rear discs through misuse of the parking brake.' I'd add to that: make sure the engine does not 'surge' in traffic (there was an engine management problem with some pre-1996 models), insist on a new 'cat test' MOT ('cats' are £517.76 each, plus VAT, and there are two), and watch out for scabrous, oxidised alloy wheels which signify a lack of care by the previous user. De-catting may be on the cards for a pre-August 1992 model (talk to BBR on 01280 702389). This, combined with BBR's Interceptor ECU, will give better performance and fuel consumption at very little added cost to the environment. Try to buy newer and higher mileage rather than older and lower mileage (an older car is, after all, an older car).

Montego gone?

" I understand that Rover Montegos have now gone out of production, which is a shame. I have owned two Montegos – an 'H' reg and a 'K'. Both have served me well. They are commodious automatics with power steering and a large boot. Above all, bought secondhand at two years old, they were reasonably priced. Can you recommend other makes which are reasonably priced at two years old and are roomy with automatic transmission and power steering? Why did Montegos go out of production? "

Rover did continue producing Montegos long past their 'sell-by' date – until demand declined to the extent that continuing to produce the cars in small numbers became uneconomical. A lot of people sneer at Montegos, but, when they ran well, there was much to recommend them. A recent model very similar to the Montego was the Daewoo Espero (it even looks a bit like a Montego, despite being Chevrolet Cavalier based). You should be able to get a two-year-old, 20,000-mile, automatic, air-conditioned 1.8CDi for between £5,000 and £5,500.

Back seat height limit?

" I have three children aged 12, 10 and 6 and, for ferrying them and their friends about, need a seven-seater. However, we also use Motorail which

does not take MPVs, so it has to be an estate car. I made enquiries about the new Peugeot 406 Family Estate, but have been informed there is a height limit of 3ft 6in. in the extra seats and therefore this will be unsuitable for our needs. The choice now seems to be between a Volvo or a Mercedes estate, but because my budget is around £17,000, these would have to be secondhand. Bearing in mind the restrictions imposed by Motorail, what do you recommend?

I think there may have been an element of miscommunication here, as 3ft 6 in. (or 1150 mm) is the *minimum* height for rear-seat occupancy, not the maximum height. The reason for this is that child seats cannot be used in the rear seat and a child smaller than 3ft 6in. might not be properly protected by the seat belts and head restraints. The 406 is now available with a very advanced 'common rail' direct injected diesel engine, and this is the best choice. Renault also does a seven-seater Laguna 2.2 TD Family Estate with aircon for £17,935. Secondhand seven-seat Volvo 850 and Mercedes 'E' class estates can be hard to find and often sell at a premium. But Volvo does offer a bargain basement V70 Torslanda estate, and Motorhoods of Colchester do seven-seat conversions for most estate cars (tel: 01206 796737).

Load and people carrier

I need to carry heavy and bulky items in connection with some land I own. On different occasions I also need to carry four large and elderly adults in comparative comfort. I have a Mondeo 2.0GLX estate which I will be looking to trade in for a replacement. By then, the Mondeo will be 3 years old with 60,000 miles and I will have £10,000 to add. What should I be looking at?

Look very seriously at a Ford Galaxy, VW Sharan

or Seat Alhambra (all the same vehicle with different ranges of engines and trim). Going by current trends, your Mondeo should be worth £5,500–£6,000 as a part-exchange next March, which will be more than enough to finance a 'nearly new' Galaxy. The good news is you only need five seats, and five-seater Galaxys tend to be the orphans of the category. The best bet of the lot from your point of view would be a five-seater Galaxy, Sharan or Alhambra TDI model with air conditioning. Also take a look at the cheaper Peugeot Partner Combi, the Renault Megane Scenic, or wait for the Vauxhall Zafira DI.

At the double

" *My 'everyday' vehicle is an old VW Caddy pick-up. I love its load carrying versatility, but bemoan its lack of seats. There seems to be an increas-*

ing number of 'double cab' pick-ups appearing on the roads, and one of these would solve my problem. However, they all seem to be four-wheel-drive, which I do not need. Does anyone make a cheap two-wheel-drive, diesel, double-cab pick-up which is available in the UK? "

Yes, Tata does, in the form of its Loadbeta double-cab turbodiesel which made an appearance in the May 1997 issue of *Diesel Car & 4×4* magazine. The vehicle is built in India and powered by an Indian 1,948 cc turbocharged and intercooled version of the PSA XUD engine. For a brochure, call 01262 402200.

Mr Softy

" *Many thanks for your recent help in locating a good Talbot Horizon. You will recall that the sole reason I sought such a car was its very comfortable suspension. I have a serious back condition (five discs fused, more discs clapped out) and other readers may have a similar very real reason for seeking a car with a comfortable ride. I wonder if you could use your column to seek nominations for cars with the most comfortable ride, in hatchback and family sizes?* "

This reader had been badgering me for years over this, but he makes a reasonable request. I nominate the Citroen Xsara, Citroen ZX, Peugeot 306 and Honda Civic five-door/Rover 400 four- or five-door in the low/medium category, and the Citroen Xantia, Audi A4, new Audi A6, Renault Laguna, Renault Safrane and Citroen XM among family-sized cars.

Tiny four-door

" *I purchased a Rover 111 Knightsbridge last year, as my wife wanted a small car to drive after my eventual demise. I have been rather disap-*

pointed at the mpg figures, and also at the lack of space for back-seat passengers. Is there another small car with four doors and more room in the back, but no wider? Perhaps a diesel engine would be preferable, as I understand the catalytic converter on petrol engines used mostly for short journeys is liable to need replacing after a short time. "

There's not much room in the back of the Daihatsu Move, but a bit more in the Suzuki Wagon R +, and the new Daewoo Matiz got a very good-write up by Mark Bursa in *The Daily Telegraph* 'Motoring'. Cheapest micro car is the Perodua Nippa at under £5,000. But go up in size slightly and the best-designed small car of the lot is the Fiat Punto 5-door, closely followed by the VW Polo. A diesel Punto or Polo with power steering might suit you best – and I guarantee you will be amazed at how easy it is for the stiff and elderly to get in and out of the Fiat.

Rover to Honda?

" *I am planning on part exchanging my 92K Rover 216SLi automatic for either a nearly-new Honda Civic automatic or a new Rover 400 automatic. My garage tells me it can get me a better deal on the Rover. I am retired, drive about 8,000 miles a year and am looking for reliability, comfort and a reasonable degree of economy. The 1997 BBC Top Gear/J.D. Power Customer Satisfaction Survey left me confused. It appears to damn the Rover with faint praise, but then* Top Gear *magazine comments 'the Rover 400 is rather good news', and goes on to praise its comfort. Perhaps this refers to 'N' and 'P' registered cars and Rover has been transformed since the survey. Given the rash of red dots awarded the Civic, there seems to be only one conclusion, but is there?* "

Something significant appeared in the 'Buying Cars' pages of *Autocar* magazine of 28 May 1997. It quoted an extract from a Toyota dealer's letter to a customer telling him how to complete a 'customer satisfaction questionnaire' as follows: 'It is vital you understand the implications of your answers ... we need to achieve 80 per cent ... filling in the "good" or "fair" boxes does not help us achieve that'. Until The Data Protection Act allows true random selection of car owners, the possibility of this sort of thing influencing a good result will remain (though, of course, if owners don't like their cars at all, a letter from their dealer won't persuade them). The 1997 J.D. Power Survey covered 'M' reg. cars, and the new Rover 400 was only available for three months of the 'M' reg. year (*Top Gear* magazine used the wrong picture) – while the equivalent Honda Civic was on the market for seven months of the year, and the survey did not distinguish between UK-built and Japanese-built Civics anyway. In the 1998 Survey of 'N' reg. cars, both the new Rover 200 and the new Rover 400 still did badly, finishing up at positions 103 and 83 in the chart. Not as bad as the 'N' reg. Vauxhall Vectra, which scored just 61 points and came bottom, but not as good as Honda Civics generally, which scored 88 and made nineteenth place.

Convertible convert

" *As a recently retired person, the opportunity has arisen for me to indulge in a life-long ambition to buy a convertible. This would be used as a second car with an estimated annual mileage of 5,000. Could you please advise on a 'best buy' for about £4,500? Convertibles are thin on the ground in Penrhyndreudraeth, so do you know of any garages which stock this type of car in my price range? Finally, a considerable time ago, owners of convertibles were advised to keep them in garages. Security where I live is not a problem, so is this still good advice?* "

Sun's blazing. Skies are cloudless. Everyone's wearing shorts. You couldn't have picked a worse time to try and buy a convertible. In 1996, a reader from Petworth sold a very nice 1984 BMW 320i Bauer cabrio for £3,750. But the most solid bet available in quantity is either a VW Golf GTi or a less powerful 'Clipper' cabriolet. Only a handful of RHD versions of these were ever fitted with power steering, so if this is a necessity you'll need to budget an extra £1,000–£1,200 for a TSR system (01278 453036). In the summer, any convertible at a sensible price (and even quite a few at ridiculous prices) simply sails off the forecourts. The only answer is lots of hard work checking the classifieds in local papers, *Trader* magazines, *Exchange & Mart*, *Top Marques* and *Classic Car Weekly*. The Golf has one of the best hoods available, but it costs thousands of pounds, so, yes, you would be well advised to keep it in a garage. However, never garage the car when the hood is wet.

Three-wheeling

" I am about to purchase my first car. I recently passed my driving test and am looking for a three-wheeled car with two wheels at the front and one at the rear. Where can I buy such a car? I have heard that some do not have reverse gear. What is the legal position on this? "

The first Morgan re-creation was the Triking, launched in 1979, with a Moto Guzzi V-twin. The original price was £4,500 complete (it rose since), but from 1981 the Triking was also available as a kit. With the 950 cc 71 bhp Guzzi engine, the Triking would do 121 mph and 0–60 in 7.8 seconds. By 1992, 100 had been built. (Triking Cyclecars, Marlingford, Norwich, Norfolk NR9

5HU, tel: 01603 880641.) There are various other 'two at the front' three-wheelers: the Lomax, with a Citroen 2CV flat twin (tel: 01384 410910); the JZR with a 500 cc Honda V-twin (tel: 01254 760260); the Tri-Pacer, also with a 2CV flat twin (tel: 01373 461589); the Gaia Deltoid, with various motorcycle engines (tel: 01292 387834); the Mumford Musketeer (tel: 01453 832707); the Berkeley Bandini, with a Mini engine (01509 845807); the Hudson, with a Renault 5 engine (tel: 01603 434762); the Falcon, once more with a 2CV flat twin (tel: 01373 473695); the Blackjack Avion, yet again with a 2CV flat twin (tel: 01326 574464); the BRA Super Sports, with a 500 cc or 650 cc Honda V-twin (tel: 01302 323325); the Morford Flyer, with a Renault 5 engine (tel: 01223 207814); and the most sophisticated of the lot, the Grinnal Scorpion, with four-cylinder BMW 'K' Series power (tel: 01299 822862), as owned by Lord Strathcarron. Latest on the scene are Honda 250 cc replica Isettas and Messerschmitts, known as the 'Zetta' and the 'Schmitt', from Tri Tech Autocraft of Preston (tel: 01772 468317). As long as the vehicle weighs less than 8 cwt, VED is at a special three-wheeler rate. (The 'no reverse' rule was for 16-year-olds who, like myself, started off in a three-wheeler, passed the test, then had to pass a second test to drive a car with reverse gear.)

A taste of the sea

" *Could you recommend a car for our 26-year-old daughter who has just gained her PhD in marine biology? She needs to visit beaches for her work, but she also goes camping quite often and has a large dog, so she would need reasonable space behind the rear seats. She has been looking at a new Kia Sportage, but I do not know much of their track record.* "

The Kia Sportage is not bad value, but if she's prepared to spend £14,000 on a new four-wheel-drive, a Subaru Impreza would be a better bet. Remember beaches can be treacherous places even for 4×4s. Sticking with two-wheel-drive, all that salt water and salt air will play havoc with the bodywork of a car which has not been galvanized. Fiats have, and £8,000 buys a 'nearly new' Fiat Punto 85 with power steering and the new 1.2 litre 16v engine. £6,000 buys a nearly new Punto 60S with less kit. To my mind, the clever design of the Punto still beats that of any other small car.

Punto purchased

" As a mum with two children aged 10 and 14, my two door Vauxhall Nova was just too small. I had no clue as to what to change it for because every friend had a different idea. So can I just thank you for recently recommending a Fiat Punto 5-door to a reader who wanted a small car with lots of room in the back? I've just bought one and it's perfect for children plus all their clobber. "

Good choice – glad to be of help.

Don't have much money

" I haven't a lot of money to spend, but I need an estate car to carry two kids, the wife, myself and all the impedimenta that goes with being a father. I fancy a Volvo. They seem safe, roomy enough to take the pram, and I am told they go on for ever. What should I buy? I am not bothered about age or styling. I just want good, safe and reliable motoring. Would you advise me to buy an automatic? "

What you write about Volvos is generally, though not always, true. The trouble is that though the 240/260 range drive like something out of the 1950s, they have a strong following and prices can be very firm. I recently saw a 77,000-mile 91J pre-cat 240GL automatic estate sell at auction for £4,775. The '700' series is a bit better (perhaps better looking) and sells for similar money – but try to avoid a car with a catalytic converter and all the extra expense this entails. By far the best estate of this size is the Mercedes E Class, but prices reflect the fact and the 200 and 230E automatic are a bit under-powered. If you're looking for something in the £1,000–£2,000 range, a good bet is the old 'over-hanging engine' VW Passat estate. You'll need muscles to steer a 1.6 or 1.8 without PAS, but the 1,900 cc five-cylinder cars with power steering tend to go on and on and all are far nicer to drive than an old Volvo. I wouldn't dismiss a good car with an autobox, but I wouldn't go out specifically to find one.

Shoestring Passat

" *I'd like to add my 1984 VW Passat five-cylinder to your record of cars run on a shoestring. Excluding VED, petrol, oil and insurance, but in-cluding the purchase price, my Passat has taken me 13,000 miles in a year for the grand sum of just £600. This is actually less than a friend of mine had to pay to renew the ECU of his Ford Probe. I use genuine VAG parts for essentials – water pump, oil filter and timing belt. But others such as a front spring, rear shock absorbers, radiator, boot carpet, electric window switches, jack and wheel wrench were all either pattern parts or came from a VW breaker.* "

This proves that with the right car, plus ingen-uity, patience and a willingness to get your hands dirty, it can be done. Buying the right car at the right time and then selling it at the right time can also mean motoring for free – but this is a lot harder than it used to be, especially bridging the gap between spring and autumn. Fortunately, though ordinary cars are still too expensive in the UK, most people regard the pleasure of owning a nice new niche model as something worth paying a lot of money for. Paradoxically, it's letters like this that make late VWs so expensive to buy secondhand.

Motoring philosophy

" *My wife kindly gave me your* Book of Motoring Answers *as a Christmas present. I found it fascinating and thought that, in return, you might be interested in my motoring philosophy. Most people would like cheap, reliable motoring, and I believe this can be achieved by running old, simple cars. The benefits are cheap, third party insurance, low to no depreciation, and cheap servicing and repair because there is less to go wrong. Rust problems can be minimised by timely use of 'Supertrol' (from Minor Developments, tel: 01562 747718). Among other vehicles, for the past 14 years we have run a 1979 Fiat 127 1050L which has now covered 133,000 miles and recently returned 46.1 mpg on a 485-mile trip. My wife bought the car when it was six years old and initially I hated it. But since it became mine five years ago I have been amazed by its stamina. It always starts, can be driven to its maximum speed for mile after mile, and can be repaired easily with no special tools. It is also difficult to get less than 38 mpg. Fancy Spares (01935 872772) are good for cheap spares which are new, unused Fiat UK stock. Whenever work is required it is always done to the highest standards with no skimping. This, plus preventative maintenance, has resulted in no on-road breakdowns.* "

Back in 1980 I bought one of these 'nearly new' from a Fiat salesman's wife for a daily two-way cross-London commute between Wimbledon and Camden Town. In terms of doing exactly what I bought it to do, it was one of the best cars I have ever run and was absolutely brilliant in

London traffic. A few minor problems (sticky starter motor, duff driveshaft joint) were fixed FOC under the free 3-year warranty. The engine (built in Brazil to run on alcohol) was very tough. The gearbox was a bit rattly, though, and the hatchback top started to rust in just two years. But after 20,000 miles of mostly commuting, the engine was still as sweet as a nut, and it was far nicer and more fun to drive than the early Polo and Fiesta which were its main rivals. In February 1997 we ran a story about a pair of Fiat Pandas in Alston, Cumbria. One had done 200,000 miles and the other 209,000.

Short, high, and easy to load

" I have been very satisfied indeed with Nissan Prairie cars. I would now like something smaller in length, particularly as the Prairie is too long for our present garage – but with the same attributes of high-level seating for ease of access, a slide-in luggage area and power steering. A Suzuki Vitara has been suggested, but I neither need nor want four wheel drive. "

Early Prairies were 13 ft 5 in. in length; later models were 14 ft 4 in. Assuming you are referring to the latter, a Mitsubishi Space Runner at 14 ft 1 in. may be the answer. They drive and handle quite well, and the automatic does more than 35 mpg. Next, at 13 ft 6 in., is the Renault Megane Scenic (the turbodiesel is best), but, though this has a multi-position rear shelf, there is a slight lip over the rear sill. A Daihatsu Grand Move is a possibility at 13 ft 3 in., but it's a strange-looking car. Shrinking further, a Fiat Punto SX 5-door with optional PAS is 12 ft 4 in. This is the easiest car to get in and out of that I know, but again there is a lip over the rear sill. Finally, three tiny boxcars are the Daihatsu Move at 10 ft 8 in., the

11 ft 2 in. Suzuki Wagon R + which has power
steering, optional four-speed autobox and a very
sophisticated 996 cc 16v 65 bhp engine, and the
11 ft 6 in. Daewoo Matiz.

The long and the short

" *I have a 1987E Ford Fiesta 1.1. My wife, who is 5ft 1in., drives it quite
happily as she can easily see over the instrument binnacle. We though of
part-exchanging it for an 'M' reg. Fiesta, but she cannot see over the top
of the steering wheel of that model. I should be grateful for your advice as
to what to buy at 2/3 years old, up to say £6,000 in price. It must not be
significantly wider than the current Fiesta or we will not be able to get it
into out garage.* "

It may surprise you, but I'm going to recommend
you forget secondhand and buy new. The car to
buy is a Seat Arosa 1.0 which comes complete
with power steering and a three-year warranty.
An essential extra in your case is the 'Comfort
Pack', at £245, which comprises rear parcel shelf,
boot trim, pollen filter, centre console, better seat
trim and, crucially, very good height-adjustable
seats. Combined with the height-adjustable steering wheel, these allow most people from the
tallest to the shortest to drive comfortably and
safely. The Arosa also has a surprisingly good ride
quality – and is built by Germans in Wolfsburg.

Entry to Gentry

" *I have a 240,000-mile Peugeot 305 Estate which is now on its last legs
(rather like me). I am interested in replacing it with a Peugeot 205
'Gentry' model, which has automatic transmission, power steering and
large front doors to help me get in and out. Where can I obtain details
such as road tests, etc., of this model?* "

The Peugeot 205 Gentry was based on the last 1992/93 Peugeot 205 1.9GTis with a detuned, catalysed 122 bhp engine. A similar, automatic version of the 309GTi was also produced, though the 309 'Goodwood' was not necessarily an automatic. I can't find any road tests listed anywhere. A good 205 Gentry automatic is extremely rare, so, if you don't need the performance, a late 205 1.6XL automatic with power steering will be much easier to find.

Trunk call

" I run a 1996 VW Passat TDI saloon, the most economical car I have ever owned. My daughter's school trunk (910×510×350 mm) and tuckbox (510×28×32 mm) both fit in the boot, but next year number two daughter will also acquire the same quantity of luggage. Will the new Passat estate cope with the volume and allow four of us to travel together? The school run is a 480-mile round trip, so trailer or roof rack are ruled out – as is a Transit van, due to my children's perception of its lack of 'street cred'. "

VW tells me that the load area of the new Passat estate is 1,125 mm long × 1,204 mm wide × 458 mm to window height or 900 mm to roof height. I would never encourage an estate car owner to load above window height for more than a short trip, but, happily, you won't have to.

Boot for trunks

" I read the 'Horses for Courses' section in your Book of Motoring Answers, and now have an unusual request. Please will you suggest a medium to large hatchback that could seat three adults comfortably while accommodating two school trunks measuring 900 mm wide by 350 mm high by 500 mm deep? I am aware of many estate cars that can answer this call, but am thinking of saloon cars or hatchbacks such as Volvos and Saabs.

Ideally I would prefer a diesel. I should add that there will be extra soft luggage in addition to the trunks, such as sports bags, stereos, etc. **"**

The Saab 9-3 2.2 TDI arrived in Spring 1998 and has a big boot with a lower loading sill than the 900 model it replaces. It also offers a huge improvement in front-end grip and steering 'feel' over the 900. A used Saab 9000CD 2.3 eco turbo should be able to accommodate both trunks inside its boot and deliver 32 mpg on a long run, which is near-diesel economy for a car of this size. (Take a tape measure along to a Saab dealer before you commit yourself.) An estate car is far easier to load with objects like this, and an old-shape Mercedes 300D TE is probably the best bet of the lot. (Always watch your back when loading heavy objects like trunks into cars, because it's all too easy to slip a disc. I speak from experience.)

3xD

" *I am considering buying a Vauxhall Astra 1.7D, 'L' or 'M' reg., as I have read that the Vauxhall diesel engine is second only to the XUD found in Peugeots, Citroens and Rover 200s. Your comments on the mechanics of the car and especially the engine would be much appreciated.* **"**

You could be referring to one of three 1.7 litre engines. The standard non-turbo Astra diesel was a 1,699 cc diesel version of the GM Family 2, which developed 59 bhp and was fairly ordinary. But Vauxhall also fitted a turbocharged, intercooled and catalysed 1,686 cc 81 bhp Isuzu engine to the Astra, Cavalier and early Vectras. Though lacking the torque of a turbocharged XUD, I think this engine is smoother and can be more economical. The timing belt also seems to last unusually well, but its Achilles heel is a combined alternator and brake vacuum pump which costs a fortune to replace if either function fails. The final Astra engine was introduced in September 1994 for the 1995 model year (distinguished by a 'V' grille). This is a low-pressure turbocharged version of the old 1,699 cc GM engine which puts out 67 bhp and makes the car both quicker and more economical. Since all 1995 model year Astras also had power steering, this is the model to go for.

Two-horse race

" *Having driven virtually every type of car over 35 years I have decided to 'down-shift' to the simplicity of a Citroen 2CV. I know of no other car which blows hot air from the engine onto its front tyres. making it great for driving up and down snowy hills. Should I go for an early one, or a late Portugese-built car capable of running on unleaded? Also, could you give me the address of the 2CV Owners' Club and of that chap you have written about who re-builds 2CVs?* "

The club address is 2CVGB, PO Box 602, Crick, Northants NN6 7UW. The restoration specialist is Garage Levallois, Wicks Farm, Ford Lane, Arundel, W. Sussex BN18 0DE, tel: 01243 555556. The good thing about these restorations is that they use a new galvanized chassis which is not significantly heavier than the original. There are other galvanized chassis, but their substantial weight can prove too much for the car's 602 cc two-pot. As for engines, yes, you will be better off in the long run with a Portugese 2CV engine, already fitted with harder valve seats to take unleaded.

Alfa 146

" *I am considering buying an Alfa Romeo 146 Twin-Spark 1.6. I think I can get hold of a secondhand one with not too many miles on the clock. My question is, how reliable are they and how much do spares cost in percentage terms, say in relation to a Rover 416? Would it cost more to run than the Rover?* **"**

A very limited number of ex-rental 146 1.6 Twin-Sparks are feeding through via Fiat's BCA Fiat auction programme. Much, much better, of course, is the two litre 146 Twin-Spark with its 'quick rack' steering. At least one reader suffered a litany of minor faults on a secondhand Alfa 146L flat-four. 'N' registered 145s and 146s with the old flat-four engines did not do well for 'problems' in the 1998 BBC *Top Gear*/J.D. Power Customer Satisfaction Survey, and were beaten by the Rover 400 Series. But if you do get problems, these are covered by a three-year warranty as against Rover's one-year warranty.

Polo SDI?

" *I recently purchased a VW Polo saloon with a 1.9 litre 'SDI' diesel engine, giving 64 bhp. The Polo hatchback has a 1.9 litre diesel engine, also with 64 bhp. Does the SDI unit offer some improvement over the hatchback's engine, or is the change of name purely cosmetic? I assume the up-market engine produced by VW is the TDI?* **"**

For the best combination of performance and economy, 'direct injection' has long been the way for diesel engines to go.

For the best combination of performance and economy, 'direct injection' has long been the way for diesel engines to go. The Polo hatchback has the 'old' 64 bhp indirect-injection, non-turbo diesel engine. But the saloon and a version of the Caddy van have a direct-injected, non-turbo diesel engine, designated the 'SDI'. Power and torque are exactly the same, at the same engine speeds as the 'IDI' engine, but economy should be better. When *Diesel Car &*

4×4 magazine tested the SDI saloon, they achieved 52.5 mpg – significantly better than the 47.4 mpg from the lighter 'IDI' hatchback. So you've bought the right car. In VW nomenclature, 'TDI' indicates 'turbo direct injected', and these engines also have an intercooler. Power outputs are 90 bhp or 110 bhp with 149 ft lbs or 155 ft lbs of torque respectively. The TDI 90 engine is an option on the Polo Caddy van in Spain, while the Seat Ibiza can be had with either – and it really flies, while delivering fuel economy in the 55 mpg bracket. Direct injected engines are also kinder to their oil than indirect injected engines, but I know from experience that a VAG TDI 90 bhp with oil changed at stipulated 10,000 mile intervals was only good for 150,000 miles.

MX5 values

" What will the new Mazda MX5, which arrived in April 1998, do to the resale value of existing MX5s, some of which carry the Japanese badging of 'Eunos Roadsters'? "

When Shigeharu Hiraiwa persuaded the Mazda board to sign off the MX5, he used two main arguments. One was that, because less material was needed, it would cost less to build than the Mazda 323. The other was that, because there were no other comparable sportscars in world markets, it could be sold for considerably more than a 323 and would therefore be much more profitable. Hiraiwa-San was right. But, of course, everyone else watched what Mazda did and then tried to do the same. Now, world markets are positively flooded with both volume and specialist sportscars. As well as the MX5 we have the Alfa Spider, BMW Z3, Fiat Barchetta, Honda CRX, Kia Phoenix, Lotus Elise, MGF, Mercedes SLK, Porsche Boxter, Renault Sport Spider, Suzuki C2 V8, Tommykaira ZZ, Morgan, TVR and many more. So, inevitably, while depreciation of sports roadsters will remain slower than for mass-market hatchbacks, MX5s will no longer have things all their own way. As from July 1998, all 'grey import' secondhand RHD Mazda Eunos Roadsters under three years old were subject to an expensive Single Vehicle Approval test before they could be registered, and trade imports were subject to a quota of 50 cars a year. But, during the two to three years before this, the market was inundated with 'grey import' Eunos Roadsters, sometimes shipped in, all taxes paid, for as little as £4,000 but sold for considerably more. The market has found out that these cars are not all they seem, and this more than anything else is having a depressing effect on prices.

Scenic aspects

" *I run a small family retail business and, for the past twelve years, have always bought Toyota Corolla estates. I am now thinking of switching to a Renault Megane Scenic 1.6RT. My Toyotas have all been very reliable and have held their value well. Do you think that a Megane Scenic will be as reliable and hold its value as well as a Corolla estate?* "

On the basis of past performance, the Corolla estate has to be the best bet for these two criteria. But there are only two versions on the UK market – the 1,332 cc Sportif estate at £12,755 and the 1,975 cc GSD estate at £14,610. In contrast, the Scenic is a unique design which spans three basic trim levels, petrol or diesel engines, and numerous sunroof and air-conditioning options. (A super-economical direct-injected turbodiesel Scenic arrived in spring 1998.) In short, there's more to get excited about. But don't expect the Scenic to be as reliable as the Corolla.

Taxi!

" A French family I met on holiday wish to buy a secondhand London taxi. For fun, not for business. Who should I refer them to? "

'All London Cabs' have 50 for sale from £1,000 to £10,000 (tel: 0966 379831). Also try London Central Cab Company (0171 501 9998) and London Cab Sales (0171 703 4330). These are not recommendations, merely numbers plucked from the 'Taxis' section of *Exchange & Mart*, where your friends will find many more. There are two basic types of London taxi: the Carbodies FX type and the Metrocab. A good source of Metrocabs is George Wilson of Viking Garages, The High Street, West End, Southampton SO30 3DS, tel: 01703 473773.

Town cars

" I think I may have found a much cheaper alternative to the Swatch car. It is the JDM Titane, a smart looking, eight-foot-long, two-seater hatchback, powered by a 523 cc Yanmar diesel engine. I sat in it and headroom was fine for my 6ft 4in. height. If we are in the European single market it seems ridiculous that we cannot purchase such vehicles and use them in the UK without expensive modifications. The manufacturer is JDM Simpla Constructeur, 12 rue Paul Langevin, – BP 19–49241 AVRILLE CEDEX, tel: 0033 2 41 21 13 59, fax: 0033 2 41 42 71 98. "

If JDM has full European Type Approval, there

should be no problem. And since the car will be built from bought-in components, it should be a relatively simple matter to source left-dipping headlamps and 'mph' speedometer, and to switch the rear foglamp from left to right. French law allows automatic microcars such as this, with very restricted performance, to be driven without a licence. As a result there is a strong demand for them, particularly from drivers with drink driving bans, and at around £4,000 they are relatively expensive to buy. But it's also the sort of vehicle that could be ideal for people who need personal transport without all the baggage of a full-size car. Left-hand-drive allows kerbside access and is no hardship when driving because the cars are virtually incapable of overtaking anyway.

Better cruiser required

" *If I can get a good deal I expect soon to exchange our Metro 1.4GTa, by which time it will be three years old and will have done 30,000 miles. My wife and I are both retired and we both drive it. We clock up our highest mileage driving to and from our flat in the Highlands of Scotland two or three times a year, and we are starting to find 3,500 revs at 70 mph a bit tiring. Could you please suggest some five-door hatchbacks with higher gearing?* "

The Metro 1.4GTa was discontinued in September 1992 and the GTa 16v in December 1992. So yours must be the 'special edition' GTa of June 1994. The Metro 1.4 is geared at 19.9 mph per 1,000 rpm in fifth. Some small hatchbacks that do better than this include: Citroen Saxo/ Peugeot 106 1.4 (22.3); Ford Ka without PAS or aircon (23.5); Ford Fiesta 1.4 16v (22.4); Honda new Civic 1.5 (24.3); Honda new Civic 1.5 V-TEC (26.2); Mazda 121/Ford

Fiesta 1.25 automatic (24.7); Renault Clio 1.9RLD (24.0); Seat Arosa 1.4 auto (22.8); Seat Ibiza TDI (28.8); Vauxhall Corsa 1.0 12v (23.1); Vauxhall Corsa 1.5TD (24.3). My personal favourite of this lot is the new Seat Ibiza TDI which, even in my hands, managed more than 54 mpg, including cold-start school runs and high-speed cruising.

Miles per thousand

" A query in your book mentions miles per hour per thousand rpm in top gear as a means of indicating how long-legged a car is for relaxed motorway cruising. Could you give me these figures for the current Honda Civic 1.6 SRi coupe, the Nissan 200SX and the Nissan Primera GT? "

Figures in mph/1000 rpm: Honda Civic 1.6SRi, 23.3; Nissan 200SX, 23.2; Nissan Primera GT, 21.6. The figure for the Primera SRi is a slightly more relaxed 23.6. Of course, these figures don't tell the whole story, because quite a few engines are at their sweetest cruising at 4,000–5,000 rpm. It's a bit different for diesels which don't rev beyond 4,500 rpm, developing their peak torque so low down that they can often pull a top gear giving 28–30 mph per 1,000 rpm. *Autocar* magazine lists these figures for every car it has tested recently.

Xedos?

" I have recently been impressed with the looks and classy interior of a Mazda Xedos 6 2.0 auto SE, three years old with a mileage of 15,000. As I am unable to obtain an AA report on this model, could you give me your opinion? Also, is it true that Japanese cars cost more to insure and that spares are pricey? "

I have to confess to a certain bias here, because back in 1992 I did some freelance work for the European launch of the Xedos 6. I fell in love with the styling of the car immediately, and I'm not the only one. In a 1997 *Classic & Sportscar* magazine poll, Karl Ludvigsen voted it the most beautiful saloon car he had ever owned: 'The quality and consideration given to every detail of its exterior are unmatched in any other volume production saloon today.' I remember a BMW 3-series (full of BMW salesmen) pulling up alongside me in a Xedos, and the Xedos made the 3-series look like a brick. Under the bonnet the turbine-smooth quad-cam 2 litre V6 is great, too. This revs to over 8,000 rpm in standard form, so it's easy to see why Ford chose the unit to power its first generation of Mondeo Touring Car racers. Handling, alas, isn't up to the quality of the 3-series, but it can be worked on. And do make sure there really is some air conditioning behind the a/c button (early cars had the button, but no aircon). *Autocar* magazine published a road test of the Xedos 6 SE manual on 10 June 1992, and one of the Xedos 9 automatic on 19 January 1994 (Haymarket reprints hotline: 01235 534323). Yes, insurance is a bit stiff at Group 16 (same as a BMW 328i), mostly because of the high cost of body repairs. And, yes, mechanical parts are also fairly expensive, but compensated for by an excellent reliability record. I worry a bit about a three-year-old 5,000-mile-a-year car, and would rather see you spend the same money on something newer with more miles and some three-year manufacturer warranty remaining.

Reliable retirement car

" *On retirement, ten years ago, I traded in my Granada for a 'pre-used'
Jaguar Sovereign only 18 months old via a Jaguar main dealer. It cost me
an arm and a leg in repairs too numerous to list. I then traded the Jag in
for a Rover 820Si, which rattled and leaked oil despite being only 12
months and 6,000 miles old. I traded that in for a 'Network Rover' 820SLi
6 months and 4,000 miles old. After a further 18,000 miles in two years
this has had to have new exhausts, new discs all round, new oil seals to the
cam cover, new tyres. Now the radio needs replacing. Is there no reasonable car of quality on the market that will give some reliability to someone who averages only 10,000 miles a year? What would you suggest?* "

Faced with the same question from our father eight years ago, my brother and I both said 'Mercedes 190E 2.0 auto'. But, instead of a 'nearly new' 2.0 litre 190E, he was persuaded by the Mercedes salesman into a two-year-old 190E 2.6 auto. Since then, he has done more than 140,000 miles in the car (now showing 160,000) with very little expenditure other than routine maintenance. Yes, there have been a couple of exhausts, several sets of tyres and a new set of valve stem oil seals. But no water pumps, alternators, timing chains, steering racks, batteries or even an autobox overhaul – and the car still manages 28 mpg. On the basis of this, my advice would be to look for a 2–3-year-old Mercedes or BMW with a six-cylinder engine. You will have to fork out occasionally, because exhausts do go on a lightly driven car, catalytic converters don't last for ever, discs do rust, tyres do wear. It's also far better in the long run to over-maintain the car with an extra oil change every year than to under-maintain it by sticking to fleet-based extended oil change intervals.

Secondhand 911

" What are the possibility and practicality of running a secondhand Porsche 911 as an everyday car? I have no first-hand knowledge of the 911, but I gather that a well maintained low-mileage example is good for a considerable further mileage, reliably and with low running costs. I had in mind an older two-wheel-drive 911 (1987–90), obviously with a full service history and probably 40,000–60,000 miles on the clock. What are 'ballpark' fair prices? Would a private buy be better than one from the specialist trade? Are there any tips or pitfalls you may be aware of? Do you know of any independent servicing specialists? I cover about 10,000 miles a year. "

Older 911s are generally reckoned to be the most practical 'junior supercars'. They do, however, require high levels of skill to drive safely at high speed or in poor weather conditions.

Older 911s are generally reckoned to be the most practical 'junior supercars'. They are extremely well built and tend to be both more reliable and far less expensive to run than a Ferrari. They also require high levels of skill to drive safely at high speed or in poor weather conditions. The best examples to buy are those which have been second or third cars owned by good drivers who have not taken them on too many 'track days' at racing circuits. You want one that has been used regularly in summers rather than winters, though the galvanized bodies resist rot well. And you're likely to find the best at franchised Porsche dealers or people who specialise in servicing and selling Porsches (Yellow Pages) but nothing else. Pricey problem areas are exhaust systems and heat exchangers (around £2,000 for pre-cat cars), clutches (around £1,000, because it's an engine-out job), and valves. (These cars don't take kindly to being revved hard from cold.) Fuel consumption is on the high side (16–20 mpg). Watch out for ill-fitting panels denoting repaired accident damage. Two other giveaways of repaired accident damage are brand new rear wing stays and a rear reflector full of condensation. Avoid targas and cabriolets for everyday use, and think seriously before buying a Tiptronic. If you can find a car in the mileage range you want you'll pay £19,000–£22,500 for an 88/89 Carrera, and £1,000 more for the big-wing 'Sport'. I personally much prefer the Carrera 2 (1990 model year onwards) for its more vice-free and easily exploitable handling, but that comes from lack of enough experience of the older model. For one of these in the mileage range you want you'll pay upwards of £26,000, and in standard form these do have catalytic converters. If you want to pay less (up to £10,000 less), seriously consider an LHD car imported from Germany (Nick Faure: 01483 414800). There's no reason why a full German service history should be any worse than a UK history, but watch out for evidence of high mileage which has been clocked back. The risk of theft will be a problem, and your insurer will insist on a full Thatcham Category 1 alarm/immobiliser system. Don't push the car without having taken some high performance driving lessons. Chariots is a good Porsche specialist in your area, but join the Porsche Club on 01608 652911. For parts, tel: 0121 782 2345.

Suitable supercar

" I'd like to run a 'supercar' as an everyday vehicle and, as I cover around 25,000 miles a year on business, it has to be both practical and reliable. To a budget of £25,000, my shortlist came down to a 1989 Porsche 911 Carrera 2 or a 1994 TVR Chimaera 4.0. Having driven both, the TVR won hands down. It is much quicker, handles better, is more economical (25–28 mpg), cheaper to service and maintain (full dealer service £300 versus £600 for a 911), has a beautifully finished cabin, is more practical (bigger boot) and, to top it all, it's 100% British. "

TVRs (or 'Trevors', as they are known) inspire fierce loyalty among owners. Buying one is like joining a club, and part-exchanging it for the next is akin to renewing your membership subscription. It would be nice to see Peter Wheeler (TVR's hands-on boss) get some sort of acknowledgement in the New Year Honours for continuing to build successful British sportscars in a British-owned factory, instead of flogging the whole shooting match to the Germans, the Americans or the South Koreans.

Rear legroom

" *My wife has a circulation problem in one leg, and often prefers to sit in the back seat where she can stretch out and 'spread herself', which is impossible in the front. We had a Volvo 740, and now have a Granada Scorpio which has good leg room, is reasonably comfortable and offers me all the modern equipment such as aircon, cruise control and electric this and that. I would now like to change, but have not found anything with the Scorpio's rear legroom. I would also like to keep under £25,000.* "

The Renault Safrane 2.5 litre 'Executive' would seem to fit the bill. Plenty of rear legroom, good ride quality, all the bells and whistles, reasonable economy and also surprisingly quick from A to B. The Peugeot 605 has the best rear legroom of this class of car and is such a slow seller you should be able to get a very good deal on a used example. The new Mitsubishi Galant 2.5 litre V6 estate is a great looking car, well built, very comfortable, good to drive, with a super autobox and absolutely loaded with kit. The new Audi A6 has a soft, un-Germanic ride, but rear legroom is a lot tighter. Alternatively, take a look at an MPV. Galaxy Ghia and Sharan Carat models are six-seaters with four 'captain's chairs' in the back. But the most reliable is the Honda Shuttle 2.3iES, which has two big armchairs plus a bench in the back, air conditioning, automatic transmission and is very good to drive. (The seven-seater LS version, also with aircon and autobox, is £2,000 cheaper.)

Baleno recommendation

" *I am an avid reader of your excellent column. You often make buying recommendations, but I have yet to see you recommend the Suzuki Baleno. I have just bought a 1.6GLX saloon and am amazed at how much quality car I got for £9,200. This offer price means I have a silly fish emblem and a 'go faster' strip to put up with, but even the normal price of £10,700 (excluding radio) is very good value for the specification and the three-year warranty. I couldn't find anything to compete with it when looking for my first new car for 16 years.* "

The Baleno Estate got a mention on p. 274 of the previous *Daily Telegraph Book of Motoring Answers*, and the saloon (voted 'Ladies Choice' at the 1996 Motor Show) is on p. 285. *Autocar* magazine's verdict was: 'packed full of equipment for very little money'.

Blonde out with 'Nippa'

" *I saw a young blonde lady driving a small car which looked like a Cinquecento, but was badged 'Nippa'. It was a nice silver colour. What car was that? Is it a new test model?* "

It's a Perodua (pronounced 'Per-odd-wah') Nippa, a Malaysian-built update of the five-door Daihatsu Mira, with the same 42 bhp 847 cc three-cylinder engine as the Cuore and the Move. Its big plus point is price – just £4,999 on the road, including a year's reduced rate VED and a two-year warranty, for the EX version, or £5,499 for the better-equipped GX. They undercut the Seat Arosa 1.0 and have five doors, but are not as comfortable and don't have power steering. So far, 28 franchises have been appointed. For more information, speak to Jutta at Perodua on 0181 961 1255. (*Autocar* did a comparison test on 24 September 1997 – Haymarket Reprints: 01235 534323.)

Over sized and over here

" Round about Motor Show time you ran a story about Cadillacs being imported to the UK once again. Unfortunately the motoring section was missing from my copy of the paper, so is there any way I can get hold of a re-print? Having owned Cadillacs in the past I am very interested in prices and performance. "

Howard Walker's test told us that the 301 bhp Seville STS does 150 mph and 0–60 in 6.8 seconds. The price is £39,750 on the road, including conversion to rhd. GM is also importing a range of lhd Chevrolets. These include: Camaro 3.8 litre V6 coupe five-speed £17,800, auto £18,800; Camaro V6 convertible five-speed £21,325, auto £22,325; Camaro Z28 V8 £22,725; Blazer 4×4 five-speed £22,075, auto £23,075; Corvette 5.7 coupe auto £36,525, six-speed £37,675; and Corvette 5.7 convertible auto £40,425, six-speed £41,575. I'd better emphasise that these prices are for the UK Type Approved cars seen at the 1997 Motor Show. GM has gone to great pains inserting amber and plain white sections into light lenses to comply with UK lighting regulations, and has made numerous other modifications to ensure that the cars are fully UK road legal.

Felicitations

" *Comments, please, about changing my 1986 Fiesta diesel, which has given very good service, for the new Skoda Felicia hatchback with the 1.6 litre petrol or 1.9 litre diesel engine.* "

By coincidence a Felicia diesel arrived at my doorstep the morning after your letter. First impressions were: good quality paint; good fit of body panels; strange, old fashioned, single-plane door and ignition key; well-made interior of good-quality plastics designed to look 'cheaper' than that of a VW Polo; flat, low, non-height-adjustable seat and steering wheel; well-weighted power steering; handling a pleasant surprise – slightly better than the Polo in the dry, but the steering loads up in extreme conditions and the front wheels can let go a bit suddenly in the wet. John Kerswill, former editor of *Diesel Car & 4×4* magazine, did a 'Coals to Newcastle' economy marathon in one, achieving 84.3 mpg on a drive to Prague. He liked it so much he bought it. Sticking to 60 mph on a long run, most drivers should be able to get close to 60 mpg from this car. Round town, expect 45–50 mpg. The answer is, yes, definitely go for the diesel.

Small, but comfy

" *We run two small automatic family cars, a VW Jetta and an 'old shape' Rover 216 automatic. My husband now wishes to purchase a slightly smaller car which is very comfortable and which has automatic transmission, power steering, central locking, electric windows, electric mirrors and, most importantly, extremely comfortable seats. We have looked at most of the smaller cars available, but to no avail. We have also started to look at larger cars, and the only ones which seem very comfortable, but far too large, are the Volvo S70, the Honda Accord and the BMW 3-series. The new Rover 400 is a possibility. My husband cannot see out of the Volvo S40 due to the position and thickness of the screen pillars. Do you have any ideas?* **"**

The Citroen Xsara 1.8SX or Exclusive automatic has a very comfortable ride, and a cleverly designed 'B' pillar which means none of the side impact problems which put back the launch of the VW Golf Mk IV. In fact the Xsara bristles with useful, sensible features such as black-faced three-piece bumpers, the sections of which can be replaced at low cost, automatic air-conditioning, doors which click open to three positions, and much more. A better automatic is the Rover 200 1.6CVT, which drives very nicely indeed but sits the driver relatively high in order to give room under the seat for rear passengers' ankles.

Seven-up

" *Having watched Quentin Willson extolling the versions of high-mileage BMW Seven Series cars on BBC 'Top Gear', my husband is thinking of changing our 'L' reg. Peugeot 405GRDT for one. We would be thinking in terms of a 'J' or 'K' reg. 730iSE or 735iSE. Can you tell us roughly how much more our running costs are likely to be and whether they really are a viable proposition? My husband really needs a larger car as he is 6ft 6in. tall and weighs 16 stone, and he'd like a comfortable retirement car.* "

Quentin Willson is a sharp, opportunist buyer who bagged this car at the tail end of an auction he was attending with a film crew (the crew effectively cleared the hall of any 'faces' who might have thought about buying the car to clock it). Nevertheless, a late 1980s pre-catalytic converter Seven Series can be a fantastic buy, even for those without Quentin's legendary buying skills. They are beautifully built, and if something goes wrong the parts are not outrageously expensive compared to the Peugeot. For example: ABS pump, £751 (Peugeot, £823); ABS computer, £480 (Peugeot, £675); ECU, £681 (the Peugeot 405GRDT doesn't have one); exchange engine £2,150 (Peugeot, £1,986); exchange autobox, £1,950 (Peugeot, £1,428); steering rack, £875 (Peugeot, £585). All prices are before VAT. Obviously, your fuel costs will be double those of the Peugeot, insurance is likely to be twice the price, and routine maintenance will be dearer, but independent BMW specialists and parts suppliers such as Euro Car Parts and German & Swedish help control the cost even of this. For a high-mileage Seven, try Cowie Autopoint, London Street, Smethwick, Birmingham, tel: 0121 558 5141; Motor Nation, Mackadown Lane, Garretts Green, Birmingham, tel: 0121 786 1111; Car Supermarkets, A5 Watling Street, Cannock, Staffs, tel: 01543 506060; The Great Trade Centre, 40–45 Hythe Road, White City, London, tel: 0181 960 3366; Venture, 333 Western Avenue, London W3, tel: 0181 745 3000; Venture, 80 Ruckholt Road, London E10, tel: 0181988 5000. Remember that our current government might be considering additional taxes on cars with large engines as part of its Integrated Transport Policy.

Occasional six-seater

" Every time one or other of my sons visits with his wife and two children I wish I had a six-seater so that we did not have to take two cars on outings. Could you please advise if there are any cars with six seats which are about the size of the Megane Scenic or the Nissan Prairie? "

The six-seater Toyota Picnic springs instantly to mind as ideal for your family picnics (they also seem to handle quite well, judging by the one I followed the other day). The last of the Nissan Prairies was available with seven seats, but these are rare and most have been snapped up for conversion by mobility specialists. The seven-seater Mitsubishi Space Wagon 'feels' slightly smaller than other MPVs. The Daihatsu HiJet takes six, but I'd be a bit worried about its stability with six adults on board (the Daihatsu Move in our November 1997 'tall cars test' sits its four passengers much lower and is consequently more stable). The forthcoming Bravo-based Fiat Multipla is a six-seater, and the Astra-based Vauxhall Zafira will take seven at a pinch. Alternatively, contact Motorhoods of Colchester, who do 'occasional' seven-seater conversions for estate cars (tel: 01206 796737).

Rare animal

" I am writing to seek your help in finding a 1991/92 Daimler Double Six Series III. Screening of newspapers and placing advertisements has so far drawn a blank. The car I am looking for should be in 'concours' condition with everything in good working order, a relatively low mileage, no more than two owners and no history of accidents. Left-hand drive is acceptable. "

I handed this task straight to Robert Hughes (01932 858381), who happens to be one of the country's top independent specialists in the marque and who found the reader an excellent car. Hughes has written a fine book on Jaguars and Daimlers from 1960–1970 (ISBN 0-7137-2713-6), published by Blandford, price £25. Another good specialist to try is David Marks of Nottingham on 01159 405370.

Peace and quiet

" The main attributes I am seeking in a new car are low noise levels at motorway speeds, good rear-seat comfort for three growing teenagers, and a purchase price of less than £20,000. Where can I find advice on noise levels? "

Autocar magazine has included interior noise levels at idle, 30 mph, 50 mph, 70 mph and during full acceleration in all its road tests since the magazine's September 1994 revamp. I thought that the new Passat TDI 110 was quiet at speed, but *Autocar* recorded 69 SPL Db (A) against 65 for a Citroen Xsara 1.8, 67 for a Vectra TDS, 68 for a Passat 20v Turbo, 68 for a Toyota Avensis 1.8GS, 68.2 for a Peugeot 406 2.1TD Estate, 72 for a Primera SRi and a Mazda 626 2.0 GSi, and 77 for a Primera TD. To get this into perspective, *Autocar*'s equivalent figure for a Bentley Turbo RT was 70. *Autocar* published a special two-week Christmas 1997 issue with a 1997 Road Test Yearbook which includes interior noise levels, and will probably do the same at Christmas 1998. If you missed these at the newsagents you can order a copy from Haymarket Reprints on 01235 534323.

Max legroom

" *I want to buy an estate car with plenty of legroom for the back seat passengers. As I cover approximately 18,000 miles a year I was thinking of a secondhand diesel about one year old. The A6, Omega and XM look reasonable, with the XM appearing to be good value for money, but I know nothing about them.* "

I used to enthuse over the XM 2.1TD estate, but build quality up to 1995M was a bit iffy and, though the engine is economical, it is very difficult to work on. I think your best bet is an old-shape VW Passat TDI estate, which sacrifices some load space in favour of giving the rear passengers excellent legroom.

Renault 4 replacement

" *I have a 'B' registered Renault 4GTL which has done 70,000 miles, is clean with no rust and has been regularly maintained. What are your thoughts on keeping it, selling it, where to find someone who might cherish it, whether or not there is a club and, if I do sell it, what can I replace it with?* "

The GTL was the last of the Renault 4s and came with a five-bearing 1,108 cc engine putting out 47 bhp to help it keep up with the traffic. I get a couple of letters a year from readers who sorely miss this model. One of them jetwashed then 'Waxoyled' his every spring to keep rust at bay. There is a Renault Owners' Club, which is not R4-specific but which might help you find an enthusiastic new owner for yours. The address is 89 Queen Elizabeth Drive, Beccles, Suffolk NR34 9LA. 'Glass's Guide' to older car values gives a trade value of £350 for one in good condition, but I reckon an enthusiast would pay £1,000. Potential replacements include a Perodua Nippa, a Daihatsu Move (ridiculous looking, but surprisingly good fun to drive), a Suzuki Wagon R or a Daewoo Matiz. Citroen launched the Berlingo Multispace in the UK last Spring, at £11,995. Aother former Renault 4GTL owner feels that his Skoda Felicia 1.3LXi estate is the ideal replacement.

Seven-seater specialist

" *Our Sierra estate has done us well, but we now have four young children and need more seats. Unfortunately my budget of £8,000 excludes the many new 7-seater MPVs on the market, but in any case I would prefer an estate car. This seems to bring the choice of forward-facing 7-seaters down to between a Peugeot 505 Family and a Renault Savanna 7-seater. Which do you recommend in terms of overall running costs? And where do you suggest I look for one?* "

A specialist such as Shadoxhurst Garage, near Ashford in Kent (01233 732811), will offer the best choice of 505 Family and Renault Savanna seven-seaters in your price range. For economy, go for a diesel. Obviously, you could do better searching the sites, the auctions and the private ads, but because these vehicles are comparatively rare, the cost of finding a bargain will very probably outweigh any saving. You should also try any Mitsubishi agent for an early current-shape Space Wagon. If he hasn't got one, Mitsubishi has a nation-wide stock locator system to help find the right vehicle.

Reliable £3.5k estate

" *I'm looking to buy a reliable estate car for my upholstery business and have approximately £3,500 to spend. Size-wise I'd prefer an Astra to a Volvo or a Mondeo. What would you recommend?* "

If you buy an ex-ministry car at auction, remember you won't be able to drive it away until it has been registered.

Three years ago I bought an Escort Mk IV LD estate for a customer and it proved to be 100% reliable. But I think you'll do better with an Astra Merit diesel estate. Call BCA on 01252 878555 to find out when they are holding their next ex-government vehicle sale, check what the first few go for and bid on the basis of that. Make sure you go for the 1995 model-year car or later, which have 'V' grilles, power steering and a small, light-pressure turbo. Do, however, remember that you can't drive away an ex-ministry car, so you will either have to leave it at the auction site until you have registered it, or arrange for it to be delivered to an address with off-road parking.

Female executive express

" *Many women must share my wife's problem: a senior position within the organisation qualifies her for a lease car, which she enjoys driving, but she has little time or inclination to research available models. She needs a car which is stylish, nippy, Astra/Vectra size, four seats, five doors and will not let her down either mechanically or socially. The budget is £13,000 to £17,000-plus, for which she would expect PAS and ABS. She would do most of her driving here in Dorset, home of the narrow twisty road, but will undertake the occasional long-distance motorway thrash. What current or soon-to-be-announced models can you recommend?* "

Try and get an order in for a VW Golf Mk IV GTi five-door, a GTi Turbo five-door or a VR5 five-door. If there are no prospects of getting one soon enough, then check out the Mazda 323F 2.0ZXi V6. Also take a look at a Peugeot 306 XSi 2.0 16v five-door with aircon. The Rover 200 218iS 16v five-door has the biggest door pockets for handbags, etc. (surprisingly important due to the increasing number of smash and grabs). There should also be a hot new 2 litre Astra by the time you read this, and, of course, the stunning new Ford Focus. Remember, tax on a company car is based on list price plus delivery, so the higher this is, the more an employee pays in car benefit tax.

The right kombination

" *I drive a 'K' reg. Ford Courier van with a 1.3 litre petrol engine. I make a daily round trip to work of 38 miles on winding A roads. The van is normally empty, but now and again I need the space for carrying furniture, timber, bicycles, etc. We are expecting a baby in March, so will have one too few seats for family outings. On trips to Europe I have peered into the backs of similar vans to mine and seen seats, usually with one or more side windows beside them. I can't afford to buy a new Courier Kombi, so what should I do?* "

If you are running the van as a private car and have paid and not re-claimed the VAT, there is nothing to stop you having it converted to a 'Kombi' type estate by a company such as Motorhoods of Colchester, tel: 01206 796737, or any of the companies specialising in wheel-chair transport conversions for the disabled such as Brotherwood Mobility on 01935 872603. But The Post Office bought five hundred Ford Fiesta Courier Kombis for transporting teams of postmen and the mail to outlying areas, and it may well be that some of these are coming up for sale secondhand. Check with your nearest motor auction houses, such as CMA Dursley on 01453 542939, or RBB Leominster on 01568 611166. If you can find a big Post Office depot in your area, you may even be able to buy one direct. BT may also have a few, and since they sell direct it's worth phoning 01772 250741.

Which estate?

" My son, who is abroad, has asked me to find out for him which of the following three cars would be a best buy from the point of view of long life, reliability and safety. The three cars are: Mercedes C250TD Estate, Mercedes E300TD Estate, Volvo V70 2.5 TDI Estate. "

If he has the money, the Mercedes E300TD Estate is easily the best of the bunch on all counts. It's the only diesel Jeremy Clarkson has ever endorsed. An ordinary C Class did quite badly in the NCAP impact tests, but the C250TD is still a good car. The Volvo will beat the C Class on safety and is likely at least to equal the E Class, but, though it's a tremendous car to drive (I prefer it to the V5), its straight-five Audi diesel's days may be numbered as this very good engine has now been replaced in the Audi A6 by a V6 TDI and only lives on in the VW Caravelle.

A car to pass on

" *For some time I have been in the habit of buying a new car which I keep for six or seven years then sell on to members of my family who would struggle to find a well-maintained secondhand car at a price they could afford. I'm ready once more to buy a new car and am torn between something interesting and nippy for occasional long journeys and the fact that recent retirement means a drastic reduction in annual mileage. My last three cars have all been Japanese – a Nissan Sunny, a Toyota Corolla and a little Suzuki SC100 'Whizzkid'. I have enjoyed their comfort and reliability. At 5ft 1in. I have also found the seat adjustment in these cars much more suitable for small people than some others I have tried. Please advise on a five-door hatchback capable of carrying my dog or my golf clubs, at preferably not more than £12,000.* "

I recently helped a neighbour of similar size find a similar car. She insisted on air conditioning and was used to Japanese reliability having owned two Micras and a Shogun TD, so it would have been foolhardy to steer her away from the inevitable Colt or Corolla. Her budget would not stretch to a new Colt 1.6 with aircon, but, with no part-exchange, the local Toyota dealer was prepared to give her a very good cash deal on a Corolla. Eventually she settled for a new Corolla 1.6GS three-door (which has aircon and sunroof as standard) for £12,000. Silver and the three-door body seem to suit this model best, but you should be able to negotiate a five-door for no more than an extra £500. (I was very impressed with the treatment my neighbour received at the Toyota agent, McCarthy of Weybridge.)

Range Rover DSE auto?

" *I am considering purchasing a secondhand Range Rover DSE auto-*

*matic. The shape, spec. and all-purpose nature appeal to me. What are
likely to be the pitfalls?* **"**

What do you want to use it for? Off-road and on
bumpy tracks, this vehicle is nothing short of
brilliant. No other 4×4 is either as effective or
as supremely comfortable (though the Discovery comes quite close). It really is an off-road
limousine. On the road, though, the acceleration and general performance are almost un-
believably pathetic, especially acceleration out
of a junction – you really do need a big gap. I
wouldn't try towing with it either, as it has
enough trouble lugging its own weight along.
Happily, J.J. Fearn (01629 732546) does a conversion for the Range Rover's BMW diesel engine which puts power up to 196 bhp and torque
to 300 ft. lb., but it still needs to be kept above
2,000 rpm to feel the benefit. (See *Diesel Car &
4×4* magazine, April 1998.)

Small 5-door auto with PAS

" *I am a single woman of 80 years old and now require a smaller, lighter
car than my present Volvo 340SE automatic. The new car must have automatic transmission, power-assisted steering, a sliding/tilting sunroof, five
doors (including hatchback), folding rear seats, a reasonable size boot, a
radio/cassette, some form of side impact protection, economical petrol
consumption, automatic locking and a price up to £10,000 or thereabouts.
Could you advise as to what is available?* **"**

Remember, you may be able to get a discount,
so don't be too shocked at the list prices I am
about to give you. A Citroen Saxo 1.4SX automatic at £10,820 on the road, a Daihatsu
Charade 1.3GLXi five-door auto at £11,005
OTR, a Fiat Punto 60 SX Selecta at £10,557 OTR

(including tilt/slide sunroof); or a Peugeot 106 1.4XL five-door auto at £10,965 OTR (with tilt-only sunroof). The Punto is the easiest to get in and out of, and is well recommended by readers, but it has developed more than its fair share of gearbox problems.

Micra *versus* Polo

" *The last three BBC 'Top Gear'/J.D. Power Customer Satisfaction surveys put the Nissan Micra streets ahead of the VW Polo, yet the latter seems to depreciate much less. Any explanation, please?* "

The public values the Polo higher, and there is a combination of reasons for this which include VW's UK marketing policy, its award winning advertising, the perception of 'German' quality (Polos are built in Spain) and, last but not least, the fact that the public prefers the way the Polo looks. No disrespect to the Micra, which is an excellent little car with a jewel of an engine as long as the oil is changed regularly.

Hatchback with 'class'

" *My husband and I are both 70-plus, with all the usual arthritic problems, and we need to change our car. I am very impressed with all you say about the Fiat Punto, but my husband won't even look at it. He wants something with status. So, please, what is next best? We expect to pay about £10,000.* "

A VW Polo. A friend of mine recently reckoned 'a bottle-green three-door Polo with a sunroof is the most middle-class car in Britain. If she could afford one, that is the one and only car Hyacinth Buckett would be seen being driven

around in.' My friend had a point. Three doors rather than five doors says it's a second car. Bottle green is the right colour. And a sunroof says you can afford the extra cost. However, because of the status Polos provide for their occupants, used prices are outrageously high, so, unlike Puntos, these cars are best bought new.

Heaven on wheels

" I have to replace my company car, spending up to £25,000 (though I could go to £27,000). I drove an Alfa 156 2.5 24v and have fallen in love with it. The trouble is, my fleet manager says Alfas are expensive to maintain and have low residual values! Surely this can't be true, given that they have a three-year warranty and their build quality is much better nowadays. I even heard mention of a magazine article that said that 156 residuals would be 3% better than a BMW's. Would you check this out for me please? "

After a wonderful 700-mile weekend with an Alfa 156 2.5 24v, I can fully understand what you're going through. It's the most exciting-looking saloon car there is, has hooligan acceleration, drives like a dream and turns heads wherever you go. (The 'Police Alert' optional spoiler may also turn the wrong sort of heads.) The Alfa is a work of art, the BMW is a pinnacle of Teutonic throughness. You choose the Alfa because the aesthetics override the known qualities of the German car. So, while the BMW 3-Series (especially the four-cylinder cars) merely say you're a conformist company person, not prepared to stick your neck out, the Alfa brands you as brave, exciting, perhaps a tad dangerous, and with impeccable taste. It's the difference between pure and acquired cool. Build quality of the Alfa feels the equal of the VW Passat or 3-Series but, more important for residuals, the first year's official UK imports are restricted to just 4,000. First 156 residual value predictions were more cautious than you suggest, but all fleet residuals are likely to be affected by UK new car prices falling into line with those in the rest of Europe anyway. In any case the benefit tax you pay for personal use of your company car is directly related to its list price. So put your foot down. Since you're literally paying for it, you should have a right to choose what you're paying for.

Heart or head?

" *I have a red 1994 BMW 320i Coupe with sun roof, full leather sports seats, M-Tech body kit, 17in. OZ alloys, 37,000 miles and full BMW service history. I'm thinking of changing it this year and have test-driven an Alfa 156 2.0 Twin-Spark and a VW Passat 1.8 Turbo Sport. I found the Passat a bit bland but offering better boot space for golf clubs. I like the Alfa to drive, but is it the best long-term purchase?* **"**

Put it this way, if you want to feel inspired every time you open the garage doors, go for the Alfa. The 2.0 Twin Spark is probably a better everyday compromise than the 2.5, which, though wonderful, is a bit of a hooligan. Best colour so far seems to be 'Silver Grey', but I'd love to see one in Alfa's 'Silver White Metallic'. After an all-too-brief affair with the Alfa 156, the Passat took quite a bit of going back to because it simply isn't a car you can reach the same plane of emotional involvement with. But its competence is unarguable, especially with Sport suspension and wheels. Mine was a five-speed Tiptronic, which works brilliantly apart from the logic of the Tiptronic shift – forward for upshifts and backward for downshifts. Your BMW has the older iron block, which is free of the troubles of the later 323/328 alloy block, so this could make the car more saleable.

Passat disappointment

" *In September 1997 I took delivery of a new VW Passat 1.8 20v SE auto with climate control. Compared to my previous Vauxhall Carlton automatic I am most disappointed with the new car. The Carlton gave a very smooth ride, was comfortable, had a silky automatic box which added to the luxurious ride, and was economical. In contrast, I find the Passat uncomfortable, with a very hard ride (despite replacing the 'V'-rated tyres with 'H'-rated Michelin Classics). Its automatic gearbox behaves all the time in the manner the Carlton's did in 'Sport' mode. The car is much noisier. And it is terribly thirsty: 26.1 mpg recorded on its computer over the 4,000 miles travelled so far. I feel I must cut my losses and replace the car, but its one good feature, climate control, I would certainly want again. So what do I replace it with? Logically I should have an Omega, but* *the model with CC was too expensive, and I wanted a slightly smaller car to give me more garage room. I tow a small caravan three or four times a year, so I need a reasonably powerful engine, but overall I am used to 'a comfortable, gentleman's carriage'. Your recommendations, please.* ”

Others have been complaining about the Passat 1.8 automatic, too. Main gripes are the way the nearside front roof pillar and mirror obscure vision when turning right out of a side road (they have a point), a whine from the four-speed autobox, low twenties fuel consumption in town. Our test Passat 1.8 Turbo Tiptronic did 28 mpg overall over 768 quickish miles. You should do some proper brim-to-brim tests. Another factor is that VW odometers tend to be very accurate, whereas those of other makes overestimate mileage by as much as 10%. The April 1998 issue of *Top Gear* magazine rated the Passat as having the best ride and handling compromise in its class, and, having travelled many thousands of miles in various Passats myself, I can't agree with your comments about the ride. Even my mum likes it, and she hates my dad's Mercedes 190E. But help is probably at hand in the form of the Audi A6, which shares the same floorpan as the Passat but has much 'softer' suspension. The model I'd go for if I were you would be the 165 bhp 2.4 30v V6 with Tiptronic gearbox. Then you could decide when you want it to change gear. Find a combined VW/Audi agent and you should be able to negotiate a sensible part-exchange deal.

Talking of torque

“ *Due to my illness, my wife is now the only driver in our family. Her driving style requires exceptionally high torque at low revs. The new VW Golf*

Mk IV TDi 110 and the Toyota Avensis TD both produce about 150 lb. ft. at approximately 2,000 rpm. Are there any others? **"**

Knocking the socks off everything is the new Citroen Xantia Common Rail TDI (to be known as the 'HDI') which stonks out 147.5 ft. lb. of torque at 1,350 rpm, rising to a massive 184.39 at just 1,500 rpm. Torque remains at 147.5 ft. lb. or more from 1,350 rpm right up to 3,800 rpm, and maximum bhp of 110 is delivered at 4,000 rpm, which should make it a brilliant engine capable of pulling a high final drive and delivering class-leading economy.

Automatic diesel MPV

" *I wish to purchase an automatic, diesel, seven-seater MPV with air conditioning. Does any manufacturer make such a vehicle for sale in the UK?* **"**

A VW Sharan TDI 110 S four-speed auto has all this as standard for an on-the-road UK price of £21,042, which includes a three-year warranty.

Horse and car

" *I am looking for a car that is reasonably economical fuel-wise, has a bit of style, is good for daily short journeys and monthly long journeys of 250 miles, and is also able to tow a horse trailer from time to time, the all-up weight of which is 1,250 kg. I can spend up to £15,000 and envisage something 2–3 years old. I'm thinking of a BMW 318 tds Touring. Is this suitable for my requirements, particularly for towing? Have you any other suggestions?* **"**

Not many hills where you live, so a 318 tds might be able to manage the trailer. The trailer's weight is within the 1,375 kg towing weight limit recommended by *Diesel Car & 4×4* magazine for this car. Finding one won't be very easy though, and don't expect typical BMW performance from this car. According to *Diesel Car*, the 0–60 time for the saloon version is 13.4 seconds, but you can expect around 40 mpg. What else? A Xantia 2.1TD is faster, more economical, arguably more stylish, handles better on country roads, the estate comes with three proper rear seat belts, and the self-levelling suspension makes it better for towing. If you ever find yourself having to tug the horse-box out of a muddy field, however, you're likely to be better off with a Subaru Impreza 2.0 or a Forester 2.0 four-wheel-drive. You won't get the fuel economy, but you probably will get out of the field without the aid of a tractor.

To auto or not to auto?

" *My 77-year-old father drives approximately 10,000 miles a year in his 'N' registered Rover 420. He is considering buying a VW Golf Mk IV when they become available. I would welcome your opinion on this and I would like also to know if I am right in trying to persuade him of the advantages of an automatic, especially as he has a stiff shoulder and anticipates continuing to drive for another three years. He thinks that with an automatic there will be too much to go wrong.* "

Golf Mk IV is fine. Good choice. Well built. Standard ABS. I'm not so sure about suddenly putting someone who has spent sixty years driving manuals into an automatic, because they can get confused and fall victim to 'unintentional acceleration syndrome'. VW has recognised this condition and fits all its automatics with a gear selection system that requires the footbrake to be applied for the lever to be moved from 'P' or 'N' to 'D' or 'R' unless the car is moving, in which case the lever can be moved from 'N' to 'D' without having to touch the footbrake first. Your father is right in thinking that there is more to go wrong with an automatic. You have to balance the cost of replacing the ATF every year against the cost of replacing a manual's clutch every six or seven years. Diesel automatic fans will be pleased to know that there is a Golf Mk IV TDI 90 automatic to rival Vauxhall's Astra 2.0DI automatic.

£20k Jag or £20k BMW?

" *I am now retired and within the not-too-distant future will have to relinquish the use of a leased car. My wife and I feel we deserve a bit of luxury in our old age, but don't think it prudent to purchase a new car at this end of the market, so I am considering a 3–4 year old BMW 7 Series or a Jaguar XJ, up to £20,000. What do you think of these choices, bearing in mind we will be doing about 8,000 miles a year? What other makes should we consider? And would you recommend purchasing at a franchised agent, a specialist dealer, privately or at auction?* "

The current-shape XJ is reckoned to be much more reliable than its predecessors over the first three years and, bought carefully, your money stretches to one of the earlier six-cylinder cars. The BMW would have been a good choice were it not for a question mark about the longevity of its Nickasil-lined bores, especially when the car is subjected to short runs from cold on relatively high-sulphur-content petrol. Some Sevens have been modified with steel-lined bores (a major operation involving a new engine block and pistons). So the only way I'd touch one of these would be from a BMW franchise offering a long warranty on the engine.

The other model to think about is a Mercedes – either an E Class or a smaller-engined S Class. Mercedes agents will be the most expensive, but should offer the best warranties. If instead you buy from a specialist dealer, privately or at auction, it's pot luck, with the most risk presented by the auction purchase. Your other option is to buy a secondhand LHD car in mainland Europe, preferably Germany. Because of the relative strength of Sterling and the relative flatness of the German secondhand market, a LHD BMW or Mercedes could be half to two-thirds the price of an RHD car in the UK. It is likely to have been driven properly on German autobahns and therefore less prone to suffer the 'short-run syndrome' so common on low-mileage UK-market cars.

Golf to 320i

" *My wife wants to change her car. She has at present a 'C' reg. Golf CL which has only travelled 50,000 miles and which she has owned for nine years. It has been totally reliable and used daily. After* Top Gear's *glowing report on the model, would £1,500 be a reasonable asking price if sold privately? As to its replacement, I have been offered, through work, a colleague's ex-company car which is a three-year-old BMW 320i with 120,000 miles on the clock. It has been BMW-agent serviced and still looks and feels almost new. The asking price is under £8,000. Given my wife's annual mileage of 3,000–5,000, would such a car prove reliable? Are there any serious costs imminent, such as catalytic converter or engine management system failure? For the same sort of price we could buy a two-year-old Mondeo or Xantia. Your views would be welcomed.* "

A price-tag of £1,500 is a bit on the high side for the Golf, but it's worth advertising at this price. If you get several nips, you may obtain the full asking price. If response is luke-warm, you may have to drop £100 or so in negotiation. But your first priority should be to grab that 95M BMW before somebody else does. Assuming it has metallic paint and either a sunroof or aircon, and especially if it's an 'SE', it's a bargain. Demand for iron-block Three Series sixes is increasing due to worries about bore wear in the later all-alloy blocks (corrected from February 1998 production). Your first service job should be to wean the engine onto a fully synthetic oil such as Mobil 1 or Esso Ultron and, because your wife's low mileage is likely to include a high proportion of short runs, change this oil and the filter twice a year. Most imminent failures are likely to be valve stems seals (changing all 24 will be quite expensive). The car's 40,000-mile-a-year regime will have been good for the 'cat', but this, too, could well give out within the next couple of years. I wouldn't anticipate early ECU failure. If BMW-agent service bills start to frighten you, find an Autotechnic or a good independent specialist. Properly looked after, this car will go on and on and on.

IMPORT/EXPORT

Poundstretchers

Many thousands of readers enquired about benefiting from the relative strength of Sterling by buying a car in France, Belgium, Spain, Holland or Germany and personally importing it. A story in the Telegraph *of 14 February 1998 mentioned pre-tax savings of up to 54%, and this was followed by Kevin Ash's story about how he managed to save £5,000 apiece on the purchase of two Alfa 156s.*

Other readers have asked about 'grey' imports from Japan: new cars with exotic specifications such as the Subaru Impreza WRX; and used Japanese cars of which by far the most popular is the Mazda Eunos Roadster (sold in the UK as the MX5). What follows is the situation as understood in August 1998. Please remember that, by the time you read this, things may have changed. If there is a shift towards genuine free trade, official car prices within the UK would have to fall by around 20%. If Dutch and Irish registration tax was imposed on exports, prices would inevitably rise.

Manufacturers and official importers have been resisting any reduction in the huge premiums consumers have to pay to buy in one European country rather than another – and for that matter to buy in Europe rather than the USA or Japan. An official Japanese importer led a delegation to Transport Minister Gavin Strang to make sure that independent imports of non-EU Type Approved Japanese and American cars were limited to a cumulative quota of just fifty of any one model in any year. VW lodged an appeal with the European Court of First Instance against a £70 million fine imposed on it by the European Commission for preventing Germans and Austrians from buying VWs in Italy where they were cheaper than in Germany. (UK prices are around 30% higher than their equivalents in Germany.)

Chancellor of the Exchequer Gordon Brown has expressed disquiet that cars should be 20% cheaper in the USA than in Europe, and he was immediately reminded that cars are 20% to 40% cheaper in Europe than they are in the UK. Despite the fact that the European Commission constantly mon-

itors the situation, most manufacturers have maintained restrictive trade practices. What happens next will depend on Karel van Miert's decision that UK quota restrictions on imports are illegal under EU law.

Buying in Europe

Some cars are significantly cheaper in continental Europe than they are here. In general, the greatest percentage savings can be made among mass-produced, oversupplied cars. Different VAT rates and the imposition of a high registration tax in countries such as Holland affect the 'on-the-road' prices. For example a Ford Fiesta 1.25 three-door may be £7,726 in Holland, compared to £7,028 in Spain and £9,145 in the UK. A basic 1.8 litre 20v Audi A4 is £17,242 on the road in Holland, compared to £15,200 in Spain and £19,016 in the UK. A Mercedes base C200 Classic is £19,985 in Holland, compared to £19,960 in Spain and £22,245 in the UK. A Mercedes C250TD is £24,061 in Holland, compared to £22,600 in Spain and £24,245 in the UK. And a base Passat TDI 90 is £14,871 in Holland, compared to £12,348 in Spain and £16,540 in the UK for the slightly better-specification 'S'. These are tax-paid prices – subtract 17.5% Dutch BTW plus Dutch BPM

Registration Tax (variable up to 30%), or a straight 16% Spanish VAT, then add 17.5% UK VAT. (Rates at Dfl 3.3 and Ptas 250 to £1.)

   In countries such as Holland and Ireland, which impose heavy registration taxes, big savings can be made by buying at the pre-tax price, importing to the UK and paying UK VAT. A typical Dutch pre-tax price breakdown is as follows:

- BMW 525TDS, no extras   Dfl54,882
- Extra for right hand drive   Dfl1,020
- Extra for 'on the road'   Dfl1,350
- Temporary export plates   Dfl300
- Typical ferry costs   Dfl400
- Total   Dfl57,952
  - @ Dfl 3.3 to £1   £17,561
  - UK VAT @ 17.5%   £3,073
- Total cost   £20,634
  - UK list, UK spec. excluding VED   £26,051
- Saving (excluding radio, etc.)   £5,417

On the same basis, for a Peugeot 306 TD a reader was quoted Dfl30,479 (£9,236 @ Dfl3.3/£), plus VAT, total £10,852 + VED + £25 UK registration fee, plus plates (Leon Van Bruniesse at Netherlands Car Trading, Utrecht, tel: 0031 3024 75100). I was quoted Dfl35,000 for a LHD VW Golf Mk IV GTi 20v Turbo with aircon by the VW agent in Leerdam (0031 3456 16424), to which I would have to add the cost of export plates, continental insurance, ferry costs and UK VAT, but the dealer told me that whether he could supply the car would depend on the outcome of VW's appeal.

   Alfa Romeo has issued its continental dealers with a 'right hand drive' price list. A Belgian price breakdown is as follows:

- Full UK spec Alfa 156TS   Bfr717,404
- Metallic Paint   Bfr14,876
- Sub total: Bfr729,280
- Less 6% discount   Bfr688,000
- Transit Plates   Bfr10,000
- Total   Bfr698,000
  - @ 60 Bfr to £1   £11,633.33

	Ferry Costs	£150
	UK VAT @ 17%	£2,062.08
●	Total cost	£13,845.41
	UK List	£17,537
●	Saving	£3,692

The dealer in this case was the Alfa Romeo agency in Ghent, salesman Koen Quintens, tel: 0032 893 04930.

Calais Renault dealer DAC has set up an export sales desk for RHD Renaults and has been offering them at an average 25% less that the UK price, after accounting for UK VAT. Talk to Stephan van der Broeck, Diffusion Automobile Calasienne, 58/60 avenue de Saint-Exupéry – B.P. 154 – 62103 Calais, tel: 00 33 321 19 15 58, fax: 00 33 321 19 15 59. Also at Calais Carrefour Hypermarket.

In all cases, the warranty is as in the country of purchase, so will be 1 year rather than the 3 years for some makes in the UK.

Illegal restrictions

Asking for right-hand drive usually causes problems. Any order for a right-hand-drive car in a left-hand-drive country could be delayed – not to frustrate RHD buyers but because the ordering system and production allocations are not set up for it. Under the EU Treaty of Rome it is supposed to be illegal for a manufacturer to refuse to supply any EU citizen with any car in any EU state. It is not illegal for such an order for a RHD car in a LHD country to be delayed or for a reasonable extra charge, such as £500, to be levied for RHD. Genuine waiting lists for cars in demand, such as the Alfa 156 and the VW Passat, can be as long in Europe as they are in the UK. And, of course, by the delivery date, the favourable Sterling rate may have reversed. But try for a RHD Ford Mondeo and there is no reason why you should not be able to get it within a month (LHD and RHD Mondeos are all built in Belgium.)

We were refused a RHD Seat Ibiza TDI in Holland on the grounds that RHD Ibizas simply were not available in Holland (Seat is owned by VAG). But we were quoted Dfl26,036 for an Ibiza TDI 110 GT 3-door, complete with air conditioning, Certificate of Conformity and export plates, a price that translated to £9,284 in the UK with UK VAT paid.

If you encounter any definite refusals to supply you with a car, report the matter to: Karel van Miert or Dieter Schwartz, DG IV, European Commission, 200 Rue de la Loi, 1049 Brussels, Belgium.

Buying in the UK

If you have a friend living in, say, Paris, you could try going to a dealer out of your area and asking for an 'export sale' RHD car, saying you're a temporary ex-pat living at your friend's address. When the car arrives, you'll get it at close to the pre-tax French price for a RHD car. Give your real address as an accommodation address in the UK and the car will be temporarily registered to you at this address. All you then have to do is pay the UK VAT and 'import' the car back into the UK. The full UK warranty will apply. But do be sure to pay the VAT within 30 days of taking delivery.

Booklets, Documents and Procedure

Anyone seeking to import a car should apply for booklet P12, 'How to Permanently Import your Vehicle into Great Britain', from the DETR·VSE1, Zone 2/01, Great Minster House, 76 Marsham Street, London SW1 4DR, enquiry line: 0171 271 4800; booklet SVA1, 'The Single Vehicle Approval Scheme', from Vehicle Standards & Engineering, at the same address, tel: 0171 271 4561; and VAT Notice 728 from your local Customs and Excise/VAT Office, or tel: 01304 224370.

If importing from another EU country, open a foreign currency account at your bank in the appropriate currency. Then order relevant car magazines for the country in which you want to buy – Auto Motor und Sport for Germany, Auto Week for Holland, Coche Actual or Autopista for Spain, Irish Auto Trader for Eire –and start phoning dealers with the intention of buying a car already in stock, either pre-tax or with the forms to reclaim the local taxes. (One very good reason for choosing Dutch or Irish dealers, of course, is that they all speak English.) Once you have located a car, send your deposit by telegraphic transfer (which takes three days). When the car arrives at the dealer, obtain the VIN number and arrange for the car to be insured in the UK on the VIN. (If your insurer won't do this, brokers ABM will, tel: 0181 681 8986.) Send the rest of the money by telegraphic transfer (once again allow three working days), take a flight to the relevant country, get the dealer to fix you up with 'export plates' and insurance, and make sure that the car comes with an EU Type Approval 'Certificate of Conformity' or you won't be able to register it in the UK. Then simply drive to the nearest ferry. When you land, if you have not already filled out VAT notice 728, go through the red channel and get one. (You have up to thirty days to pay – no longer.)

If you have bought a LHD car it's a relatively simple matter to change over the lights and foglamp, get the speedo altered to mph by Reap Automotive Design (0181 863 2305), have the car inspected and have it registered via your local VRO. With Europe-wide Type Approval for European cars from January 1998, there is no need for an SVA for a new European car, but you must make sure you get a 'Certificate of Conformity' with it, otherwise it will be subject to SVA.

If you order a car from a dealer in mainland Europe, the biggest worry you are likely to face is that he may demand a substantial deposit – of up to 30%. If his franchise is pulled or he goes bust before you take delivery of your car, the situation is the same as in the UK. Your deposit becomes one of the assets of the company and you will be way down the list of creditors, so you'll be unlikely to get it back.

Agents

The alternative is to use an agent, such as the very helpful Carfax International, tel: 0181 288 3536. If you do, make sure the final price (or price parameters) are pre-agreed in Sterling, in writing on the contract. Write down the exact specification you are contracting to buy on the contract (don't make the mistake one reader made of 'assuming' a VW Sharan would automatically come with seven seats and a driver's manual in English), and also make sure that any deposit you make is either paid by credit card or paid into a 'client' or 'escrow' account from which you still have some chance of getting it back if the worst comes to the worst. Other agents include Park Lane on 01420 544300, Origin Euro on 0181 696 0999, PCA Car Brokers on 01892 516261, Eurocar on 0800 068 0303, Euro Continental Cars on 01703 470208 and Auto Liberté on 01491 412468. Though agents get you through the hoops, they do, of course, charge for their services, and your saving on the car will be greatly reduced.

A further source is cancelled RHD export orders. Since the economies of RHD Pacific Basin countries collapsed, UK companies have specialised in diverting RHD exports to the UK. Included are Park Lane on 01420 544300, Trade Sales of Slough on 01753 773763, and Hughes Motor Co. Ltd on

01202 381888. The problem is, because they were scheduled for export out of the EU, these cars might not come with an EU Type Approval Certificate of Conformity and are therefore subject to a Single Vehicle Approval Test. A further problem (as the law stands as laid before Parliament on 8 April 1998) is that if these cars are imported by agents, only 50 of any one make and model can be SVA-approved in any one year. Importers and the EU Commissioner are obviously fighting to get this restriction lifted.

Japanese Imports

The strong pound has also made secondhand RHD imports from Japan spectacularly cheap. There is an auction of used Japanese imports every month in Dublin (Windsor Car Auctions, Bewlgard Road, Dublin, tel: 00 351 1 4599 300). Specialist importers include: Warrender of Bolton, tel: 01257 427700; Orbis International (part of Sidney Newton plc), tel: 0181 965 9666; John Boyd, tel: 01840 213010; Windsor Motor City, tel: 00 353 1 4061 000; Keith Chapman at Far East Services, tel: 01322 529647; Park Lane, tel: 01420 544300; MMC International Holdings Ltd, tel: 0181 656 1555 (website: http://www.mmc-intl.com); AJR Trading, tel: 0161 723 3748; Intercar, tel: 0181 203 3399; and Direct Vehicle Rental, tel: 01902 353393. From a list of cars which were shipped on the Asian Beauty out of Nagoya in March 1997, I worked out some examples of UK-landed trade prices, shipping and all taxes paid: 1990 Eunos Roadster (Mazda MX5) £3,976; 1992 Mitsubishi Galant 2.0 V6 £5,636; 1991 Toyota Celica Turbo £7,325; 1994 Toyota Celica Cabrio £8,838.

But I advise great caution, because these are Japanese-specification cars and are not necessarily suitable for use in the UK. When ECUs are electronically interrogated, the information is in Japanese. Low mileage in a Japanese car may also mean countless hours idling in Japan's notorious traffic jams, which wrecks engines. A useful appraisal of the situation is provided in Automobile Buyers Services Technical Information Sheet 27, from ABS, Adelphi Mill, Grimshaw Lane, Bollington, Macclesfield, Cheshire SK10 5JB, tel: 01625 576441 (ABS Vehicle Inspections: 0345 419926). You should also speak to Martin Dix at Intech (01264 773888) because he knows what is needed to get individual models through the SVA test. Though the SVA test did not become compulsory until 1 May 1998, an official SVA certificate is the only sure way to know that any grey import you buy is likely to pass a future MOT. A three-year-

old grey import with a dodgy MOT could be as illegal to drive in the UK as one with no MOT at all.

The test costs £165 for cars and £60 for vans and is available at Ministry HGV testing stations. The SVA procedure will recognise overseas approvals, such as the American Federal Motor Vehicle Safety Standard. SVA Inspection Manuals, which give full details of the test, are available, priced £25, from The Vehicle Inspectorate, PO Box 12, Swansea SA1 1BP.

However, the biggest problem is the SVA quota restriction applied to these cars. Any non-EU Type Approved car up to three years old (proof is required of the car's age) imported by a private individual will be subject to an SVA test, and there is no restriction on the numbers of cars imported by private individuals. But non-EU Type Approved cars up to ten years old *imported for re-sale* will not only be subject to SVA, but the cumulative quota of that model that can be imported, tested and registered is restricted to 50.

By April 1998, the cumulative total of most Japanese imports, even Subaru WRXs, had already been exceeded. So do not under any circumstances buy a Japanese import which has not been SVA tested and registered or you may find it cannot be. (As before, naturally the importers are fighting this restriction and the DETR has kept the matter 'under consultation', so it may have been relaxed by the time you read this.)

Bringing a car back from France

" *Since I retired six years ago I have been living in France, and I bought a 1993 Peugeot 309 'Vital' 1.9 diesel which has now covered 80,000 kms. I intend to return to the UK soon and bring the car with me to use to try and find a suitable place to settle. I understand there are certain garages in the UK which specialise in the purchase and sale of left-hand-drive vehicles and would appreciate any information as to their location. As an alternative to selling, would converting the car from left-hand drive to right-hand drive be a viable proposition?* "

This will be a genuine 'personal import' with no tax to pay, and you should have no trouble eventually registering the car to a UK address. You have twelve months to do this so will need to make sure that your French insurance covers you, otherwise you'll have to insure the car by its VIN number. You need the leaflets mentioned earlier in this chapter. The best specialist I know of for left-hand-drive cars is The Left Hand Drive Place, Whitney Road, Daneshill, Basingstoke, Hants RG24 8NS, tel: 01256 461173. Unless you can find a RHD 309 with severe rear end damage to cannibalise (preferably one with power steering) and a small garage to do the work at a low labour rate, a left-to-right conversion isn't worth doing.

Buying a British car abroad

" My daughter in Italy is buying a UK-registered, taxed and MOT tested car. Her problem is that she will not be leaving Italy to return to the UK until late August, but the MOT and VED run out at the end of July. Is there any way around this problem? "

If the car has been in Italy for more than twelve months, then it is illegal for it to remain on a UK registration. If it has not, and your daughter officially 'resides' in the UK, then she can use the registration document to register her keepership of the car to her (or your) UK address. (However, it would still be illegal for the period the car is 'kept' in Italy to exceed twelve months.) Your daughter then faces a 'grey' period between the end of July and the end of August. On landing in the UK, it will be legal for her to drive the car directly to a pre-arranged MOT test, after which she should be able to use the VED reminder (which will arrive in mid-July) to re-tax the car at a post office retrospectively as from 1 August. The other problem, one you have not mentioned, is insurance: in order to re-tax the car in the UK at a post office, this also needs to have been arranged in the UK.

Illegal export

" *I have a 'D' registered car which I have owned from new and which remains in excellent condition. However, with it being worth very little, I decided to take it to my cottage in France and use it when on holiday. Now, twelve months on, I have a problem. I am unable to re-insure it as it now needs an MOT. I do not want to bring it home every year. Please can you tell me how I can be covered for a maximum 1,000 miles a year? Does the French 'Control Technic' qualify as an MOT? French insurance is very expensive.* "

What you have done is technically illegal because a foreign car is only allowed to remain in any EU country for twelve months, after which it must be registered to an address in that country. You now have two choices: register the car to yourself at your French address, put the car through the French 'Control Technic' and insure and tax it in France; or bring it back to the UK every six months, use one of the six-monthly visits to MOT it, and insure and tax it in the UK. Insurance Brokers such as ABM, tel: 0181 681 8986 (highly recommended by readers with slightly unusual policy requirements), can fix you up with a Norwich Union policy which provides for extensive use in Europe.

Secondhand imports

" *Some time ago, you covered the personal import of new cars from mainland Europe. You concluded that for ordinary cars there may be some savings to be made, but there could be a long wait for a RHD car ordered from a continental dealer. But what about secondhand cars? And how could I import a secondhand Mercedes 190?* "

As long as Sterling stays up against the DMark and the Franc and continental Europe remains in comparative recession, it makes sense to buy

There is no VAT or import duty to pay when you import a car more than six months old, and on which local VAT has already been paid, from another EU country.

used left-hand drive cars in Europe, particularly sports cars such as Porsches, Audi Quattros, Corrados and Mercedes SLs. Two specialists who can do this on your behalf are Simon Howarth on 01932 850244 (mobile: 0370 946944), and Richard Able on 01787 479346. Nick Faure carries a selection of LHD Porsches (01483 4148000). If you want to try it yourself, you need the booklets referred in the introduction to this chapter. There is no VAT or import duty to pay when you import a car more than six months old, and on which local VAT has already been paid, from another EU country. But if it's less than three years old, make sure it comes with an EU Type Approval Certificate of Conformity or you won't be able to register it without going through SVA.

Speedo correction service

" I have followed all the correspondence on the matter of personal car imports, and I've read the relevant section in your book. Now I am about to try it. In May I shall take delivery of a new Mercedes outside the EU. Then I shall bring the car back to the UK and pay duty and VAT. Being RHD and LH dip, and absolutely standard, the car will comply with SVA in all respects except one: the speedo will read in kilometres. The cost of changing a Merc speedo is probably too horrendous even to think about. Is there a simple solution such as an acceptably calibrated and easily fitted stick-on disc? With the chances of personal imports increasing, there may well be a market for such an easy option. "

Speak to Julian Reap of Reap Automotive Design, 4 Radnor Road, Harrow, Middlesex HA1 1RY, tel: 0181 863 2305. He specialises in colour-coding instrument clusters and either silk-screening transfers or fitting new dial faces to kilometre speedos. Once a speedo has been screened, new dial faces are available from stock, but the process of creating a new one can take up to six days and it will mean supplying Reap with the speedometer rather than the car. Prices are from £65 plus VAT. Changing the odometer from kph to mph is usually a separate job, of varying complexity. Some electronic odometers can be switched over easily; others are more difficult. Mechanical odometers are best left alone.

The Irish question

" I am hoping to buy a new car in the Irish Republic. Part of the reason is the artificially low pre-tax price of cars in Ireland to allow for high new car taxes (29.9% registration tax plus 21% VAT) and part is due to the strength of Sterling against the Punt. If I proceed, the car will have to be ordered specially and delivery will not be for six months. So how do I buy at today's advantageous Sterling rate? And what rate will I get after commission – the 'tourist rate' or a different rate? Where best can I exchange the currency? And how do I compensate for loss of interest on my UK investments? "

Though Sterling is presently 10% ahead of the Punt, the two currencies reflect each other much more closely than, say, Sterling and the Peseta. If you buy foreign currency when Sterling is very strong you usually get the best rate at a bank of the country the currency of which you are buying. Or you can open a foreign currency account at your own bank, transferring money to and from it at the commercial rate, but the interest you get will reflect the base rate of the foreign country rather than the UK base rate. You have no choice but to take a gamble – either buy your foreign currency now or speculate on Sterling going higher. When you buy in Ireland at the pre-tax rate, you pay UK

VAT at 17.5% on entry to the UK (payable within thirty days). Tel: 01304 224370 for details and VAT Notice 728. You lose benefits such as a three-year manufacturer warranty, but can save several thousand pounds even on a UK-discounted price. To insure the car on its VIN number, talk to a good broker such as ABM on 0181 681 8986. They will arrange a cover note showing the chassis number.

Cross-channel swap

" I will soon be going to live permanently in France and have a problem which must also face anyone else planning to do the same thing. I have a two-year-old right-hand-drive Citroen ZX which has the balance of a five-year, 60,000-mile warranty to run. I would like to part exchange this for a left-hand-drive Citroen Berlingo Multispace to be registered to my French address. Obviously a French Citroen dealer will not want a right-hand-drive UK-registered ZX, but does Citroen operate any kind of scheme enabling me to effect the part-exchange in the UK? "

Yes. Speak to Sam Williams of Citroen London West in Brentford, tel: 0181 987 4000. He specialises in export and military personnel sales, and should be able to work out a deal for you.

Figaro, figaro, figaro!

" I have just become the proud owner of a very unusual car. It's a Nissan Figaro which I bought locally from a dealer and fell in love with at first sight. I would like to discover some more information about the car. Can you tell me, please: when they were first produced; how many were made (I've been told it was a limited edition); how many came to the UK; how much they cost new; what Nissan model they were based on; whether I can get a handbook in English (mine is in Japanese); and what colours they came in? I hope you can help me or refer me to someone who can. "

You're in celebrity company, as Vanessa Feltz, Betty Boo and Mrs Jonathan Ross also have Figaros. They were the last and best of a series of retro-styled cars which began with the 1 litre Mk 1 Micra-based Be-1, progressed through the 1.5 litre Sunny based S-Cargo van and 1.0 litre Micra-based Pao utility car, and ended with the turbo-charged, air-conditioned, automatic 1.0 litre Micra-based Figaro. As far as I can remember, the Figaro was built from 1991 to 1993 but was limited to 10,000 units, and prospective buyers were chosen by lottery. There are estimated to be less than 100 in the UK, all 'personal' grey imports. Prices reflect the 'want factor' and scarcity, and currently run at between £15,000 and £18,000. Colours are grey and cream, or pastel green and cream – similar to the colours of the 1950s Goggomobiles which inspired the Figaro. There is a book, 'Nissan Micra 1983–1992', price £9.95, which may help, and a Haynes Manual for the Mk 1 Micra (code: H0931), price £11.99. (Mill House Books on 01205 270377, or Delta Press Ltd on 01442 877794.) For servicing and repairs, go to: Intech GB, Thruxton, Hants, tel: 01264 773888, who have the necessary workshop manuals. They can also recode the radios to UK frequencies. Talking to Martin Dix of Intech, I discovered that they have already put quite a few Japanese 'grey imports' through the new Single Vehicle Approval Test and know exactly what is needed for a pass.

Twingos completely legalised

After a number of appeals in the column, I now possess a list of suppliers of all the components

Left-hand-drive Twingo Matics with PAS would be ideal vehicles for the disabled, because they would then have a small, inexpensive, very versatile vehicle they could get out of much more safely kerb-side.

needed to make Renault Twingos completely UK legal. VCA-approved left-dipping headlights can be supplied by David Benton, Broadmeadows Garage, Padstow Road, Wadebridge, Cornwall PL27 7LS, tel: 01208 812046, at £150 a pair delivered. Mph and kph speedometers with installation kits can be supplied by Peter Hass, Twingo Direct, HMS Ltd, TLF Unit 4, Castle Lane Industrial Estate, Melbourne, Derbyshire DE73 1DY, tel: 01332 864659, at £224.50, plus postage and VAT. Fitting is easy, but callers can have the units fitted by HMS for no extra charge. All that then remains to do is to move the rear foglight over from the left to the right. It has often struck me that left-hand-drive Twingo Matics with power steering would be ideal vehicles for the disabled, because they would then have a small, inexpensive, very versatile vehicle they could get out of much more safely kerb-side.

Suppliers other than those already mentioned include: (South): Auto Europ, c/o 7 Clementine Close, Beltinge, Herne Bay, Kent CT6 6SN, tel: 01227 769700, fax: 01227 741257; (Midlands): Studio Imports UK, Alscott Park, Stratford-upon-Avon, Warks CV37 8BL, tel: 01789 450480; (Wales): Dafydd Williams, Garreg Lwyd, Penrhyndeudraeth, Gwynedd LL48 6AW, tel: 01766 770203; (France): Stephan van der Broek, Diffusion Automobile Calasiene, 58/60 avenue de Saint-Exupéry – B.P. 154 – 62103 Calais, tel: 00 33 321 19 15 58; (Spain): Inaki Martin Dominguez, Twingos Aragon, Calle Sagrada Familia 3, 2 – esc, 3-B, Zaragoza 50 012, Spain, tel. (mobile): 00 34 09 06 02 13, fax: 00 347 623 4917 weekdays, 00 347 656 2366 weekends; Paul Cross, Dragon Car Hire S.L., Calle Poeta Salvador Rueda 29, 29640

Fuengirola, Los Boliches, Malaga, tel: 00 345 247 5360, mobile: 829 447 192 (UK office: Bridge Frame, Dean Street, Stalybridge, Cheshire SK15 2JD, tel: 0161 303 8317).

For details of the Twingo Club, write c/o Dave Thornton, Renault Twingo UK Register, 30 Cranmer Avenue, Ealing, London W13 9SH, tel/fax: 0181 932 3396.

Spanish import?

" *I am considering buying, in Spain, a basic Fiat Cinquecento at a cost of around £4,200. If I were to bring it back to the UK (I can afford to wait for six months) what would I have to pay besides the cost of the RHD lamps and mph speedometer?* "

You'd also have to shift the rear fog lamp from the left to the right, buy a set of number plates and pay for your UK road tax. But apart from this, as long as it comes with a CoC, that's it. At the rate of Ptas250 to £1, I make the cost of a basic Cinquecento 900S to be £4,361, including 16% Spanish VAT, which works out at £3,759 before tax. If you bought the car free of Spanish tax, VAT would be due on this on entry to the UK. So, say the shipping cost pulled the price up to £3,900, you'd be looking at £4,600 plus the lights and the speedo for a left-hand-drive car. Since, by April 1998, RHD 8,000-mile 'R' reg. Cinquecento SXs in metallic colours were selling at auction for £4,425, the exercise you propose doesn't seem worth it.

Paying by Czech

" *I have just returned from the Czech Republic where I was amazed at the prices of cars. These are some examples: Ford Ka, £4,800; Toyota Corolla,*

£6,750; Citroen Xsara, £6,800; Skoda Octavia, £8,000. These prices include recoverable tax at, I believe, 22%. HM Customs & Excise tells me that I must pay European Import Duty at the rate of 10% on the pre-tax price, plus VAT at 17.5% on the trade price plus 10%. Would this be the cheapest way of purchasing a new car, or would, say, Holland be cheaper, bearing in mind any discounts for cash available in any of these countries? "

As long as you don't mind left-hand drive and you are buying from dealer stock rather than having to order and wait for delivery, this may well be the cheapest way to buy a car. However, in the Czech Republic, you are not protected by any EU Consumer Laws. I doubt that the cars would be covered, even by the manufacturer warranty, in the UK and, with no EU Type Approval CoC, you may not be able to register the car in the UK. A car bought in Holland would be EU Type Approved, and discounts on Dutch list prices for LHD cars are typically 6% to 10%.

Wrong kind of import

" *I recently returned from Poland after working there for 18 months. Whilst there I bought a Polish-built Fiat Cinquecento 900S with left-hand drive, paying all relevant Polish taxes. I returned to the UK in August 1997 and, in order to get it registered and insured in the UK, I applied for and received Transfer of Residence Relief. My problem now is twofold. Having got another job abroad in Dubai I want to sell the car, but I am unable to do so unless I pay UK import duty and VAT or wait a year from when it was re-registered. Is there any way round this? If the answer is no, then what is the best way to sell a left-hand-drive car in the UK, and how much might I get for it? The car is 'N' registered and has done the equivalent of 20,000 miles.* "

What a mess you've got yourself into. When you imported the car last August it was worth about £3,500 all taxes paid. So any tax you pay should be as a proportion of this; in other words, 17.5% VAT amounts to £521.28, while 10% European import tax would be £270.79. In early 1998, in LHD form with all UK taxes paid, the car is worth £2,750 to £3,000. In the short time you have available it's going to be difficult to offload this car, non-tax-paid, to someone taking it back to Poland (where the taxes are paid) or to someone taking it out of the EU. But Peter Rushforth at The Left Hand Drive Place might be able to help, tel: 01256 461173.

Spanish Saxo

" Recently we asked you about the ride quality of small hatchbacks, and you advised us to try the Citroen Saxo. My wife and I joined a queue at 9.30 on Monday morning at Citroen Palma de Mallorca to find four sales-men selling the full range that was on offer. We had a test run and bought the basic Saxo, which at current exchange rates (Ptas250/£1) worked out at just £4,750. We are very pleased with the car. Many thanks. "

Yes, readers, you did read that correctly: £4,750. It must have been a special cut-price model, though, because the cheapest 1.1X Saxo lists at the equivalent of £5,873 in Spain and £8,165 in the UK (though Citroen soon responded with a 1.0-litre Saxo at £6,995). The UK price usually includes at least a year's and sometimes two year's insurance and remains open to negotiation with the franchise. The closest we can get to your deal in the UK is the Perodua Nippa EX, now £4,999, plus VED and including a two-year warranty.

UK motoring costs

" I have just returned from a tour of the continent, where I was aston-

ished to find the following equivalent prices for a litre of 95Ron 'premium' unleaded: Switzerland, 50p; Austria and Germany, 56p; Northern France, 62p. In 42 years of motoring I cannot recall a time when French petrol was cheaper than it is in the UK. Also, while waiting at traffic lights opposite a BMW dealer in Wangen near Bodensee I spotted a Z3 Roadster offered at the equivalent of £15,500 and an 8-Series coupe at £16,500. Though everyone keeps saying this is due to the strength of Sterling, the pound is still not as strong against the DMark and the dollar as it was in the mid-1980s. I would be interested in your comments. **"**

We Brits are being collectively ripped off and we're suckers for putting up with it. A litre of unleaded in Spain is just 48p. In Bali, it's 5p.

American imports

" *Do you have any information on the importation of used vehicles from the USA? I am considering buying in America and then importing to this country. Can you offer advice on UK duty and tax and shipping procedures and costs? Also, do you have details of auction sites on the US East Coast?* **"**

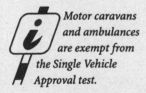
Motor caravans and ambulances are exempt from the Single Vehicle Approval test.

There is 10% European import duty to pay on the invoice price of the vehicle plus the shipping costs, then a further 17.5% UK VAT to pay. Unless the situation suddenly changes, all private imports up to three years old (you must be able to prove the precise age of the vehicle) are subject to a Single Vehicle Approval test at an HGV station, which costs £165 for cars and £60 for the less severe test for commercials. Motor caravans and ambulances are exempt, and any other privately imported vehicle over three years old is exempt but must pass a UK MOT (including emissions testing) before it can be registered. The appropriate two leaflets are: 'How to Permanently Import your Vehicle into Great Britain' (Department of Transport leaflet

P12, December 1996) and 'The Single Vehicle Approval Scheme' (leaflet SVA1, also December 1996). Both are available from Department of Transport VSE1, Zone 2/01, Great Minster House, 76 Marsham Street, London SW1 4DR, tel: 0171 271 4800. A good shipper is Mann Motor Ships (tel: 01703 237711) which imports from Jacksonville, Charleston, Baltimore, New York and Halifax to Southampton and Liverpool, using Wallenius Lines. Mann only uses roll-on roll-off ships, but you can have a car shipped as deck cargo or fully containerised. Expect to pay between $495 and $625 to ship a 'one-off' average-size car. You'll also have to pay US wharfage of $75–$85 and UK wharfage of about £30. Insurance has to be negotiated with a Stateside broker. British Car Auctions' head office, tel: 01428 607440, can put you in touch with ADT in the USA, while the CMA head office, tel: 0113282 8606, can put you in touch with Manheim Auctions.

INSURANCE AND WARRANTIES

LHD insurance

" Why do insurers discriminate against left-hand-drive cars? I recently insured a Chevrolet Corvette and was amazed at the disparity between the quotes. One broker even told me the insurer 'would have to load it because it was left-hand-drive'. Why? I am a careful driver with no points on my licence, no accidents, and I am over 30 years old. Who does the best insurance deals on LHD American cars? "

American Car Imports (0181 889 4545) tell me that about ten brokers specialise in American car insurance. One of the best is Peter Lewis of Badbury Insurance, Southampton, tel: 01703 232223. The big insurance companies, such as Norwich Union, are very well aware that owners of American cars tend to take great pride in them. Other left-hand-drive insurers are: Bradford and Hatcher on 01473 211951; and NFU Mutual, which is happy to cover European and Japanese left-hand-drive cars.

Excessive excess?

" I would like to draw your reader's attention to the practice of certain car rental companies of charging a £100 'excess' when even the slightest damage occurs during a rental – even if it was not the renter's fault. My son hired a car from Hertz in August which suffered some very minor

damage that he thought could be polished out, but he was still charged the £100 compulsory damage excess. **"**

I checked this with Hertz. These things take time to process, but, having inspected the car, Hertz decided that the damage was so slight it was not even worth pursuing the third party's insurer. Your son's credit card account has been re-credited with the £100 'excess'.

Well connected

" *I thought you might be interested in my experience with my car insurers. I have a comprehensive policy with Sun Alliance Connections which I took out because it was very competitive on price. Recently my car was stolen. In less than three weeks I had not only been quoted a very fair price in settlement, but I had also received the cheque – together with a very welcome £150 towards the cost of hire cars in the interim. Connections' quotation for covering a replacement car of higher value was also very reasonable. Friends in a similar position, but with other insurers, have told me of protracted delays, sometimes lasting several months. So far as I am concerned, Sun Alliance Connections is definitely 'flavour of the month'.* **"**

Nice to read this (especially as I used to do a bit of work for Sun Alliance before the merger. However, since your letter came totally 'out of the blue' I feel it's not unreasonable to print it). To be totally fair, a reader from Edgware also reports good claims experience with Guardian Direct. Price alone is not the only criterion in choosing a car insurance policy.

Extended warranties

" *I have just taken delivery of a Ford Ka and, yes, it's everything the pun-*

dits have praised. However, I was strongly pressed by the salesman to take out an extended warranty with service cover. This shook my confidence, as I would not expect to have to replace tyres, brakes and exhaust at the second service. The total package is £377, which includes the cost of the first two services. But, of course, had I bought a Nissan Micra, it would come with a three-year, 60,000-mile warranty at no extra cost. "

So would a Mazda 121, which is effectively a Ford Fiesta with different badges and trim, built on exactly the same production line. But the imposition of 17.5% VAT on separately purchased extended warranties is likely to shake this matter up. Manufacturer warranties included in the price of the car are already subject to this tax, so an aftermarket warranty, which used to be a method of VAT avoidance, now offers no tax saving. Nor does a warranty 'included' in the price of a used car but invoiced at far more than the dealer actually paid for it. I quite like the idea of Ford's 'Service Cover B', which includes the cost of brakes, tyres and exhausts as well as servicing. For your £377 you're then getting even more peace of mind than you would with a free inclusive three-year, 60,000-mile, warranty – and, since Fiestas and Kas can go through brake discs rapidly, you're covered.

Don't settle for less

" *Your readers should be aware that, subsequent to an accident which is not their fault, they may be able to claim for the fact that their car is worth less after accident repairs than it was before the accident. After a crash (for which the other driver was fined £75), through my solicitor I successfully claimed compensation for the diminished value of my car. Initially I had suggested a figure of 5%, but the consulting engineers recommended 10%. In making my case, my solicitor quoted the following precedents:* Payton v Brooks 1974 *(before Lord Justice Ormrod);* Brightmore v Eaton

1986 *(before Judge Crowther QC) and* Watson v Aston Hackney Turvey 1991 *(at Leeds County Court). Part of the judgment of this last case reads:* 'The Diminution in Value occurs immediately after the accident damage has been repaired. From that date, the motor car has a diminished value which remains with it for the rest of its existence. The diminution does not arise upon the sale of the car. It is my view, therefore, that the damages for Diminution in Value to which a plaintiff is entitled is the difference between the price the plaintiff would obtain if he sold the car immediately after the repairs had been completed and the price he would have obtained on that date if the car had not been involved in an accident.' In the event, my case was settled out of court with an amount for Diminution in Value included in the settlement figure.* "

The great thing about this is that it enables an owner left in a disadvantaged situation as the result of another driver's negligence to force the other driver to make right, just and proper redress. (For help, see 'Crash Victories', below.) The same is not true, however, if your are fighting a settlement offered by your own insurer for damage you have inflicted on your own vehicle. Then your own negligence, and the precise terms of your insurance policy, may be cited against your case.

Crash Victories

A reader who has dealt with around five hundred cases claiming for 'Diminution in Value following Repair Work' has sent me a file of judgments and is very experienced in cases of this kind. He is a professional, and fees would need to be agreed. But any reader who thinks he or she has a good case should contact D. Griffiths of Cotton Griffiths and Co., Consulting Engineers, Automobile Accident Claims Assessors and Valuers, 880 Stockport Road,

Levenshulme, Manchester M19 3BN, tel: 0161 225 5813.

Agreement seems to have been reached that the diminution percentage should be age-related – for example, 10% of the trade value where a car is less than one year old with less than 12,000 miles, 5% where a car is less than two years old with less than 25,000 miles, and 2.5% where a car is less than three years old with less than 50,000 miles. The award should also allow for the extent of the repairs – up to 20% when a new car has been extensively repaired down to 2% when an older car has had minor repairs. Diminution in value of accident-damaged 'classic cars' obviously requires different criteria.

Another Automobile Accident Claims Assessor is J. Hill, The Claims Bureau, 58 Dinsmore Road, Balham, London SW12 9PS, tel: 0181 673 9988. The number for the Insurance Ombudsman Bureau is 0171 928 4488; and that for the Association of British Insurers, 0171 600 3333.

Uninsured losses

" I had an accident in August 1997 which was not my fault but, because my insurer settled 50/50 with the other party's insurer, I have been left out of pocket. I supplied full details of the accident to my insurers together with witness statements, yet I have still lost out. Where did I go wrong? And how should I approach this the next time? "

It's too late now, but what you should have done is immediately refer the matter to a Claims Assessor or a specialist solicitor. A firm recommended by readers is Easthams Solicitors, and I spoke to Andrew Eastham to find out what is and isn't possible in such cases. First, it needs to be understood that such specialists will only get involved where the client is not at fault, where there is a genuine and recoverable 'uninsured loss', and where the third party responsible for the damage is properly insured. Their enquiry officers will establish this during the first telephone conversation. Depending on whether a client is insured 'Third Party', 'Third Party, Fire and Theft' or 'Comprehensive', uninsured losses could include any of the following: loss of earnings; hire of a car or loss of use of the damaged car; repairs to the damaged car; diminution of value of the damaged car after repair; personal injuries; ambulance fees; damage to other property (such as clothes or belongings in the car); taxi fares to and from hospital; insurance excess; increase in premium as a result of the claim; and 'reasonable expenses' (not including the client's costs of corresponding with them). Easthams Solicitors' two addresses are: Continental House, 292–302 Church Street, Blackpool FY1 3QA, tel: 01253 299222; and 10th Floor, Leon House, High Street, Croydon CR9 0TE, tel: 0181 681 5464.

Crash, bang, wallet

" *I recently had an accident which resulted in my insurer writing off my car. I then purchased a replacement, only to find that this particular insurer would not cover it. The insurer did refer me to another insurer which would cover the new car, but would not refund the balance of my premium. So, having taken out insurance in November, not only did my insurer get a £200 policy excess but kept the remaining £133 as well. This is doubly galling because, had I been able to stay with the insurer, I would not have lost this £133. What can I do about it?* "

Nothing. But this raises an important point many other readers may not be aware of. When you take out any insurance policy, you pay a premium for cover over an agreed period. If you make a claim at any time during this period, then cancel the policy, you are not entitled to reclaim any 'balance' of premium for the rest of the period. If, however, you cancel a policy having not made a claim, you are entitled to a pro-rata refund minus administration charges. The lesson to be learned from this is to ensure that a replacement car can be covered under your existing policy before you buy it.

Warranty racket?

" *Last year we bought a 'K' reg. Astra Estate with a three-year Warranty Holdings warranty on specified parts. To keep the warranty valid, basic servicing that my husband would have done has had to be carried out by a garage. At the last service we were advised that the head gasket needed replacing and, although it is a specified part, we have found that we are not covered for the full cost of the job. Warranty Holdings will only pay for the ICME book time of 2.6 hours labour, and will not pay for replacement cylinder head bolts nor for the cost of replacing the timing belt – even though we were told this had to be replaced as part of the job. So, although Warranty Holdings will pay £133.42 of the bill, we still have to find £102.73.* "

In fact you don't have a warranty, you have a mechanical breakdown insurance. And the truth is, Warranty Holdings has honoured a fair proportion of the cost of the total repair. Even though the cylinder head bolts and timing belt had to be replaced, you are now in a better position than you were before. The timing belt would have had to be replaced at some time anyway – at a cost not far short of the £102.73 you were asked to pay – and you can now look forward to three years and 36,000 miles before you need to replace it again.

Unwarranted claim?

" *In March 1995 I bought a low-mileage 1994M Ford Mondeo 1.8LX from a nearly new specialist for £9,495. I was also encouraged to take out a two-year extended warranty, which I did. Then, in December 1996, the car was diagnosed as having a worn ring gear on the flywheel and I made a claim on the warranty. I was asked to supply service history dates and mileages and, having done so, was advised my claim was invalid because I had the 70,000-mile service carried out early, at 66,543 miles, and thus invalidated the warranty. I would be grateful if you could take this matter up and print this letter as a salutary lesson to motorists before they consider effecting this type of insurance.* "

The manufacturer-scheduled service intervals for a Mondeo 1.8iLX are 10,000 miles apart and, while this is pushing it in my view, you have at least been covering a beneficially high mileage in a short time. But the service intervals the insurers told me you gave them were: 19 September 1995 at 17,090 miles; 8 November 1995 at 40,090 miles; 28 February 1996 at 53,707 miles; 15 May 1996 at 61,295 miles; 25 September 1996 at 66,543 miles and 13 November 1996 at 84,086 miles. There is some confusion as to whether the car had done 17,090 miles when you bought it (on 27 March 1995) or on the date the extended warranty came into force (19 September 1995), and you might like to clear this up because otherwise there appears to be a 23,000-mile gap between the first and second services. But the 13,617-mile gap between the second and third services, and the 17,543-mile gap between the fifth and sixth services, are each enough to disqualify claims under the terms of the warranty. If this is incorrect, and you can demonstrate that the car was in fact serviced at maximum intervals of 10,000 miles, the insurer will reconsider your claim.

Salvaging a 'write-off'

" *I own an 'E' reg. Renault 11 and, as a result of an accident, the car was damaged beyond economic repair. I decided I would retain the salvage of the car and have the repairs done myself. The valuation was agreed at £1,925. The argument I have is that the engineer who assessed the damage and the value told me that the salvage value he would put on it would be 20%. I then went ahead with the repairs, and the independent engineer who examined the car afterwards suggested that a reasonable salvage value for the car would be £200–£350. Subsequently my insurer, Direct Line, informed me that as far as it is concerned the salvage value is 35% of the £1,925. As a result, I am £289 out of pocket.* "

I can understand the urgency to get the car back on the road and hence the hasty repair. But the fact is, Direct Line has a deal with several salvage companies which take its repairable insurance damage write-offs – and they pay 35% of the settlement figure for every car. What the

Always check with the insurance company precisely what the salvage value will be before authorising repairs on your insurance damage write-off.

salvage companies lose on the swings they gain on the roundabouts. That's the deal, whatever independent assessment may be made of the car's salvage value, and Direct Line's rather good settlement figure is partly based on getting 35% of it for the salvage. (You can't have it both ways.) The moral of all this is to check with the insurance company precisely what the salvage value will be *before* authorising repairs on your insurance damage write-off.

Insurance database

" *It appears that the Motor Insurance Bureau has proposed a single computer database of all privately held car insurance policies. The proposal suggests terminals at all police control rooms, immediately accessible to traffic officers and even 'beat' officers who call in, to be funded entirely by the MIB. It seems that the MIB believes that the cost of this would be more than met by the resulting increase in the number of insurance policies issued.* "

This is a very good idea, and will certainly help motorists who feel they have been let down by the police when the insurance of a driver who damaged their property was later found out to be invalid or fake. But, if we are going to go this far, we might as well go further. First, reform the Data Protection Act to make vehicle keepership information accessible to everyone. Then replace the antediluvian 'tax disc' system with vehicle detail 'smart cards'. The smart card would contain all the vehicle's V-5 details, the period for which it is taxed, the period for which it is MOT certified, the period for which it is insured, any outstanding parking tickets and road traffic offences against the vehicle – and the mileage when anything was done to the vehicle. Once the technology was in place, a new Road Traffic Act would need to be passed compelling the smart card details to be to be entered into a terminal whenever the car is MOT tested, re-taxed, re-insured, stopped by the police, or ever enters a garage, tyre dealer or bodyshop for any work at all. The database would, of course, need to be protected so that a lower mileage than the previous mileage recorded would immediately set off alarm bells and could not be recorded.

Classic Golf insurance

" I have a 1982 Mk I Golf GTi with a mildly modified 150 bhp engine, and uprated suspension, wheels and brakes. I only drive it 5,000 miles a year, so have been looking for a cut-price 'classic' policy, but I can't find one as none of the insurers I have approached will cover modified cars. Any suggestions? "

What? Not in Club GTi? How dare you drive a Mk I without joining the club? (For an application form, write to Sean Grenyer, Club GTi Membership, PO Box 2747, Brighton.) Advertising in *Rabbit* (the club's magazine) is a specialist insurer offering discounts for Club GTi members on both standard and modified cars. Call John or Kerry on 01792 650933, 01685 383838 or 01792 872664 after office hours. Also advertising in *Rabbit* are Herts Insurance Consultants on 01279 506090, but again you need to be a member to get the Club GTi discounts (membership is only £20 a year).

Private 'warranty'

" The warranty on my January 1994 Audi 80 stipulates that it must be serviced at a franchised dealer and thus ties me down to franchised deal-

er prices. Is it possible to buy a private warranty which would allow me to shop around for services when the current warranty expires in October? **"**

For a private used-car 'Mechanical Breakdown Insurance' ('warranty' is a misnomer), try: OneQuote Respond on 01452 529969; Motor Warranty Direct on 0800 731 7001; and AA Personal Warranties on 0990 225600. When you buy one of these MBIs direct, you only pay 4% Insurance Premium Tax rather than the 17.5% that must now be charged by dealers selling MBIs with cars. Motor Warranty Direct also covers items such as air-conditioning compressors, direct ignition units, fuel injection airflow meters and warm-up regulators, ABS pumps, electric window motors and many other items not covered by some MBIs. Remember, though, these are all insurances, not guarantees. Both the price of cover and the amount of cover depend on the underwriting risk involved.

Knight in shining armour

" *I want to buy a secondhand car for my 24-year-old son. As I have a limited budget, I think this will have to be a private buy. A friend told me about a warranty scheme she had seen advertised under the name 'White Knight'. Would this protect my purchase?* **"**

First, understand that all a secondhand car warranty can ever be is a form of insurance policy ('Mechanical Breakdown Insurance' is the correct term). For an insurance underwriter to meet any claims on such a policy, there must have been nothing wrong with the car when it was sold. They will not meet 'warranty' claims for faults which were already present. White Knight recognises this by creating a contract between vendor and buyer in which the vendor lists all of the car's major parts in good working order and White Knight covers them with its MBI. If any of these parts fail within twenty-one days, White Knight then either pays for the repair or has the AA inspect the vehicle in order to decide if the fault was present when the car was sold. If it was, the vendor is held liable for the repair. After these twenty-one days the buyer has cover for the remainder of the six- or twelve-months warranty period purchased. The plan can be used to cover any car up to 10 years old and up to 110,000 miles, the cost is fixed at £99 for six months or £149 for twelve months, and the policy can be taken out either by the vendor or by the purchaser. To obtain a contract form with full instructions, call: 0870 601 6055.

Insurance Saga

« Saga Motor Insurance advertises 'Because it is widely recognised that driving ability improves with age and experience, many insurance companies now offer a discount to people aged 50 and over. But at Saga, we believe you deserve more than just a discount. We only offer our motor insurance policies to car owners aged 50 and over.' My annual premium for 1996/97 was £260.77. The renewal notice last month asked for £362.82. The reason given for the increase was my postal code and my age of 76. »

Insurance premiums have risen over the last year and are likely to rise again now that insurers are expected to fund the cost of NHS injury treatment. Excesses (the amount of a claim to be paid by the policyholder) are also set to rise. But whenever a driver is hit with a premium hike such as this, it's a good idea to shop around. First point of call should be a good broker, such as ABM on 0181 681 8986 or Rauch and Stallard on 01702 348261. Another reader recommends Age Concern Insurance Services (Motor Department), Halford House, 2 Coval Lane, Chelmsford, Essex CM1 1TZ, tel: 01245 351540.

'Engine lifetime'

" *In your column and in your first book you frequently exhort car owners to have their engine oil and filter changed at least every six months. Yet when I wrote to Volvo about this, I received the reply: 'With modern, high-tolerance oils and the latest low-friction design of engines, as fitted to your 1.6 litre car, it is entirely acceptable for oil to remain in the engine for up to one year or 10,000 miles, whichever is the sooner.' The letter goes on to state: "Certainly, you will lose the benefit of Lifetime Care if an intermediate oil change takes place outside the Volvo dealer network. Clearly, we would not have the guarantee that the correct oil and filter would be fitted.' So how do you square this with your advice to change the engine oil and filter at least every six months?* "

If you read the 'Lifetime Care' warranty description you will find that it does not mean your lifetime, merely a reasonable 'life' for each component. So I phoned Volvo to ask what a reasonable 'life' would be for one of its Renault-derived 1.6-litre engines. The answer was: 'Engine failure at 100,000 miles is not unreasonable.' So, if you want your engine to last 100,000 miles, do as Volvo says. If you want it to last a lot longer, do as I say. And if you want to keep your 'Lifetime Care' up to 100,000 miles, have the intermediate oil and filter changes carried out by a Volvo agent.

Out of line

" *Our neighbour crashed into our Jeep Cherokee 4.0 LTD SE, admitted responsibility, and the car went back to the Jeep franchise for repair. Now it has steering and handling akin to riding a bar of soap in a wet bath tub. And no one wants to take responsibility. The repairers say there is nothing wrong with the car, even though it has gone back to them twice, and the insurers are saying that because my wife picked the car up we have accepted that the work has been done satisfactorily. What can we do?* "

If the insurers really said this, they're lying. Morally and legally you are entitled to be put back into the position you were immediately before the accident. The problem may simply be caused by excessive 'toe-in', which can make many cars feel like you described. The steering box may be loose. (Cherokees were recalled because of this possibility, and my neighbour's had to be repaired twice.) Or the chassis and suspension may be out of alignment and you would need to ascertain this by taking the car for an alignment check, which will cost you £150–£200 (speak to Autolign on 01604 859424, or Popplewells on 01992 561571). You should also contact an insurance assessor to act on your behalf (for telephone numbers, see 'Crash Victory' earlier in this chapter).

'New-for-new' catch

" *In August, our 9-month-old Polo 1.6GLX was damaged by another car. Our insurer's approved repairer supplied us with a courtesy car, but, after inspection, our Polo was written off and the courtesy car was returned. Since our insurer operates a 'new-for-new' policy for write-offs less than a year old, it ordered a new 1.6GL model for us with optional ABS and passenger airbag to bring it up to GLX specification. We are still waiting for this replacement, as the VW agent not only cannot give us a delivery date, he cannot even tell us when the car will be built. Since I need a car for work, we have now run up well over £1,000 in hire car costs, yet the third party's insurer refuses to pay more than £1,000 for this. What is your advice?* "

Insurance policies do not usually provide for 'courtesy cars' other than during the period the policyholder's car is being repaired.

Insurance policies do not usually provide for 'courtesy cars' other than during the period the policyholder's car is being repaired. (These cars are provided by the repairer, not the insurer.) You are the innocent party here, and it is the responsibility of the third party or his or her insurer to put you back in the position you were immediately before the accident. If this involves finding an identical car to your original Polo 1.6GLX, then this is what they should do. But since you have opted for a new car and since delivery of this new car is the problem, I doubt that the third party can be held responsible.

End of warranty inspection

" *Our February 1998 Peugeot 106 will come to the end of its manufacturer's warranty in February 1999. To ask the Peugeot agent to carry out a thorough check before the warranty runs out would seem to be asking too much, because it would hardly be in the agent's interests to find a lot wrong with the car. So how can we find an impartial party to carry out such an inspection so that we can submit the car to the agent with a list of things to be put right before the warranty expires?* "

This is good thinking, but it does, of course, assume that the independent inspection will find enough wrong to be fixed under warranty to justify its own cost of between £50 and £150. Useful numbers for used car inspections are: AA, 0345 500610; ABS, 0345 419926; RAC, 0800 333660; Green Flag, 01254 355606; or check in Yellow Pages for a cheaper independent engineer. Remember, these inspections involve no dismantling, so for the same outlay or less you might be able to get a small local garage or MOT testing station to make a more comprehensive check, including emissions. In this case, you are not looking for a time-consuming written report – merely a short list of faults to be put right under warranty.

Searching questions

" *My wife and I have insured our cars through AA brokers since as far back as 1988. For a recent renewal, my wife received a document entitled 'Statement of Insurance', with over forty personal queries and statements, some queries too ambiguous to answer correctly and some statements simply incorrect. Repeated efforts have failed to persuade the AA's computer to print out a corrected form. The 'Statement' states that it forms the basis of the Contract of Insurance, and that failure to disclose information, or false information, could invalidate the insurance. But could one be contractually certain of no error in a detailed answer to questions such as 'Have you ever been convicted of any motoring offence?', or 'Have you ever suffered from any illness?' Bad contracts leave the contractors vulnerable, so the effect of this document is that we feel our insurance is no longer reliable. Can you advise as to whether the AA Statement can be ignored as inept administration with no significant place in law?* "

I checked this out with the Association of British Insurers. The law over contracts of this type is that, once a motoring conviction is 'spent' (for example, three years after a fixed penalty speeding conviction) you don't have to enter it on the form, and it would be illegal for a claim to be refused because you had not entered a 'spent' conviction. For the illness question, simply write 'no serious illness', or list any serious illnesses and state 'minor illnesses not entered'. For the mistakes, correct them on the form and keep a photocopy of your corrections. If the AA's clerks cannot get round to correcting the information held on the AA computer, then you cannot be held accountable. However, do check that none of this misinformation has led to an increase in your premium. Another reader, who happens to have a 'non-English' name, recently complained about being asked how long he had resided in the UK. This is an entirely legitimate standard question, because a driver unfamiliar with UK road signs, with the UK Highway Code, and even with driving on the left, is statistically more likely to have an accident resulting in a claim than a driver who has resided and driven in the UK for more than five years.

Third Party, Fire and 'Not Insured'

" I recently discovered that, because my husband's car was stolen in England by deception, it hasn't 'really' been stolen – and the loss is therefore not insured. Is not the insurance company playing the same deceitful game? It sounds jolly like it to me. Even the police are uninterested, despite the fact that they have traced the car. Or maybe I'm just thick. Perhaps one of your readers could enlighten me. The day that legalised theft was discussed I must have been absent from school. "

If a car is taken while the keys are in the ignition, most insurers will turn down a claim on the grounds of contributory negligence. If you let someone take a test drive without first making sure that your car is insured for 'any driver', or that the driver is insured on his or her policy, then you are taking an enormous risk (it's a common deception for the 'buyer' to nick the car while you swap seats to give him a test drive). Finally, if you sell a car and the buyer takes it away, only for the buyer's cheque later to 'bounce', of course the loss is not insured, because in UK law the car has not technically been stolen. The buyer is merely in breach of contract (and this, by the way, is a civil matter over which the police have no jurisdiction).

Land of litigation

" I am going to spend seven months of next year touring North America in my camper van. Negotiating shipment of the van to and from the USA has been no problem at all, but insurance is proving to be a nightmare. Every UK broker I have asked says it is better to negotiate cover in the USA. Most US brokers said I'm better to negotiate cover in the UK before I leave. I have now received one quote from a US broker for Third Party and Public Liability insurance, which is ten times the rate I pay for comprehensive cover in the UK. I expect to pay extra, but I think I am being seriously ripped off. "

The main reasons are the vastly increased risk of litigation in the USA and the huge size of personal injury claims. Insurers also see a far greater risk in insuring an inexperienced foreign driver in a vehicle with its steering wheel on the wrong side. The ABI's suggestions are, first, to see what kind of deal your own insurer can come up with, second, to see what help your motoring organisation (AA, RAC etc.) can offer, and third, to keep shopping around. Finally, it will also make sense to check the cost of hiring a camper in the USA for seven months, because this may work out cheaper than shipping and insuring your own and, of course, removes the risk of breaking down in a country where no parts are available for your vehicle.

GEM to the rescue

" I have declined to renew my breakdown cover with Green Flag National Breakdown because of unacceptably large premium increases over the past couple of years – and because my letter seeking an explanation was ignored. I have been told of the existence of an organisation thought to be called The Guild of Experienced Motorists. It is believed that this Guild restricts membership to those whose age exceeds 50, and it pro-

vides several interesting offerings, including breakdown insurance at more acceptable rates. Can you confirm its existence and provide an address or phone number, please? **"**

I phoned GEM on your behalf at 4.30pm on Christmas Eve, and I'm delighted to report that, not only was my enquiry answered promptly and with charm, but that an information pack was dispatched by the next available post. The Guild of Experienced Motorists is best known for its 'V' badges with the number of years the holder has been driving in the centre. But it imposes no lower or upper age limits, and is available to all. Membership costs £13.50 a year, or membership including breakdown recovery insurance £44.50 a year. (Members organise their own recovery from an approved list, then claim the cost back.) The Guild of Experienced Motorists, Station Road, Forest Row, East Sussex RH13 5EN, tel: 01342 825676.

Two drive cheaper than one

" *In December 1997 I sought an insurance quotation from Commercial Union. It duly arrived, giving a figure of £137.77 which assumed that both me and my wife would be driving. I pointed out to Commercial Union that my wife did not drive, and was then very surprised to receive a quotation for £181.48 for the same cover, but for myself as the only driver. How can this be?* **"**

It is a simple matter of insurance underwriting risk. Commercial Union has discovered from its claims records that a couple both driving the same car represent less risk than a single person driving the car. For this reason they introduced their 'Dual Driver Policy' at a lower premium than a standard (single driver) policy. Readers who want to check the price of a Dual Driver Policy should Freefone 0800 115116.

When it's a 'write-off', should you write off?

" *Recently my car was declared an 'insurance damage write-off'. My insurers sent me a form purporting to have been issued by the DVLA, requesting me to send them the insurance certificate, MOT certificate and entire V-5 form not completed or signed. However, on the V-5 it expressly states 'You are required by law to notify DVLC if you sell the vehicle'. Not wanting to break the law, I therefore completed and signed the tear-off slip and sent it in to the DVLC. Was this correct?* "

No. I checked with the DVLA and, while it did not issue your insurance company's form, it had approved the wording. So if your car is an insurance damage write-off and your insurer asks you to send the documents unsigned and uncompleted, this is the correct thing to do. You are not in effect transferring ownership to the insurer. The insurer merely acts as your agent in disposing of the write-off, which will be graded according to repairability on an insurance damage register. This does not mean that wrecks can be returned to the road in an unroadworthy condition. It merely means that an insurer may write a car off when the cost of restoring it to a condition acceptable to the policyholder exceeds a percentage of its value. Some damage repair specialists may be able to put the car safely back on the road at a far lower cost and then sell it to a buyer who is prepared to accept it as 'damaged/repaired'.

Saintly progress

" *I seem to remember that there used to be an organisation, operating under the name of 'Saint Christopher', that offered insurance against the loss of one's driving licence. Does this organisation still exist? And do you have any details?* **"**

Yes. St Christopher DriverPlan, IOMA House, Prospect Hill, Douglas, Isle of Man IM99 1PU, helpline: 0800 919639. For a premium of £192 a year, it provides cover of up to £1,200 a month to pay for chauffeur services, taxis or trains in the event of disqualification through points 'totting up' or speeding, revocation of licence due to ill health, inability to drive due to injury, or towards the cost of hiring a car if yours is stolen or damaged in an accident. More limited cover of up to £200 a month is available for an annual premium of £51. St Christopher will not provide cover against being banned for drink-driving offences.

Four-by-four for daughter

" *My daughter is 28 and wishes to purchase a 4×4 vehicle. She has been driving for eight years as a named driver on my policy which carries maximum no claims discount. As she would be insuring the 4×4 in her own name, would her record on my policy have any effect on the premium?* **"**

Your insurance record has no bearing on any discount your daughter will achieve. She may get an 'introductory' discount, and her driving record and age will help, but basically she'll be starting from scratch. A good insurer for 4×4s is The National Farmer's Union Mutual (01420 83516), but your daughter should still use a broker such as ABM (0181 681 8986) or First (05001 05001) to shop around for the best deal on her behalf.

LEGAL MATTERS AND CONSUMER RIGHTS

Your rights under the Act

The Sale of Goods Act (1979) was modified by The Sale and Supply of Goods Act (1994), which more tightly described what was meant by the requirement for the goods to be of suitable quality and 'fit for the purpose' for which they were sold.

It states:

'Where the seller sells goods in the course of a business, there is an implied term that the goods supplied under the contract are of satisfactory quality ... Goods are of satisfactory quality if they meet the standard that a reasonable person would regard as satisfactory, taking account of any description of the goods, the price (if relevant) and all the other relevant circumstances.' (This differentiates a garage or even a trader operating from home from a private vendor. A trader operating from home cannot hide from the obligations as outlined above.)

'... The following are in appropriate cases aspects of the quality of goods:

(a) *Fitness for all the purposes for which goods of the kind in question are commonly supplied.* (For example, it is reasonable to expect a Rover Metro 1.1 to operate adequately on shopping trips, the school run and leisure trips. It is not reasonable to expect it to pull a large caravan or to run all day at 100 mph.)

(b) *Appearance and finish.*

(c) *Freedom from minor defects.* (For example, it is reasonable to expect a new car to be free from minor defects such as small scratches and paint chips. It is not reasonable to expect a secondhand car to be.)

(d)   Safety. (For example, it is reasonable to expect the brakes, steering and suspension of a new or secondhand car to be safe, taking account of the nature of the deal and the price paid. It would not be reasonable to expect an old car, bought as a 'non-runner' with no MOT, to be safe.)

(e)   Durability. (For example, it is reasonable to expect a new or second-hand car to run properly without breaking down and without falling apart for a reasonable period of time, taking account of the nature of the deal and the price paid, and provided the buyer has maintained it properly and not abused it. It would not be reasonable to expect a £200 banger to be immediately capable of a long journey.)'

But these terms do not extend to '*...any matter making the quality of goods unsatisfactory...*

(a)   ...which is specifically drawn to the buyer's attention before the contract is made. (If defects are pointed out to you by the vendor, you cannot later reject the car for those defects.)

(b)   ...where the buyer examines the goods before the contract is made and which that examination ought to reveal. (If you are given a good chance to inspect the car and fail to notice a very obvious fault, you cannot later reject the car for that reason. However, a professional buyer is expected to know what to look for and to inspect the car much more carefully than a private buyer.)'

The Act then defines what is meant by "acceptance".

Goods are accepted where the buyer intimates to the seller he has accepted them or when the goods have been delivered to him and he does any act in relation to them which is inconsistent with the ownership of the seller. (So, start using a car as your own, without the permission of the seller, and you are deemed to have accepted it.)

But where goods are delivered to the buyer and he has not previously examined them, he is not deemed to have accepted them until he has had a reasonable chance of examining them. (So, if you order a car on the basis of a test drive or viewing of another in the showroom, you are not deemed to have accepted the car you ordered until you have had a reasonable chance of inspecting it.)

The buyer is also deemed to have accepted goods when after the lapse of a reasonable time he retains the goods without intimating to the seller he has rejected them.

The buyer is not ... deemed to have accepted the goods merely because he asks for or agrees to their repair by or under an arrangement with the seller. (So, if you ask the seller to put right a fault and the seller does put it right, you are still not deemed to have accepted the car.)'

Case law

Rejection under the Acts

There are a number of examples of case law on this section of the 1979 Act. In Bernstein v Palmerston Motors 1987, *the engine of Mr Bernstein's new car failed after three weeks and 120 miles. Palmerston Motors fitted a new engine, but Mr Bernstein still attempted to reject the car. When it went to court, Mr Bernstein's case failed. But in* Rogers v Parrish 1987 *the buyer tried to reject a Range Rover after six months and 5,500 miles for a catalogue of faults, including defective oil seals, gearbox defects and body problems. His case was upheld on appeal by the Queens Bench. Against this, in 1995 in Scotland, the case of a buyer who tried to reject a car after ten months (and two minor accidents) was rejected on appeal. And in* Carlisle v Lane 1996, *which concerned a used Range Rover alleged to be older than indicated by the date of registration, the case failed on appeal on the evidence because the buyer was adjudged to have been told the car was older than its registration date at the time of sale. In yet another, more recent case, the buyer of a VW Polo was held not to have rejected the car, because he kept possession of it rather than returning it to the dealer he sought redress against.*

Termination of a Purchase Contract

A more recent case, Johnson v HWM 1997 *(Kingston Crown Court) set another precedent.*

Mr J, an Aston Martin Virage owner, ordered a new Virage in October 1988 during the heady days of supercar speculation. He was required to put down a deposit of £20,000 of which VAT was charged as a proportion be-

cause, unlike an 'option to buy', his deposit constituted a part-payment for the car.

In 1989 Mr J decided he would like a more powerful car, and changed his order to the Vantage model. Then, over the years (there was a very long waiting list) he began to change his mind again, and, in 1993, asked to cancel the order. HWM refused to refund his part payment and instead suggested he took a new Virage which, by that time, had been uprated.

Mr J then launched a campaign against HWM alleging that, amongst other things, the Vantage was not a full four-seater and the car was not what he ordered because the automatic gearbox of Vantage models was retro-fitted. (In fact, a Vantage is merely a highly modified Virage and shares the same body shell as the Virage which Mr J already owned.)

HMW tried to settle the matter out of court, but could not reach agreement, so the case went to court.

On 15 August 1997 the judge found for HWM. Mr J not only lost his £20,000 deposit, interest on the deposit and HWM's loss of profit, he was also ordered to pay HWM's legal costs and court fees as well as his own. The precedent set here is that, in between the time of order and delivery, a manufacturer can change the specification of the car for whatever reason, whether it be legislation, development, changes of parts suppliers, or whatever.

Misrepresentation

C.M. of Dover had a dispute with a Mercedes salesman over the paintwork of a secondhand 300TE he purchased in October 1992. No instance more perfectly confirms my advice to avoid litigation for damages over and above a reasonable settlement offered by a dealer.

C.M.'s case hinged on the salesman's description of the car as 'an original one-owner car which [his garage] had supplied new to that owner and serviced'. The car, new in 1990, had a lot of extras to justify the price of £22,950 – partly paid by a part exchange allowance of £10,995 for C.M.'s older 300TE. But the word 'original' was important to C.M. because the newer car was in a shade of solid red, the pigment of which is notoriously difficult to match.

After two years, C.M. noticed that the paint on the nearside front wing and door had 'bloomed' to a different colour from the rest of the car. It later transpired that, early in the car's life (at fourteen weeks old), the paintwork of those two panels had been damaged by a golf trolley and they had been resprayed by the selling garage at a cost of £213.47, which included replacing the grille.

In April 1995, the garage offered to 'cut back' the bloomed paint, but C.M. declined. He demanded that the garage either took the car back and refunded the original purchase price, supplied him with a better car, or paid him £5,000. This figure was based on a perceived 'trade guide' price difference between the two cars involved in the original transaction, plus £800 'damages'.

On getting no satisfaction, C.M. issued a County Court summons for £900, representing the difference in trade value between an 'original' 1990H 300TE and one with repaired damage. The case was heard by District Judge Morling in the Ashford County Court on 12 December 1996 (Mulloy v Darren Dawkins). The judge agreed that the car was not 'original' and should not have been described as such – particularly where the golf trolley damage had been repaired at an earlier date by the selling garage and the information was on its records. But, in finding for the plaintiff, the judge awarded a mere £500 in damages and costs on Scale 1. This left C.M. more than £5,000 out of pocket and, though he was able to recover part of this after a Taxation Hearing, his loss was still considerable.

So, though a case of 'misrepresentation' was proven against the salesman (and may set a precedent for other similar cases), C.M. has still lost out. It could be argued that, in the circumstances, C.M.'s claims were less than 'reasonable' and the system punished him for this. But as long as the costs of legal action in the UK can outweigh any benefit, even when a case is proven, private individuals are ill-advised to take a case such as this as far as C.M. did. Unless you have money to burn, it is especially ill-advised to pursue any matter through the courts on 'a matter of principle'.

Mercedes Benz UK has taken the view that the case should never have gone to court and, according to C.M., has written to the selling garage asking it to refund to C.M. the balance of his costs as a 'gesture of goodwill'. However, since C.M. has asked Mercedes Benz UK to review the franchises of both the selling agent and another MB franchise which the agent called in as an expert witness, 'goodwill' may be a little thin on the ground.

Falling out with a restorer

If you consign a car to a restorer and then fall out with him, the relevant precedent is Peter Troy Davies v Anthony K. Divey (Peterborough County Court).

Troy Davies claimed that in January 1994 he took out a contract with Anthony Divey who trades as Triking Cyclecars to restore his car for a price of £1,791. He then paid £2,000 in advance, and in June 1994 he paid a further £400 to Triking Cyclecars. The plaintiff relied upon the implied condition of the contract that work would be done using all reasonable care and skill and that parts supplied would be of merchantable quality. He claimed that the defendant had failed him in each case, enlisted the help of the legal department of Which?,and relied on an RAC report carried out five months after he had collected the car from Triking. The plaintiff had refused to have his vehicle inspected by the RAC before he removed it from Triking's premises. After collecting the car on 28 April 1995 the plaintiff had faxed and demanded a refund of £3,301.90 on 2 May 1995. The refund was to be paid by 9 May 1995, and he later increased his demand to £4,300.

He made a claim on 30 January 1996, and issued a summons on 16 February 1996. Triking filed its defence and counterclaim on 22 March 1996, but the plaintiff did not respond to this until 12 June 1996. Action commenced in the Hitchin County Court on 21 October 1996, and was later transferred to the Peterborough County Court, a transferral which the plaintiff had opposed.. After various delays, the plaintiff presented his case, but was absent when District Judge Cernik heard the defendant's evidence on 12 August 1997.

The defendant's case was that there was never a written contract. He agreed he had collected the plaintiff's cyclecar in order to look it over and give the plaintiff a general idea of what could be done within the plaintiff's available budget. He then presented a fax sent to him by the plaintiff on 1 March 1994 listing a number of 'things to be done', which stated: 'Tony, if you can give me an idea of the cost of the above I will then know how much of my budget I will have left over to do the items below. As said on the phone, I am away from the end of March/April/May and possibly June, so there is no rush to get the job done. I suggest you look at it as one of those jobs to be done when things are a bit slack … There is no rush for the job. I don't even care if you can't start on it till your six orders are complete.' The plaintiff's fax then went on to mention other jobs he would like doing, including a complete respray, a re-trim of the cockpit surround, the fitting of a removable head, some new side pipes and stainless steel silencers and two replacement rocker box covers. He paid the defendant £2,000 as an advance, but not on the basis of any quotation. After costing the work and making a number of adjustments to what the plaintiff had requested, the defendant had quoted that he could perform a number of tasks for a price of £2,450, as long as time was not of the essence.

A first attempt to respray the vehicle was unsuccessful, due to concealed accident damage which the defendant had not found on his first inspection.

The Judge declared himself satisfied that 'at no time did the defendant agree to undertake a complete restoration' and that the 'all-important fax of 1 March referring to things to be done and other jobs that he would like to do are entirely inconsistent with a complete refurbishment. ... I formed a clear impression that the plaintiff was something of a perfectionist and found it less than agreeable to have anything to do with something that was in effect a compromise. ... The notice that he gave by letter of 21 April 1995 to complete the job on 24 April 1995 was clearly unreasonable. ... The plaintiff did not challenge the defendant's case that the defendant had wanted an independent expert called there and then (before the car was removed from his premises). ... He then commissioned his report from the RAC on 8 September which was a good five months later."

Working from a large number of photographs taken by the defendant during the restoration, the Judge decided that the vehicle inspected by the RAC was not the same vehicle presented by the plaintiff after restoration that May. Parts were missing and wear was in evidence that would not have been possible in the five months since the restoration, during which the plaintiff had anyway claimed he had been unable to use it. As a result the Judge stated, "I frankly find it difficult to attribute any degree of reliance upon the remainder of the Plaintiff's evidence ... I believe the Plaintiff got what he paid for. What the Plaintiff did after that in the presentation of this case suggests to me an attempt to distort the true facts and mislead the Court. ... I dismiss the Defendant's counterclaim, but the Plaintiff must pay the costs thrown away by the Defendant to include the hearing on 21 April ... a total of £495."

This seems to represent a victory for restorers working to contracts where time is not of the essence and presented with dubious claims by their clients.

Falling out over a sale 'on consignment'

Case No 96BUS188 between Richard John Leeson and Classic Automobiles of London Ltd went to trial in the Central London County Court on 13 August 1997.

In R.L.'s words, 'I had known the defendant for many years and in 1996, over a very enjoyable lunch, I agreed to allow his firm to sell a recreated Bugatti Type 40 of mine, constructed from original parts, for a net return to me of £50,000. The verbal agreement we reached also allowed me to sell the car myself at no commission to his firm on the basis of "first past the post" and I informed the defendant that some interest had already been expressed as a result of an advertisement in the Bugatti Owners' Club newsletter. Within a few days I received a call from one of the defendant's salesmen that he had an offer of £30,000 plus an Austin Healey he considered to be worth at least £20,000. I turned down this offer which was followed by a revised offer of £40,000 which I also declined. By that time, a potential purchaser I had spoken to some time previously expressed a more serious interest in the car and wanted to fly out to the UK to view it. This he did, by arrangement with the defendant's firm, and on the day he made me a firm offer of £50,000. He then expressed his satisfaction with the deal to the defendant's sales manager, and we returned to my home in Surbiton to complete the sales agreement and receipt. Two days later, I spoke to the sales manager about the sale and he told me that the car had already been sold earlier on that day to a purchaser who took out an option on it several weeks before and had now offered the full asking price. The case went to trial and when it was heard I was totally vindicated. But, unfortunately, it was not possible to "undo" the deal between the defendant's firm and the person to whom it sold my car, so my purchaser was disappointed.

Judgement was in favour of R.L., and Classic Automobiles of London Ltd was ordered to pay him £50,000, plus interest at £5,633.44, plus most of R.L.'s costs. What this case illustrates is the absolute necessity to put all such deals and any subsequent alterations in writing, so that any dispute can be easily resolved without the enormous cost of going to court (in this case estimated at more than £100,000).

My advice

The Retail Motor Industry runs a conciliation service for disputes between its members and used car buyers where the purchase was made less than twelve months previously. (It will not become involved in disputes over new cars.) The telephone number is 01788 538316/538317, but the RMI will only arbitrate where the dispute remains private, with no involvement of solici-

tors, Trading Standards officers, TV or the press. Alternatively you can discuss the matter with your local Trading Standards Office.

However, my advice is to think very carefully before you engage a solicitor and try to pursue the seller for costs over and above the amount you paid for the car. Where dealers agree to a refund, they are likely to stick their heels in over such costs. When a refund is agreed, a dealer will usually ask the recipient to sign a receipt stating that the refund is 'in full and final settlement', to preclude any further claims. This is often the best you are going to get.

If you fight the dealer for costs all the way to an Appeal Court hearing, not only may you lose the refund, you may find yourself landed with £10,000–£15,000 of court and solicitors fees – on top of a nerve-wracking delay before the Appeal hearing.

It's criminal

" *In December 1995 I purchased a 'nearly new' 'M' reg. MPV from a franchised dealer for £15,990, paid in full, with no finance involved. Twelve months later the car was involved in a serious accident resulting in it being declared a damage 'write-off'. Subsequently our insurer offered us £15,000 in settlement. Later, having heard no more from our insurer, I called them and discovered, to my horror, that two cheques had been issued. One, for £4,500, to us. And another, for the balance, to a finance company. I later discovered that a hire purchase agreement had been entered into on the car on 8 December 1995, the day after we paid for the car in full, and that repayments had been made by a car hire firm owned by the franchisee. This franchisee wanted us to authorise payment of the £9,500 insurance cheque to the finance company, promising to repay the money to us. We refused and instead asked him to clear the finance debt so that the full insurance cheque could be paid to us. He did, but his cheque bounced, and despite clear contravention of Section 27 of The Hire Purchase Act 1964, the insurer still acted as if the finance company had a claim on our vehicle. Fortunately, the franchisee paid off the finance with a bank draft and the settlement was finally transferred direct to our account the following day. We are hoping to replace the original MPV with a Galaxy, and in complete contrast the Ford dealer could not have been more helpful – even loaning us a car for the three weeks during which this debacle was taking place.* **"**

On the facts you presented, this looked like a clear case of financial fraud to me, so I passed the correspondence straight on to the manufacturer. It may have been that the franchisee got himself into a cash-flow problem while clearing cheques for cars sold for the new year, and raised cash from the double sale of your car. The fact that his first cheque to the finance company bounced tends to confirm this. The dealer who pulled this stunt is now in deep trouble.

Taken advantage of?

" *A very elderly lady friend of mine recently bought a 'G' reg. Ford Escort from the local garage for £1,500. She has subsequently been told she should have paid no more than half that amount. The car is not in particularly good order, and within three weeks of buying it the gearbox needed attention (it still slips out of reverse) and the steering is very heavy. I fear my friend has been badly taken advantage of. She traded in her small Daihatsu for £200, but did not see the Escort before buying it because she trusted the man. She has a bad back, and so the car is really unsuitable for her. She cannot afford to trade it in as she would lose so much money on it, and though she is not at all well off (in fact, rather poor), she is of that age (late 80s) and generation which does not complain and she says she will just have to live with her mistake. Is there anything she or I can do, such as get some of the cost refunded or obtain a more suitable replacement car?* "

£1,500 is not a lot of money for a 'G' reg. Escort five-door unless it is in very poor condition. (A 90G five-door Popular with 66,000 miles 'trade books' at £275 more than this, and the 'retail' price is around £2,500.) Nevertheless, the Sale and Supply of Goods Act 1994 does give some protection to people who buy goods 'unseen' which turn out to have a fault – even if the seller is able to put the fault right. The problem is a lack of case law on this point. It's worth talking to your local Trading Standards Office to see if any pressure can be brought to bear on the garage, but, before you do this, you or your friend should have a calm, quiet word with him. He has a small business in a small village and good relationships with the local people are essential for his survival.

Well and truly done

" I recently purchased a used car from a franchised dealer, and paid £180 extra for a six-month 'approved' warranty. Two months after purchase, the ECU and ignition unit failed. This was not covered by the guarantee, but the dealer gave me a 10% discount on the £341 replacement cost. Surely a guarantee should not only list what is covered but should also list what is not covered. "

On these bald facts, and assuming the car was less than five years old and cost you more than £3,000, I think you've been well and truly skinned. You have paid £180 for an allegedly 'manufacturer approved' mechanical breakdown insurance which did not even cover the ECU and which probably did not cost the dealer more than £50. Not only that, the car broke down sooner than you could reasonably expect it to. Under the Sale and Supply of Goods Act 1994, I think a judge in a Small Claims Court would very probably find in your favour. Speak to the Trading Standards Office which covers the garage, then I think you should be able to work out a better deal with the dealer. If, however, the car was a ten-year-old banger costing less than £2,000, you're on shakier ground. In these circumstances a judge may not consider it reasonable for nothing to go wrong with the car during the first two months of ownership.

Compensation not forthcoming

" I enclose copies of correspondence with Ford Motor Company, together with a copy of the company's reply. This relates to my Ford Escort 16v, first registered in April 1995 and which I bought 'nearly new' with 250 miles on the odometer in August 1995. At 25,000 miles, the car started missing badly, particularly when cold, and the problem was diagnosed as sticking valves. The problem has now been solved at a cost of £419.09, but, because the problem is not uncommon, I feel compensation is due from Ford. Any assistance you can provide will be greatly appreciated. "

As Ford's Customer Assistance Centre explained to you, you bought a car on which the original manufacturer warranty had been cancelled. It is highly likely that the car was a 'Customer Service Return' – a car rejected by the first buyer under the terms of Ford's Commitment programme. These cars are subsequently auctioned off to the trade by British Car Auctions, where the reason for their rejection is made clear and where it is stated whether or not the original manufacturer's warranty has been withdrawn. Either this was explained to you when you bought the car and was reflected in its price, or it was not. If not, your remedy lies with the dealer who sold you the car, not with Ford. That said, there is a general problem with some 16v Fords and Vauxhalls of valves sticking when the cars are started from cold. The reason, as Ford explained to you, is tight valve and valve guide tolerances, coupled with variations in the quality of unleaded petrol. If this is refined from relatively poor quality base stock and does not contain enough of the right detergent additive, gums and tars form on parts of the fuel delivery system, particularly the inlet valve stems, and the valves can stick. To overcome the problem of owners using cheap petrol, Ford has revised the valve stem and guide tolerances on its Zetec engines, and allowed more lubrication of the stems via the stem seals. But the oil company Texaco guarantees that when its CleanSystem 3 petrol is used problems such as sticking valves simply won't happen.

Sneaky MOT repairs?

" For more than 40 years I have maintained my cars and prepared them for their MOT tests. I recently took my Peugeot to a garage and left it for its MOT. En route to the garage I re-tested the brakes and confirmed they were in good working order. The garage later phoned to say that a rear wheel brake cylinder was leaking and also that the alternator belt was split. I had no option but to agree to the work. A little later, a second call informed me that the garage had 'found' the other rear brake cylinder to be leaking and that the brake shoes needed replacing. What a lucky coincidence! The total cost was £327. This must surely be a dead ringer for any rogue's garage, as it is very easy to initiate a leak if necessary. "

Your letter will infuriate every MOT tester who reads it. But, since you are a professional engineer (C. Eng; M.I. Mech E.), I can only assume that your professional preparation for the car's MOT included thoroughly checking the alternator belt, lifting the car on a garage hoist to check the rear brake cylinders thoroughly, using a 'rolling road' brake tester to check the efficiency of the brakes properly, and removing the rear drums to inspect the rear brake shoes for wear. If you did all this and found no faults, then you have clearly been ripped off.

Pull the other one

A reader whose brother obtained a Ford Mondeo TD estate car at a big discount under the Ford Employee Privilege scheme tried to involve me in a campaign to extract compensation of £16,289.70 and a new Ford Galaxy from the Ford Motor Company.

The registered keeper of the car (the reader's brother) ignored three brake vacuum safety recall notices on the car, sent to his address on 1 November 1995, 26 January 1996 and 23 February 1996. Then, on 12 March 1996, the reader, who was driving the car at the time, had an accident as a partial result of brake failure. He sent me a massive file of complaints about this and the standard of accident repairs to the car, plus two further complaints. One, that the clutch slave cylinder failed (again the subject of a recall). Two, that the 'engine and gearbox cracked open while travelling on a motorway'. Ford ascertained that the car had missed at least two services and as a result may have been down on oil when this happened, but nevertheless gave the reader the benefit of the doubt and paid for a new engine and gearbox to be fitted. Had the car been serviced on time it is also likely that the recall work would have been carried out while the agent's service department had the car – and therefore none of the situations leading to the reader's complaints would ever have arisen.

The reader demanded compensation for 'whiplash' injuries and for having been sold a car not 'of satisfactory quality' under the Sale and Supply of Goods Act 1994 – and, instead of leaving it as a matter between Ford's insurer and his own insurer, or seeking redress through the courts, tried to involve the national press and BBC 'Watchdog'. He failed.

Steering struggle

<< *We recently purchased a Citroen ZX Avantage diesel estate car from a Citroen agent, only later to find that its lack of power assisted steering makes the car very tiring to manoeuvre. Though this was not apparent during the test drive, we feel that this deficiency should have been made clear to us at the time of purchase. We definitely discussed the desirability of power steering during the pre-sale discussion. However, the dealer's attitude has been uncompromising. I have also written to Citroen Cars (UK), and Hereford Trading Standards. Any help you can give would be much appreciated.* >>

All Citroen Avantage diesel hatchbacks have been fitted with power steering as standard from June 1992. However, when estate versions were launched in March 1994, power steering was an optional extra on the Avantage estate, presumably to keep the list price as low as possible, and only became standard on that model in June 1995. Under The Sale and Supply of Goods Act, 1994, you might not be entitled to reject the car because you did road test it before you bought it. But you say you paid £9,995, and I have to tell you that 'book retail' for a 95M Avantage diesel estate with 27,000 miles at the time you bought it was £7,550. Even a 95N model, which had to have power steering, was only valued at £8,350 with 22,000 miles. Since you paid so heavily over the odds, and since the dealer has since valued the same car at a mere £8,000 as a part exchange, I thought the dealer was morally bound at least to retro-fit power steering to it – something he could do at a net cost to him of around £600. (This matter was later resolved when Citroen

UK offered to cough up £500 for PAS to be installed, but, rather than this, the dealer offered to swap the 14,000-mile 'N' reg. Avantage D Estate plus the £500 for a 16,000-mile 'M' reg. Aura TD Estate – an arrangement my correspondent was happy with.)

Big bang

" *My 69-year-old mother has a 1994 Peugeot 405 Turbo Diesel Estate, which she has owned since new and which has a full service history. Six weeks after a service, at 42,000 miles, a con rod broke, smashing through the sump. The car is not covered by warranty and Peugeot has shown no interest. An AA inspection found no explanation (the timing belt had not snapped). The Peugeot agent charged her £4,392 to repair the engine. Has she had a raw deal?* "

Yes. An independent specialist would have been able to replace the engine block of this car with a secondhand one from a crashed car for around £1,500, and the agent should have made your mother aware both of this and of the costs she faced by having the car repaired by its workshops. A well-written letter to Peugeot Customer Care explaining the full circumstances and the outrageous cost of the repair may elicit a better response than you have received so far.

Not what it seemed

" *I wonder if you would let me have your opinion on whether I have a case against a garage that sold me a car which has done around 10,000 miles more than the garage claimed. On 20 September 1997 I part-exchanged a 28,000-mile 1992J Ford Fiesta 1.1LX 5-door for a 39,000-mile 1993K Peugeot 205 GRDT. The odometer reading is itemised as 39,000 miles on the invoice, under which a statement reads 'All mileages are checked by IMVA and are correct unless otherwise stated.' I received £3,395 in part exchange for the Fiesta and paid £2,379.75 to make up the price of £5,774.75, which included 6 months VED and 12 months MBI by 'Motor Cover'. The actual odometer reading of the car was 13,600 miles, but I was told it had been fitted with a new speedometer, that 39,000 miles was the true mileage, and that it has a full service history. When I collected the car I was told that the service history had not been found, but that a copy of the history up to December 1995 had been obtained from Peugeot Contract Hire. When I checked this, I found that the speedo reading on the last entry in December 1995 was 33,615 miles, so even if the speedo had been replaced the next day, the true total mileage would have been 47,215 miles. I then contacted the second owner, who could not remember when the odometer failed but thought it was at at least 35,000 miles, making the total 48,600. I now have a car that has more mileage than I intended to buy and may become more expensive during the 12 months or so I expect to keep it. Who do you recommend I contact at the garage about this? And what sort of recompense should I expect?* **"**

This is a clear case of deception because of the false trade description – whether the garage intended to deceive you or not. Clearly there has either been no IMVA check on the mileage, or the previous owners contacted by IMVA have not responded. Report the case to the Trading Standards Office covering the garage locality, then speak to the sales manager of the garage. On the date of the deal, according to Glass's Guide the trade value for your Fiesta was £2,750 and retail for the Peugeot (with 49,000 miles) was £5,275, making the 'cost to switch' £2,525. So, despite not getting what you thought you were getting, you have had a good deal. The Peugeot is at the mileage when it needs a new timing belt, new camshaft end oil seal and new timing belt tensioner. If the dealership fits these and offers you a free 6,000-mile oil change, plus a free annual service, I think that would square the situation fairly and enable you to tell the

Trading Standards Office that the matter has been amicably resolved.

Clocked?

" *In April 1997 I purchased an August 1989, 71,000-mile BMW 325i Convertible from a specialist in Winnersh. The car was standard apart from an M-Tech bodykit, 16in. alloys and full external respray in BMW Neon Blue, but the hood and leather interior were beginning to show signs of wear. Prior to purchase I had an ABS Vehicle Inspection and an HPI report. Both were satisfactory. I was also told that the car had a long MOT, but this was not available due to a cherished number transfer. (When I eventually received the MOT it had run out.) I was also told that the car had a full service history, but this has still not been provided. I paid £10,400 for the car. My plan is now to take County Court action to recover the difference in retail value between the car with full service history and without. Could you please advice what this difference would be?* "

Between £1,000 and £1,500. But you've got me suspicious, because the circumstances you describe are precisely the way a clocked car can be dumped on a member of the public despite all the precautions you rightly took. Fancy wheels and bodykit, recent respray, but a well-worn interior and hood, cherished number transfer and no service history? By transferring the number, the dealer can get rid of the previous keepers' details on the V-5. But if a previous keeper is listed which is not the dealer, first get in touch with that person and ask him to confirm the mileage on disposal. Also get in touch with Berkshire Trading Standards to see if they have a file on the dealer. And, because you are the registered keeper of the vehicle, you can obtain a list of all previous keepers within the rules of the Data Protection Act. Write to: Fee Paying Section, DVLA, Swansea SA99 1AL, enclose a cheque for

£5 made out to 'Department of Transport', ask for a list of all previous keepers, and give the current registration, the pre-transfer registration and the VIN (chassis) number of the car. Once you get the list you can start contacting the previous owners in the hope that they will tell you the mileage of the car on disposal. Don't go to court until you have this information. If you find out that the car has been clocked, Trading Standards will probably take out a criminal case against the dealer which, if necessary, you can follow up with your civil case.

Post-sale lawsuit

" In July 1977 I sold my much cherished Jaguar E-Type 2+2 Series 1 to fund some college fees. I advertised it in Classic & Sportscar *magazine, priced at £1,250 less than the magazine's estimate for a 'good' example at the time (£10,750 as against £12,000). The person who bought the car haggled the price down to £10,000 after pointing out various 'faults', one of which was the fact that the oil pressure gauge showed only 20 lbs at running speed and nearly zero at idle. I told him it had always been like that ever since I purchased the car three years previously. After road testing the car and satisfying himself, the chap came back a week later with the money. Two weeks later, he phoned to ask for his money back (which by then had disappeared into college fees). Now I have received a court summons for £2,500 for a bottom-end rebuild of the engine. Please can you advise me if I was responsible and, if so, whether or not the person who originally sold me the car was responsible? "*

This is a private sale not subject to the laws which govern a sale by a trader. It may be that the purchaser has issued his summons through the Small Claims Court, in which case you have to decide whether you are prepared to allow a District Judge to arbitrate or are prepared to fight the case in a County Court. If the bill of sale contained the wording 'accepted as seen and tested', I can't imagine that the purchaser would have a case in the County Court. If he won, it would also set a very dangerous precedent whereby people could make private purchases then sue private vendors for faults at a later stage. But Small Claims Court decisions, which do not set legal precedents, can go either way, and I can't predict what sort of decision the Judge will deliver. My instinct is to think that you are faced with a try-on, but common sense dictates that you should obtain proper legal advice from a trusted solicitor.

Attempted blackmail?

" *In June 1996 I bought a 40-month-old, 50,000-mile Audi S2 from a West Country Audi franchise for £20,000, allowing for part exchange. I asked for a list of five faults to be put right. Two were, but I am still concerned about the level of attention to discoloration of the alloy wheels and stone chips and the fact that, after the offside fog light lens was replaced, the nearside lens was found to be cracked. I also noticed a squeak from the driver's electric window. Later, during July and August, I noticed that the backlight for the clock did not work and that the rear ashtray was broken. The supplier agreed to remedy these. I also noticed that the first aid kit and warning triangle were missing, but the supplier has not agreed to replace these. The supplier agreed to allow my local Hertfordshire Audi dealer to replace the ashtray and clock bulb – and I also asked this dealer to replace the nearside foglamp and solve the squeak in the driver's window. When I went to pick up the car, half an hour after the garage had closed, I refused to pay and the matter remains unresolved. I have written a letter in which I state: "Other avenues for me to explore would be to write to The Times and Telegraph motoring sections who I am sure would appreciate a good story, and no doubt some seriously bad publicity for Audi." I would be pleased if your intervention on this matter would hasten a solution to this situation, as I am now getting pretty fed up with it.* "

It may well be that Audi will 'nip this in the bud' and cover the £197.28 owed to the Hertfordshire franchise. But let's get two things straight. I am not here to help readers blackmail the motor trade over a dubious claim. And a dispute with one franchised dealer is nothing to do with any other franchised dealer. These dealers both tell me that, though the ashtray replacement was authorised by the West Country dealer, nothing else was. And that, when you booked the car in with the Hertfordshire dealer for the four items of work, you did not tell them that they were to be paid for by another dealer. However aggrieved you may feel, this is not the way to behave, and it renders you open to justifiable legal, and possibly also criminal, action by the Hertfordshire dealer. (You have effectively 'stolen' from that dealer a foglight, a clock bulb and their work on the window.) When you bought the car it was 40 months old and had done 50,000 miles. Minor discoloration of alloy wheels and a few stone chips are normal on cars of that age. Though expensive, it was not a new car and could not reasonably be expected to appear new in every respect.

MAINTENANCE

The secrets of long life

" *I have a six-year-old manual Volvo 240 estate with 80,000 miles on the clock. It is in immaculate condition, both bodily and mechanically, and I would like to keep it that way as long as possible. I recall a story in 'Telegraph Motoring' some time ago about a Volvo which had done more than 400,000 miles. I know you recommend changing the engine oil every 3,000 miles, but what about the oil in the gearbox and back axle? Should these be changed? And what is your opinion of engine oil, gearbox oil and petrol additives such as Slick 50 and STP in prolonging component life?* "

Automatic transmission fluid and filter should be changed every year, brake fluid and power steering fluid every two years, and coolant every two years unless you switch to a Trigard-based pre-mix coolant in which the corrosion inhibitors last four years. It will benefit a manual gearbox and diff to change the oil every 2–3 years, and – though I have to confess I have never bothered to do this myself – it's a good idea to change it after the first year, as a Mondeo-owning reader found (see 'Granulated Gearbox' on p. 307). The secret of the 400,000-mile Volvo's (and the 520,000-mile VW Passat's) engine life is never to let it get cold. The more a vehicle is used, the more miles its engine will cover. Record-breaking high milers always clock up at least 40,000 miles a year. A Kenlowe Hotstart engine preheater will help in this respect – tel: 01628 823303. I prefer to use a fully synthetic or semi-synthetic engine oil, but readers who put

Slick 50 in their engines swear by it. STP supplied case histories of a 172,000-mile Fiesta 1.1 and a 200,000-mile Fiat Uno 1.0 Fire, both of which got there using STP engine oil treatment. I have some STP gearbox oil additive in the box of the car I'm driving now. I also believe in petrol additives such as fuel system cleaners, particularly when combined with an octane enhancer which many older engines seem to need to compensate for the lack of octane in 'premium' unleaded and 'low-lead' four star.

DIY car

" *I have a 1995N Skoda Felicia GLXi. I understand that VAG is very firm in refusing to sell manufacturer workshop manuals and data to the public. I also rang Haynes, who told me they had made their plans until the end of 1997 and these did not include a manual for the Felicia. But, if a sufficient number of owners made known their desire for a manual, they would consider publishing one. Please could you ask all Felicia owners who want to do their own maintenance to write to Haynes and register their interest?* "

The reason why VAG will not sell workshop information to the public is fear of manufacturer liability should anything go wrong as the result of a home repair. Haynes had not published one in 1997 because the Felicia had been out for less than three years and all were covered by a three-year manufacturer and dealer warranty which home maintenance would have disqualified. But the Felicia is very much a home maintenance car, as was the Favorit for which Haynes also published a manual. So Haynes does expect to publish a manual for the Felicia by Christmas 1998. Haynes Publishing Group, Sparkford, Yeovil, Somerset BA22 7JJ, tel: 01963 440635.

Oil changes

" *I bought a new Peugeot 106 in mid-February and immediately invested in a Haynes manual. The manufacturer recommends oil changes at 9,000-mile intervals. Haynes says 6,000 miles. The manufacturer states that tyre pressures should be 33 psi. Haynes says 29 psi. Who is right?* "

Haynes manuals are not intended to enable owners of new cars to start fiddling with them and thereby invalidating the warranty. This particular manual will have been written for the original Peugeot 106, launched in 1991, which had 6,000-mile service intervals, rather than the newer model, launched in 1996, which has 9,000-mile intervals. The 9,000-mile oil change is really intended for fleet cars which do more than 20,000 miles a year and will therefore have an oil change twice a year or more. It's foolhardy for a private motorist to expect ordinary mineral oil or even semi-synthetic to last 9,000 miles or a full year, so it's only sensible to change it more often. As for the tyre pressures, you don't state which model of 106, or whether you are talking about loaded or unloaded – all of which affect the pressure the tyres should be inflated to.

Workshop manual

" *I have a 1984 VW Caravelle with a water-cooled four-cylinder petrol engine. I cannot get a workshop manual for this model, and not having one means I cannot challenge any servicing work done by a franchised dealer which I feel I have been let down over. VW Customer Care tells me I must consult my dealer, so is of no help in this.* "

Though VW is pretty good about its older cars, it's a bit much to expect an automatic right to 'customer care' for a thirteen-year-old vehicle, and I'm surprised you're still taking it to a franchised dealer with which you are dissatisfied. A specialist in the Good Garage Guide section may be more appropriate for a vehicle of this age. Mill House Books (01205 270377) can sell you a factory workshop manual for VW Transporters from 1982, including water-cooled models, for £15.95 plus p&p. There is also a Haynes manual at £10.95 for pre-1982 air-cooled models. (Tip: The water-cooled flat four needs coolant changes every two years, otherwise the long studs which hold head, cylinder blocks and crankcase together tend to corrode badly and the engine eventually falls apart. The first signs of this are water leaks.)

All steamed up

A number of readers have written to ask why, on 8 March 1997, I advised the owner of a Saab never to have the engine steam cleaned. The reason is that the high-pressure water or 'steam' hits engine components at a force they were never designed to withstand. As soon as moisture gets into components such as the engine management computer, the fuse box, the ABS management system, the direct ignition system on a Saab or the plethora of relays and connectors under the bonnet of any modern car, it begins to do damage. The damage may be immediate, or it may be a gradual corrosion of a component or contact. The other effect of steam cleaning is to disqualify any anti-perforation warranty in the region of the engine compartment as the process removes some of the protective waxes on body parts, over electronic components or on parts of the engine itself.

Service intervals

" *In October 1996 I bought a 1993 Rover 820i. It had done 72,000 miles and had been serviced in April of that year. The car has now done 80,000 miles. The official service interval is 12,000 miles. It has now been a year since the car was last serviced, but it is 4,000 miles short of the next service mileage. Is it advisable to service the car because it has been a year since the last service, or can I wait until the car has done 84,000 miles? I don't want to line the dealer's pocket unnecessarily.* "

You will if you carry on at this rate, because the car could rapidly need a new engine. Read the service guide a bit more carefully and you'll see it says '12,000 miles or 12 months whichever comes first'. But in my view, this is still far too long an interval when a car is new, never mind when it's more than four years old. In short, the car needs servicing immediately. It probably also needs a new timing belt, which caution dictates should be changed every three years or every 36,000 miles (particularly on the Rover 800). The coolant should also be changed, as should the brake fluid and, if the car is automatic, the ATF fluid and filter. The oil and filter should then be changed every six months or every 6,000 miles whichever comes first, the ATF fluid and filter every year, and the brake fluid and coolant every two years unless you replace the coolant with a Trigard-based MPG solution, which should be good for four years.

The pits

" *I am about to have a wooden garage built so that I can preserve and work on my classic Triumph Stag. I would like to incorporate an inspection pit, but the thought of digging out such a big hole, lining it with bricks or cement, plus the probably damp working environment do not appeal.*

Is there any form of 'kit pit' on the market that I could simply drop into a dug out area? **"**

Yes. It's called the Mech Mate Motor Pit, it's RAC approved, and it's made of moulded one-piece GRP by Truckman (who make Truckman Tops for pick-up trucks). The basic price is £515 plus VAT, and delivery costs £55; Truckman Ltd, Unit C6, Baker Street, Gloucester, tel: 01452 332233, email: truckman@compuserve.com. To dig an accurate pit, a reader from Tewkesbury suggested employing the local gravedigger who, one hopes, is not too busy with his main job. Another reader warns of the danger of explosions from petroleum gases, which are heavier than air and tend to collect at the bottom of inspection pits.

When to change oils?

" *I was very interested in the piece in 'Telegraph Motoring' on the 1,000,000-mile BMW and the use of Mobil 1. I am about to take delivery of an Audi A3 1.8T Sport and would appreciate your advice. I have read that with a new car it is as well to retain the original oil until the first 10,000-mile service to allow for a little wear so that the engine can bed in. At the first service, a change to fully synthetic oil is to be advised – but would Mobil 1 or Magnatec be a better bet? I drive 500–600 miles a week, mainly on motorways, and set off very early each day so the engine tends to be very cold on start-up.* **"**

You're right about allowing the engine to bed in. Some mechanics recommend as long as 30,000 miles, especially with VAG TDI diesel engines. But you also need to watch the state of the original oil over those first 10,000 miles. VAG's factory fill is a special brew using a synthetic base and reclaimed, reprocessed oil. With the turbo, in the summer, this oil is going to get very hot indeed, and at the first sign of coking (turning black) it needs to be changed. The first refill with fully synthetic will 'suspend' hydrocarbon particles from the bedding-in oil and may turn light brown fairly quickly. But the second refill with fully synthetic should stay clear and should last 7,500 miles. I'd go for Mobil 1 because it is 0W–40, and as a result will lubricate your Audi's 20 valves and its turbo bearings more quickly from a cold start. Once the car is run in, don't be tempted to run it to its rev-limiter too often. The resulting misfire will hot-spot the car's catalytic converter – something manufacturers allowing 'track testing' of their catalysed cars have been finding out. Subsequent to my test, the million-mile BMW withstood a week of being thrashed round the International Circuit at Silverstone by eighty different drivers during the Fleet Show and clocked up another 10,000 reliable miles in the hands of many different drivers in the year to follow.

How to wreck an engine

" I read a recent letter in your column about oil changes and, having encountered a related problem, would be grateful for your advice. I own a secondhand 'E' reg. Mercedes 230TE, purchased at 42,000 miles and which has now done 108,736 miles. At the 102,000-mile oil change in November 1996, it was recommended that I brought it back again at 108,000 for an earlier oil change than I have been used to. Then, the week before I was going to take it in, the oil light came on and the car stopped. An AA man told me the engine was completely dry of oil and was wrecked. Is it possible that this could have happened with an oil change having been performed at the 102,000 mile service? Also, if the engine is re-built, what mileage can I expect from the car before further problems develop? "

Your letter is not untypical of many from Mercedes owners, who seem to think their cars are bullet-proof. The most likely explanation is that your engine's valve stem seals gave up the ghost and let engine oil into the combustion chambers where it was burned. But any owner of a car with 100,000 miles on the clock who does not check the engine oil level at least once a week is asking for trouble. Now you face a bill of around £4,000 for a recon or around £5,000 for a new engine. I'd go for a new engine – preferably with the later 'Duplex' timing chain. If you have the oil and filter in this engine changed every six months or 3,000 miles (whichever comes first), the engine should last 350,000 miles or more. If the new engine comes with the earlier 'Simplex' timing chain (as on your present engine), to be on the safe side the chain will need to be changed every 60,000–70,000 miles.

How much to change a light bulb?

A reader from Shepperton has rightly reminded us all that when our car is in for a service at a franchised agent and the agent rings up to ask if we want to replace minor items such as a light bulb, we say, 'No thanks, I'll buy the bulb and do it myself.' He was hit a total of £25 in parts, labour and VAT, just to change a stop-light bulb.

Day of the jack oil

" *I own a 1953 1250 cc MG 'Y' saloon which is fitted with the Jackall jacking system. Can you please tell me where I can obtain the correct red oil that used to be sold by Smiths?* "

Castrol Crimson has the correct lubricity. Castrol runs an excellent helpline for questions such as this on 01954 231668.

Handy for handbooks

" I recently bought a 1978 Alfa 1600 Spider, but it has no handbook. Where can I go for one? And please could you also supply the address of the Alfa Romeo Owners' Club? "

Star of the film 'The Graduate' (do you think Katherine Ross would have gone off with Dustin Hoffman if he drove a Chevette?), and the car in which Kirk Douglas tried to kill himself in 'The Arrangement', the classic Alfa Spider managed an extraordinary lifespan of almost 30 years. (Useful tip: watch out for the top of the 'B' pillar when you get in or out – it can stab you in the back.) Handbooks are £8.95 plus p&p from Mill House Books on 01205 270377; workshop manuals are £12.95 for the Autobook and £36.95 for the factory issue. Another good supplier of workshop and technical manuals is Delta Press of 8 Billet Lane, Berkhamsted, Herts HP4 1DP, tel: 01442 877794. The club's address is Alfa Romeo Owners' Club, 97 High Street, Linton, Cambs CB1 6JT, tel: 01223 894300.

Age-related problems

" I have just bought a 1987 BMW 316 with only 7,860 miles on the clock and garaged since new. It achieved its mileage in only the first five of its ten years, and since then its only outings were to the local BMW dealer for an annual inspection. Apart from a minor dent, the car looks virtually new and the motor still feels 'tight'. What problems am I likely to encounter which are the result of age rather than mileage? "

Anything rubber, and anything in contact with a liquid containing water, deteriorates with age – even if kept in a well ventilated garage.

Anything rubber and anything in contact with a liquid containing water deteriorates with age – even if kept in a well ventilated garage. First job is to replace the timing belt, which BMW recommends changing every three years even if the car only does a small mileage. With the belt off, it makes sense to change the camshaft end oil seal and the belt tensioner. Petrol left in the tank may have condensed and separated, causing problems in the fuel injection system, so it would be a wise move to have the tank and fuel system flushed out. Check all hoses, then flush and reverse-flush the entire cooling system until any trace of rusty water is gone, and re-fill with a Trigard-based pre-mixed coolant. Replace the brake fluid and power steering fluid. If the car is an automatic, replace the ATF and filter; if manual, consider replacing the gearbox oil. Add engine flush and replace the oil with either mineral oil or semi-synthetic, not fully synthetic at this stage because from your description the engine is not yet run in. Once the engine has loosened off you can make the switch to fully synthetic. I would guess that your first failure is likely to be the water pump or the fuel pump which, like a central heating pump, tends to gum up when not used. If the coolant has not been regularly replaced as part of the annual inspection, the corrosion inhibitors in it could have degraded and there could be corrosion in the area of the cylinder head, gasket and the top of the cylinder block. Any emulsified oil on the inside of the oil filler cap or steam coming out of the exhaust when the engine is hot is symptomatic of this problem. Unless the battery has been kept fully charged, you're also likely to need a new one of those, too.

Grease monkeys

" *Here's a warning about sloppy servicing. After a recent service, we noticed a creaking noise from the hinges and door stay of our car. They looked to be well-covered with that white spray-on grease used nowadays. But when I wiped the grease away with a rag, I found the metal underneath was red with rust. The grease had obviously been sprayed over the parts when they were damp and instead of protecting them had prevented the moisture from drying out.* "

Well, you won't go back there again, will you?

Plugged

" *Can spark plugs be used indefinitely as long as they have no visible wear and are kept clean?* "

No, because the insulation eventually breaks

down or cracks, causing 'arcing' and consequent misfires. Because just one misfire can lead to the destruction of a catalytic converter, owners of cars with cats are advised to have their spark plugs checked at least every 10,000 miles and to change them at least every 20,000 miles.

Top tips

" *Could you pass on a couple of tips to your readers? I find that the best windscreen cleaner is cheap toothpaste. It gets rid of diesel film very well indeed. Another tip is to tie a length of 5 amp fuse wire around the screen washer bottle so you will know where to find it (the length of wire, that is!). Fuse wire is excellent for clearing out blocked screen washer jets, and you can also use it to replace the screws which fall out of spectacles or sunglasses.* "

Thank you for these useful tips. Perhaps we'll see the one about the fuse wire and spectacles appearing in 'Viz' or a forthcoming McDonalds commercial.

VAG injector cleaner

" *Some time ago I'm sure I read in your column of a 'magic' product sold by VW dealers to clean fuel injectors. The parts department at my local VW franchise denies that it has ever been on sale, yet on the service counter is a notice stating that it was automatically used as part of a service. Where can I get it? I have a feeling that my 73,000-mile, 'J' reg. Mk II 16v could do with a dose.* "

Why does a GTi run so much better after a service at a good VW dealers? Because, apart from the service, it receives a dose of injector cleaner which, like most injector cleaners, also just happens to contain an octane enhancer. The stuff I have comes in a white 150 ml bottle, and the dose is 50 ml to 50 litres petrol, poured in before the petrol (VAG code number G 001 700 03). But it also carries the 'hazchem' mark and, because the cap is not child-proof, may not generally be on sale. Try Autocavan Components Ltd, 103 Lower Weybourne Lane, Baldshot Lea, Farnham, Surrey GU9 9LG, tel: 01252 333891. They don't sell the concentrated stuff to the public, but do sell a 300 ml one-shot treatment with a child-proof top, price £5.45. Other fuel injector cleaners such as STP contain pretty much the same recipe and also make your car feel as though it has been given a new lease of life.

Cut-price maintenance

" Very soon after we bought our 'G' registered Renault 5 it required a new cylinder head gasket, which was fitted under warranty. The coolant itself was rusty brown and very probably original. A few weeks ago I saw you recommend coolant changes every two years with MEG coolants and every four with Trigard-based MPG coolants. So I cut the piece out and showed it to my Renault service manager. He confirmed that the service record book covering the expected life of my car made no reference to coolant changes at any age or mileage and it was not their practice to change coolant regularly – although he did agree with your reply. Does Renault's coolant contain some magic ingredient that others lack? Or is the maintenance schedule at fault? "

Leasing, rental and company fleets buy around 70% of all new cars sold in this country and part of the 'whole life costs' of a fleet car are its servicing costs. This explains why oil change intervals have been changed from 5,000 miles or six months to as much as 12,000 miles and twelve months, and why brake fluid changes, automatic transmission fluid changes and coolant changes tend to be ignored as part of maintenance schedules. The fleets run these cars for a maximum of three to four years, during which the cars tend to remain reasonably reliable. Only after this, when the cars find their ways into private hands, does the damage caused by skimped maintenance schedules become apparent. If you don't believe me, check the recommendations made in any Haynes manual to owner/drivers which are designed to keep cars running reliably for far longer than any fleet has ever required. Until the UK public finally cottoned on, we were paying around 25% too much for our cars in order to finance fleet discounts. And the fleets were palming us off with their cast-offs, which may have been 'maintained to the manufacturer's standards' but have not been maintained to the standard a wise owner would adopt. (Vauxhall has introduced a pre-winter cooling system service which involves checking and pressure-testing the entire system and draining and re-filling with fresh coolant at an all-in price of £29.95 at participating dealers.)

Mitsubishi manual

" *I have acquired a 1991 Mitsubishi Galant 1.8 GLS. Do you know if anybody produces a maintenance manual for this model (Haynes do not, it seems), as I prefer to do my own maintenance?* "

A manual for the 'E30' Series Galant (1988–91) is available via any Mitsubishi dealer from The Colt Car Company Ltd. It is published by Peter Russeck Publications Ltd, Little Stone House, High Street, Markow, Berks. Haynes does a manual for the American-market Mitsubishi Cordia, Tredia, Galant, Precis and Mirage (-

excluding V6) 1983–93. The catalogue number is H1669, price £11.95 including post and packing from Delta Press Ltd, 8 Billet Lane, Berkhamsted, Herts HP14 1DP, tel: 01442 877794, or Mill House Books on 01205 270377. But the technical data in the American manual is for catalysed versions only.

Back to the 'Landy'

" *My son, aged 15, is developing an enthusiasm for tinkering with cars – an enthusiasm I do not share. A friend has recommended the purchase of an ageing Land Rover as a vehicle which would suit a beginner to car mechanics and one he might be able to try safely off-road before his seventeenth birthday. Would this be a wise purchase?* "

When doing mechanical work on an old car, always wear disposable gloves and a face mask to protect against the carcinogens found in old oil and asbestos brake dust.

Yes, very much so. Though part-time four-wheel-drive, old Land Rovers are mechanically straightforward and there is enough information available about them to fill a library. Realistically, you'll probably be looking at a Series II, and a good starting point would be the Haynes manual (code H0304, £11.95 from Delta Press on 01442 877794). Next step would be to join your nearest Land Rover club (addresses in one of the many Land Rover and 4×4 magazines at newsagents). Parts are reasonably priced. But do look out for chassis rot before buying, particularly at the rear of the vehicle. Make sure your son always wears disposable gloves when working on it (there are nasty carcinogens in old oil and brake dust), make him wear a face mask when dismantling the brakes (asbestos), and make him wear goggles or safety glasses when grinding, welding or brazing. I don't want to put a damper on things, but as for driving 'off-road', I presume you are referring to private land. It would be illegal to drive on common land or any public place. 'Byways' are officially classed as roads and vehicles are forbidden from 'bridle ways'.

Moly slip-up?

" *I have used Molyslip for years and am a true believer in the benefits of Molybdenum Disulphide. I am now about to change my car, so I wrote to Holt Lloyd to ask if Molyslip E was compatible with synthetic oils. Their reply was: 'It is completely compatible with the new synthetic oils and can be used in diesel engines and turbo-charged engines provided they run on conventional oils.' I also note that Mobil says that Mobil 1 oil can prolong the life of a catalytic converter.* "

Molyslip has been the saviour of many an older engine and gearbox filled with conventional oil. I continue to use it and the STP equivalent in gearboxes. But I'm not convinced about using it in conjunction with fully synthetic oil. Having driven a BMW that had done more than 1,000,000 miles on Mobil 1 at over 100 mph on two occasions (on test and race tracks) I can confirm that the oil does its job, but 7,500 miles is the limit between changes. Whether Molyslip provides enough lubrication for an engine to run longer on a partially degraded oil is another matter altogether.

Switching batteries

" *I recently bought a car at auction and am very pleased with it. An absolute bargain. The only defect, which was pointed out to me, is that one of the cells of the original battery is duff. It was also pointed out that the radio is coded, the code is unknown and changing the battery will lose the code. My local audio centre has quoted £80 to £100 to recode it. What should I do?* "

Readers should first check with a franchised agent that what I propose will not blow any circuits (it shouldn't). What you do is get the battery fitter to take a pair of jump leads and *bridge* the battery while it is being changed. First, use the jump leads to connect the positive old battery lead to the positive terminal of a good third battery. Then do the same negative to negative. Unfasten the battery leads of the old battery, replace with the new battery, connect the battery leads to the new battery firmly, then disconnect the jump leads. The radio circuit should remain unbroken and the codes should be retained.

Early test is best

" *Just a reminder from a very experienced MOT tester that January and August are our busiest times of the year, for the simple reason that more new car registrations take place in January and August than any other months of the year. A three-year-old car coming in for its first MOT can be tested up to a month earlier than the day of the month it was first registered, yet the MOT will be dated to apply from the date it was due. (You will need to take along the car's V-5 to prove the date of first registration.) For example, a car first registered on 17 January 1995 could be tested at any date back to 17 December 1997 and the MOT would still run for a year from 17 January 1998. Similarly, a car with a current MOT can be tested up to a month early and can be sent away with a 13-month MOT, but only if the current MOT is submitted with the car before the test.* "

This came from the ever-helpful Ted Craker of The Bromley Test Centre, 107 Southlands Road, Bromley BR2 9QT, tel: 0181 460 6666. Ted also advises a pre-check by a garage, and points out that getting an MOT a month before the end of a car's three-year warranty could well point up defects repairable under warranty before the warranty expires. Good on you, Ted.

Trickle charging

" Is there any kind of battery charger which can be left permanently connected to a car in storage to keep the battery fully charged without damaging the car's ECU or alarm/immobiliser? "

I finally found one: The Airflow Battery Conditioner, which is used and approved by BMW UK. I had to buy my own, price £40, at The Motor Show and have connected it to the battery of a car I use infrequently with excellent results and no problems. However, you must follow the connection and disconnection procedure to the letter. Airflow UK, Crown House, Faraday Road, Newbury, Berks RG14 2AB, tel: 01635 569569. I have seen similar, cheaper battery conditioners advertised but can't vouch for them. Definitely don't buy anything connected via the cigarette lighter/accessory socket.

Assault on battery

" I parked outside a shop for five minutes to make a purchase, and when I returned to my car it failed to start. The battery had collapsed without warning and the only thing that would work was the radio. In fifty years of motoring, when batteries have failed on previous occasions they always gave a warning. Why not now? "

Your type of motoring has changed. A good car battery, such as a Delco Freedom, will last 10–15 years as long as it is always kept fully charged. Conversely, a battery in a car used for short runs, which never puts back what starting takes out, may last no more than eighteen months because the battery progressively loses its capacity to hold a charge. Starting takes more out the battery than anything else (particularly cold starting) so, though a battery may still be up for playing the radio, it may not have the power to turn the engine. Get a Delco Freedom Battery from a Vauxhall parts department and an Airflow Battery Conditioner (see 'Trickle charging' above), and you can leave the battery on charge whenever you put the car in the garage. That's what I do with little-used cars.

Six monthly services

" *In a recent reply, you told us 'No engine oil is capable of surviving both summer and winter without some degree of contamination, while 12 months is plenty of time for brakes to deteriorate alarmingly'. Surely the manufacturer's norm is 10,000 miles/12 months these days? There must be many of your readers out there who are now wondering what to do in this respect. Can you please enlarge on your views and also tell us whether you are recommending a mid-year oil change notwithstanding the maker's instructions?* "

I recommend an oil and filter change at least every six months or 3,000 miles (whichever comes first) if using ordinary mineral oil; at least every six months or 5,000 miles (whichever comes first) if using a good semi-synthetic; and at least every six months or 7,500 miles (whichever comes first) if using a fully synthetic. The fact is, the two greatest engine killers are dirty oil and degraded coolant. Dirty oil allows premature engine wear. Degraded coolant allows corrosion of the cylinder head gasket and generally inside the engine, the sludge from which eventually blocks waterways or the radiator and causes overheating. (Coolant should be changed every two years, or every four years if using a Trigard-based coolant.) Engine remanufacturer H.V. Arnett of Doncaster (01302

323931) wrote to confirm this, adding that long oil-change intervals were especially injurious to low-mileage cars.

A really handy handbook

" While clearing out some old family bits and pieces I came across the original 1955 order form and invoice for my sister's first car – a new Austin A30. I also found the owner's handbook. Perhaps these details might fill an odd space at some time, and if you know of an A30 Club, its members might be glad to have the documents. "

Thank you very much indeed for your generosity. The handbook is a model of clarity – the best I've ever seen and an object lesson in how to explain complicated mechanics in simple terms to owners who, through necessity, have to work on their cars themselves. Among the writing and design team were Ivor Greening, Gordon Bennett, Alan Jones, John Collins and Rowland Harrison. Thanks for helping me find them to Barney Sharratt, who wrote the definitive book on the model, *Post War Baby Austins – A30, A35 and A40* published by Osprey and, though out of print, still to be found at specialist bookstalls at motoring events. Thanks also to Graham Cole of the Austin A30–A35 Owners' Club. If any readers would like to join the club, the address is, Ivydene, Allett, Truro, Cornwall TR4 9DW, tel: 01872 273938.

HONEST JOHN'S LIST OF 'NEARLY-NEW' SPECIALISTS

Remember, most 'nearly new' mass-market cars are ex-rental or from 'fast rotation' fleets. The availability and prices fluctuate wildly according to supply and demand, and big manufacturers such as Ford and Vauxhall have now cut back the number of cars they register through rental fleets and 'fast rotators'. You may save as much as £9,000 on cars in the £20,000-plus bracket – but the saving on small cars may be as little as £2,000.

Beware of 'customer service returns' which can be faulty new cars rejected by customers, taken back by the manufacturers and auctioned off to the trade. And beware of Fiats lacking a 'red key' for the alarm/immobiliser system.

- **London:** The Great Trade Centre, Hythe Road (off Scrubs Lane – the original 'Car Supermarket'), White City, London NW10, tel: 0181 964 8080 (cheap, advertises in *Exchange & Mart* and the *Thames Valley Trader*). Hertz Car Sales, Gillette Corner, Brentford, tel: 0181 560 1202. MAXCAR, Concord Point, 3 Concord Road, Park Royal, London W3 0TQ (off A40), tel: 0181 752 8500 (like CARLAND, Lakeside, but insurance not included in price). Car Supermarkets, Hayes, off Parkway (M4 J3).

- **South:** Trade Sales of Slough, 353–357 Bath Road, Slough, Berks SL1 6JA, tel: 01753 773763 (cheap 'Deal 1' prices; even cheaper 'Deal 2' prices are after £500 minimum part exchange, plus £99 and only for cars sold on finance). CARLAND, Lakeside, Weston Avenue, West Thurrock, Essex RM20 3FJ, tel: 0800 783 3366 (high prices include a year's warranty and comprehensive 'any driver' insurance).

- **Midlands:** Car Supermarkets (The Motor House), A5 Watling Street, Cannock, Staffs, tel: 01543 506060 or 0990 289227 (1 mile from M6 J11). Car Supermarkets, Ravens Way, Northampton (next to Billing Aquadrome), tel: 01604 401333. Motor Nation, Mackadown Lane, Garrett's Green, Birmingham, tel: 0121 786 1111 (advertises in *The Book* car price guide). Bristol Street Motors, 156–182 Bristol Street, Birmingham B5 7AZ, tel: 0121 666 6003 (Fords only). Rayns of Leicester, tel: 0116 261 2200 (Fords only).

- **Wales:** Car Supermarkets (formerly Empress Cars), Langland Way, Spitty Road, Newport, Gwent, tel: 01633 284800 (advertises in the *Star* on Saturdays). Ron Skinner and Sons, Roundabout Garage, Rhymney, Gwent, tel: 01685 842642.

- **North-East:** Reg Vardy Motor Zone, Stoddart Street, Shieldfield, Newcastle-upon-Tyne NE2 1AN, tel: 0191 232 3838.

- **North West:** Fords of Winsford, Wharton Retail Park, Weaver Valley Road (off A5018), Winsford, Cheshire, tel: 01606 861234, faxback: 0891 715970. Carcraft, Molesworth Street, Rochdale OL16 1TS, tel: 01706 32041. Reg Vardy Motor Zone, Albion Way, Salford, Lancs M5 4DG, tel: 0161 737 7333. Reg Vardy Motor Zone, 608 Penistone Road, Sheffield S6 2SZ, tel: 01142 834949. Reg Vardy Motor Zone, Chancellor Lane, Ardwick, Manchester M12 6JZ, tel: 0161 273 2273. Car Supermarkets, Middleton Road, Middleton, Manchester (M62 J18); Car Supermarkets, Nottingham, on A38 (1.5 miles from M1 J28).

- **Scotland:** Reg Vardy Motor Zone, 5 Seafield Way, Seafield Road (between Portobello and Leith), Edinburgh EH15 1TB, tel: 0131 669 3000.

NEW CAR PROBLEMS

MG grief

Soon after its launch I received eight letters of complaint about quality problems with the new MGF. The first, which lost an Army officer serving in Bosnia most of his leave, was caused by a melted Lambda cable – the result of a very high speed run on the autobahn. Because the MGF's Lambda probe is fitted in the exhaust manifold, it's worth checking from time to time that the cables from it are not touching the hot pipework. Further complaints were received about paint quality, door and mirror handles falling off, missed assembly jobs, loose gearshift, water leaks into the cabin and the poor design of the folded hood cover retaining straps. After this flurry of activity I received a lot of letters from owners praising their MGFs and no further complaints at all, so I think we can put most of this down to teething troubles. Any owner not satisfied with the car or dealer fixes should Freefone Rover Cars Customer Service on 0800 620 820.

Saxo seats

" *I have a new Citroen Saxo SX with which I am almost completely satisfied. My sole problem is the driver's seat. I have tried every permutation of adjustment, but even on the shortest journeys I develop an ache across my shoulder blades. Can you recommend any of the several types of seat cushions available, or a satisfactory alternative?* **"**

> Your problem is probably due to the severe offset of the pedals in relation to the seat and steering wheel in order for the pedals to clear the offside wheel arch. Peugeot 106s, Rover Metros and Rover 100s have the same problem. The answer is to allow for this in the way you sit and hold the steering wheel.

Drummed out

" *On 6 September 1996 we purchased a VW Passat 1.9TDI estate car (old model) from the local VW agents. This car is very rarely driven (and has covered just 1,030 miles) due to the most terrible drumming noise coming from the back once the rear windows are opened. The agents have had the car in, and they declare that the noise is 'typical for this car'. I am, of course, not at all satisfied that a leading car manufacturer places on the market a £16,000 estate car with this glaring fault. My husband wrote to VW, but sadly we have received no reply. Why have these cars been allowed to be marketed under what I can only describe as a form of 'sharp practice'? Am I the only one being taken advantage of?* **"**

> If this is the only fault, I have to tell you that 'drumming' is normal when the rear windows of an estate car are opened. Opening them allows a volume of air into the car which can't then get out, causing the 'drumming' effect in the rear load area. If you want to drive with the windows open, you may find that opening one front window and partially opening the opposite rear will help. (When a car has a sunroof which causes 'drumming' when open, it usually helps to open one or both rear windows slightly.) But, generally, the more aerodynamic

the shape of a car, the more you are likely to experience drumming with the windows open. If your Passat is fitted with air conditioning, opening the windows causes a pointless waste of fuel. However, if you really want to drive with open windows, a company known as Clim Air markets wind deflectors for windows and sunroofs. Clim Air UK, 1 Station Parade, Station Road, Sidcup, Kent DA15 7DB, tel: 0181 309 7744.

Scorpio bonnet warning

A reader from Basingstoke has written to warn of problems with the bonnets of the controversially styled, post-January 1995 Ford Scorpio. His bonnet catch gave way and the bonnet came open at 45 mph. He attributes this to corrosion of the bonnet safety catch due to its vulnerability to the elements through the grille. (Apparently salt corrosion caused throttle assembly problems, resulting in a partial recall.) Scorpio owners would be well advised to check the operation of the bonnet safety catch and spring and to grease it thoroughly.

Get-out clause

" *I have ordered a new Jaguar XK8 Coupe, and now find that whilst I can get it into my garage I can't actually get out of the car. I do not want a convertible, I cannot enlarge the garage and I am reluctant to move house. Is there an alternative car I should consider, or is there some sort of gadgetry that can help me with my predicament?* "

The problem will be the length of the door in relation to the seat. If there is any room at all on the left hand side of the car, then you might be able to purchase some short lengths of rail similar to those used in the Ford Direct refurbishment plant. Drive the car onto wheel carriers on the rails, open the window and push it away from the wall on the driver's side. Then move the driver's seat back to its rearmost point. This might, just, give you enough room to open the door sufficiently to get out. Try motor factors and garage equipment suppliers for the rail system. The Garage Equipment Association Helpline is on 01327 312616.

Ka trouble

" I purchased a Ford Ka in January 1997. When the car was delivered, it was pointed out to me by the dealer that it had defective paintwork. I was assured that, under the Ford Commitment scheme, wheels would be put in motion for me to receive a replacement Ka. Since at no stage did I believe this would not happen, I took delivery of the defective car. The dealer then raised the matter with Ford Customer Assistance, but was advised that a replacement would not be available under the Commitment programme unless three attempts had been made to rectify the paint problem, all of which had failed. I am now at an impasse with the dealer and with Ford. I want what I believe I was promised. "

Any right of redress under the Sale and Supply of Goods Act 1994 is against the supplier of the car, not the manufacturer.

The dealer was wrong to make the promise he did before clearing it with the Ford Motor Company. The terms of Ford's Commitment changed in April 1996, and from that date no longer allowed a free thirty-day exchange for any reason. Now the only reason for a replacement is if three attempts have been made to fix the same fault, all of which have failed. This does not affect any rights you may have to reject the car under the Sale and Supply of Goods Act, 1994. But any rights you do have under this Act are against the supplier of the car – not against the manufacturer. In fact, the Ford dealer that sold you the car has now lost its franchise. But since the AA has agreed that the damage is repairable, under the terms of the car's one year warranty, Ford has agreed to meet the costs of the repair, and the costs of a courtesy car while this is taking place, at the Ford dealer of your choice.

Peugeot exonerated?

" My 1995 Peugeot 306 1.8 XT automatic suffered piston slap when it had done only 18,000 miles. The Peugeot franchise, Rochester Motor Company, provided a loan car while repairs were carried out, all at Peugeot's expense. Then, at 32,000 miles, the piston slap became evident again. This time, RMC advised me to contact my local Peugeot dealer, Hounslow West Motors, who gained approval for the engine to be virtually rebuilt, again at Peugeot's expense. In 30 years of motoring I have never had such excellent service from a car manufacturer or its dealers. Well done, Peugeot. "

I'm very glad to hear it, because this does prove that, if a Peugeot is properly serviced by the manufacturer's franchises, the manufacturer might be willing to pick up the bill when out-of-warranty problems occur. There was a known problem with the piston skirts of PSA 1.8 litre 8-valve engines, which may be why you received the help you did. But this will be of no comfort to a reader from Warminster who was hit for a preposterous £4,392 bill when the engine of her 42,000-mile 1994 Peugeot 405 turbodiesel threw a rod and received no help whatsoever from Peugeot (see 'Big Bang' on p. 462). I felt that, before the work was carried out, she should at least have been advised of the cheaper option of a secondhand replacement engine.

Non-franchised Fiat

" In April I bought what I thought was a new Fiat Punto 75SX from what I thought was a Fiat dealership. Soon after, we discovered it had been supplied with the wrong set of keys, in particular the infamous 'red key'. Because of this the engine control unit, the key code box and all the locks on the car had to be changed. In the process, the dealer must have dislodged part of the driver's-side electric window winding mechanism, with the result that on our holiday the window jammed down and because we were nowhere near a Fiat franchise repairs were delayed. I wrote to Fiat asking for compensation for our ruined holiday, and it was only then I discovered that the dealership had lost its Fiat franchise before it sold me the car as new. Fiat's two replies to my letters indicated that the loss of the keys, the changing of the ECU and locks, and the subsequent window problem were all the responsibility of the dealer which sold me the car. But how was I to know it was no longer a Fiat dealer? "

The dealership seems to have done all it could to remedy the situation. But in law (Sale and Supply of Goods Act 1994), the dealer, not Fiat, must bear responsibility for the car to have been of satisfactory standard at the time of sale. Whether it is worth trying to pursue the dealer for any compensation for your unhappy holiday experience is another matter, but it seems that by allowing the repair to the window mechanism under warranty despite the circumstances, Fiat itself has done the honourable thing. You can tell a non-franchised Fiat specialist from a Fiat franchise by the fact that the non-franchise is not allowed to use the Fiat logo. In your case, it would seem that the dealer lost its franchise round about the same time, or shortly after, you bought the car, which explains the confused situation, but Fiat is looking into how an ex-franchise continued to behave as if it was still a Fiat agent.

Over the top

" *On 1 August 1997 I took delivery of a Renault Megane Scenic 2.0RXE, the specification of which is supposed to include roof bars which are indispensable to me. These were not fitted. On 14 October I was told that the bars were still not available, so I wrote to Renault UK and the problem dragged on into late January. I would appreciate your advice as to what action I should now take.* "

Renault Customer Services explained in its letters to you that it had a supply problem with these roof bars. (They had proved to be substandard, and in some cases had actually bent.) Renault has now found an alternative supplier which has developed roof bars to an acceptable standard and these should by now be starting to arrive in the UK. Once sufficient supplies are here, Renault agents will fit the new bars to any RXE models that came without them and will also replace the sub-standard bars fitted to earlier RXEs. Please be careful about what you load onto the roof of this vehicle. Though the Scenic did very well in the stability tests we conducted in late 1997, any tall vehicle must be loaded with heavy weights on the floor and only light items above waist height. Extra special care should be taken over roof loads, as the 'pendulum effect' could make any tall vehicle dangerously unstable. I certainly do not recommend using a roof box with this type of vehicle. Unless it is 'manufacturer approved' (as was the bike rack in the Scenic commercial), using a roof box or roof bike rack could also invalidate the car's insurance.

Vectra troubles

" *I purchased a Vauxhall Vectra SRi just over two years ago and it has now covered 19,000 miles. It has been into Vauxhall agents some 19 times with various problems – from severe vibrations to deciding to drop its gearbox oil onto the M4. It has had two new clutches, new gearbox (they say), new flywheel and various electrical components. I could go on and on. Vauxhall offered a free second year warranty because of all the trouble after I complained bitterly. This has now expired, but the vibration has returned, together with difficulty in changing gear between reverse and 1st and between 1st and 2nd. I have taken the car back to a Vauxhall agent and his opinion is that the vibration is from a loose exhaust or baffle plates and that there is no fault with the gearbox. What can I do? I am not a member of a motoring organisation.* "

Vauxhall has done the right thing in providing a free second year warranty, but why not a third year warranty? The work done by the dealer will also have been very expensive because to separate a Vectra engine from its gearbox they both have first to be removed from the car, and this can be a six-hour job. I'd keep cajoling. If Vauxhall doesn't look after private owners who have paid 'full pop' for its cars, then those private owners will stop buying Vauxhalls. You're probably due for some new front tyres by now. Try Pirelli P6000s.

Missionary position

" *My son is a medical missionary, working as a surgeon in a small hospital in Beraga, Tanzania. The position he finds himself in is that he purchased a Land Rover 110 TDi Station Wagon new from a UK specialist with donations from various church and charitable organisations, and exported it to Tanzania in January 1997. He now finds that the weight of the spare wheel on the rear door is causing the door to crack. Before ordering the vehicle, my son had noticed that most LR Station Wagons in East Africa had the spare wheel mounted on a separate swing-out carrier rather than directly onto the rear door. He asked about this and was assured that the vehicle ordered would come with the latest strengthened door. He has asked the agents in Dar Es Salaam whether anything can be done under warranty, but has not yet heard anything. Is there anything you can do to expedite matters?"*

I'm delighted to report an immediate and positive response from Land Rover. Both a new, strengthened door and a separate swing-out rear spare wheel carrier are to be fitted to the vehicle FOC by the Tanzanian agents, CMC Land Rover. Many thanks to Fred Pearce of the Rover Group Export Service.

ODDBALLS

Registration date

" In which country were registration plates first used, and when? "

> France, Interior Department Seine under the Paris Police Ordinance on 14 August 1893. International 'country' plates were introduced in 1926. (Answers kindly supplied by the library of The National Motor Museum, Beaulieu, tel: 01590 612345.)

Drive-in

" We live in a very modest terrace house and are thinking of having hard-standing built in front of the house and the kerb levelled off for access. Will this give us a right of access? Others in the road have had this done and there appear to be no problems. "

> I know from experience that the council will insist there be adequate space in front of the house to accommodate a medium-sized car with ease. The council will also insist on adequate sight lines (no trees in the way). But, if the council agrees, the dip in the kerb will constitute an entrance and you will be within your rights to call the police to have anything blocking it towed away. Remember, however, that the more reasonable you are about this, the less likely you are to get a brick through your front window.

Stolen Volvo 440

" *My brother's 'F' registration Volvo 440 Turbo was stolen from a busy multi-storey car park, where it had been surrounded by a variety of more modern, more valuable cars. Is there something about this model Volvo which makes it specially worth stealing?* "

Two things. One is that it could be easier to steal than the more modern cars because it lacks their relatively sophisticated alarm and immobiliser systems. The other is, it was stolen for a robbery. After all, it's reasonably quick, and who would suspect a Volvo 440, even if it did contain four big blokes with stockings over their heads?

Sound tests

" *Does any organisation publish measurement of sound levels inside cars, at 'driver's ear'? I am interested in buying a quiet car, but test drives don't cover all road conditions and it's difficult to remember one against another.* "

Autocar does.

Increasing girth

" *I am considering the purchase of a new BMW 5-Series as, though my present 525 is only two years old, it lacks air conditioning. However, the new models are 3in. wider than their predecessors and, including the door mirrors, are 6ft 6in. wide overall. As my garage has standard 7ft doors, the clearance would be only 3in. either side. I also note that most manufacturers quote a body width excluding the added width of the door mirrors. Do you think that your readers would appreciate a warning of this before changing cars? This trend towards increased width will surely affect many people. A neighbour of mine who drives a Ford is unable to use his garage without first folding the driver's door mirror, and is staring at the choice of either re-building his garage or changing the car.* **"**

This is a point which has been raised before, but you are right to raise it again. Worst affected are owners of some 1930s semis, the garages of which were built to a width to accommodate an Austin Ten and simply can't cope with any modern car wider than a Skoda Felicia. I, too, have the 7ft door problem and have been forced to fold the door mirrors of Ford Mondeos and Fiat Tipos to be sure of getting the cars in without a scratch. The overall widths listed in useful data pages such as those of *What Car?* magazine rely on manufacturers' data, which may or may not include the mirrors. However, owners of the Chrysler Neon need have no worries. Its door mirrors fold electrically at the touch of a button.

Daytime running lights

Twelve readers responded to a letter complaining about Volvo's 'daytime running lights', and to a man (for they were all men) not one approved of them. One from Tidworth felt that what makes sense in Scandinavia, where winter nights last most of the day and cars are few and far between, does not make so much sense for the rest of Europe. While fully approving the daytime use of headlights on small vehicles such as motorcycles which might not otherwise be seen, he felt that a car's daytime running lights, on a clear day, could be both distracting and give the impression that the car was flashing its lights either as a warning (as per the 'Highway Code') or as an unofficial means of telling another driver 'I've seen you, so please proceed'. This view was echoed by several others. A reader from Bridgend supported the concept of bright side lights as daytime running lights, as on a Saab, because they have no reflector. The problem with the Volvo system is that the running lights are basically dipped beams with a sharp cut-off, and any bump in the road can give the impression that the driver is flashing his (or her) lights. EC legislators, please take note. (I still receive an average of two letters a week complaining about Volvo's 'daytime running lights', particularly on S40s and V40s.)

Carrying the can

" *I have just changed my old five-door car for a new three-door car, and have two problems with the new one. The first is that the nozzle of my five-litre reserve petrol container is too wide for the restricted entry of the new car. I know I can buy a new container with a narrower nozzle, but resent having to replace a still serviceable container with a new one. The second is that in a three-door car, the seatbelt is a long reach. I have seen devices which 'hand' the seatbelt forward in Daewoo three-door cars, but who makes them?* "

I hope you are not carrying a 'reserve supply' of petrol in a can in the car. Please, just think about this for a moment. The car has a petrol tank capable of safely containing 40, 50, maybe 60 litres of fuel, so why do you need to carry five litres in a separate can? Premium unleaded can 'go off' in a matter of months. If you run a catalysed car dry, it could misfire when you re-prime it, destroying its catalytic converter. And, of course, there is a danger in carrying fuel in a car in an unsecured container – especially if an accident occurs. Carry a can in the car by all means if it makes you

feel better, but an empty one. As for the seat-belt question, I have warned about this in the past. The smaller doors of a four- or five-door car and the closer location of the seatbelt can make it much better for a stiff or elderly person than a two- or three-door – especially when trying to get out in confined spaces. Accessory shops sell the sprung arm device you have seen, which is also standard kit on the Vauxhall Calibra.

Road racing

" *What is happening to the A65 every Sunday? It appears to turn into a race track for motorbikes, and the police are nowhere to be seen. I have had several scary experiences of being dangerously overtaken by bikes at speeds considerably over the limit. This road is far from straight and is quite busy. What is going on?* "

The A65 runs from Junction 65 of the M6 in Cumbria to Otley in West Yorkshire. What was 'going on' was that a combined force of Northumbria and Cumbria police got very heavy with bikers who traditionally used the glorious A686 and A689 to get the most out of their bikes and themselves. Some of these bikers lacked the skill to be safe at the speeds they were reaching, accidents and even deaths occurred, and the police were compelled to put a stop to it. I've seen Escort Cosworth, Volvo T5 and Cavalier Turbo patrol cars, plus 'disguised' police Cavalier Turbos and Honda motorcycles, all working together to stop these Sunday runs (I was on my way to walk the fells). The inevitable result is that the bikers have moved on. It would be nice if the British could use some National Lottery funds to open a really good, really challenging road circuit available to all on payment of a small fee, like the Nurburgring in Germany. But I'm afraid there's a fat chance of that happening.

RAC veteran

" Next year, a friend of mine will have completed 50 years as a member of the RAC. Is this a record, and does the RAC recognise this achievement in any way? "

It seems not. I phoned the RAC, only to discover that more than 63,000 have enjoyed over 50 years membership.

Within tent

" We are desperately looking for a temporary garage structure in order

to protect our car in the winter. We aren't allowed to build a garage, so we need something appropriate that keeps the snow and ice off the vehicle. I remember some years ago seeing a waterproof cover that unfolded like a fan and deployed a dome-shaped shield over the car. But despite extensive enquiries, I can find no source. "

'The Quality Portable Garage' costs from £150 including VAT for a small one and is available from The Canvas and Nylon Company, 'Our Way', North Street, Winkfield, Berks SL4 4TF, tel: 01344 882539. Rigid frame Canvas/PVC garages that would also make good 'shops' for autojumblers are available from All Weather Shelters (UK) Ltd, 1 Crossways, Everton, Lymington, Hants, tel: 01590 644255, priced from £566 plus VAT for an 8ft x 16ft shelter.

Spilled milk

" *Three weeks ago, a four-litre milk container emptied itself into my car (the top was faulty). The supplying supermarket offered to pay for the cost of cleaning, but I was unable to find a valet service. I have since spent every weekend trying to clean the car to no avail. The smell is quite unbearable. What can I do?* "

This is the worst smell to pervade a car. It even out-stinks old dogs (known in the trade as 'crocodiles' for their nasty habit of eating the seats). The answer is first to get rid of the bacteria by scrubbing with a solution of bicarbonate of soda, then get rid of any remaining pong with an odour neutraliser by the name of 'Nodor', from Town and Country Chemicals of Poole, Dorset, tel: 01202 700094. It's always sensible to put cartons of milk upright in a plastic supermarket bag and hang the bag on a window winder to keep it upright. The new BMW

5-Series has a hook in the boot specifically for shopping bags, while the Ford Ka has a deep bottle holder in the floor between the two rear seats. Three-door Citroen AXs and Berlingos have bottle holders in their door pockets. Having your milk delivered by the milkman avoids this problem entirely.

After this letter and my reply appeared in the column, many other readers came up with their own suggestions, most of which I have tried. Anything that kills the bacteria, such as bicarbonate of soda, vinegar, 'Milton' baby bottle steriliser (apropyl alcohol), methylated spirit (a bit dangerous!) obviously makes sense, as does 'Vaxing' the seats and carpet. But 'Nodor' (which now contains an antibacterial agent) gets rid of any lingering odours that these methods leave behind. I'll give another example. In the heat of last summer, a Renault Megane Scenic was delivered for testing with an unpleasant smell inside. After the smell had lingered for several days, I removed the removable seats and eventually isolated the culprit as one which still bore indentations from a child seat. The occupant had obviously had an 'accident'. A few drops of Nodor neutralised the stink within minutes and without any more effort proving necessary. Doggy smells. Fried onions. Smelly shoes. Tobacco smoke. It's really good. It really works.

Clockwatchers

A number of readers have written to suggest means of checking the accuracy of speedometers and odometers. One from Bridgwater pointed out that, though both the odometer and the speedometer work off the same cable, speedo accuracy also depends on the strength or weakness of the speedo magnet and hairspring. He suggests driving at a constant indicated 60 mph and timing how long it takes to pass seventeen 100-metre markers (i.e. sixteen spaces). The time (he says) should be one minute, and the number of seconds taken divided by 60 will give the ratio of indicated speed to true speed. Whether a driver can keep to a constant indicated 60 mph for this distance is of course another matter. Another reader, from Droitwich, took the manufacturer's figure of 23.5 mph per 1,000 rpm in fifth gear for his BMW 323i and compared speedo and rev readings with the true calculated speed at 50 mph, 60 mph and 70 mph. Yet another, this time from Newcastle upon Tyne, suggested that because 74.56 mph = 120 kph = 2 kilometres per minute, then at this exact speed you should pass eleven 100-metre posts (i.e. ten spaces) in 30 seconds. If you don't, the speedometer is either too fast or too slow, but usually works out at between 5.9% and 8.6% too fast. Finally, a reader from Grantham suggested that a far better way would be to borrow his yachting friend's hand-held Global Positioning System set, set it to measure 'SOG' (speed over ground) and obtain an instant, 100% accurate, real-time readout of true speed to compare with the speedometer. The Satellite Navigation Systems fitted as options to some new cars should, of course, also be capable of doing this.

Origins of the AA

" Am I right in thinking that the origins of the AA stem from the actions of a certain Surrey Justice of the Peace, a Colonel Mowbray Saut, who was

advanced in imposing restrictions on motorists in the early part of the century? Certain motorists got together to warn others of where police speed traps lay in waiting, and from this the AA was eventually formed. "

Yes. The Guinness Book of Car Facts and Feats (ISBN 0 85112 2078) tells us that 'The Automobile Association was formed in 1905 expressly to provide "Scouts" to warn motorists of hidden "police traps".' From another source I learned that the first AA patrols were young lads on bicycles who wore 'AA' badges on circular discs, one side of which was white and the other red. If they showed the white background, the road ahead was clear. If they showed the red background, there was a speed trap ahead. This was ruled to be legal *outside* a speed trap because the patrol was merely warning AA members to keep within the law. But in 1906 a speed trap near Guildford was altered without the patrol's knowledge, so that he actually gave the warning within the trap itself. In the ensuing prosecution it was ruled that the use of AA patrols to warn motorists of speed traps was an illegal interference with the police. The AA got round this by instituting its rule: 'If an AA patrol *fails* to salute you, stop and ask the reason.' This gave the patrol an opportunity to say words such as, 'Sorry, didn't see your badge. By the way, take it easy for a mile or so. Dodgy road surface.'

'No entry' at the Motor Show

" *A big 'thank you' to Honest John for restoring an eight-year-old boy's faith in human nature. We visited the 1997 Motor Show one Saturday in October and bought our entry tickets. My son Andrew, who is particularly interested in Porsches, approached the Porsche stand and asked a rather stern looking man if he could look at the cars. He was rebuffed with the comment that access to the stand was only allowed for current Porsche owners or those with a specific invitation or a Porsche credit card. Even Ferrari allowed controlled access to its stand. So thank you for gaining access for Andrew to the stand and for taking responsibility for him while he was there.* "

In fairness to Porsche, it is trying to sell its cars, and if it allowed unlimited access to the stand it would be overrun. So I'd like to thank the Porsche security man for actually allowing us on. But maybe there are a couple of lessons to be learned here. First, eight-year-old Andrew may, one day, be able to afford a series of Porsches of his own. If all he remembered of Porsche was a brusque rebuff at the 1997 Motor Show, this might forever taint his attitude to the marque. Second, I well remember my first Motor Show, in 1959. Not only were kids welcomed onto most stands (including those of the coachbuilders), but special efforts were made to cater specifically for youngsters. BMC even produced a special *Eagle*-like kid's comic detailing the design history and production of the Mini which had been launched a few months previously. Okay, in 1997 everyone who visited the Nissan stand got a balloon, and SEAT did a great line in brochure bags. But the show as a whole could hardly be described as 'exciting', and more effort should have been made to send paying punters home feeling good and dreaming of the day they could finally afford one of the beautiful cars they had seen, touched and sat in.

Cruise night

" *I have heard that there are now new organisers for the Guildford Cruise of American Cars and Hot Rods, and that it is held right through the winter. Please could you confirm this?* "

Yes. A reader from Surbiton kindly sent me all the relevant details. The Guildford Cruise is held on the evening of the first Sunday of every month at the American Roadhouse-style Burger King in the Ladymead Retail Park situated between Guildford town centre and the A3 Guildford by-pass. Organisers are: Noel and Pin Bowman, tel: 0181 423 0549, mobile: 0585 068556; and Dave and Jennie Palmer, tel: 01264 363295. Resident 1950s DJ (no records later than 1959) remains Rockin' Roy Hunt, tel: 01483 539474. Others on the Cruise Committee are Lynn Price, tel: 01483 539474; Graham Small, tel: 01276 858017; and John George, tel: 0181 398 6485.

Left hookers

" Can you settle an argument about when the USA introduced left-hand drive and shifted to driving on the right-hand side of the road? At a local steam rally, my curiosity was aroused by a Stanley steam car with right-hand drive. The owner of the car claimed that Henry Ford was responsible for the changeover, but an American friend thought this was unlikely. "

The rule of the road in both the USA and Europe was to drive on the right, and the driver of the 1886 Benz Patent Motorwagen (which had tiller steering) quite logically sat on the left. But, as steering wheels began to appear, most turn-of-the-century cars were driven from the right, including Henry Ford's own 1903 Model A and his 1906 Model K. However, following Benz practice, the first American car with a steering wheel instead of a tiller was the 1901 Columbia which steered from the left. The 1903 Autocar also steered from the left. And when Henry Ford launched the Model T in 1908 he decided that it, too, should steer from the left. In his book, *Cars: Early and Vintage 1886–1930*, G.N. Georgano writes, 'As in other matters, where Ford led, the rest followed – and within ten years right hand drive was practically extinct on American cars.' Only a few luxurious American cars retained right-hand steering. Pierce Arrow kept it up to 1920 because the company felt it helped a chauffeur to alight more quickly to open the sidewalk-side door for his masters. In Europe, though cars drove on the right, no Bugatti ever had left-hand drive, and Lancia only switched in 1956 to meet demand from the USA. Canada switched from RHD to LHD in the early 1950s, and Sweden switched over in 1967. If Britain had switched too, it would never have been possible to hike

UK car prices to 25% more than the average for the rest of Europe.

Soft tops

" *There seems to be some confusion regarding the term 'cabriolet', as applied to a type of car body. I had always understood that a cabriolet was a car which had conventional saloon doors and windows, but the canvas roof rolled back in the manner of a Fiat Topolino or a Citroen 2CV. The title 'cabriolet' now seems to be applied to all manner of convertibles, such as Fords, Vauxhalls, Volkswagens, etc., which do not have these features. Is this correct? And could you also explain the difference between a Sedanca de Ville and a Coupe de Ville?* "

I'll try and list as many different types as I can think of:

- Cabriolet: A two- or four-seat drop-head coupe on which part of the roof structure remains permanently in place – as is the case with the VW Golf cabriolet.
- Convertible: Generic name for any car with a fully-folding top where no part of the top is left in place when the roof is folded.
- Coupe: A fixed-roof car with two or four seats, usually with rear head and legroom compromised for styling reasons.
- Coupe de Ville: A formal but close-coupled hard-top town car, sometimes with only two doors.
- Drop-Head Coupe: Two- or four-seater with snug folding top, winding windows, and window frames which stay in place with the top down.
- Estate Car: A car with squared-off bodywork aft of the front seats and doors at the back that open to roof height.

- Folding-Head Saloon: Saloon car with a folding or roll-top canvas centre to the roof (as per the 2CV).
- Landaulette: A limousine with a folding canvas or leather hood over the rear passengers, but a fixed roof over the driver.
- Limousine: A large car with the driving compartment separated from the rear passenger compartment by a glass screen.
- Phaeton: American term for what the English understand as a 'tourer'.
- Roadster: Open two-seater car with rudimentary foul-weather equipment – usually a frame which needs to be assembled and a hood stretched over it. Roadsters used to have side screens rather than winding windows.
- Sedanca: A car with two doors and a removable top over the chauffeur's seat, but a fixed roof over the rear passengers.
- Sedanca de Ville: A car with four doors and a removable top over the chauffeur's seat, but a fixed roof over the rear passengers.
- Saloon: A fixed-roof car with four or more seats and plenty of headroom in the rear.
- Shooting Break: A car with squared off bodywork aft of the front seats with doors at the back that open to roof height.
- Station Wagon: A car with squared off bodywork aft of the front seats with doors at the back that open to roof height.
- Tourer: Four-seater roadster, usually with a folding top but only rudimentary protection at the sides.
- Traveller: A name used by Morris for a Station Wagon.

PARTS AND ACCESSORIES

Tracking down a track rod end

" *I have a 'J' reg. Dacia Duster Diesel and am trying to locate a track rod end for it. Despite contacting advertisers in* Exchange & Mart *(the importers have moved on from their previous address) I have been unable to find this part. Could you please help?* "

This vehicle was based on the old Renault 12 which continued in production in Rumania. Renault dealers may be able to supply some parts but the numbers of two alternative Dacia parts specialists from *Exchange & Mart* are: 01702 713206 and 01303 812727.

On the shelf

Several readers have recently asked if they can obtain more robust luggage covers for hatchbacks and estate cars. The answer came in the February 1997 issue of *Diesel Car & 4×4* magazine (always a useful source). A range of 'extremely strong' parcel shelves is made by Autoshelf UK (tel: 01562 742247) priced from £29.95. But please remember that piling things on top of a luggage cover restricts your vision, causes reflections and can be dangerous.

Cover-up

" *Recently I part-exchanged my five-door Honda Civic 1.6iLS auto for a Honda CRV ES Auto in order to benefit from the CRV's ease of entry and exit. I am also quite impressed with its build quality, comfort and performance. But I'm not happy with the flimsy luggage cover provided by Honda as an optional extra. Does any accessory company specialise in a luggage cover 'roller blind'?* "

Yes, the 'Covertech' roller luggage cover from Clim Air UK, 1 Station Parade, Station Road, Sidcup, Kent DA15 7DB, tel: 0181 309 7744. It comes in four different widths, 48 in., 51 in., 53 in. and 55 in. (125 cm, 130 cm, 134 cm or 140 cm) and costs £99.95 including VAT. For people who like to drive with the windows slightly open, Clim Air also offers TUV-approved car side window rain deflectors, at £49.95 a pair, and sunroof wind deflectors.

Cheap parts

" *I run a Mercedes 190E which has 150,000 miles on the clock. For reasons of economy I prefer to replace such parts as silencers with non-Mercedes parts. My local motor factor tried to find a rear silencer and tailpipe section, but to no avail. Do you have phone numbers for any suppliers of such parts? I understand that there are a couple of companies specialising in spare parts for Audi, BMW, Mercedes, Porsche, Saab, VW and Volvo – all long-lasting cars which must create a demand for cheaper parts.* "

In my experience, some aftermarket parts are very good, but for others you're better off sticking either to manufacturer parts or parts made by the people who make them for the manufacturer. This is true of oil filters, timing chains, brake parts and exhaust systems. Cheap aftermarket exhausts may have only a third of the life of the 'original' part – particularly in the case of VWs. Two specialists you might like to try are Euro Car Parts on 0541 506 506, and German & Swedish on 0181 893 1688, both of which do both original parts and aftermarket parts and advertise their latest prices in *Exchange & Mart*.

Pop of the stops

A large number of readers wrote with suggestions as to why stop lamp filament failures were so common with certain makes and models of car. Some thought it was increased use of the brakes. Some thought it was the fault of lazy drivers who kept their foot on the brake pedal at junctions and traffic signals instead of applying the handbrake. Others blamed the slamming of hatchbacks. Yet another blamed poor waterproof sealing on the lamp units. But I concur with the reader who blames the poor quality of the bulbs fitted to some makes of car and of the replacements sold by main dealers. When he discovered that the bulbs of his car were failing at nine-month intervals, he checked and found they were all of Eastern European manufacture. When he replaced them with bulbs made in Germany he had no further problems. He has owned his current car, a VW Passat, for eight years and 92,000 miles, and in that time has only needed to replace one bulb. This echoes my experience of a used VW I have run for ten years and 80,000 miles and on which I don't remember ever having to replace a bulb.

Pressing matter

" Where can I get pressed aluminium number plates? I am heartily sick of having to replace my brittle plastic plates for every MOT. (Yes, I am afraid I do use my bumper as a battering ram.) "

Try Steve Hughes Number Plates on 01275 333856; Jamesigns Ltd on 01295 758355; Plates 4 YOU on 01487 831239; or Tippers Vintage Plates on 01702 553225. But please don't park near any of my cars.

Alternator anguish

" I have just been quoted £461.78 to replace the alternator on my Vauxhall Corsa 1.5D. Is this a record? "

No. The 1.5 and 1.7 Corsa and the 1.7TD Astra and Cavalier have Isuzu engines. The alternator is an imported Isuzu part and is combined with the brake vacuum pump, and these factors together make it so expensive.

Wheel trims

" I keep losing my wheel trims into the verge of the road and they are quite expensive to replace. If motor manufacturers reverted to the hub-caps of the 1950s they could save millions of pounds on the basic price of cars. They would then make a lot more money selling expensive wheel trims to those who thought they needed them. "

Not quite true. Manufacturers actually save a fortune by using cheap-to-produce plastic wheeltrims and only giving the wheels underneath a thin coat of paint. When these wheeltrims are then scrubbed off on kerbs (all too

easy in a multi-storey carpark), the same manufacturers charge £10–£30 each for replacements. The answer is to remove the expensive
wheeltrims provided by the manufacturer, keep
them in a safe place, and invest £10–£20 in an
entire set of aftermarket wheel trims. When you
come to sell your car, you can then replace the
original pristine set of trims.

Price of silence

*" Last year I purchased a Hyundai Lantra, which I think is good value
for money. However, I do find the engine noisy inside the car and wonder
if you know of any firm which specialises in noise insulation? "*

Try BJ Acoustics, 289 Featherstall Road North,
Oldham, Lancs OL1 2NH, tel: 0161 627 0873.
Their 'Sound Barrier' kit, which includes a lead-

lined engine blanket, costs £250 including VAT and delivery, but cheaper kits are also available.

Tim not-so-dim

" *Fed up with the main beam performance of my VW Golf Mk III, I ordered the 80/100 watt relay kit from Tim Stiles Racing (£94.59, tel: 01278 453036) and it came the next day. The performance on main beam is a vast improvement, but the VW's 'dim dip' system creates a problem. When the control is switched to 'sidelights' I get 80/100 watt main beam, which can cause dazzle on a 25-mile drive home along twisty but quite busy lanes. What is the answer?* "

Don't ever drive on sidelights. Switch to 'sidelights' on a Golf Mk III and that's what you get. But turn on the engine and the standard system then converts to 'dim dip', which is main beam with a very low current passing through. In the UK it is only legal to drive at night on 'dim dip' in built-up areas or outside those areas for half an hour after sunset and half an hour before sunrise, otherwise you must always use dipped beam. The only other legal use of 'dim dip' is in dull daytime weather (new Highway Code Rules 94–96). What happens on 'dim dip' in your Golf is that the new relay detects that main beams are on and gives them the full current. So your answer is to use only dipped or full beam for driving, to rewire the lighting system to get rid of the 'dim dip on sidelights', or to ditch the new relay and bulbs and go for Xenon Plus bulbs using the standard system. For details, tel: 0800 526510.

Sitting comfortably

" *Can you help with advice as to where to get economical replacement upholstery for a 1982 Mercedes 280E? There may also be a problem with the interior of the driver's seat. Mercedes dealers are a 'no go area' because their prices are astronomical. "*

Most drivers of older cars face this same problem. The driver's seat always goes first, and because of this secondhand drivers seats are few and far between at specialist dismantlers. The answer is to run through your local Yellow Pages and phone the listed 'Car Trimmers and Upholsterers'. Some will have 'menu' prices for the work; others will need to see the car to judge the amount of work required before making an estimate.

Mirror mirror

" Thank you for your personal reply regarding a replacement mirror glass for my American-built Chrysler Neon. As you suggested, I contacted AC Automotive Ltd at 247–251 Goldhawk Road, London W12, tel: 0181 741 9993, and found them most helpful. I went there last week and they had new glass made and fitted within a few hours at a cost of £25 plus VAT. A big improvement on the £320 quoted by Chrysler. "

Pleased to be of service. Another company which can help with parts and servicing of American cars is AC Delco of 19 Wadsworth Road, Unit 14, Perivale, Middx, tel: 0181 810 4595.

Long-life batteries

" In September 1997 you mentioned AC Delco as a source of parts for American cars. Is this the same AC Delco which made the original battery in my 1985 Vauxhall Astra? Despite twelve years, 107,000 miles and plenty of cold starts on wet mornings, it has never given me a moment's worry. It's the most robust battery I have ever had. "

AC Delco is owned by General Motors and you can get an AC Delco battery for a European car just about anywhere. AC Delco American of 19 Wadsworth Road, Unit 14, Perivale, Middx (tel: 0181 810 4595) specialises in American car parts and AC Delco batteries for American cars which are otherwise unobtainable in the UK.

Ka sunroof

" *I purchased a Ford Ka² in January of this year and have been very pleased with its overall performance. However, I am anxious to have a tilt-and-slide sunroof fitted. Ford tells me it is only able to offer a pop-up version, so do you know of any manufacturer of a tilt-and-slide sunroof suitable for the narrow roofline of the Ka which would not infringe the Ford warranty?* "

A roll bar incorporated into the roof structure of the Ka prevents the fitting of a sun-roof which slides back under the roof. Hollandia Weathershields make the 'approved' pop-up sunroof available through Ford dealers. They also make an external sliding sunroof which has already been successfully fitted to a number of Kas. (Tel: 0121 322 2030 for prices and local fitting agent.)

Brighter spark

" *My daughter drives an elderly Mini which continually lets her down. I would like to fit an electronic ignition kit, but have been told it is no longer possible to obtain them. Is this so? If not, where can I get one? I find your column most enjoyable. It's the first thing I read every Saturday at breakfast. My wife calls it my 'I didn't know that' column.* "

Lumenition electronic ignition conversion kits

are still available from the Autocar Electrical Equipment Co. Ltd, 49–51 Tiverton Street, London SE1 6NZ, tel: 0171 403 4334 (as any reader of *Practical Classics* magazine would have been able to tell you). Optical trigger electronic ignition (which eliminated the points system) has further advantages and is available from Barry Jacobson, CT-Spark, 78 Kirkstone Drive, Loughborough, Leics LE11 3RW, tel: 01509 261905 or 01509 505152. It costs a bit more (average £155), but carries a five-year guarantee. Remember, though, that with their distributors at the front directly behind the grille, Minis have always been susceptible to damp, and if the protective guard has fallen off (or has always been missing) a damp distributor is more or less inevitable.

£800 carburettor

" I have a 1990 Cavalier 1.6L, which I have had from new and which has covered 188,000 virtually trouble-free miles. It has proved to be a superb piece of engineering, but the automatic choke and its linkage wore, causing me a myriad of problems. My Vauxhall agent told me I had only two options: the first, a new carburettor at £800 plus fitting; the second, a manual choke conversion at £31.50 plus fitting. Naturally I opted for the latter, and the car is running perfectly again. Can you explain how Vauxhall has the gall to charge £800 for a carburettor? It seems like a ploy to avoid stocking spares which no one will buy at that price. "

Two reasons. First, as is the case in Japan (where cars are routinely either scrapped or exported to poorer countries after five or seven years), manufacturers do not regard it in their interests to encourage extended ownership of older cars (VW is one of the few honourable exceptions). Second, cost of inventory. To maintain a stock of parts for obsolete models a manufacturer has to have them specially batch-built at intervals and is then faced with the cost of stocking the parts for years. This inevitably makes such parts expensive. Happily, your dealer had a cheap solution to the autochoke problem. But if your car needs a new carburettor in the future, your best bet is to contact Webcon on 01932 788805, who manufacture a range of replacement carburettor kits, normally at prices between £175 and £300. I don't recommend a carb from a scrapper, as this may well be as worn as the carb it replaces.

Exhausted

" A Honda dealer recently quoted me a price of £110 for a new rear silencer box for my 1989 Accord Aerodeck. Several 'fast-fit' tyre and exhaust centres have quoted me a great deal less, for example £80. What's the difference? Is it generally worthwhile fitting manufacturers' replacement parts once the car is out of warranty? "

Rear silencer boxes have a hard life on a car used for short journeys, because they have to cope with masses of condensation which never dries out and which rots the steel from the inside out.

If the 'genuine' exhaust system is of higher-quality steel, thicker grade, is 'aluminised' or is stainless steel, then its life can be up to four times longer than that of a cheap mild steel 'copy' silencer. Rear silencer boxes have a hard life on a car used for short journeys, because they have to cope with masses of condensation which never dries out and which rots the steel from the inside out. This does not mean that a 'fast fit' centre can't offer you a long-life silencer. But you do need to check you are comparing like for like and not simply a price against a price. Where parts are sourced from the makers which actually supply the car manufacturer you tend to get the same part for less. But some 'copy' parts, especially brake parts, sourced from the Far East can be seriously dodgy.

Re-manufactured engines

" *On 17 January 1998 you referred a reader from Southampton to the Landcrab Owners' Club as a possible source of a replacement engine and gearbox for his 1976 Princess 1800HL. On 14 February you mentioned an engine re-manufacturer in Doncaster and an importer of secondhand Japanese engines. You might also have mentioned the Federation of Engine Re-manufacturers, which has 180 members – all of which are required to conform to a Code of Practice. Your readers can be directed to the nearest FER engine re-manufacturer by phoning 01788 538321.* **"**

Japanese secondhand engine importer API (0500 830530) is the only secondhand engine importer I have ever recommended. API and engine re-manufacturer R & E Arnett (01302 323931) both got in because of the honest advice they gave concerning engine oil changes. But your federation certainly represents a good way for readers to avoid the numerous engine replacement rip-off merchants.

Sinclair spare part surgery

A reader from Crowborough wrote to ask where he could source spare parts for his Sinclair C5. I referred him to The Battery Vehicle Society (01258 455470), who, I am pleased to report, located a source of C5 spares. It is E.S.G. Ltd, 27 Cornhill, Liverpool L18, tel: 0151 428 7408. Another reader asked about Sinclair electric motors for pedal cycles. The brand name for these is Zeta II, no licence, tax or motorcycle helmet is needed, and they give a top speed of up to 14 mph or a range of up to 30 miles (with pedal assistance) on one battery charge. More information: Sinclair Research Ltd, 13 Dennington Road, Wellingborough NN8 2RL, tel: 01933 279300.

PERFORMANCE TUNING

Interception

" As the owner of a Mazda MX5, I was intrigued by a small classified advertisement in Telegraph *'Motoring' offering 15–20 extra bhp for £495 – call BBR. Could you tell me what modification this is? Is it the same BBR which was linked to a special edition MX5? And, if I go ahead, should I tell my insurer? "*

It's our old friend the 'Interceptor 2000', a supplementary ECU which reprocesses the signals from the car's existing ECU. Originally developed for cars which could not be chipped because there was no way into their ECU, the 'Interceptor 2000' is the way forward for the Audi A8, Mazda MX5 1.6 and 1.8, Golf GTi Mk III, Toyota MR2, the latest Range Rover, the Jeep Cherokee, the MGF and now the Lotus Elise. The Elise Interceptor was commissioned by Lotus agents Bell & Colville and gives the car a much needed extra 22 bhp in the mid-range – at 4,000 rpm. There is a very good chance it will be dealer warranted and may even be adopted by Lotus itself. BBR can now chip or 'intercept' 900 different models, so are well worth a call on 01280 702389. On an MX5 the job takes four hours, so can be done while you hang around (the Silverstone circuit is just up the road). Yes, BBR did the original MX5 turbo before the

'Interceptor 2000' had been developed. And yes, you must tell your insurer.

Power mad

" My question is about power and how it is measured. Some manufacturers quote 'bhp' (brake horse power), some 'PS' (which I have been told is the same thing, and some use 'kW' (kilowatts). What is the relationship between these units? "

According to 'Glass's Guide Checkbook', one unit of bhp equals 1.014 Pferdestarke (PS) and 0.7457 kW, one PS equals 0.9863 bhp and one kW equals 1.341 bhp. You might also like to know that one unit lb. ft torque equals 1.3558 Nm (Newton metres) and that one Nm equals 0.7376 lb. ft. The public can buy 'Glass's Guide Checkbook', price £31, which gives details and brief specifications of all cars on sale in the UK for the past nine years, by calling Glass's Information Services Ltd on 01932 823823.

Cut-price BMW

" I have a 1984 BMW 316 with a 1,766 cc motor and Pierburg 2 BE carburettor. The rectangular inlet and exhaust manifold ports do not match the round cylinder head ports. This motor should improve in bhp, torque or economy (30–36 mpg) if it had matching ports and manifolds with reduced turbulence. The exhaust manifold in particular is an oddly convoluted, ugly, cracked lump of an iron casting. Where can I find information on gas flow? A book on tuning, perhaps? Where can I obtain a suitable flowed manifold, please? "

From about 1980, UK-market BMW 316s were fitted with the carburettor 1,766 cc engine instead of the old 1,573 cc engine. This 1,766 cc engine was designed for Bosch K-Jetronic fuel injection, giving 98 bhp, so the carburettor model was a cut-price version and economies such as those you describe were made. When the square-rigged E30 3-Series was launched in early 1983, the 90 bhp 1,766 cc engine continued in the 316, but power in the 318i, now fitted with L-Jetronic injection, rose to 105 bhp. Later on, in 1987–88 (and very confusingly) the 316 became the 316i and received a new 1,596 cc 102 bhp fuel injected engine and the 318i a new 1,795 cc 115 bhp fuel injected engine. I always found the old carburettor 1,766 cc engine less than satisfactory, especially on hills, but it's one of the penalties of a base-spec. cut-price car. For improved performance your answer is to upgrade the engine to 318i spec., or sell the car and buy a later 316i or 318i. For books on tuning, call Mill House Books on 01205 270377.

'Running in – please pass'

" Years ago, when I was a lad, I can remember my father having to 'run in' the family Standard 9 after it was re-bored. So far as I can recall, the instructions were to drive the car at no more than 40 mph for at least 500 miles. The instructions were, I think, much the same when I bought my first car, a Ford Anglia 1200, in 1965. Since then I have had quite a few new cars but have never been quite sure whether to 'run them in' or not. Please could you advise? "

Engines are built to far tighter tolerances than they used to be and oils are a lot better in suspending any metal that wears off during the first few thousand miles of a car's life. It's generally reckoned that a car is best run for its first 5,000 miles on mineral oil to allow some wear and 'bedding in' before switching to a semi- or fully

'Running in' a new car still makes sense, but it's best done at higher speeds than in the past.

synthetic oil. Obviously, if you thrash a car straight away, or, worse still, drive it too slowly or 'labour' the engine in too high a gear, you can create problems. Once I patiently 'ran in' a Peugeot 205GTi 1.6 105 bhp for 1,000 miles, varying the speed between 60 mph and 70 mph round the M25, changed the oil for fresh mineral oil, ran it at no more than 85 mph for another 750 miles or so, then started getting my foot down. The result was a 205 1.6 that, on the Autobahn, could hit 130 mph on the clock. So, yes, 'running in' still does make sense, but it's best done at higher speeds than in the past. It's also true that modern cars 'loosen up' considerably after around 3,000 miles, and continue to loosen up for many thousands of miles after that. I recently very reluctantly handed back a 9,000-mile Peugeot 306 GTi-6, which early road tests (not *Autocar*'s) had criticised for a 'tight' engine – yet this one would spin to 7,000 rpm – 500 rpm past its power peak – at the drop of a foot, still did 33 mpg, and was truly delightful to drive.

More muscle

" I have a 1995 model Nissan Primera 2.0E GT, bought at 5,000 miles in December 1995 and now with 20,000 miles under its wheels. Apart from a jiggly low-speed ride, it's been fine. Though I am a careful driver, I feel I could do with more torque. I have tested a few V6 models, but have not been impressed, and I'm also 'underwhelmed' by the new-shape Primera GT. Because of this, I'm considering either 'chipping' my present car, fitting a turbo, or both. I am sure the chassis could handle another 30–50 bhp. Can you recommend someone to do this? Finally, would a Subaru Impreza Turbo be a good replacement for the Primera? "

The best people to 'chip' and otherwise modify your Primera are BBR in Brackley, Northants, tel: 01280 702389. They specialise in chipping catalysed cars to gain more mid-range torque and driveability. (Remember, you must inform your insurer of any such mods.) Yes, a Subaru Impreza would be a good replacement. An Impreza WRX would be even better if you can find one that's slipped in within the SVA import quota (try Park Lane on 01420 544300 or Warrender on 01257 427700).

Chipping a diesel

" I have a 1995 Audi 80 TDI Estate with a power output of 90 bhp at 4,000 rpm. Several times I have noticed an advert in the magazine of the IAM for a 'Power Link' system by Rossiters of King's Lynn (tel: 01485 540000). This is stated to increase the power and torque of a turbodiesel, to use factory connections, to be capable of being fitted or removed in minutes, and to offer a sensational performance increase. My query is, how proven and how reliable is such a piece of kit? Rossiters tell me it is Bosch-approved and in use by several police forces in preference to changing the chip in the ECU. The increase in power is 20 bhp and fuel consumption goes down by a mile or two per gallon. Rossiters tell me it has been purchased extensively by owners of the new VW Passat TDI 90 who were unable to obtain delivery of the 110 bhp version. "

A friend of mine has a new Passat TDI 90, 'Superchipped' to 120 bhp and, subjectively, his car feels more responsive at over 3,000 rpm than the Passat TDI 110, yet still delivers 40–50 mpg (Superchips: 01280 816781). BBR (01280 702389) has developed a similar type of external engine management chip to re-map the output the of existing ECU without the need to 'open the box', which is sometimes impossible. Two others are Darley Specialist Services' TDI Powerchip (01332 553143) and Webcon's more sophisticated Torqmaster (01932 787100). Like the Rossiter kit you describe, these can both be attached or removed from the engine in minutes. VW itself brought the power up to 110 bhp in a different way, by adopting an electronically controlled variable vane turbocharger. To pull emissions back to MOT 'Smoke Opacity Test' standards, any late-model VAG diesel (Audi, Seat, Skoda, VW) with an in-car diagnostic socket can have its fuelling re-set by any competent specialist using the VAG 1552 ECU interrogator, which can also diagnose virtually any electronic fault on any VAG car with the appropriate socket.

'At the wheels'

" I feel that quoted 'bhp' figures are a bit misleading because they relate to power delivered at the flywheel rather than at the wheels. Surely it would provide a better means of comparison if 'bhp at the wheels' was quoted, preferably also in relation to the weight of the vehicle. My own car is very underrated and generally ignored by the motoring press. With a 2 litre 16v engine producing 150 bhp (at the flywheel), it has ABS, electronic traction control, twin airbags and a host of other 'extras' including air conditioning and a three-year warranty. Add to this a huge boot and you have the Seat Toledo 16v. For the same money, you could, of course, have a Mondeo or Vectra and make do with less performance and a much more basic specification. "

You're right about 'power at the wheels' figures, but it would, of course, require road test cars to visit a chassis dynamometer (rolling road). Colin Marshall at VW specialists Wheelbase of Hersham (01932 252515) has a GTi Engineering Golf Mk II 2.0 16v with some extra mods of his own, which is putting out 200 bhp at the flywheel and 175 bhp at the road wheels, so the power loss is 12.5%. Your Seat Toledo is built on the floorpan of that old 'Golf with a rucksack', the Mk II Jetta, and, with its big hole for the hatchback, is not as stiff as the Jetta. The Toledo 16v found a lot of friends in the motoring press when it was relatively new to the scene, but it has now been around since October 1991 and is due to be replaced by a new Golf Mk IV-based version in 1998. Regarding 'power to weight', although the antediluvian pre-cat 2,232 lb Mk II Jetta GTi 1.8 16v officially 'only' developed 139 bhp, *Autocar* magazine still managed to record a 0–60 of just 7.1 seconds – exactly the same as the 2,687 lb 174 bhp Golf Mk III VR6. (Both cars reached 60 in second gear.) Subtract 12.5% for power losses and the Jetta had 121 bhp per ton against 127 bhp per ton for the VR6, which suggests that the Jetta's quoted power output may have been a bit conservative. More info: Haymarket Reprints, tel: 01235 534323.

Free turbo chart

" How and where can I find all the details about turbos? What they do, how they are fitted, different types, how to drive a turbo, maintenance and possible problems. "

The best I've seen is a small wall-chart produced by Turbo Technics, of which I have sent you a spare copy. Other readers who would like to have one should write to Turbo Technics Ltd, 17 Gallowhill Road, Brackmills, Northampton NN4 7EE (tel: 01604 764005). Please enclose an address label and £1.20 in stamps to cover the cost of postage and a cardboard postage tube. Turbo Technics is responsible for supercharging the MGF VVC to 200 bhp plus and has made sure the application will also fit the Lotus Elise. Web-site: http://www.demon.co.uk/turbotec.

POWER STEERING

Heavy helm

" *I have a 1991 VW Golf Clipper cabrio, which is a wonderful car apart from the steering. Is it possible to convert to power steering? Are there specialists who can do the work?* "

This is a much-asked question. VW had some of the last Mk I cabrios imported converted to PAS by Steering Developments Ltd (01442 212918). They have now got the cost of fitting PAS to a Mk 1 Golf or Mk 1 Golf cabrio down to £1,900 + VAT using Golf Mk II parts. TSR has also been working on this for years and has built several running prototypes. By the time you read this they should have a conversion available for around £1,200. More info: 01278 453036.

New or secondhand steering

" *My Golf Mk II 1.6CL automatic will be ten years old in February. It is in sparkling condition, is serviced every six months, and has done just 22,450 miles. I would like to keep it and have power steering fitted – but have been quoted £4,000 for the work and been told the car is only worth £1,000.* "

You're being taken for a ride. Your car is worth between £1,250 and £1,750 as a private sale, and with power steering fitted could be worth as much as £2,500. The cost of having power steering fitted, using new parts, should not exceed

£1,200 plus VAT. Using used parts from a Golf 1.8GL or Golf 1.6 Driver automatic, it should be about half this price. Try TSR on 01278 453036 (VW/Audi specialist – prices from £650 plus VAT), A&C Vehicle Services of Leek, Staffs, tel: 01538 398227 (VW/Audi specialist – prices from £500 plus VAT), Power Steering Services on 0181 853 3374 (prices from £2,000 plus VAT using new parts) and Steering Developments Ltd on 01442 212918 (prices from £1,900 plus VAT using new parts).

PAS for £660

" *Some months ago you were kind enough to recommend Andy Jackson of A&C Vehicle Services in Leek, Staffs, for the job of fitting power assisted steering to my non-assisted Audi 80. From start to finish I found Andy to be a most reliable, positive and friendly person. The job was completed in just under eight hours, using secondhand parts. And the cost was exactly the same as the estimate – £660. My wife and I can once again take pleasure in driving the car. Thank you for putting us in touch with such an effective small garage.* "

That's what I like to hear. A&C's address and phone number is above under 'New or secondhand steering'. Please inform your insurer of the conversion.

Metro retro power steering

" *Some time ago I read in your column that power steering could be retrofitted to cars not provided with it when new. I would like to have such a system fitted to my 'K' reg. Metro diesel. Could you refresh my memory with the details?* "

It can be done, but it's expensive. Steering

Developments (01442 212918) do a PAS system for the Rover Metro for £2,270 plus VAT, fitted. Power Steering Services of Greenwich (0181 853 3374) also fit a system to the Rover Metro for £2,500 plus VAT. Obviously retrofitting PAS to a car never designed for it is much more expensive than retrofitting PAS to a car where it is standard on some of the model range. Steering Developments can even fit an electro-hydraulic power steering system to the Mk I Metro.

Power failure

" *My 'J' reg. VW Golf GTi went into the local main dealer for its annual service in perfect working order and came out minus the power steering. No previous problems had been experienced. But the dealer found a leak which his mechanics attempted to seal externally. After collecting the car from the service, the power steering failed completely the same afternoon and I was faced with a £462 bill for a new pump. Both the main agent and VW imply fair wear and tear. Do you consider this reasonable for a car which has covered just 57,000 miles?* **"**

Once a car is over five years old it's even more necessary for it to have an oil-change service every six months, to give the mechanics a chance to spot any impending problems.

Another reader suffered the same problem immediately after a service, on this occasion with an old-model VW Passat. I think that what happened on both occasions was that the pumps had become worn and that the correct tensioning of slackened belts during the service had finished them off. At your car's age it is normal for components to start wearing out – if not the PAS pump then something else. Also, now that the car is more than five years old, it is even more necessary than before to pop it in for an intermediate oil change service every six months rather than every year. That gives mechanics a chance to spot such impending problems as a leaking fuel pump, leaking rear brake compensator, chafed brake pipe, worn pads, ridged discs or worn strut tops before they have tragic consequences.

Cheap assistance

" *My Vauxhall Astra 1.4 does not have power steering. However, a local garage has offered to fit it for £200–£250 using Vauxhall parts. The main dealer denies all knowledge of such a conversion and would not attempt it. All they could say was a Northampton firm might do the job for around £2,000. Is this really possible? And would I have problems when I came to trade the car in?* **"**

£200–£250 is really cheap – but possible using secondhand parts. Providing it works well and there are no leaks, it will enhance the value of your car by the cost of the conversion at the very least. Remember, under the Sale and Supply of

Goods Act 1994, the work must be done to a 'satisfactory' standard and the garage would be liable if you had an accident as a direct result of a fault with the conversion. Please inform your insurer of this addition.

Power to your elbow

" My two-year-old Fiat Punto Cabriolet has developed a loud whine and rumble from the steering rack – but only when going slowly and on full lock. The local Fiat dealer tells me the rack is leaking fluid and advises a new one at £500, but a local independent garage suggests a power steering fluid additive which will expand and seal the leak. Do you think this will work? If not, do you think that Fiat will contribute to the cost of a new rack? "

Fiat might contribute, so get a decision from Fiat Customer Services one way or the other before doing anything else. The problem with power steering is it can make the driver 'too strong' and more likely to damage the rack by straining it against the lock stops or when a wheel is tight against a kerb. If Fiat decides that you damaged the steering in this way, then you can't expect any compensation. That leaves the additive, which is worth trying rather then spending £500, but you will have to monitor the power steering fluid level regularly or you could suddenly find yourself with unassisted steering.

RECALLS
1994–1998[*]

1994 Recalls

- *Citroen Xantia (May 1993–Oct 1994):* Parking brake modification.

- *Citroen ZX range (Mostly Volcane May 1992–Oct 1992 and 16v 1992–1994):* Brake pipe chafing.

- *Ford Escort/Orion 1.3 and 1.4CFi (92 VIN NE, NL, NY, NS, NT; 93 VIN PJ, PU, PM, PP, PB, PR, PA, PG, PC, PK):* Electrical check.

- *Ford Mondeo (92 VIN NY, NS, NT; 93 VIN PJ, PU, PM, PP, PB, PR, PA, PG, PC, PK, PD, PE; 94 VIN RL, RY, RS, RT, RJ, RU, RM):* Headlamp failure.

- *Honda Civic 3-door, 4-door, CRX automatics:* auto gear indicator may show wrong transmission mode.

- *Mazda Xedos 6 (VIN JMZ CA1***01100001–01119137):* Engine may stop without warning.

- *Mazda MX3 1.6 & 1.8 (VIN JMZ EC13**00100001–00113020):* Front coil spring failure.

- *Nissan Micra (Sep 92–June 94 VIN 000001–237783):* Floor may crack next to handbrake.

---

* SMMT Recall Hotline: 0171 235 7000 – ask for Consumer Affairs Department. Department of Transport Vehicle Safety Branch: 0117 954 3300.

- *Renault 19 Phase II (Apr 92–Mar 94):* Faulty seat belt pretensioners and bonnet catch.

- *Renault Safrane (Dec 91–Mar 94):* Heat shield required to protect fuel tank from exhaust.

- *Rover 800 (VIN RS 100001–117697 and RS 150000–187439):* Front seat belt security.

- *Saab 9000 (VIN N1041085–N1049024 and P1000001–P1015289):* Fuel leak.

- *Saab 9000/Turbo (VIN N1000001–N1049024, P1000001–P1042386, R1000001–R1027659):* Oil leak and faulty brake light switch on some models.

- *Saab 900 (VIN R2000001–R2028886):* Delayed braking action.

- *Saab 900 5-door (VIN R2000001–R2022754):* Cracking of driver's seat rails.

- *Seat Ibiza (1985–1991 VIN 09045074–D119002):* Fuel leak.

- *Skoda Favorit (VIN P0670305–R0916381 and P5019665–R5043486):* Wheel bearing failure.

- *Suzuki Vitara (Sep 1993–Jul 1994):* Wheel bearing failure.

- *Vauxhall Cavalier TD (Mar 1992–Mar 1994 VIN NV201488–R7560941):* Loss of braking efficiency.

- *Volvo 440/460/480 2.0 litre (440 VIN 419000–602090; 460 VIN 419001–602089; 480 VIN 586300–590058):* Airbag may deploy accidentally.

1995 Recalls

- *Alfa 164 (to VIN 6272929):* Corrosion of front suspension spring support.

- *Ford Fiesta (VIN prefix SK, SD):* Tyres may be incorrectly fitted.

- *Ford Fiesta/Escort (VIN prefix SE):* Brake lights may not work.

- *Ford Fiesta/Escort/Mondeo diesels (VIN prefix SY,SS, ST)):* Brake vacuum pump may not create enough vacuum for servo.

- *Ford Escort (VIN prefix SE, SL):* Loose rear brake cylinders.

- *Ford Escort (VIN prefix SC, SK, SD):* Possible damage to seat belt webbing.

- *Ford Mondeo:* Fuel pipe.

- *Ford Mondeo (VIN prefix RP, RB, RR):* Static sparks may occur when refuelling.

- *Ford Fiesta, Escort and Mondeo diesel (from Jun 1995):* Check brake vacuum pump.

- *Ford Maverick with Michelin 215/80 R15 tyres (VIN prefix PM, PP, PB, PR, PA, PG, PK, PD, PE, RL, RY, RS, RT, RJ, RV, RM, RP, RB, RA):* Tyres may lose pressure.

- *Land Rover Discovery VIN LJ163104–LJ172980 and LJ501920–LJ504252):* Check seat belts.

- *Range Rover (new model) (VIN LP311035–LP312917):* ABS brake hose may fail.

- *Mercedes Benz E-Class:* Passenger footrest.

- *Nissan Primera (VIN 000001–472213):* Front brake hoses may chafe.

- *Nissan Terrano II with Michelin 215/80 R15 tyres (VIN 200000–242699):* Tyres may lose pressure.

- *Peugeot 306:* Check accelerator cable.

- *Peugeot 405: (1995 model year to VIN 71339513):* Airbag may fail to inflate in an accident.

- *Renault 5 Campus 1.4 (VIN C4070510214892–C4070511788781):* Car may pull to left when braking.

- *Renault Espace 2.1TD first reg Mar 1993–Jun 1994:* Install fuse in preheater wiring circuit, re-route wiring away from main loom and install clip to keep it away from loom to prevent risk of insulation damage.

- *Saab 900 (VIN R2027373–S2009903 and S7000001–S7013081):* Welds missing from seat frames.

- *Saab 9000 (*manual with TCS): VIN N1000001–N1049024, *P1000001–P1042386, *R1000001–R1026535):* Loss of brake pressure and/or ABS.

- *Vauxhall Astra:* Fuel pipe, airbag.

- *Vauxhall Astra TD (VIN S5000001–S5241939; S2500001–S2707652 and S8000001–S8216827):* Chafing of wiring harness and possible fire risk.

- *Vauxhall Combo van, Corsa, Astra, Cavalier and Omega:* Static sparking during refuelling.

- *Vauxhall Astra:* Airbag may fail to inflate in an accident.

- *Vauxhall Omega 16v (VIN R 1000001–S1155206):* Fuel feed pipe may chafe. Reposition and clamp into place.

- *Vauxhall Frontera (VIN NV500400–RV628644):* Faulty bonnet safety catch.

- *Volvo 760 (VIN 37400–39877 and 16300–38007):* Battery short circuit leading to possible fire risk.

- *Volvo 850 (VIN 078000–120420 and 175000–220678):* Fault with jack which could allow the car to fall.

- *VW Golf/Jetta 1.6 & 1.8 1983A–1989G:* Bypass valve to be inserted into heater pipe; heater matrix to be replaced if degraded.

- *VW Golf GTi, 16v, VR6, Convertible (VIN 1HPW 439315–1HSW 418237 and 1ERK 000001–1ESK 025159):* Headlamp failures. Headlight switch on RHD models can overheat, leading to headlight failure. 28,000 cars affected.

- *VW Passat (VIN 3ARE 0000001–3ASE 142536):* Headlamp failures.

1996 Recalls

- *Citroen ZX ('facelift' model from Jun 1994):* Faulty seat belt pretensioners and, on cars so fitted, faulty airbag sensors.

- *Daewoo Nexia (to May 1995):* Check engine bay wiring harness routing (helpline: 0800 060606).

- *Ford Fiesta (Mar 1989F–Sep 1990H):* Check for possibility of front seatbelt inertia reel locking mechanism failure.

- *Ford new Fiesta and Courier van (1996 model year – 47,500 cars):* Check for faulty piston seal in hydraulic clutch master cylinder. Check for contamination of brake fluid and incorrect front brake hose routing.

- *Ford Mondeo (all):* 'Free recall' (as per *What Car?* Sep 1996 p. 132) to replace sticking valve stem seals – work will usually be carried out when car is in for a routine service.

- *Ford Mondeo (1996 model year with hydraulic clutch – excluding V6):* Check, replace if necessary clutch master cylinder/slave cylinder. Check front brake callipers.

- *Ford Galaxy (Apr 1996–Jul 1996):* Check for overheating of brake system.

- *Ford Galaxy 2 litre with air conditioning (Jan 1995–Feb 1996):* Aircon compressor may seize up.

- *Ford Scorpio (Aug 1994–Jul 1996):* Check for sticking throttle due to corrosion by road salt.

- *Ford Scorpio (Feb 1996–Mar 1996):* Rear axle mounting may loosen.

- *Hyundai Lantra: (1991–1996):* Check for fracture of rear suspension bolt.

- *Mazda new 121 (Fiesta-based) (1996 model year):* Check for faulty piston seal in hydraulic clutch master cylinder. Check for contamination of brake fluid and incorrect front brake hose routing.

- *Mercedes Benz C-Class:* Check for sticking bonnet catch and safety catch which may lead bonnet to fly open.

- *Mercedes Benz E-Class:* Airbag may inflate on wrong side.

- *Mitsubishi Colt, Shogun and Sigma (1991–1994):* Check for loss of brake fluid.

- *Peugeot 306 (Jul 1993–Feb 1996; 150,000 cars):* Underbonnet wiring may chafe leading to short circuit and fire.

- *Peugeot 405 (Sep 1993–May 1995):* Check for seepage of fuel from feed pipe.

- *Peugeot 406 1.8i and 2.0i petrol:* Free upgrade of engine management chip if owner complains of 'rough' running, flat spots and lack of power on hills.

- *Peugeot 806 (Sep 1995–Oct 1995):* Check airbag trigger.

- *Porsche 911 (1989 –1993):* 54,000 cars worldwide recalled (2,966 in UK) to check universal joint in steering column which may fail. Early signs are noises or free play in the system.

- *Proton Compact:* from October 1995: Fuel pump can allow fuel to leak when tank is brimmed.

- *Renault Espace – on original tyres (Mar 1991–Oct 1992):* Check for separation of tyre tread.

- *Renault Laguna and Safrane (May 1994–Aug 1994):* Automatic transmission may lock up.

- *Renault Laguna and Safrane (Jul 1994–Dec 1994):* Airbag warning light may be faulty.

- *Renault Laguna (Apr 1996–Aug 1996):* Fuel injection system computer may be faulty.

- *Rover 400 (new model):* Driver's seat lock does not always click into place properly. May mean seat slides when car is being driven. Most likely on cars with several drivers where seat is moved to and fro.

- *Rover 600 (Dec 1994 and Dec 1995):* Check to ensure steering rack mounting bolts are secure – sympton of problem: stiff steering.

- *Saab 900 convertible (1993–1995, old model):* Check for loss of steering control.

- *Seat Toledo (1993–1995):* Cooling fan motor may seize.

- *Toyota Carina E:* Anti-roll bar linkages may fail (first sign is a rattling noise). Covered under 3-year warranty. Only affects 2% of cars.

- *Vauxhall Vectra (Aug 1995 –Feb 1996; 40,000 cars):* Check front seatbelt mounting bolts and tighten if necessary.

- *Vauxhall Frontera Sport:* Fit heat shield between exhaust system and petrol tank (fire risk). Replace catches for removable roof section.

- *VW new Polo (to June 1996):* Steel wheels may lead to loss of tyre pressure.

- *VW Golf/Jetta 1.3 (1983A–1989G), 4-cylinder VW Passats and Corrados (1988F–1989G):* bypass valve to be inserted into heater pipe; heater matrix to be replaced if degraded.

- *VW Golf, Passat and Corrado VR6 (1993–1995):* Cooling fan motor may seize.

- *Volvo 440, 460, 480 (1991–1995):* Fire risk from faulty electrical connections.

1997 Recalls

- *Audi A3, A4, (1997; 1996 model year), A6 (Feb–Mar 1997):* Check front seat belt top mounting height adjusters.

- *Audi A6 2.8 V6:* rumoured recall issued in April concerning driveline.

- *Audi 80, A4, A6:* 50,523 cars recalled due to possibility of inadvertant deployment of airbags.

- *Bentley Azure:* 101 cars recalled due to danger of fire from a short circuit.

- *BMW E36 3-Series (from Jan 1996):* Tighten stub axle bolts.

- *BMW E36 3-Series (77,000 cars):* Possibility of corroded steering shafts.

- *BMW 2.8 litre 6-cylinder engines:* Possibility of premature bore wear, not mileage or age related, repaired under warranty. (Not an official recall.)

- *BMW M3:* Faulty bearings in Variable Valve Timing mechanism can deposit shards of metal in engine. Official recall. 400 cars affected.

- *Citroen Saxo:* Driver's seat.

- *Ferrari F355:* 120 cars recalled due to fire risk caused by possible fuel leak.

- *Fiat Bravo/Brava – 17,000 cars:* Petrol may contaminate brake vacuum diaphragm leading to loss of power assistance.

- *Ford Mondeo 24v (1 Aug 1994–14 Jun 1996; 9,000 cars):* Free official recall to replace catalytic converter closest to exhaust manifold.

- *Jaguar XK8:* Rear suspension.

- *Jeep Cherokee (Jan 1993–1997 model year RHD; 19,200 cars):* Check for stress fractures around steering box mounting.

- *Jeep Grand Cherokee:* 2,536 cars recalled due to danger of fire from a short circuit.

- *Chrysler Jeep:* 567 cars recalled due to possibility of inadvertant deployment of airbags.

- *Land Rover Discovery – 22,723 vehicles:* Possibility of failure of RHS door latches.

- *Mercedes Benz, all cars with 'Brake Assist' – 170,000 cars worldwide:* The 'Brake Assist' system, which is designed to apply the brakes fully in an emergency, may give too much 'assistance' during light braking. 1997 recall to disconnect the system. Supplies of modified component available from early 1998.

- *Mitsubishi Colt:* 213 cars found to have potentially defective braking system.

- *Peugeot 106 – 15,821 cars:* Ignition switch harness may foul on steering column.

- *Peugeot 306:* possible starter motor fault on 1996 model cars. Free replacement.

- *Peugeot 306:* 2,060 cars found to have potentially defective braking system.

- *Peugeot 406 – 13,412 cars:* Ignition switch harness may foul on steering column.

- *Peugeot 406:* 333 cars found to have potentially defective braking system.

- *Proton Persona:* 1,797 cars found to have potentially defective braking system.

- *Renault Megane and Scenic:* 7,434 cars found to have potentially defective braking system.

- *Renault Laguna – 12,494 cars:* Engine ECU may malfunction causing exhaust manifold to overheat and set fire to bulkhead insulation.

- *Rolls Royce and Bentley:* 29 left-hand-drive cars found to have potentially defective braking system.

- *Saab 900 (all current shape models – 21,661 cars):* Corrosion on the throttle housing can cause a sticking throttle. Relevant parts to be replaced with brass items which cannot corrode.

- *Seat Alhambra:* Brake problem.

- *Suzuki Vitara:* Steering fault.

- *Vauxhall Corsa/Astra/Vectra (1993–1996, 1.4 and 1.6 16v only; 27,000 cars):* Possibility of faulty cambelt idler pulley which can snap cambelt.

- *Vauxhall Astra 1.4 litre models:* Oil pump may fail. Vauxhall will replace faulty component free of charge on cars less then three years old. Will consider part-payment for older cars, but not for engine damage as a result of continuing to drive with the oil light on indicating no oil pressure.

- *VW Golf Mk III (single headlight models – 9,700 cars):* Jan 1997 recall – headlight switch on RHD models can overheat, leading to headlight failure.

- *VW Golf Mk III and Vento (1994–1997; 150,000 cars):* September 1997 recall for headlamp modification for all cars.

- *VW Golf Mk III and Vento with electric front windows – 16,000 cars:* Insulation on power cable may chafe and short-circuit. Needs protective shield in cable opening of door.

- *VW Sharan:* brake problem.

- *Volvo 850 (1996 and 1997 model years):* Check for sticking throttle.

1998 Recalls

- *Audi A3:* 2,822 cars recalled due to possiblity of rear seat belt fixing brackets cracking.

- *Audi A4, A6, A8:* 4,574 cars built between August 1997 and February 1998 recalled due to possibility of jammed throttle.

- *BMW E30 3-Series (1983-90):* 170,000 UK market cars recalled because valve in radiator cap may seize up and over-pressurise cooling system.

- *Chrysler Voyager and Grand Voyager (old model not marketed in UK except by mobility specialists):* Recall in USA after fatalities due to faulty rear door latches. Voluntary recall in Europe.

- *Citroen Xsara:* 14,000 owners of cars built September 1997 - February 1998 notified that may be a delay in airbag inflating in the event of an accident.

- *Ferrari F355:* Possible fault with steering column bolt.

- *Ford Fiesta (Jul 1995–Jun 1996; 67,000 cars):* Possibility of brake failure due to front brake pipe chafing on bracket. Modified pipe and bracket to be fitted to both front brakes. (Announced radio 12/2/98.)

- *Ford Fiesta, Escort. Mondeo, Scorpio (with passenger airbag, Aug*

1996–Feb 1998): Passenger airbag may go off while car is stationary.

- *Ford Explorer:* Oil pump recall notice issued January 1998. Explorer TSB's (Technical Service Bulletins) include curing transmission shudder. Accelerator may be jammed open by the driver's floormat.

- *Jaguar XK8 and XJ8 (Jul–Oct 1997;11,221 cars):* May suffer sudden deceleration due to weak retention bracket on accelerator cable. Extra clip 'costing pennies' solves the problem. (Announced on radio 7/2/98.)

- *Lotus Esprit:* 200 V8 models recalled for new timing belt, idler pulley bearings, new clutch and 5th gear locknut, cost to Lotus at least £1,500 per car. Also check rear alloy wheels for hairline cracks.

- *Porsche 911 Carrera (1998 '996' model: 540 UK cars):* Wrong size pulley fitted driving ancilliaries drive belt which may slip affecting PAS, brakes, water pump and alternator.

- *Renault Laguna:* 'Plip' key transmitters can go out of sequence due to static or fiddling with them in the pocket. Improved 'plip' key transmitters now available free of charge to Laguna owners. (Per BBC 'Watchdog' 12/2/98.)

- *Renault Laguna diesel:* Cambelt tensioner may lead to premature failure of cambelt - to be checked as a TSB item at services.

- *Renault Laguna:* 17,000 cars recalled due to possibility of 'inadvertant deployment of airbags'.

- *Vauxhall Corsa diesel (K to N reg.; 26,000 cars):* Live cable may rub against bonnet hinge, lose insulation and cause a fire. (Helpline 01189 458500.)

- *Vauxhall Corsa 1.0 12v (P to R reg.; 8,000 cars):* Cable may touch engine inlet manifold. (Helpline 01189 458500.)

- *Vauxhall Vectra (all 200,000 built before July 1997):* Handbrake cable subject to premature wear. Modified cable free replacement service.

- *Vauxhall Vectra automatics:* In-service modification to autobox ECU mapping.

- *Vauxhall Sintra:* Catches for removing the seats may sever fingers. Covers to be fitted to seat release lever mechanism.

- *VW Passat: (May–Nov 1997; 11,450 cars):* Recall due to potential fault affecting front seat belts. Involves replacing complete belt units.

RESTORATION AND SPECIALISTS

Registering a rebuild

" *I wonder if you would have the time to run through the attached file of correspondence on my Saab 96 V4 GLS. The car was built in 1979 and I have owned it for fourteen years, since it was originally imported in 1982. Before I rebuilt the car it bore the registration mark LGK 916Y, from the original date of importation (rather than the build date, as is the current system). The rebuilt car retains its original body/chassis, apart from bolt-on replacement wings, etc. It has its original engine, gearbox and springs. But the rear axle was replaced in 1986 and I have converted it from LHD to RHD so it has a replacement steering assembly. The Local DVLA VRO has inspected the car twice, but insists on re-registering it with a new chassis number and a 'Q' plate. How can I get a clear statement of their basis for doing this and challenge it?* "

On the basis of its inspections, the DVLA has now allocated the car a new chassis number (contradicting the number stamped on the actual 'chassis') and a 'Q' plate, and has voided both the original registration LGK 916Y and the registration MOO 778J from which some 'donor' parts such as the steering rack and column came. But on the basis of the DVLA's leaflet INF26 'The Registration of Rebuilt or Radically Altered Vehicles and Kit Cars', I agree with you – the car appears to qualify to keep its originally allocated number-plate. To qualify to keep an original registration the car must notch up 8 or more points from the following list:

- Original chassis or both sub-frames and bodyshell, or a replacement bodyshell supplied new by the manufacturer: 5 points

- Original suspension   2 points

- Original axles   2 points

- Original transmission   2 points

- Original steering assembly   2 points

- Original engine   1 point

So, even if replacement shock absorbers disqualify the suspension, and despite the change of bulkhead (as long as the bulkhead bears the chassis number of the rest of the chassis), your car should still score 8 points. Demanding that you change the chassis number makes no sense to me and forces you to 'ring' the vehicle.

Corvette re-cons

" *In Bob Murray's article about Corvettes, he quoted Tom Falconer as stating that 'a complete engine re-build would cost well under £1,000.' I have been quoted £3,500 locally. So who is Tom Falconer, and how does one get in touch with him?* "

Tom Falconer runs Claremont Corvette, and, with six books to his credit, is the UK's top Corvette expert. He confirms that a 'tired engine', already out of the car, could be rebuilt with new rings, mains, ends, camshaft, lifters and timing gear for a total of around £1,000. More work, such as a rebore, balancing, chemical cleaning and painting or plating would naturally cost more. Claremont Corvette is based at Malling Road, Snodland, Kent ME6 5NA, tel: 01634 244444.

Camper restoration

" *I have a 1971 'bay window' VW camper which I have been slowly renovating over a period of years. Unfortunately it is exposed to the elements all year round which undoes my efforts to remove the rot and causes more serious corrosion. I have a 'Waxoyl' injector, but, being a pensioner, can no longer afford 'Waxoyl' itself. Is there a cheaper alternative? Should I fill the cavities with old engine oil? The vehicle is used for short-break touring holidays and is in no better than average condition. Is anything likely to hasten the day when it becomes uneconomical to use? Finally, you recommended a make of remould tyres some time ago. What was the make?* "

A big problem with VW Types 1 and 2 left standing for long periods outside is corrosion above the oil level in the gearbox caused by condensation, so it's a good idea to use the vehicle as much as possible.

Try Dinitrol. Bob at Morriespares in Epping is an agent (01992 524249). A big problem with VW Types 1 and 2 left standing for long periods outside is corrosion above the oil level in the gearbox, caused by condensation. So it's a good idea to use the vehicle as much as possible. It would be a good idea to join The VW Type 2 Owners' Club for the help, advice and general support membership can give you. (C/o P. Shaw, 57 Humphrey Drive, Charford, Bromsgrove, Worcs B60 3JD, tel: 01527 872194.) The remoulds I mentioned are Technic.

Golf and Scirocco rebuilds

" *Some time ago you wrote about a company which could supply parts for VW cars, in particular the Scirocco range. I believe you wrote it was*

*possible to rebuild or to have rebuilt a complete car. Could you send me
the address and details of the services they offer?* **"**

The company is TSR Performance of Bridgwater,
Somerset (tel: 01278 453036) which has issued a
catalogue detailing its services. The company's
main business is performance modifications, but
it also offers a restoration service for Mk I VW
Golfs and Sciroccos. Not cheap, of course, but a
good restoration never is. But other VW specialists such as Wheelbase of Hersham (01932
252515) will undertake a full restoration of cars
like the Mk I Golf GTi.

Radio days

" *Some time ago 'Telegraph Motoring' published an article about a firm
in the Bristol area that restores old car radios. Sadly I did not keep a note*

of their name and address, but now have need of their services. Thanks for a great motoring section. It's the best part of the Saturday Telegraph. **"**

The firm you refer to is either Car Radio Repair and Restoration Service, 10 Westview, Paulton, Bristol BS18 5XJ, tel: 01761 413933, or Vintage Radio Services, 37 Court Road, Frampton Cotterell, Bristol BS17 2DE, tel: 01454 772814. Another, nearer to you, which specialises in Radiomobiles from 1930–1975, FM conversions, period aerials, eight-tracks and car record players, is The Vintage Wireless Company, 15–17 Britannia Road, Sale, Cheshire M33 2AA, tel: 0161 973 0438. Yet more specialists include Evets Classic Cars of Derby on 01332 363981, the Midland Magneto and Electrical Co. of Nottingham on 0115 955 2233, and Sandy Lane Garage of Fleet on 01252 615244.

Boring question

" *I have a 1984 Opel Manta 1.8S hatchback. The ATE master cylinder is leaking and new cylinders are not now available. I have managed to obtain a secondhand temporary replacement, but would also like to have the original refurbished so it can be refitted. Do you know of a specialist firm which carries out such work, including reaming of the cylinder bore if necessary and the fitting of oversize seals?* **"**

Try Classicar Automotive, Unit A, Alderley Road, Chelfont, Cheshire SK11 9AP, tel: 01625 860910.

SAFETY

Kids in cars

" *Time and again we see sickening pictures of small cars in which groups of teenage friends have been killed. Could you start a campaign to make young novice drivers aware of the effect of heavily loading a small car? Cars in the Mini or Fiesta categories, particularly those a few years old, are often affordable runabouts appealing to newly-qualified youngsters aspiring to their first set of wheels. Unfortunately, while these are nippy and controllable cars with only one or two people in them, with two or three passengers in the back the picture changes. The centre of gravity is moved back and up so that the car starts to roll on bends and the steering becomes heavy and unresponsive. Braking distances are also much longer. These effects can be compounded by elderly suspensions, tyres near their legal limit or economies on maintenance. If a young driver finds this out the hard way on a dark damp night when concentration and reactions are adversely affected by a long evening at a disco and a group of pals in the car, then the consequence is only too likely to be yet another distressing set of photos in the local rag.* "

One problem is that kids are far less afraid of stealing cars or driving under-age than they were when I was their age. But the reason why law-abiding kids drive ancient Metros, Unos and Fiestas is the enormous cost of insuring anything else. Insurance companies could take an initiative here by offering lower rates to new drivers who take the post-test 'Pass Plus' course and insure a car with a high *Which?* magazine safety rating. They should also offer new drivers who pass additional safe driving tests, such as Advanced Driving (0181 994 4403), the chance of being a named driver of their father's or mother's bigger, safer car at an acceptable premium.

Tough luck

" On 13 June 1997, The Daily Telegraph *carried pictures of Miss Melville Smith's Volvo 940 estate car after its collision with Camilla Parker Bowles's Ford Mondeo. Why is the Volvo a 'write-off'? Is it because insurance companies find it cheaper to write cars off and pay low amounts in compensation to their clients? Last year, my six-month-old Toyota, which had cost me £11,500 new, was said to be a write-off and I was offered just £8,500. Fortunately there was a clause allowing me a new replacement if my car was severely damaged in its first 12 months. However, I later discovered that my Toyota had been repaired and exported. I think that new cars are very poor in accidents despite all their so-called safety factors. There's too little metal in modern cars. Oh for my old 1947 Rover 75 which, in an accident 45 years ago, suffered no more than a bent mudguard.* "

I, too, ran a P3 Rover in the 1960s and, having jacked it up on numerous occasions via the internal jacking points, can testify to the sheer weight of the thing. The point is, modern cars are designed to crumple progressively – sacrificing themselves to protect the occupants. Roads are better, cars are better and the standard of driving is now far better than it was in the 1930s, 1940s and 50s – and testament to this is the fact that, despite the number of licensed vehicles on UK roads having risen from 2,000,000 in 1931 to 26,200,000 last year, the number killed on our roads last year was half the 1931 figure. If we all read Paul Ripley every week, thought a bit more about our driving, and drove with more consideration for other motorists whatever we think of their standard of driving, we could halve this figure yet again.

Airbags

A number of readers watched a 'World in Action' TV programme about the dangers of airbags to shorter drivers who are forced to drive close to the steering wheel. I did not see the programme but, as far as I can gather, some of the content must have come from the USA. There, larger-than-European-size airbags are fitted to many cars as a substitute for seatbelts rather than a complement to seatbelts. US airbags also fire off at impacts of 5 mph rather than the 15 mph impact speed in Europe. US manufacturers are reported to be offering the option of a switch to switch off airbag activation, but the worry about this must be liability. It could be argued in a court that someone who was killed in a car could have been saved if they had not been able to de-activate the airbag. My advice would be for shorter drivers who need the seat to be close to the pedals in order to drive to recline their seats slightly so as not to sit too close to the steering wheel (this is also good ergonomic advice) and not to worry themselves unduly. An airbag is far more likely to save their lives than to kill them – particularly in Europe where a much heavier impact is required to set them off than in the USA. Pipe smokers, however, should not smoke their pipes while driving an airbag-equipped car.

Crash test results

" My husband was recently in an accident and his car was a write-off. Having seen the extent of the damage, I now want to replace my Citroen ZX with a different five-door hatchback. Can you please tell me what is available and in particular their relative safety in the event of an accident? My budget is not unlimited and I had been thinking of a Clio, but I read somewhere that it did not perform particularly well in a crash test. "

The RAC, AA, DETR and three other national and independent testing organisations have joined forces to test cars for occupant safety in the event of a crash, under the title 'Euro NCAP'. At the time of writing, seven 'superminis' and thirteen 'upper medium' cars have been tested in a 40 mph offset front impact and a 30 mph side impact. Of the superminis, the Ford Fiesta and VW Polo were awarded three stars; of the 'upper medium' cars, the Volvo S40 was awarded four stars and the Ford Mondeo, Nissan Primera, Renault Laguna, Vauxhall Vectra and VW Passat were each awarded three stars. The full report is in the '*What Car?* Buyers Report 1998', which costs £4.95 from newsagents. 'Lower medium size' cars, such as the VW Golf, were tested by NCAP in May 1968. Top performers were the new VW Golf Mk IV (fitted with standard side airbags), the Renault Megane and the Audi A3. Those that earned three stars were the Citroen Xsara, Peugeot 306 and Toyota Corolla. The Daewoo Lanos, Fiat Brava, Honda Civic five-door and Hyundai Accent all earned two full stars or less. Meanwhile, Mercedes has overcome the A Class 'elk test' problem and has made it a much better car in the process. It is anticipated that, due to its double floor, the A Class will fare particularly well in the NCAP side impact test. Remember, NCAP tests do not measure the relative likelihood of the cars being involved in an accident due to handling, roadholding or braking deficiencies.

Proper seat belts

" *My daughter has a boy of eleven and twin boys of seven. She and her husband can only afford a Skoda Felicia Estate, which means one boy will have to used the centre lap belt. On TV it has been shown how lethal these can be, so she has bought a bar to be fitted behind the back seats onto which a shoulder harness can be anchored. Is there no way of safely sitting a child in the middle of a back seat?* "

Yes. All the cars I am about to list come with three proper lap and diagonal rear seat belts as standard equipment. They are: Alfa 156 (£97.53 option), new BMW 5-Series, Citroen Xantia Estate, Ford Mondeo from 1997 Model Year, Land Rover Freelander 5-door; new Mazda 626 from July 1997, Mitsubishi Galant from 1998 model year, New Nissan Primera SLX, Peugeot 306 Sedan, Peugeot 406, Renault Laguna from 95M, Renault Megane and Scenic, Renault

Espace from 1997 model year, 'new' Rover 200, Rover 600 from 1997 model year, Rover 800 4-door from 94M, Saab 900 from 94L, Saab 9-3, Saab 9-5, Toyota Camry from 1997 model year, Toyota Corolla from July 1997, Toyota Avensis, New Vauxhall Astra from April 1998, Vauxhall Vectra from 1997 model year, Vauxhall Omega, 1998 VW Golf IV (£100 optional extra), new VW Passat (£100 optional extra), Volvo S40, Volvo V40, Volvo S70, Volvo V70, Volvo 850, Volvo 940, Volvo 960, Volvo S90, Volvo V90.

SECURITY

Alarming

" *My new Ford Fiesta 1.25LX is fitted with the optional extra of central locking which also incorporates the Ford perimeter alarm. I understood this set industry standards for security, so approached my insurer with a view to obtaining a discount on the basis of the security package. I was then told that the system I had purchased was only classified as a theft deterrent, and if I wanted to obtain an insurance discount on the basis of the car's security system it would need to conform to a level known as 'Thatcham 1'. What is the specification for 'Thatcham 1'? And can the Ford system be modified to meet it?* "

The Fiesta 1.25LX is in The Association of British Insurers (ABI) Group 5, which is already a low group and is assessed partly on the basis of the 'Thatcham 2' security system provided as standard. Thatcham is the ABI's laboratory which tests the effectiveness of security systems. Thatcham 2 systems are immobilisers. Thatcham 1 systems are combined alarms and immobilisers which provide a high degree of security. The Fiesta's optional central locking and perimeter alarm can be upgraded with back-up battery power, etc., to Thatcham 1 standards. Your nearest Thatcham-accredited installer is Mike Stokes Tyre and Battery Supplies in Bournemouth, tel: 01202 294230. The system is the Laserline 993, price £279.95 including fitting and VAT. It operates remotely, is guaranteed as long as you own the car, and Mike Stokes can offer you a free demonstration.

Enterprising immobiliser

" *The police are buying 'Interceptor' immobilisers from us. Your readers will be astounded to find they can buy the most effective, advanced immobiliser for only £38. Let them know.* "

This came with a mass of testimonial support. The 'Interceptor' consists of a small box which can be hidden virtually anywhere in the engine compartment or behind the dashboard of the car. It intercepts the cable from the ignition switch to the coil (or any other vital electrical cable). A third cable is connected to an earthing point and a fourth to a secret metal touch point insulated from the metal of the car body. Switching off the ignition arms the system. To disarm it, you touch the secret touch point with one hand and the metal of the car body with the other. More information from Enterprise (Europe), PO Box 427, London SE25 6RT, tel: 0181 771 2935. At the time of writing, it is not Thatcham-approved, so is unlikely to result in an insurance premium reduction. But if it stops your car being stolen it has done its job. Fitting is extra (instructions provided) and involves about an hour's labour by an experienced fitter.

Immobiliser rip-off

" *In December 1997 you mentioned the excellent Enterprise 'Interceptor' immobiliser – which very effectively immobilises a car at a cost of a mere £38. I wrote for particulars, but found that the space for 'local installer' had been left blank, so I phoned the company to ask why. The reason, I was told, was that some unscrupulous outfits had been charging up to £180 to fit it, so the company now gives full fitting instructions and leaves it up to the buyer either to choose an installer or fit it himself.* "

Thank you for this tip. Another reader, from Portsmouth, whose garage charged £41 to fit the immobiliser, found it would not work because his skin was too dry. Wetting his fingers before touching the secret contact points solved the problem. For more information, or to order one, see 'Enterprising immobiliser' above.

Look, no steering wheel

" Could you let me know the name and address of the manufacturer of the removable steering wheel featured in your Motor Show issue? Unfortunately I wasn't able to get to the show. "

This is the 'Snap Off', as fitted to Ford rally cars, by Raid Steering Wheels of 8 Morris Road, Daventry, Northants NN11 5PD, tel: 01327 706881.

Not remotely

Following a letter about battery life in keyfob radio remote immobiliser activators, the makers of 'Foxguard' immobilisers have kindly offered the following advice:

- Do not buy the cheapest and expect the best results.
- Have the system installed by a reputable dealer.
- Read the handbook.
- Do not let your children play with the radio transmitters as a way of keeping them quiet.
- Do not expect the keys to work on-board ferries, next to radio stations or after they have been dropped in puddles or pints of beer or put through a washing machine.

Another reader added that he tests for a weak battery by checking the range at which his remote fob will disarm the immobiliser. This will work with some systems, particularly older 'infra-red' types, but not with many of the new 'ungrabbable' radio systems which are designed only to work close to the car. Readers should be aware of The National Vehicle Security Helpline, run by The Association of British Insurers, on 0990 502006.

Surveillance aids

" *While a car is parked in a driveway or garage out of view, it provides a far greater level of security if the car can be seen from inside the house. Kits connecting a single closed-circuit camera to a domestic television are now available for as little as £149.95, including post, packing and full instructions. A quick flick on the remote to the TV channel dedicated to the camera will instantly reveal any intrusion, and, if connected via a video recorder, the trespass can be recorded for evidence.* "

This makes sense. Readers interested in the system should contact D. Prescott, ID Business Ltd, 8 Mill Street, Ormskirk, Lancs L39 4QD, tel: 01695 580343.

Stolen radios

" *In the past five years I have had four car radios stolen. The most recent was a removable-front model, so only half of the radio was stolen. Almost all new cars have radios fitted as standard, so where is the demand coming from for all the stolen radios? A cynic might think that the replacement car glass companies buy them up, but I'm sure this cannot be the answer. Where do they all go?* "

Older radios can be protected from theft by a cable lock which loops through the steering wheel and locks in the cassette socket.

Into 'bangers' fitted with DIN sockets via 'car booty' sales. And for export. For example, the police in Amsterdam told me that the sacks of radios stolen in Holland go to Turkey and Pakistan in exchange for drugs. Happily, most new radios are now made in odd shapes, designed to fit only one make and model of car. But older radios can be protected by a cable lock which loops through the steering wheel and locks in the cassette socket.

'Red Key' problems

" *In January my wife purchased a 'P' reg. Fiat Cinquecento with 3,211 miles on the clock from a Newcastle dealer. The salesman told us the car was bought in from a rental or finance firm and pointed out that the 'Red Key' was missing, but that it might be sent on by the previous owner later. He also told us that if we lost the only black key we were given it could cost £500 for a new ECU/immobiliser unit and a complete change of locks. I subsequently read an article which said that without the 'Red Key' a Fiat agent could not gain access to the engine management system to carry out a service. Is this correct? Would it be worth contacting the previous owner shown on the V-5 in order to try and obtain the 'Red Key' from them? Is this a common occurrence?* "

When Fiats which should have 'Red Keys' turn up without them at auction they bid to between £500 and £750 less than similar Fiats with a Red Key. Some outfits claim to be able to programme new keys for the cars, but, because of the rolling code system, I have yet to see any evidence that they really can do this. So it's worth hunting high and low for your Red Key and even offering employees at the company which owned the car previously a £50 reward for finding the right key. You have no redress against the dealer, because he was entirely straight with you and the price you paid probably accounted for the lack of Red Key anyway. In fairness, both I and BBC TV's 'Watchdog' have issued warnings about Fiat Red Keys before. Fiat has certainly come up with a very effective security system. (Ford Red Keys are a different matter, and replacements can usually be obtained for around £40.)

Car security shock

" *Recently I saw a snippet in a magazine about a steering wheel security bar that emits a 120-decibel alarm when tampered with and which also pumps 50,000 volts through the hands of anyone unwise enough to touch it. The article gave a price of £200, but no information as to the manufacturer or where it could be obtained. I want one. Do you have any information?* "

There's nothing more irritating than reading about something then finding no information about how to get it. Fortunately, when *Diesel Car & 4×4* magazine ran its item about the Auto Taser it included a phone number, 01254 55892, which I checked. After clamping to the steering wheel, the device is activated by remote control. *Diesel Car* reported getting a 'very nasty shock' from it, but also pointed out that a brave and skilled thief can pick the lock fairly easily. But it certainly has a deterrent function, and it is legal. Price: £169.95.

Alarm? So what!

" *My French friend's treasured five-year-old BMW was recently nicked from a car park outside a large French supermarket. It was alarmed and also had an autolock device. There was no trace of broken glass. I have a Peugeot 406 which has a keypad immobiliser but, unlike the 306 I had before, does not have an alarm. I also use an autolock brake-to-gearlever 'visible deterrent'. As I spend a lot of time in France, I am quite worried – but, of course, should be equally worried about the car being stolen in the UK. How effective is the immobiliser? Is the autolock any good? Should I get an alarm and, if so, which one? Have you any advice for your readers as to how best to reduce or, better still, prevent car theft?* "

In my view, though it is a stipulation to qualify for Thatcham Category 1, a car alarm is a total waste of money, because all it does is annoy people and run down the car battery. In Amsterdam, a drug addict can walk down a street filling a sack with every nickable car radio and setting all the alarms off in the process, without anyone paying the slightest attention. Peugeot keypad immobilisers qualify as Thatcham Category 2 immobilisers. As far as I know, the Enterprise 'Interceptor' immobiliser is yet to be beaten and at £38 (DIY-fit or pay a garage) has to be the security bargain of the year.

Corrupting influence

" *The remote locking system of my 1996N Toyota Carina E started to go wrong two weeks ago. I replaced the battery of one of the keyfobs, but still found that the fob intermittently failed to unlock the car. Toyota has sent me instructions to cure this which involve partially dismantling the fob and pressing one of the buttons of the dissembled fob. I am very annoyed that I have to go through such a fussy business and think that, under the terms of the warranty, Toyota should come up with a better long-term solution.* "

The low-frequency radio signal from the fob to the receiver in the car is being corrupted by a higher-frequency signal occurring nearby. There is now an EU directive which seeks to eliminate electronic interference but, of course, this can't work retrospectively for every piece of equipment which emits radio signals or an electronic field. If the problem occurs in a place where it did not occur before, such as your driveway, then someone has probably moved a piece of equipment such as a computer into the area. You could try parking the car in a slightly different place or the opposite way round. If the fault occurs on the open road, the AA advises pushing the car 20 yards from where it failed to start and trying again. If this fails, then the method described by Toyota will discharge the extraneous charge and allow the system to reset away from the source of corruption. Toyota later found out precisely what form of external interference is upsetting its systems and altered its keyfob transmitters. One other tip: a sharp upwards movement while pressing the keyfob button and holding it close to the car door has often worked for me when simply pressing the button did nothing.

Fobbed off

I've been given a clearer explanation by members of the Radio Society of Great Britain of why so many drivers have trouble with keyfob-operated electronic immobilisers – one which leaves egg all over the faces of our lords and masters in Brussels.

Before their EMC Directive of two years ago, all very-short-wavelength transmitters used to arm and disarm immobilisers operated in the UHF waveband at 418 MHz. Because this is a protected waveband in which only very-low-power transmissions exist, there is only a minimal chance of mutual interference. But when the EU issued its Directive, it settled on an immobiliser frequency of 433.92 MHz, with a maximum permitted unlicensed power of 0.25 mW.

Unfortunately, in the UK, 433.92 MHz is in

the middle of a band used by the MOD for its MOULD national radio network, and the MOD is the primary user of this band. For Radio Amateurs there is an internationally allocated band of 430 MHz–440 MHz. In the UK, Radio Amateurs are classed as secondary users of the band, but powerful signals exist from UK and continental static and mobile radio stations. Trafficmaster also uses the 433 MHz band and it, too, is classified as a secondary user.

The Wireless Telegraphy Act of 1949 requires that secondary users of any waveband *must* accept interference. And since keyfob transmitters are required by the EU directive to operate at the extremely weak power of 0.25 mW, they will almost always be overridden by a stronger signal.

A reader from Marlborough tells us that the signal receivers in car systems are of very poor quality and are unable to filter out radio signals on frequencies which adjoin 433.92 MHz. These overload the front of the transmitter so it cannot 'hear' the signal from the keyfob. He compares it to two people trying to whisper to each other in the midst of a football crowd after a goal. His tips are, first, to hold the fob as close as possible to the receiver (something we've all done). Second, to wait in case the stronger signal decreases in strength or stops. Third, to get into the car with the key and move it to another location where the fob will disarm the immobiliser.

The other problem is synchronisation of the rolling codes of Thatcham approved immobilisers. The car's receiver knows that the next signal it should receive should be based on the previous signal received. But if one of more of these are blocked by a stronger signal, the code sequence goes out of step and the receiver ignores any further signals from the transmitter fob. There are various routines to re-synchronise the fob transmitter, which usually mean opening it and pressing two buttons at the same time, but may be more complicated.

My Marlborough correspondent suggests that car buyers should insist on a system that operates on 418 MHz rather than 433.92 MHz. He recommends that owners with problem systems operating on 433.92 MHz seek legal advice as to the 'satisfactory quality' of their systems under the 1994 Sale and Supply of Goods Act. (I would warn readers that getting redress under the Act is easier said than done, but there may be a basis for a Small Claims Court action.) Finally, he feels that the AA and RAC should press the DTI to persuade Brussels to remove the 433.92 MHz immobiliser allocation.

A reader from Newbury sent me an extract from *Radcom*, the magazine of the Radio Society of Great Britain. This tells us the RSGB has formed an EMC Committee which is campaigning for an improvement in the performance of 433.92 MHz vehicle radio-activated key entry systems. The 'RAKE' group has produced a document entitled 'Guidelines for Manufacturers of Vehicle Key Systems'. Contact the Radio Society of Great Britain, tel: 01707 659015, email: D.M.Lauder@herts.ac.uk.

STARTING AND RUNNING PROBLEMS

Hesitant GTi

"I own a 1983 VW Golf GTi Mk I, which is in excellent condition apart from three rust spots, and which has done 115,000 miles. My problem is one of hesitation and reduced acceleration. The original reason for this was moisture in the petrol from a rusted fuel filler pipe. But despite flushing the tank many times and fitting a new fuel pump, the problem persists. Who can I turn to? Unfortunately, as we are expecting a new baby, I may have to sell the car anyway, but if I can't get more than £2,000 I will keep it. What do you think it is worth?"

Good Mk I Golf GTi 1800s are already appreciating, but the rust spots bother me. They need urgent attention. As for the hesitation, have you changed the fuel filter? Have you checked for air leaks into the injection system? Have you checked the diaphragm pressure switch (at the front LHS next to the fuel meter on top of the air filter)? Have you checked the second fuel pump (one is under the floor; the other is in the boot)? Have you checked the spark plug leads and distributor? Have you tried a good injector cleaner (VAG's own 'G001 700 03' is one of the best there is)? Have you tried switching to a petrol with good detergent content, such as

Texaco CleanSystem 3 4-star? (Never use premium unleaded in this engine.) If all this fails, try Andy Jackson in Leek (01538 398227) or Derek Boardman in Manchester (0161 681 0456), and join Club GTi anyway by sending a SAE to Sean Grenyer, Club GTi Membership, PO Box 2747, Brighton BN1 2NP.

The Home Service

" Suggestions in your column as to why a 'Hesitant GTi' was hesitant were correct, but I'd have got there before you. The car was displaying the classic symptoms of a ruptured vacuum advance unit diaphragm. The test is to remove the pipe from the unit to the inlet manifold, fix another short piece of pipe to the unit, and suck. If you can suck through it, the diaphragm is perforated and needs to be replaced. I am a mobile engine tuner operating a 'Computer Tune' franchise. You have never recommended people like me. Now I know some mobile tuners are cowboys, but

there are also some good, dedicated people out there – like me. How about giving us a mention? **"**

> Readers in the Gravesend area who want to give him a try should call B.A. on 01474 535201 (mobile 0802 201593). He offers full engine tune-ups from £31.50, and 5,000-mile services with tune-up from £54.50.

Sick VR6

" *Seven months ago my son bought a secondhand VW Golf VR6 with 40,000 miles on the clock for £13,250. Though he is otherwise delighted with the car, it has let him down on no less than five occasions. It simply stops without warning, but can be re-started again after a short rest. I consider the car dangerous and unroadworthy and, without being dramatic, feel that the lives of my son, daughter-in-law and two grandchildren are at risk. The garage he bought it from has offered £11,000 in part-exchange for something else but, on my advice, my son is not prepared to take the car back unless the fault is corrected. Please can you offer any advice which will lead to a safe and amicable outcome.* **"**

> Rather than 'lose' at least £2,250 for seven months motoring, your son would be better advised to have the car looked at by the country's top experts at diagnosing peripheral faults on VR6s (BBR, tel: 01280 702389). One known trouble spot is the fuel pump on early cars. But the problem could be caused by high resistance in any of a number of electrical components, causing the connection to get hot and eventually separate. VR6 engines are among the toughest and most reliable in current production. The Hampshire constabulary did 170,000 trouble-free miles filming dodgy drivers in its dark blue Vento VR6, and racing VR6s usually last a whole season without needing a strip-down.

Intermittent faults

A number or readers came up with alternative reasons why the VW Golf VR6 discussed in the previous letter had suffered an intermittent fault which caused the engine to stop but then be capable of a re-start after a few minutes. My reply gave the most likely reasons for this problem with a VR6, but some other reasons for intermittent faults on other cars are as follows:

- **Carburettor icing** The air entering a carburettor needs to be heated because, at speed, condensation in the air can freeze in the air intake, restricting the orifice and cutting off the air. Once the car has stopped for a short time, the residual heat of the engine melts the ice and the car can be re-started. If water-heated, check water pipes; if electrically heated, check electrics. If the air filter trunk has a 'summer' and 'winter' setting, switch it to the winter setting so it picks up hot air from the exhaust manifold.

- **Faulty carburettor** The Pierburg carburettors of older VWs can suffer loosening of the brass needle valve seat when the engine is hot. This leads to flooding of the carburettor, leading in turn to an over-rich mixture which makes the engine difficult to start. Stripping the carb, pushing the needle valve seat firmly home, and peining the surrounding aluminium to keep it in place, will solve the problem for a while.

- **Faulty fuel pump or relay** An electrical contact in the relay to the fuel pump or in the fuel pump itself could break or 'dry out', causing intermittent misfires in a fuel-injected car. After correction, the condition of the catalytic converter (if fitted) should also be checked.

- **Air leaks in the injection system or the diaphragm pressure switch**

- **Blocked exhaust system** In pre-cat days, rust caused by condensation inside one of the silencer boxes could eventually block passages inside the exhaust, preventing the car from 'exhaling' and thus stopping the engine. The same can happen if the ceramic core of a catalytic converter breaks up and blocks the rest of the exhaust system.

- **Badly-routed cable** An electrical engine management cable routed over a part of the engine subject to movement could rub the insulation from the cable, leading to a short.

- **Faulty contact or internally broken cable** Any engine management system cable suffering such a fault can lead to intermittent breakdowns; for example: 'the earth contacts at the plenum chamber to rocker cover were producing a short circuit cause by two unsecured bolts on the rear rocker which had become stripped' (Alfa 164 Cloverleaf).

- **Dried-out coil or ignition system contacts** The remedy for this is to check all contacts and clean where necessary.

- **Coil failure**

- **Spark plug or spark plug cable failure** The insulation of the cables from the distributor to the spark plugs can eventually break down, but first try cleaning any accumulated dirt from the outside of the cables as this can harbour moisture which diverts the high tension current.

- **Dirt in fuel** Swarf or rust in a steel fuel tank can block the fuel pipe or fuel filter, causing an excess of back pressure.

- **Fuel line air lock** Often due to a sticking gravity valve, this can stop a carburetted car where the fuel is sucked by an engine-driven pump rather then pumped from the tank by an electric pump.

- **Blocked fuel tank breather (pipe or filler cap)** By preventing air being drawn into the fuel tank to replace the fuel sucked out, this can stop a car.

- **Faulty inlet air temperature sensor** Part of the 'choke mechanism' on a fuel-injected car, this sends messages from which the ECU decides to enrich or lean-off the fuel/air mixture.

- **Faulty fuel flow meter or air flow meter** This can cause intermittent or total failure in a fuel-injected car.

One reader, from Dorchester, came up with a novel reason for intermittent failures – one I had not encountered before. His heavy house keys were on the same keyring as the ignition key, and the motion of these caused the key to move slightly in the ignition switch, separating the contacts. A new ignition switch solved the problem.

Unreliable Volvo 340

" *I bought a 1989 Volvo 340GL 1.7 for reliability. It has covered 48,000 miles during which time I have been stranded twice, on the last occasion a few days after a service by the Volvo agent. Both times the fault was in the distributor cap. But the garage informs me that checking the distributor cap is no longer part of the service schedule. How can this be so, if it was part of the service schedule originally?* "

An extraordinary number of British people bought these old Volvo 340s under the illusion that they were 'buying into' the legendary Volvo reliability. In fact, the cars are designed by DAF, assembled in Holland, and mainly had Renault engines. (Only the 2-litre models had Volvo engines.) Your car either needs a new distributor cap and a set of plug leads (they can start to 'arc' after 6–7 years), or a new waterproof cover for the distributor to prevent condensation 'shorts'. There's no reason why a Renault agent or any competent local garage can't do the job if you feel that the Volvo agent has let you down.

Skoda sorted

" *Though I tried injector cleaner in my Skoda Favorit, this did not cure its 'pinking'. But Jean Pierre Ltd, my local Skoda dealer, was able to identify the cause: 'The clearance between the butterfly valve in the fuel injector system and the end of the accelerator cable was not correct'. Now the car goes like a bird and is a joy to motor in. Is there any book I could buy which explains fuel injection systems?* "

Thanks for your report, because it all adds to the information bank. Mill House Books can supply various fuel injection manuals (besides a truly vast number of other automotive titles – ask for the 1997 catalogue), tel: 01205 270377.

Bosch Fuel Injection and Engine Management (£21.95) should cover your car. The comprehensive tome is *Electronic Fuel Injection Manual – A Troubleshooting Guide for European, Japanese and Korean Vehicles.*

What a sucker

" *Crossing a ford recently, which was not deep enough to reach the floorpan of my Volvo 480 turbo, enough of a wave was created for water to reach the air intake and cause £1,320 of damage. Though the car is still under warranty, Volvo refused to foot the bill.* "

The same thing has happened to drivers of Renault Espace turbodiesels – and drivers of Citroen Xantia turbodiesels who failed to raise the car on its suspension before negotiating a flood. Before driving into any deep water, all car drivers, particularly diesel owners, should familiarise themselves with the height of the air intake.

Oily Volvo

" *I enclose copies of my letters to Volvo and Volvo's reply. In essence, I bought a January 1993 Volvo 440SE 2 litre, with a recorded mileage of 17,687, on 1 February 1996. Since then, the car has covered a further 10,600 miles, but has consumed 13.7 pints of oil in the process. Volvo's agent told me that when customers reported excessive oil consumption by 2 litre Volvo 440s and 460s, the engines were fitted with replacement piston rings – and that this had, in fact, been done to my car. I also get the impression that this engine is no longer being fitted to Volvos. Volvo has offered me a new engine at 50% of the cost as a 'goodwill gesture', but I do not feel that this is a reasonable offer.* "

There was an acknowledged problem with this engine, and the solution was 'Mod 2371' – effectively a new set of piston rings. But the problem had tended to be compounded by the way Volvo 440/460 owners drive the cars. Your car's low mileage on purchase implies a fair amount of short journeys from cold starts – precisely when the greatest amount of engine wear takes place. If the car was also driven gently and never revved above 3,000 rpm, it would not have bedded in properly, and this can lead to heavy oil consumption. In the circumstances, Volvo's offer is generous. You will be getting a new engine in a four-year-old, 28,000-mile car, at 50% of cost, so the 50% you are being asked to pay is a fair price for the betterment you will gain. You are right that production of the Volvo 440/460 has now ceased – to clear the production lines for the S40 and V40.

No choice

" *You often advise readers that short journeys from cold starts are bad for a car and, though I totally agree with you, I feel I should point out that many of us have no choice. Rather than take the car for an extended run every week or so, I think the best advice to get rid of accumulated condensation inside the engine is to change the oil very frequently – every three months, or every 2,000 miles, whichever comes first. Treated in this way, my present 1988 Astra, which has done 68,000 miles, still uses no oil in between changes.* "

The gearbox, the catalytic converter and the rest of the exhaust system need heating through regularly to evaporate cold-start condensation inside them.

This is sound thinking for a pre-cat car and something I have, in fact, advocated in the past. But it won't save the gearbox, the catalytic converter and the rest of the exhaust system which need heating through regularly to evaporate cold start condensation inside them. That's why I recommend a regular run of 10–20 miles. A Kenlowe 'Hotstart' engine preheater will also help on petrol and diesel engines alike – around £150 from Kenlowe on 01628 823303. (Make sure there is adequate underbonnet space for it to fit before ordering it.)

Faltering Fiesta

" *I know little about the workings of a motor car, but in July 1996 I bought a Ford Fiesta LX diesel, first registered on 6 March 1996 and used as a hire car in Guernsey, where it had done 2,100 miles. Though apparently serviced on its return, after driving the car for a mile I realised it lacked power and all was not well. I took it back and the garage found that the exhaust pipe was kinked. This was replaced. By the 7,500-mile service there was still a good deal of exhaust smoke, but the garage checked the emissions and pronounced them okay. Recently the car has become unresponsive again and I am wondering if 2,100 miles with a kinked exhaust has damaged the engine in some way. A new air filter helped, but did not completely cure the sluggishness.* "

The 'kink' was probably caused when the car was loaded or unloaded from the ferry – either on its outward or homeward-bound leg. I wouldn't worry too much about this. What I would do is replace the air filter, which may be clogged up, then dose the car with some injector cleaner such as Millers DieselClean Plus (for stockists, call 01484 713201) or STP Diesel Injector Cleaner. Once you have added this to the diesel, give the car an 'Italian tune-up' (give it a bit of stick) and this should clear its throat, restoring the lost performance.

Tappety

" *I own a 1996N Ford Mondeo 1.8i. As with most overhead cam engines, mine is noisy when starting from cold. I refer to the chatter from the top of the engine which I assume is from the hydraulic tappets. The car seems to be particularly noisy when cold, but the noise goes away as the engine warms up. Would an additive help? And is the noise normal?* "

As you say, the reason for the noise may be that the oil is not pumping up and cushioning the hydraulic tappets quickly enough, and this could be because the oil is too thick or too dirty, or that the wrong oil filter without a non-return valve has been fitted. So, first job is to have the oil and filter changed, using a light and at least semi-synthetic oil (preferably fully synthetic Mobil 1 0W–40) and a new Ford filter. If the noise persists and lasts longer than a few seconds, then the cause could be the petrol you are using. Many car owners foolishly search out the cheapest petrol they can buy and end up with poor quality fuel with an inadequate detergent content. This leaves gums and varnishes on the valve stems, causing them to stick in the guides.

Shell and Texaco CleanSystem 3 have adequate detergent content. The only additives likely to solve the problem you describe are fuel system cleansing petrol additives – made by STP, Wynn's, Comma, Redex and many others. But before you use any of these on a relatively new car, take advice from the car's manufacturer.

BMW V8 trouble

" *In November 1992 I bought a new BMW 730i V8. I was very pleased with it and decided to keep it on my retirement – expecting it to last for many years at an annual mileage of 6,000–7,000. Recently, at just 47,000 miles, the car failed to start. The AA could not solve the problem and the car was towed to my local BMW agent. Three days later, I was told the car was running again. The problem had been cylinder wear, which meant oil was being burned and contaminating the spark plugs. I was shocked to be presented with a bill for £3,535.33 for repairing the engine. £64.62 of the bill was for replacement air-conditioning gas, later paid for by the agent. BMW at first offered to pay 50% of the parts cost, then 100%, leaving me to pay £916.50 for labour. Are you aware of any reason why such wear should occur at such a low mileage? It seems to me that either the material used to line the cylinder walls was deficient or the cylinder lubrication system was inadequate, but neither the agent nor BMW will give me an explanation. Can you shed any light on this?* "

This is a familiar alloy-block BMW problem. Some months ago, Andrew English and I tried a 100,000-mile 94L 730i V8, the same model as yours, and thought it drove beautifully. Then, a few months ago, another reader wrote about having experienced similar problems to yours. This reader was in the habit of starting his car up solely to move it in or out of the garage. Subsequently, *Autocar* magazine ran an item in May 1997 about the problem, and confirmed that it seemed to occur with small numbers of the original BMW 2,997 cc and 3,952 cc V8s fitted to 5-Series and 7-Series cars. (In 1996, the 3 litre V8 was increased in capacity to 3,498 cc and the 4 litre V8 to 4,398 cc.) To quote *Autocar*, 'The car maker blames the high sulphur content in UK petrol, which it says has caused some engines to lose compression.' The same problem was then reported to occur with BMW's all-alloy 323/523 and 328/528 six-cylinder engines. BMW says the corrosion is caused by the high sulphur levels in some UK petrol and the way the engine management system protects the catalytic converters after a cold start. This can leave incompletely burned petrol in the combustion chambers and leaking down the bores if the car is not driven a sufficient distance to get to running temperature and burn the fuel off. A very high-quality fully synthetic oil such as Mobil 1 0W–40, changed at least every six months or every 5,000 miles, should help enormously in this respect. However, I should add that, in many other cases, BMW has relented and paid the labour as well as the parts costs for the necessary repairs.

Down on power?

" *I have a 14-year-old 'A' reg. Audi 80 Sport which has now done 88,000 miles. After a chassis dynamometer test, I was told that peak power had dropped from 112 bhp to 98 bhp and peak torque from 118 ft lb. to 91 ft lb.. I was also told that this was mainly due to weak springs on the bob weights of the distributor, necessitating some retardation of the ignition. A new distributor costs £318. Would this produce a worthwhile increase in power and torque, or is the fall-off more likely to be due to general wear and tear? It has also struck me that many drivers of older cars may be unaware that their engines are pinking due to distributor wear rather than to the reduced octane of the fuel they are using.* "

No need to pay an Audi agent £318 for a new distributor. You should be able to get one from a Bosch agent for around £100. Or try Autocavan on 01252 333891, Euro Car Parts (mail order) on 0541 506506, The German Car Co. on 01702 530440, or German and Swedish on 01281 893 1688. It is possible that you might get some 'pinking' at low revs due to a faulty mechanical advance, but remember that the 112 bhp and 118 ft lb. are the original power and torque outputs of the engine at the flywheel, not at the wheels. Having turned the transmission, the power at the wheels measured by a chassis dynamometer is never as much as the power at the flywheel measured by an engine dynamometer.

Strangled by cat

" After 125,000 trouble-free miles in a Ford Escort XR3i 1.6 litre cabriolet, owned for eleven years, I decided to trade up to a newer one. I part-exchanged it for a catalysed 1.8 litre 16v cabriolet with just 20,000 miles on the clock. Now, in place of a lively, flexible and impressive car, I have a lacklustre vehicle with all the sparkle of a suet pudding. When I brought this up with the vendor, a Ford agent, he agreed with me and said it was because of the catalytic converter, which in effect meant I now had a de-tuned engine. Is it still beyond the wit of designers to come up with something which is acceptable both to the environment and to the driver? And is there any way of getting round the problem? "

Because of the increased exhaust back pressure they cause, 'cats' do rob an engine of 5–10% of its potential power output. But whether your Escort 1.8 16v will outperform the old car depends on its designated power output. Between January 1992J and April 1993K, the car was offered with power outputs of 103 bhp or 128 bhp. From April 1993K (oval grille) the car was only

If the cat has hot-spotted and begun to disintegrate, it will have partially blocked the exhaust system, and the resulting increase in back pressure will make the car feel very lethargic indeed.

offered with the 128 bhp engine. Then, from August 1995N to date (1998R) the car has only been offered with 113 bhp. Whether your car performs as it should depends on everything being in order under the bonnet and under the car. If the cat has hot-spotted and begun to disintegrate, it will have partially blocked the exhaust system, and the resulting increase in back pressure will make the car feel very lethargic indeed. Get the dealer to sign the invoice stating that the car is performing to specification, then get it tested by your local experts, Southern Carburettors of Wimbledon (0181 540 2723).

Lena the Carina

" *I own a Carina E, and for twelve months I have been endeavouring to get a problem sorted out for which Toyota tell me there is no solution. Under certain conditions, the 'lean burn' should revert to a 'normal burn', giving extra power when needed. With my car, this no longer happens. I have been told that when the car's ECU was interrogated, no fault could be found. Yet my car still lacks overtaking power. Have any of your readers experienced the same problem?* "

I obtained some more details from the writer of this letter, including an MOT cat test printout. This showed his 1.6 litre engine running at Lambda 0.998 at 2,607 rpm, and proved that it was capable of running at a 'normal' stoichiometric air-to-fuel ratio of 14.5 to 1. (Toyota seems to have altered the test rev. range from 2,400–2,600 rpm to 2,350–2,650 rpm). I also inspected a copy of Toyota's 'Driver's Guide' for Carina E 1.6 models. This states that 'The engine is most fuel efficient between 3,000 and 4,000 rpm'; that 'If you want to accelerate quickly it is better to use small throttle openings and high revs rather than low revs and wide throttle openings'; and that 'It does not pay to accelerate in the region below 3,000 rpm unless at very small throttle openings.' It points out that, above 4,600 rpm and above a 60% throttle opening, the lean burn valve opens and 'you will feel the surge of power'. It also states that the way to get good acceleration from low revs in a low gear is to lift off and reapply the throttle to the same position as before. In the past I have had complaints from readers that the transition from lean to normal burn was not a smooth one, but no-one had reported that they could not get the power when needed. In this instance the next logical step would be to get the car put on a chassis dynamometer to have the power at the wheels checked. At 5,000 rpm, even after power losses through the gearbox, this should not be significantly less than 90 bhp.

Slow-starting diesel

" *Perhaps you can help me with a problem which my local Ford dealer has been unable or unwilling to solve. My company inflicted a 1994 Escort diesel on me a couple of years ago. At about 55,000 miles it started taking a long time to start from cold. I follow the correct starting procedures, and the glowplugs were replaced at the last service with no improvement. I have now started to use City Diesel instead of Esso, but this has not improved starting. Any ideas?* "

A West Country reader had this same problem with a Fiesta for years and nobody seemed able to solve it. Finally, he tried an independent diesel specialist and the fault was traced to a very small air leak in the inlet manifold.

Start–stop Volvo

" *We have been very satisfied purchasers of 'nearly new' Volvos for many years now, but are not so satisfied with our present car. It is an 'L' registered 850GL 20v estate, purchased two years ago. The problem is that if you ever make the mistake of stopping somewhere, switching the engine off, then switching it on again to move it a few yards, if you then switch it off for a second time in short succession it simply will not start again. RAC rescue patrols know what to do, but Volvo tells us it is a problem associated with poor-quality unleaded petrol and they can't do anything about it. Because of this, when the time came we changed our other Volvo, a 740, for an Isuzu Trooper instead of a Volvo 960. But we have kept our ancient 200,000-mile 240 which never lets us down. Have you come across this fault with the 850 before?* "

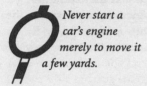

Never start a car's engine merely to move it a few yards.

Yes, and with BMWs, Nissan Micras and many other moderm cars. It is the engine management system protecting the catalytic converter from unburned petrol. One solution might be to run the car on better petrol than you do or give it a real treat by running it on 'Shell' or 'Texaco CleanSystem 3' Superunleaded. The other is never ever to start the car's engine merely to move it a few yards. Check the car's handbook to see if it warns you about this.

Oil pump failure

" *I own a petrol-engined Peugeot 405GL which a mechanic told me needed a new oil pump. The only obvious sign of trouble was the oil light going on and off intermittently for two months before the engine started rattling. The gauge sender worked perfectly. The mechanic said it would be cheaper to fit a reconditioned engine as the engine would have to come out anyway to fit a new oil pump. Two other garages said the same, with one adding that engine damage would push up the price. Even though I know how much parts and labour can cost, is a reconditioned engine at £1,245.50 really a cheaper option? The car is 'J' registered with 93,500 miles and had been trouble-free up to this point.* "

How many times do I have to repeat this? When the oil light comes on you must stop. It means the engine lacks oil pressure, because either the pump has failed or the engine is losing oil. Without oil pressure, the oil will not circulate and will not lubricate the engine, which is why your bearings began to rattle. One reader who ignored the oil light in a Spanish hire car was hit for £2,000 by the rental company for a new engine. If the engine you have been offered is a genuine Peugeot reconditioned engine, then £1,245.50 is reasonable. Your other option is to have the engine rebuilt by a member of The Federation of Engine Re-Manufacturers (tel: 01788 576465). The FER Code of Practice avoids problems associated with engines reconditioned by cowboy outfits.

Stammering Orion

" *I have a 1990H Ford Orion 1.6 Ghia EFi. I am having problems when in fifth gear, as the engine loses power causing a judder. This can happen at any speed, but mainly at around 40 to 50 mph. My friend has tried replacing the ECU but to no avail. Any suggestions?* "

There could be a lot of reasons for this, but it's most likely that it is the ECU which is at fault – it's a notoriously duff unit on this model and concurrent XR3is. BBR (01280 702389) and Superchips (01280 816780) both offer solutions to this specific problem.

Sudden cut-outs

" *A close relative was driving a 'J' registered BMW 316i along the overtaking lane of a very busy stretch of elevated dual carriageway with no hard shoulder, when it suddenly cut out. With great difficulty he managed to edge the car to the nearside lane and as much as possible onto the narrow pavement. He put on the hazard flashers, opened bonnet and boot and erected the warning triangle, then called the RAC. It turned out that the ignition box had completely failed, rendering the car suddenly useless. The total cost of the repair was £700, to which BMW refused to contribute on the grounds of the car's age, stating that the failure was due to 'normal wear and tear'. But the car has been serviced regularly every 3–4 months. So my questions are, what use is such frequent servicing when a component like an ignition box can suddenly fail? (My Volkswagen only needs servicing once a year.) And, is ignition box failure a common problem with BMW cars?* **”**

Solid-state components cannot be 'serviced'. They are usually totally reliable, but when they fail it is almost always without warning.

Modern cars need a full service once every 10,000 miles or once a year, whichever comes first. But if the owner wants them to last and wants faults such as leaking brake pipes, worn pads, etc. spotted before they cause an accident, the car needs oil and filter changes and 'inspections' more often – at least every six months, in my view, with an oil change either every six months or every 3,000 miles if using mineral oil, every 4,000–5,000 miles if using semi-synthetic oil, or every 6,000–7,500 miles if using fully synthetic. The quicker the car clocks up the mileage, the closer to the higher limits you can push these oil changes. And, of course, the more often the car is up on a ramp, the more chances there are of faults being picked up before they represent a serious danger. Solid-state components cannot be 'serviced', however. They are usually totally reliable, but when they fail it is almost always without warning. BMW 316s and 318s are generally very reliable (though 'J' reg. models still had timing belts which need to be replaced every three years). Another quite common fault which can stop a car in its tracks with no prior warning is failure of the fuel pump relay.

STORING A CAR

Open-air winter storage

" Next year I will be leaving my car in an 'open-air' parking compound near Heathrow airport for nine weeks during February and March while I jet off to sunnier climes. The car is a two-year-old Citroen Xantia turbo-diesel, regularly serviced and lubricated with Millers XFE semi-synthethic oil. What precautions should I take to ensure that the car does not suffer problems after nine weeks inactivity, outside, in winter weather? I am sure your answer will interest many other readers who escape the English winter blues. "

This is a terrible thing to do to a car, but no worse than thousands of new or 'nearly new' cars suffer every year. The exposed area around Heathrow is particularly cold during the winter, so make sure your antifreeze is capable of protecting the engine to at least 30 degrees below zero. If your battery is in good condition, the run down to Heathrow should leave it in a fully charged state, and it is more likely to retain enough charge to start the car if left disconnected (check with your Citroen dealer if you can use a 'slave' battery to keep the clock, radio code and alarm/immobiliser running). Battery condition is particularly important with a diesel, due to the huge slug of power they take to heat the glow plugs and then turn an extremely high compression engine. (Leave jump leads in the car, but remember you won't be able to jump start it from most petrol-engined cars because they can't deliver enough wallop.)

Change the oil and filter before your trip down. Get some lock antifreeze. Spread some silicone grease around the door seals in case the doors get frozen up. Ask your dealer about protective wax to protect the paint from bird droppings (particularly if it's a metallic with lacquer coat). Leave the hand brake off and the car in first gear to help prevent corrosion of the rear discs. Some parking compounds keep the keys and move the cars around. This can be a good thing as long as they leave the engines running long enough to put back what they take out of the batteries, but it can, of course, leave a lot of condensation inside the exhaust systems.

Left standing

" *I recently bought a new Peugeot 406GLX with air conditioning, alarm, immobiliser and catalytic converter. In February I will be out of the country for five weeks, leaving the car in a friend's driveway. I had intended asking him to start it up and leave it idling now and again, but in view of the damage this may cause to the catalytic converter, is there a different precaution I should take?* "

Far better to insure the car for your friend to drive it and ask him to take it for a ten-mile drive every week, preferably involving a bit of motorway or dual carriageway where he can drive it at a reasonable speed, and with the air conditioning on. This will re-charge the battery, keep the aircon pump free of gunge, and should dry out any exhaust system condensation from the cold start.

Car cryogenics

" *My son has one of the last old-shape Saab 900 low-pressure turbos,*

which he bought in 1993. He now has to leave the country to work overseas for a year and is stuck with the quandary of what to do with the car. He wants to keep it. Should he garage it? And, if so, is there any particular care which will have to be administered prior to and during this period? "

During the summer it will be better for the car to be driven a reasonable distance occasionally. (Do you know anyone with trade insurance and trade plates who could do this without the necessity to tax and insure the car?) During the winter it will probably be better to lay the car up. Briefly, prior to laying up, completely drain and thoroughly flush the cooling system and refill with a pre-mixed MPG Trigard coolant such as Comma Coldstream, which lasts four years rather than the two years of conventional MEG coolants and the year or less of methanol coolants. Renew the engine oil and filter, grease the battery terminals with petroleum jelly, don't garage the car unless it is thoroughly dry (best to take it for a long run immediately prior to laying up to evaporate any condensation in the exhaust system), and don't blip the accelerator before switching off (this leaves unburned petrol in the exhaust system). A new product which helps prevent corrosion in cylinder barrels by absorbing condensation is Stortech Storage Plugs, which replace the spark plugs (remember to number the leads when you remove them). These cost £16.95 for a set of four from Richbrook International on 0171 381 0777, but make sure the reach is right for a Saab 900 16v head. When you leave the car, either disconnect both terminals of the battery or buy an 'Airflow' battery conditioner, follow the instructions, and leave it connected. Unlike a conventional battery charger, the 'Airflow' keeps the battery fully charged but not overcharged with a very low amperage current which does not interfere with the car's ECU, immobiliser, or any other electronics. It's £40 well spent, and is available from Airflow UK, Crown House, Faraday Road, Newbury, Berks RG14 2AB, tel: 01635 569569. Store the car in a dry, well-aired garage, shed, barn or warehouse (the more air around the car the better). Consider investing in a dehumidifier or a 'Carcoon' (tel: 0161 737 9630). Leave the windows slightly open. Cover the car with a cotton sheet. Pump the tyres about 5 psi over pressure and push the car backwards and forwards occasionally to prevent the tyres flat spotting. Give the battery a top-up charge once a month, press the clutch and brake pedals a few times every fortnight. There's not much you can do about the brake discs rusting except to store the car when dry in a dry place. Leave the handbrake off to prevent the cable stretching and the

To re-start the car after a lay-up, first turn the engine over with a wrench or turn it over using the starter motor with the ignition disconnected. This will circulate some oil before the engine is fired up.

rear brakes seizing on. Don't leave the car with a lot of petrol in the tank, as this will evaporate and degrade, and when you fill up to use the car again be sure to fill the tank with top quality petrol, such as Shell Super or Texaco Cleansystem 3 Super. When you want to re-start the car, either turn the engine over with a wrench or turn it over using the starter motor with the ignition disconnected to circulate some oil before firing it up.

Storing a diesel

" I drive an 'N' reg. Peugeot 306 diesel and in December I will be going abroad for six months. I would like to know what to do about my car before I lock it up in my garage. Does the oil need to be drained? Should I leave diesel in the car? The car is due for a service in November, so should I delay this until I get back and have the whole car checked thoroughly then? "

See 'Car Cryogenics' above, but the rules are a bit different for a diesel. The worst enemy of the XUD engine in your car is internal corrosion, so you should ask for the coolant to be replaced – preferably with a pre-mixed solution containing Trigard. The engine oil also needs to be replaced to remove contaminants. And before you finally put the car away, add a double quantity of a diesel injector cleaner which contains a 'lubricity enhancer' to the fuel, take it on a 20-mile drive, then top up the tank. This will ensure the critical surfaces in the fuel pump are reasonably well protected and helps prevent the fuel line getting blocked by globules of emulsified DERV caused by condensation in the tank. When you want to re-start the car, turn it over straight away to circulate some oil. Then switch off, switch on again, wait for the glow plugs to warm up, and start.

TAX

Iniquitous

" I wonder how many of your readers are aware of the punishment that awaits them should they dare to change their company car part-way through the tax year. This could happen if the car was stolen, written off in an accident or simply changed at a certain time due to company policy. Instead of the driver's total annual mileage being apportioned between the two cars, each is treated separately. If, for example, the driver has a £15,000 car for 300 days of the tax year and drives 20,000 miles, he benefits from the full 2/3rds reduction in taxable benefit. This works out at £3,499, multiplied by 300 and divided by 365, which comes to £2,875. If, for whatever reason, he then drives less than 400 business miles in a replacement £15,000 car over the remaining 65 days of the tax year, he gains no reduction for mileage and his taxable benefit on that car works out at £5,250, multiplied by 65 and divided by 365, which comes to £935. His total taxable benefit for the year would than be £2,875 plus £935, which comes to £3,810, whereas had he done the same 20,400 miles in the same car his taxable benefit would have been £3,500. "

You're right, of course, and the fleet industry is well aware of this. It's the one thing Stephen Dorrel did not correct when he acceded to a list-price-based benefit tax rather than one based on a scale charge. I have a feeling the present government will attend to the matter as part of its Integrated Transport Policy, because the present system encourages more business miles to be driven and more environmental damage to be done than is strictly necessary. Car benefit tax based on the amount of private mileage driven by the company driver rather than the amount of business mileage driven would be a far more sensible system.

Fuel tax

" *I believe it is now some years since you gave us a breakdown of the tax on fuels per litre. Now that the tax has been increased twice in the same year, could you please give us the latest figures?* "

Certainly:

Fuel (litre)	Fuel Tax	VAT	Pump Price	Fuel Cost	Tax rate	% as tax
4-Star	49.26p	11.30p	75.90p	15.34p	395%	79.79%
Unleaded	43.99p	10.11p	67.90p	13.8p	392%	79.67%
Super	48.76p	11.90p	79.90p	19.24p	315%	75.92%
Diesel	44.99p	10.41p	69.90p	14.50p	382%	79.25%
City Diesel	42.99p	10.41p	69.90p	16.5p	324%	76.39%

Vehicle fuels, along with booze and fags, are a select group of products on which we pay a tax on a tax.

'VAT-Qualifying'

" *On St Valentines Day my wife and I purchased a nine-month-old car with 9,250 miles, warranted, from a franchised agent for the marque. We arranged to pay for it with a building society cheque made out to the agent which the building society told us could not be cancelled. When we were presented with the invoice I was horrified to see that £1,895 of the agreed price was VAT, which was not mentioned before. I was under the impression that VAT was not payable on secondhand cars. The car was previously registered to a company. As this was a major purchase for us pensioners and probably our last car, it has niggled me ever since. Can you explain?* "

Nothing to worry about. When new cars are purchased solely for business purposes, for example by car hire companies and leasing companies, input VAT can be re-claimed. On disposal, output VAT must be paid to HM Customs and Excise and itemised on the invoice as a proportion of the selling price. So, if you bought a 'Qualifying Car' for £12,725 plus the cost of the VED disc, the invoice would show the purchase price as £10,830, and VAT as £1,895 (which, from August 1995, could be reclaimed by any VAT-registered business which bought the vehicle secondhand for business purposes only). A car bought by a company for an employee's use does not qualify because of the implied element of personal use. Like most other traders, I have used this as a nice little 'free loan' from the VAT man, which I did not have to repay until a month after the VAT quarter in which I re-sold the qualifying cars. Smarter traders than me made a lot of money by reclaiming the VAT on qualifying cars bought at the 'market low' of October/November 1995 which they did not re-sell until the 'market high' of January/February 1996. Many made £2,000 a car, with the purchase of every sixth car financed by HM Customs and Excise – all totally legal and above board.

TIMING BELTS AND CHAINS

Another broken belt

"Can you name any UK-manufactured 2 litre cars in which failure of the timing belt does not cause consequential damage? The timing belt of my Rover 820i failed recently after having been replaced 13,000 miles previously. The repair cost was estimated at £1,000, and I do not want to repeat this experience."

Your timing belt should not have snapped a mere 13,000 miles after it was fitted, so the fitter is probably at fault. If the belt is put on a few notches out, if it is not tensioned correctly, or if over-strong valve springs are fitted, its life will be shortened. Three UK-built 2 litre cars I can think of with a timing chain rather than a belt are the Nissan Primera petrol and the Vauxhall Astra/Vectra 2.0DI direct injected diesel. Non-diesel Nissan Sunnys and Almeras have chains rather than belts. So do current 16v Micras and 16v Suzukis. Old 2.25 litre Land Rovers, V8 Range Rovers, Jaguars and anything with the Buick alloy V8 such as TVRs and Morgan Plus 8s all use them, as do Saabs, Mercs, 2.0 litre twin-cam Sierras, Granadas and Scorpios, 2.3 litre Galaxys and Scorpios, old 2.3 litre Vauxhalls and six-cylinder Vauxhalls, V6 Mondeos, VW VR6s and V5s and all BMWs from September 1993. The six-cylinder BMW

2.5 litre diesel engine, also used in the current Range Rover and Vauxhall Omega, has a chain rather than a belt, as does the VM diesel used in the Rover 800, Jeep Cherokee, some older Range Rovers and the Chrysler Voyager. Ford Mavericks, Nissan Terranos and Nissan Patrols also use chains. The most fail-safe conversion you can buy is by Zeus, and replaces chains or belts on Land Rover four-cylinder engines with constant mesh gears (tel: 01392 438833) – and this is the standard method of camshaft drive in the Toyota Landcruiser VX 4.2 diesel.

Dyslexic diesel

" *I have owned nine Fords in 30 years, but my present Escort 1.8XL diesel will be my last. After just 21,600 miles it suffered cambelt failure, repairing the damage cost £500, and Ford would not re-imburse more than 50% of this due to the age of the car. I now need to replace it with a one- or two-year-old three-door diesel hatchback, preferably with adjustable driver's seat height and no history of cam drive failures. What do you suggest?* "

You don't say how old your car is. Cambelt failure was a problem on Ford 1.8 litre diesels in 1990 and 1991, and one reason given was over-strong valve springs. But if the car is more than four years old it was overdue a cambelt change anyway. Replace it with a DI Astra.

Belt up

" *How long would you expect a Ford Sierra camshaft drive belt to last? According to the Haynes manual, it should be replaced at 36,000-mile intervals, but according to the Ford Motor Company it should last indefinitely! As a result of the failure of this 'indestructible' component after 96,000 miles, I have been left with engine damage which cost me £295.64* " *to rectify. Ford has confirmed there is nothing in the service schedule about replacing the cambelt, and I believe the company is negligent in supplying an inadequate service schedule. The company states that the failure of the belt could have been caused by another fault such as an oil leak, and that the age of the vehicle (seven years) could be a contributing factor. I would very much appreciate your opinion on this.* "

I would expect it to last three years or 35,000–40,000 miles. Since you have a Haynes manual and have ignored its similar advice, the 'negligence' rests with you. A cambelt or 'timing belt' can last anything from a couple of miles (incorrectly tensioned or positioned) to around 100,000 miles. If the camshaft end seal or a jackshaft seal goes, oil will contaminate the cambelt and shorten its life. This is why the Haynes manuals very sensibly recommend a change at 36,000 miles or every 3–4 years – and why I do, too. Some cambelts, such as those in the Isuzu diesel engine in Vauxhalls and the Ford Zetec engine, are a bit thicker and the recommended change point is 72,000–80,000 miles and 4–5 years, whichever comes first. You were lucky that the engine damage in your case was so slight. In some cases the damage can cost £2,000 to put right.

Snap!

" *I have a January 1991 VW Polo which is driven by my wife on local trips and has covered just 16,000 miles. Despite the low mileage it has been regularly serviced, first by a VW dealer and then by the local garage. A couple of days ago, the car packed up without warning and the reason was diagnosed as a faulty camshaft drive belt. Repairs are estimated at over £300. VW does not accept any responsibility, owing to the car's age. Is it worth pursuing them?* "

No.

Broken hearted

" *In April 1995 I bought a March 1993 'K' registered BMW 518iSE, with 21,000 miles, from a BMW agent. I have used a small independent garage for servicing, and soon after the last service, at 51,000 miles, the timing belt broke causing £800 worth of damage. I took the car to the supplying agent who advised that the timing belt needed changing at 36,000 miles. Do I have a case against the independent garage, or is BMW the guilty party?* "

Once a timing belt has been in use for more than three years or 35,000 miles, the chance of an expensive breakage is increased.

Neither. A timing belt can last anything from five miles to 100,000 miles, but, once it's been on for more than three years or 35,000 miles, the chance of an expensive breakage increases. That's why I, and BMW, recommend a change at three years or 35,000–40,000 miles, whichever comes first. Later four-cylinder BMWs (from September 1993 in the case of the 316i and 318i and from May 1994 in the case of the 518i) went over to timing chains instead of belts and, of course, BMW M42 fours, M50 sixes and M60 eight-cylinder engines have been on chains for even longer.

Chains go too

" *I have owned a 1981 Mercedes 230E since new and, since I am retired, the mileage is a mere 92,000. I was interested to read in your column several weeks ago what you wrote of the W123 4-cylinder engine having a propensity to need new timing chains every 60,000–80,000 miles until the engines went over to Duplex chains in 1989. My car has the 'old' 102-series engine and has needed new timing chains at 36,000 miles and at 84,000 miles, so I am wondering whether I should follow your advice and have the oil and filter changed every six months. In the past I have only changed the oil and filter every 6,000 miles, which could have taken 18 months to clock up.* "

The infrequency of your oil changes almost certainly led to a blocked oil feed to the chain, premature wear and early replacement. Your engine may also be in dire need of a flush, which will mean changing the filter and the oil to a light, preferably fully synthetic oil, driving it around on that for 2,000 miles or three months, changing it and the filter, then changing it again after a further 2,000 miles. Look carefully and I'm pretty sure the manual will state something like 'oil changes are due every 6,000 miles or every six months whichever comes first'. Just think what would have happened if the chain had actually snapped. With this engine, you'd have faced a bill for engine repairs of between £1,200 and £2,000.

Snapped Sierra chains.

" *I purchased a 'new' Ford Sierra GLX in 1994 and the car has been regularly serviced by Ford dealers. Having reached 50,000 miles I asked why a timing belt change had not been scheduled and was told it was unnecessary because the engine has a timing chain, not a belt. Very soon afterwards, the car broke down. The timing chain had snapped, resulting in catastrophic engine damage. I was quoted £1,800 for a replacement engine. I wrote to Ford asking why a replacement timing chain had not been scheduled and, though my question was not answered, I received a 'goodwill' cheque for £640. Having been badly advised by the Ford agent I feel I should be entitled to a full refund.* "

A 1994 Sierra? Production of this car ceased in April 1993 at the latest (VIN identifier 'PP'), so your car must have been at least a year old when you bought it. It would not surprise me if the etching on the side window glass showed it to be 1992 build. Long pre-sale storage in compounds often leads to condensation corrosion inside engines. The twin cams of later 2.0 litre Sierras (and also 2.0 litre Granadas, Scorpios

Engines whose twin cams are driven by 'Simplex' chains need their oil changed at least as often as every six months.

and Galaxys) are driven by quite a narrow 'Simplex' chain. The life of this chain is totally dependent on the condition of the oil in the engine. If it is not changed frequently (at least every six months), degraded oil will block vital oilways, starving the chain of its oil supply and leading to premature failure.

Time to snap back

" *My August 1995 'N' registered Vauxhall Astra 1.8 Sport, for which I paid nearly £15,000, is currently undergoing repairs as the result of a snapped cambelt, which occurred at 28,000 miles. The cylinder head will need replacing. Vauxhall initially offered to pay 20% of the cost, then upped this to 50% of the cost of the parts. The company specifies 36,000 miles as the point when the cambelt should be changed, but mine looked like it had been ripped apart, possibly due to overtightening. The car has always been serviced on time by Vauxhall agents. I think that the least Vauxhall should do is cover the full cost of the parts.* "

Vauxhall Corsas, Astras and Vectras from 1993 to 1996, fitted with 1.4 or 1.6 16v engines, were subject to a 1997 recall due to the possibility of faulty cambelt idler pulleys which could snap their cambelts. Though your car is a 1.8 16v, it very much looks like your car has suffered from the same fault, and this should have been acknowledged by the Vauxhall agent and by Vauxhall itself. I strongly suspect that, now you are armed with this information, it will be.

TOWING

Overheated automatics

" *The subject of automatic transmissions overheating when towing came up again recently. I have a Ford Sierra fitted with the later four-speed automatic gearbox. Unfortunately, though the older three-speed automatic Sierra had a separate transmission fluid cooler, the four-speed automatic does not. Anyone contemplating towing with a four-speed automatic Sierra should have this extra oil radiator fitted.* "

A number of readers have written in about the overheating of their car's automatic transmission fluid while towing a caravan. In many cases the means of cooling the ATF is a secondary matrix within the car's engine radiator which cannot cope with the increased transmission heat caused by towing a caravan in the summer. The solution is to fit an auxiliary and entirely separate ATF cooler, and an excellent source for that is Kenlowe Ltd on 01628 823303. The company also makes slimline auxiliary electric fans and a device for pre-heating engines in winter, branded the 'Hotstart'.

Big torquing towcar

" *I need to replace my venerable Peugeot 405 1.9 (petrol), as it is not really up to towing a caravan of 1,100 GVW. I am looking for a car with good low-down torque and am considering the Peugeot 406 2.1TD, Omega 2.5TD, Toyota Avensis 2.0TD or possibly the upcoming Saab 2.2TDI. Unfortunately, the Passat 1.9 TDI 110 bhp is reported as not being a good towcar, due to inherent instability and unsuitable gear ratios. If I choose a 406, should I wait for the arrival of PSA's new HDI engine? Also, I want the car to last ten years and 120,000 miles.* "

If the report about the Passat comes from the specialist caravan press, I'll defer to it. Otherwise I'd have said it has the best combination of power and torque of any car you list apart from the BMW-powered Omega and the forthcoming Xantia/406 HDI. The new Saab 9-3 2.2 TiD with GM's 2.2 litre 115 bhp engine is much better to drive than I thought it would be (in my opinion it's the best overall package in the 9-3 line-up) and, like all 9-3s, has steering which is vastly improved over the previous 900. But peak torque of 192 lb. ft is developed between a relatively high 1,900–3,000 rpm and, because power and torque fall off sharply below that figure, the engine 'prefers' to be kept at 2,000 rpm or above. (At 1,350 rpm, for example, you're looking at just 125 lb. ft and a mere 40 bhp.) The torque characteristics of the PSA HDI, however, provides 184 lb. ft at just 1,500 rpm, with more than 148 lb. ft available from 1,350 rpm all the way to 4,000 rpm. The HDI's maximum power of 110 bhp is also developed at usefully lower revs than the GM TiD, so the HDI in a car such as the Xantia with self-levelling suspension should provide the best tow-car.

Causing queues and dazzle

" *As a vintage car driver, may I suggest that it is courteous for towing vehicles to pull off the road from time to time to allow the queue behind to overtake? Also, what can be done about the dipped headlights of oncoming cars which still dazzle?* "

A very sensible suggestion which considerate caravan owners and tractor drivers already abide by when they can. It would also be courteous for all drivers who prefer to travel at less than 50 mph on A roads not to do so in convoys but to leave enough space for an overtaking car between themselves and the car in front. Most modern cars have electric dipped beam adjusters to compensate for load or the weight of a caravan on the tow bar, but all-too-many drivers have either not found the switch or don't know what it's for. This very useful device also enables the driver of an unladen car to lower the angle of his or her dipped beams in heavy traffic so the lights do not dazzle or distract other drivers.

Motorway cruising

" *We recently acquired a 17ft 7in. motor cruiser and trailer. We are con-*

*templating changing our Peugeot 405 diesel estate for a 406 2.1 diesel es-
tate. In view of the fact that the 406 is front-wheel-drive, would you recommend it for towing or suggest an alternative?* **"**

Fine car. Great engine. But it's shared by the
Citroen Xantia 2.1TD Estate which, by virtue of
its self-levelling suspension, should be much
better for towing. (A new, more flexible and
more economical 'HDI' engine was launched for
these cars in October 1998.) If you can afford it,
a Volvo V70 TDI Estate should be good too. A
safe rule of thumb is that the laden trailer should
not exceed 85% of the weight of the car. If the
weight of the trailer is greater than the weight of
the car, then you would be much better off with
a 4×4 designed for towing, such as a Fourtrak,
Discovery, Shogun, Trooper or Landcruiser. All
trailers are prohibited from the overtaking lane
of three-lane UK motorways. Where the weight
of the trailer exceeds that of the towing vehicle,
many further restrictions apply – especially in
France, where you will be limited to the nearside lane only of the Autoroute.

A case for castration

" *I wonder how many of your readers have returned to their cars to find
a ball-shaped dent in the bumper or elsewhere. Never a note of apology or
an offer to pay for the repairs. For the third time in six years I have been
the victim of such an attack, and from the shape of the dent my car has
clearly been at the receiving end of a caravan towing ball used as a battering ram by an 'acoustic parking' enthusiast. When I see the extent by
which some towbars project, I wonder if they can possibly conform with
'Construction and Use' regulations. Isn't it high time that projecting balls
were enclosed in some sort of protective vehicle jock-strap?* **"**

You're right. Where a towing hook is removable,

a responsible caravan or trailer owner should remove it when not in use. Alternatively, he should be compelled to cover it with some form of protective box. But I certainly won't suggest that victims of towball mania go so far as to arm themselves with hacksaws. Witter (01204 341146) is the largest UK manufacturer of towbars and does make detachable towbars, tested and type-approved to EC Directive 94/20 by the Vehicle Certification Agency, price £195 plus VAT. Brink also does a range of 'Brinkmatic' detachable towbars for Audi, BMW, Mercedes, VW and Volvo, priced from £160 (Euro Car Parts, National Mail Order: 0541 506 506).

TYRES

Win-tyred

" My attempts at locating a source of 'chunky' or 'Town and Country' tyres for my Rover Metro in the specified 155/65 R13 size have so far drawn a blank. It would appear that the Metro is about the only vehicle which uses that particular size, and I have no wish to impair safety, invalidate my insurance or risk wheelarch or other damage by experimenting with an alternative size. Can you offer any suggestions? "

I put this to Micheldever Tyres who just happen to have a fitting depot in Westbury (tel: 01373 825800), which is closer to you than their base at Micheldever Station (tel: 01962 774437). True to form, they gave the most complete answer you could wish for. First, they remind us that the tyres must be fitted to all four wheels, because fitting them to the front only on a front-wheel-drive car would cause an imbalance between front and rear grip and a twitchy rear end. The correct Mud-and-Snow tyres for the Metro's 13in. x 4.5in. B rims are 145/70 R13s which slightly increase the rolling circumference from 1,625 mm to 1,638 mm, but this is within the permitted tolerance. The slightly narrower footprint helps them grip better than a wider tyre in mud and snow. The tyres, Michelin Alpines, carry a 'Q' speed rating of less than 100 mph and reduce the load capacity of the car from 365 kg to 345 kg. Their price is £49.95 each plus VAT, fitted and balanced. If you're going to keep the car, it would work out cheaper in the long run to buy a second set of four rims for the M+S tyres.

Odd tyres

" I recently asked my Vauxhall dealer to fit two new tyres to the front wheels of my Vauxhall Astra. When I went to collect the car I found that two different tyres had been fitted – a Michelin and a Kelly. I told the service manager that I did not consider this a safe thing to do, but he insisted it was perfectly OK. As the car did not feel right, I had a matching Michelin put on by my village garage. I have since written to the MD of the Vauxhall garage on two occasions, only for the service manager to call me back insisting he was right. Am I living in the past, or am I right? "

When a car is nearing the end of its life on a fleet and needs a single new tyre, it's not uncommon for the fleet to replace it with a cheap one of the same size, regardless of match. And, on the ex-Vauxhall Masterhire Cavaliers and Astras I've dealt in, it did not seem to make much difference – even on the front. (These are not the sharpest handling of cars even at the best of times.) I think what must have happened is that the garage replaced one tyre with the spare Michelin from the boot and, because it did not have any Michelins in stock, replaced the other tyre with a Kelly. If there is going to be a mismatch, I'd prefer the tyres on the front of a front-wheel-drive car to match and the mismatch to be on the back.

Full-size 'spares'

" As a farmer driving in conditions where punctures are not uncommon I need a full-size emergency wheel for my Golf. I discovered that my excellent local VW dealer, Irvines of Bridgwater, had lots of tyre-less full-

size steel wheels – rejected by the alloy wheel brigade – which they were going to 'recycle'. So I now have a full-size spare for little more than the cost of the tyre. "

Good tip, especially since a VW steel rim is usually £80. I once fitted out a Peugeot 205XLD with a set of proper-size steel wheels from a 205GT in the same way. The GT owner wanted alloys. I needed a set of wider wheels to stop the XLD going straight on at roundabouts.

Tyre trouble

" *I run a September 1994 VW Passat TDI estate car which came fitted with Kleber tyres. Due to a tracking problem and a nail in one of the rear tyres, I had four tyres replaced at the end of July 1996. I had wanted Michelin ZX or XZX or similar, but was told these were no longer made and that Michelin Classic would be a suitable replacement. I immediately noticed that the car had lost some 'thrust', the steering became stiffer and average fuel consumption increased very noticeably from 48.9 mpg to 43.8 mpg. When I complained, it was suggested I increase the tyre pressures by 2 psi, but when I did that the car bounced around. It shed a previously secure mud flap and cracked the front exhaust pipe, I believe due to the bumpier ride on over-inflated tyres. Now I am faced with driving the car 30,000–40,000 miles on the 'wrong tyres' and neither the chairman of the 'fast fit' chain which supplied the tyres, nor Michelin, seem to be willing to help me. I was informed that Michelin now makes an 'Economy' tyre, but wonder if the reason is that ordinary Michelin tyres are not economical.* "

A factor which could affect the fuel consumption of diesel engines is the recently reduced sulphur content of UK diesel. A 'heavy' diesel almost always takes you further than a 'light, clean' diesel.

There is no doubt that Michelin 'Energy' tyres do save fuel compared to standard tyres, and this was proved some years ago using a Citroen AX 1.5D. I can believe that your new tyres provide increased 'grip' (something you experience in the form of 'stiffer steering'.) I can also believe that the increased rolling resistance of the Michelins over the Klebers will have had some effect on fuel consumption. But I simply can't believe that increasing your tyre pressures by 2 psi to partially compensate would lead the car to 'bounce around', crack the exhaust pipe and shed a mudflap. Though, in theory, you might be entitled to some redress under the Sale and Supply of Goods Act 1994, I think your case would be too difficult to prove to make litigation worthwhile. What I suggest is to get the tracking checked and to continue to experiment with tyre pressures, varying the front and back pressures until you are happy with the balance of the car and its fuel consumption. (You will, of course, have to increase the pressures for load carrying – and you need a good gauge such as the Accu-Gage, £13.50 from ITC, tel: 01604 591200.) Another factor which could affect your fuel consumption is the recently reduced sulphur content of UK diesel. A 'heavy' diesel almost always takes you further than a 'light, clean' diesel.

More plaudits for the P6000

" *I recently went to Micheldever Tyres, near Winchester, to ask for advice about new tyres for my 1986 Mercedes 300SL which has completed 36,000 miles. I found them to be most helpful – and very reasonable on price. After discussion of the various merits, I opted for Pirelli P6000s. These have improved the handling, especially in wet conditions.* "

Glad to see an unsolicited testimonial for Micheldever Tyres (01962 774437), as I often recommend them. And I can confirm you have made a good choice. P6000s are also one of the quietest and longest-lasting of the current crop of new tyres. There may be a slight penalty, though. Both a Volvo S40 and a BMW 528iSE fitted with P6000s seemed to me to lack the amount of steering feel I expected.

Tyre life

" *Is there a nominal life for a tyre, from new, in miles?* "

No. It depends on make and type of tyre; whether the vehicle is front-wheel-drive, rear-wheel-drive or four-wheel-drive, manual or automatic; whether the tyre is fitted on the front or back; and the performance and suspension set-up of the vehicle. I've got no more than 300 miles from a pair of re-moulds on the front of a Minivan with racing shock absorbers – and more than 40,000 miles from a pair of Pirelli P600s on the back of a front-wheel-drive VW. One reader got more than 70,000 miles from the rear tyres of his Citroen BX, another got 81,000 miles from the rears of his Toyota Carina II automatic, and Peter Williams managed an incredible 99,000 miles from one of the rears on his 200,000-mile Fiat Panda 4×4.

Treadwear ratings

" *I will soon have to buy new tyres for my 1985 BMW 525e, size 195/70 HR14. My current tyres are branded 'Corsa', with a treadwear rating of 180, and they cost £37.50 each including fitting, valving and balancing. I have seen the same size 'Roadhog' tyres advertised at £46.35 inclusive, with a treadwear rating of 320. Does this mean that the Roadhogs will last as long as the Corsas? Will there be any drawbacks?* "

I had never heard of treadwear ratings, so I asked Brian at Micheldever Tyres (01962 774437). It seems that they are a North American requirement based on a drum test. The benchmark is 100%, so if a tyre achieves 180 the test says it will last 80% longer than the benchmark. If it achieves 320, the test says it will last 220% longer. Corsa tyres apparently originate in South America and are a relatively soft compound. 'Groundhogs' (not to be confused with the Dunlop Groundhogs of the 1960s) are a Southern Tyres 'own brand' and must have a relatively hard compound. The disadvantage of a hard compound over a soft compound is usually less grip.

Remoulds

" *I would be interested in your opinion on using retread tyres. I drive around 20,000 miles a year and am forever seeing the debris of cast-off tyre treads littering the country's motorways. I have only ever fitted new tyres, long before they reached the legal limit, and have only ever suffered two punctures. But, sitting waiting for yet another set of tyres to be fitted recently, I picked up a leaflet on 'Technic' remoulds and was quite impressed.* "

Technic's remoulds are probably the best, and regularly prove themselves in racing. But the true cost of a tyre is measured in pence per mile.

The bits of tyre you see on motorways are usually (though not always) from trucks, the operators of most of which find it more economical to run on remoulds.

The cost of replacing a tyre can be as much as £10 for fitting, balancing, new valve and disposal of the old tyre *per wheel*, in addition to the cost of the tyre itself – so if a cheaper tyre does less road miles you have to add this extra cost more often. The bits of tyre you see on motorways are usually (though not always) from trucks, the operators of most of which do find it more economical to run on remoulds. In Technic's favour, I spotted a pair of its products on the rear of a clean, 97,000-mile 1988E BMW 635CSi, which then went on to make £2,000 over 'book' at a CMA 'Top Marques' car auction.

Long-life tyres

" I have been running an 'M' reg. BMW 318i since October 1994 on Dunlop SP Sport D8M2 205/60 R15 91V tyres. I have covered 68,000 reasonably quick but careful miles. The rear tyres lasted 40,000 miles and were replaced by ATS with an identical pair. But the fronts still carry 2 mm of tread over and above the tread wear marker. This seems extraordinarily good – especially bearing in mind the fact that cars with power steering often scrub off front tyre tread due to using the power to steer while the car is stationary. A friend who drives a Volvo 850 2.5 recently had to change his front tyres after just 10,000 miles and was told by the garage that this was good. They sometimes had to change Volvo 850 front tyres at 6,000 miles. "

You have done well, but I'm afraid these tyres have now been superceded by SP 200s. If your colleague's Volvo 850 is a T5, the tyre wear experiences is about right for a manual car. John Bradley, who manages the Hampshire Constabulary fleet, ordered T5 automatics rather than manuals because they will do an average of 13,000–15,000 miles on the fronts compared to an average of 8,000 for T5 manuals.

Quiet tyres

" *After 32,000 miles I need to re-tyre my 1993 Rover Sterling. The original-equipment tyres were Michelin Xs, and I have always felt that they gave a hard and noisy ride. May I have your suggestions for replacements?* "

I'd lay the blame for the ride on the suspension of your car rather than the tyres. But the 'quietest' tyres I know of which do not have serious downsides are Pirelli P6000s. However, if a car comes with fairly 'feel-free' power steering to start with, P6000s do tend to exaggerate this. For a comprehensive 'performance' tyre track test (not a longevity test), try and get a back number of *Autocar* for 5 November 1997 from Haymarket Reprints on 01235 534323. The best place I know of to get your new tyres is Micheldever Tyres, Micheldever Station (off the A303), Winchester, Hants, tel: 01962 774437.

The dreaded side-slip

" *Both my son-in-law and daughter have experienced side-slip when driving their new four-wheel-drive Isuzu Trooper in rear-wheel-drive, particularly in wet conditions. Very sensibly, they have now decided always to keep it in four-wheel-drive. I would like to know if this is a common problem and, if so, what are the best tyres to fit to alleviate the problem?* "

We had exactly the same problem with the short-wheelbase Toyota RAV 4 we tested for our story on tall car safety in November 1997. Since the RAV 4 is designed to run in full-time four-wheel-drive, Paul Ripley felt that the principle culprit had to be the tyres, which are a compromise between off-road and road tyres, and as such don't offer the ideal sidewall flexibilty and tread pattern for road use. If your son-in-law's Trooper is not used off-road, then a road-pattern tyre will help. But he still has the comparative stability problem shared by any vehicle with a high centre of gravity and should load and drive the vehicle accordingly. Think of it as a truck, not a car, and he won't go far wrong.

Vectra tyres

By a process of elimination, and with a little help from readers, I have discovered why some Vauxhall Vectras have less grip than others, and why some create more tyre noise than others. It is mostly a matter of the type of tyre fitted. The best all round for older Vectras, and the choice of the Jim Russell Motor Racing School (01332 811430) for its 2 litre Vectra 'Super Touring' driver training cars, are Pirelli P6000s, which I have recommended numerous times before for their low road noise. Some cars do lose a bit of steering feel on these tyres, but the Jim Russell Vectras (which have non-standard rear shocks) felt far better than any other Vectras I had driven before the advent of the much-improved April 1998 Vectra SRi 2 litre. This latest Vectra shares a lot of the steering and chassis improvements of the Saab 9-3 over the Saab 900 and, like the Saab, is even sharper on Michelin Pilots or Yokohamas than it is on Pirelli P6000s.

UNUSUAL CAR CLUBS*

Allegro club

" *Please could you tell me if there is an Allegro Drivers' Club? And from whom can I obtain a handbook for my recently-acquired 1976 Allegro 1300?* "

Allegro Club International, 20 Stoneleigh Crescent, Stoneleigh, Epsom, Surrey KT19 0RP. (A full list of owners' clubs is included in every issue of *Practical Classics* magazine.) Haynes do an Allegro manual, code H0164, from Mill House Books on 01205 270377 or DPL on 01442 877794.

Nova cabrio

" *My daughter has owned a Nova Cabriolet for some years and we have come to believe it is one of only a small number produced by Vauxhall. Is it possible to ascertain production figures? If the number is very small, would this have a significant effect on the resale value of the car? Where would be best to advertise it? And where can we get a replacement hood?* "

The car was probably one of 200 Novas modified by Hutchinsons Designs Ltd, now at 92 Cromwell Lane, Tile Hill, Coventry CV4 8AS, tel: 01203 470354, which can still supply parts for these and

---

* Other car clubs listed under 'Classics and Nostalgia'.

for the Hammond and Theidie Cavalier Mk II convertible. Irmscher also did a Nova cabrio. Crayford did the same to other Vauxhall models, such as the Chevette, while a Mk I Cavalier convertible was marketed as the Cavalier Centaur. The Owners' Club is The Vauxhall Convertible Car Club, c/o Phil Homer, 43 The Ridgeway, St Albans, Herts AL4 9NR, tel: 01727 868405. If the club can't help over the hood, try Soft Tops of Bartons Green, Barras Green, Coventry CV2 4PA, tel: 01203 455477, or Hoods Galore on 0181 665 6355. On the open market, the car is worth between £1,000 in good condition and £1,750 if excellent, but the club feels it could be worth up to double that to a member. If it's an Irmscher, add £1,000 to these figures.

Capricious?

" For the past eight years we have made light use of a 1983 four-speed Ford Capri 1600 LS which we have kept as a 'reserve car' and which has now done all of 70,000 miles. I have read somewhere that cars of this vintage are becoming more valuable, yet asking prices in the local press definitely don't seem to confirm this. Is there any specialist publication where Capri fans regularly look? Are there any Capri clubs? "

Quentin Willson gave the Capri a nice boost on his unmissable TV programme 'The Car's The Star' of 27 October 1997. Though I'm a fan of RS3100s and 2.8is, I'm afraid 'cooking' 1.6 and 2.0 litre Capri hatchbacks don't press the same buttons. Enthusiasts differ, of course, and there are at least eight Capri clubs, all with their own club magazines or newsletters. Those I have the phone numbers for are: Capri Club International (01527 502066); Capri II Register (01707 336343); Capri Enthusiasts' Register

(0161 280 6177); Capri Collection (0976 375905); Southern Capri Club (0181 367 0310).

Wedges and Crabs

" I have a 1976 Princess 1.8HL. This car was launched well before its time and its lines put many modern cars to shame. It's in tip top condition but has done more than 150,000 miles, and I would like to know where to obtain a new engine and gearbox. Rover can't help. "

You need to consult (and join) the Landcrab Owners' Club International, c/o Bill Fraser, PO Box 218, Cardiff CF3 9HZ. Sadly, 'The Wedge Club' (a dedicated club for Princess-shape cars) is dead. May it rust in peace.

MG spares and clubs

" On a recent holiday in Honolulu I met a lady resident who owns a 1954 MG TF. On her last short visit to the UK she unsuccessfully attempted to purchase some spare parts, but I regret to say she did not find the Rover agents in Central London very helpful and returned home empty-handed. Can you please advise of possible sources of spares for this vehicle and also any addresses of MG owners' clubs which may be useful to her in the future? "

I'd be interested to know what reaction you'd get if you walked into a Chevrolet dealer's in downtown Honolulu and asked for a tail light for a 1954 Corvette. The best parts specialist is Naylor Bros MG Parts Ltd, Regent House, Dockfield Road, Shipley, West Yorkshire BD17 7SF, tel: 01274 594071, fax: 01274 531149. The model-specific club for 'T' Types is the MG Octagon Car Club, c/o Harry Crutchley, No. 19 Hollins Business Centre, Rowley Street, Stafford ST16 2RH, tel: 01785 251015. Your friend can also contact both main MG clubs via the Internet. MG Car Club Ltd, Kimber House, PO Box 251, Abingdon, Oxon OX14 1FF, tel: 01235 555552, fax: 01235 533755, web-site: http://www.mgcars.org.uk; MG Owners' Club, Octagon House, Swavesey, Cambs CB4 5QZ, tel: 01954 231125, fax: 01954 232106, web-site: http://www.mgownersclub.co.uk.

XR3i cabrio

" *I will shortly be selling my 1987E Ford Escort XR3i cabriolet. It was purchased new, has done just 32,000 miles, and is in excellent condition. It has been regularly serviced and I have the full history. It has only ever been driven by me and, on a few occasions, by my husband. I would be grateful if you could tell me the best source of finding out how much I should ask.* "

The XR Owners Club, which has 3,500 members. Speak to Les Gent on 01509 881015.

'Splitty' and witty

" *On a few occasions in the past you have mentioned VW 'Type 2' split-window Transporters, affectionately known as 'Splitties'. There is, in fact, a club dedicated specifically to 'Splitties': The Split Screen Van Club, c/o The Homestead, Valebridge Road, Burgess Hill, Sussex RH15 0RT, tel: 01444 241407, fax: 01444 246899, email: mikemundy@aol.com. Good, original, unrestored Splitty campers are now fetching £10,000–£12,000, and our magazine,* Split Screen Scene, *provides a useful means of selling them.* "

This is a great club magazine, full of fun as well as very useful technical help ('Splitty nitty gritty'), events, and, of course, the for-sale section headed 'Splits and pieces'. Anyone with a Splitty or thinking of buying one should join straight away.

Bubble clubs

" *I want to purchase a 'bubble car' or similar, for example a BMW Isetta or a Heinkel, and I don't know the best way to find one. Also, if I do find one, can anyone help with spares and maintenance?* "

Readers seeking something small and imperfectly formed should contact Alan's Unusual Automobiles, 56 Lechlade Road, Faringdon, Oxon SN7 8AQ, tel: 01367 240125. Clubs (your best bet for spares and maintenance tips) are: Isetta Owners' Club of GB, c/o Mick and Kay West, 137 Prebendal Avenue, Aylesbury, Bucks HP21 8LD; Heinkel Trojan Owners' Club, c/o Peter Jones, 37 Brinklow Close, Matchborough West, Redditch, Worcs B98 0HB; Messerschmitt Owners' Club, c/o E. Hallam, The Birches, Ashmores Lane, Rusper, West Sussex RH12 4PS; Messerschmitt Enthusiasts' Club, c/o Graham

Taylor, 5 The Green, Highworth, Swindon, Wilts, tel: 01793 764770; and the Register of Unusual Microcars, c/o Jean Hammond, School House Farm, Hawenbury, North Staplehurst, Kent TN12 0EB, tel: 01580 891377.

Definitely not the yacht club

" My 1978 Morris Marina 1800 has failed its MOT for the sole reason that the rear offside light unit lens is broken. Please can you direct me to the Marina Club which should be able to supply this type of spare part? "

Such is the enthusiasm for these fine examples of 1970s British motor engineering that there is not merely one club, but three: Morris Marina Owners' Club, PO Box 84, Stourbridge, W. Midlands DY8 1LW, tel: 01902 326229; Marina/Ital Drivers' Club, c/o John Lawson, 12 Nithsdale Road, Liverpool LS15 5AX; and Morris Marina Enthusiasts' Club, c/o A. Cotton. 1 Police House, St Martin's Road, Gobowen, Oswestry, Shrops SY11 3NN. Best of luck.

Toyota 1000?

" I am a student at Portsmouth University and drive a cream 'S' registered Toyota 1000 saloon. I have had it for two years and the mileage is now 60,000. I have never had any problems with it and it amazes me that a car so old can be so reliable. The few other owners I have spoken to tell me that their Toyota 1000s passed 90,000 miles with no problems. Toyota garages often don't know the model, and parts are becoming increasingly scarce. I think I got the last exhaust system in the country. Are there any parts I should buy now in case the spares totally disappear? And is there a club catering for this car? "

According to an ancient 'Parker's Guide', Toyota

1000s were imported from January 1975 to July 1978, when they were succeeded by the Starlet. If I was you I'd try to get my hands on a clutch – and a clutch cable if the clutch is cable operated. Other parts, such as brake discs, etc., may be interchangeable with those of the Starlet. But you'll get the best advice from Billy Wells of the Toyota Enthusiasts' Club, 28 Park Road, Feltham, Middx TW13 6PW, tel: 0181 898 0740.

Armstrong Siddeley

" *In the thirties, my father ran an Armstrong Siddeley saloon with a small fanlight in the roof. Over the years, however, whenever vintage cars were talked about, no mention has been made of these cars. Are there any examples still in existence?* "

Plenty. There is even an Armstrong Siddeley Owners' Club, c/o Peter Sheppard, 57 Berberry Close, Bournville, Birmingham B30 1TB, tel: 0121 459 0742. The name is the result of Armstrong Whitworth acquiring Siddeley-Deasy in 1919 – though in 1926 J.D. Siddeley regained total control of the company.

Living the life of Riley

" *The most desirable car I ever saw was a brand-new Riley Kestrel 'Big Four' being delivered to Riley agent Tom Cox in Cambridge in 1938. The Kestrel was the last of Victor Riley's designs, and this one was finished in gleaming black with 16in. wire wheels. Tom Cox did sell me a secondhand 1933 Riley 9 Monaco. I duly joined the Riley Motor Club and took part in a 24-Hour Trial which ended in Southport. Soon after, I went abroad, and then came the war which blew our lives apart, so it was only some years later that I discovered I had been awarded a solid silver napkin ring, which I still have and which is engraved 'Riley 24 1938'. If the club's records still exist I should be interested to know how I came by the award, which was received at my family home unaccompanied by an explanation.* **"**

The Riley Motor Club still exists, c/o J.S. Hall, 'Treelands', 127 Penn Road, Wolverhampton WV3 0DU, tel: 01902 773197. The Riley Register may also be able to help, c/o J. Clarke, 56 Cheltenham Road, Bishops Cleeve, Cheltenham, Glos GL52 4LY, tel: 01242 673598. I agree, the Kestrel was a lovely-looking car. In the early 1980s, my neighbour at the time and some of his mates drove an ivory Kestrel-bodied RME 2.5 to Egypt and back.

British Salmson

" *You have featured letters about French-built 1920s Salmsons several times in the past, but I thought you might be interested in a 1937/38 British Salmson, owned by Keith Clayton in Brixham, Devon, from before the war to just after. After I helped him recommission it, I drove the car quite a lot during 1946. From memory it was very nice to drive and, though performance was not startling, it was very comfortable. I wonder if it survived?* **"**

There is a club which, given a bit more detail, may be able to tell you. It is The British Salmson Owners' Club, c/o John Maddison, 86 The Broadway North, Walsall, West Midlands WS1 2QF, tel: 01922 29677.

Classic camper

" *We have relatives in Australia who have recently acquired a Chrysler Commer Camper Van, 1,500 cc, chassis number PBCM1590H, engine number 42204490, type PBCM1500VHDL. They would like to know its year of manufacture and obtain a workshop manual for it. The camper* *body was built by the Western Motor Caravan Company, Box Road, Bath, Somerset. The vehicle is on the road and in use, but needs work to restore it to first-class condition. Please can you point us in the direction of a suitable club or organisation which can help us to fill in the gaps in the van's history?* "

> Your best source of help is likely to be The Classic Camper Club, which you may need to join. Contact Steve Cooper, 40 Audley Drive, Kidderminster, Worcs DY11 5NE, tel: 01562 752432. The fact that it's a 1,500 cc rather than a 1,725 cc suggests it dates from the mid-1960s.

Datsun 260

" *My grandmother has asked me to sell her 1981W Datsun 260 automatic saloon. This immaculate vehicle has covered only 26,000 miles from new, has a full documented service history, twelve months MOT, and has been garaged all its life. My local Nissan dealer says it is worth only £500–£600, but I am sure there must be someone who would appreciate this car rather than it being sold as an 'old banger'. Is there an old Datsun/Nissan specialist?* "

> Your first port of call should be the Datsun Owners' Club, c/o 'Gullege', Imberhorne Lane, East Grinstead, West Sussex RH19 1TX, tel: 01342 321000.

Gordon Keeble

" *I was interested to see Giles Chapman's item about the Gordon Keeble Car in your 'Mystery Motors' section, particularly since my own name is Keeble. Where can I obtain further information about this car?* "

> The Gordon Keeble Owners' Club, c/o Ann Knott, Westminster Road, Brackley, Northants

NN13 5EB, tel: 01280 702311 (day), 01280 701009 (evening).

A most original Austin

" *I own a 1937 Austin 7 Ruby 'Sunshine' saloon which I bought at a Classic Car Auction and which at the time was described as 'the most original Austin 7 Ruby extant'. Its history is well documented, starting with a newspaper cutting showing it being handed over to its first owner, Sid A. Shoesmith of Manor Grove, Richmond on 1 October 1936. It then passed into the hands of Geo. H. Pitchers of Shepperton, Middlesex in June 1958. The car was subsequently sold to John Debens, who was one of the senior civil engineers to plan all of the early motorways in the UK, and he still never fails to send his car a Christmas card each year. The original tool kit is still with the car, together with a catalogue showing all the 1936 Austin models produced at Longbridge. I also have the buff registration book, the 'Handbook of the Austin 7 – price one shilling' and also the 'List of Spare Parts', first published in August 1936 and reprinted in November of the same year. The radiator muff, still in its original paper wrapping, also came with the car.* "

You must, of course, be in the owners' club, which will be very interested in your car and its detailed history. But in any case I'll use this as an opportunity to give the club address, which is: Pre-War Austin 7 Club Ltd, c/o J. Tantum, 90 Dovedale Avenue, Long Eaton, Notts NG10 3HU, tel: 0115 972 7626, email: WILCOX@seven.netkonect.co.uk. (The club for later Sevens is the Austin Big 7 Register, c/o R. Taylor, 101 Derby Road, Chellaston, Derbyshire DE73 1SB, tel: 01332 700629.)

INDEX

OTHER TITLES OF INTEREST FROM
ROBINSON and THE DAILY TELEGRAPH

Weekend Wisdom   Compiled by Eric Bailey   £6.99 [ ]
A real treasure trove of advice, tips and timesavers for problems and jobs around
the home, tried and tested by readers of the Telegraph Weekend section.

Arthritis: The complete guide to relief using methods that really work   Dava Sobel
& Arthur C. Klein   £9.99 [ ]
Two best-selling books in one volume, giving details of the treatments that have
helped most people, and illustrated, effective exercise plans. 'A truly excellent
book' Dr James Le Fanu

IBS: A complete guide to relief from Irritable Bowel Syndrome   Christine P. Dancey
& Susan Backhouse   £7.99 [ ]
Includes information on medical tests, physical and emotional problems, re-
gaining quality of life, diet, complementary treatments, helpful addresses and
much more.

Robinson Books are available from all good bookstores, or direct from the pub-
lishers – just tick the title you want and fill in the form below.

Robinson Publishing Ltd, PO Box 11, Falmouth, Cornwall TR10 9EN
Tel: +44(0) 1326 374900; Fax: +44(0) 1326 374888
Email: books@Barni.avel.co.uk

UK/BFPO customers please allow £1.00 for p&p for the first book, plus 50p for
the second, plus 30p for each additional book up to a maximum charge of £3.00.
Overseas customers (inc Ireland) please allow £2.00 for the first book, plus £1.00
for the second, plus 50p for each additional book.

Please send me the titles ticked above.

NAME (Block letters) ....
ADDRESS ....
.... POSTCODE ....

I enclose a cheque/PO (payable to Robinson Publishing Ltd) for ....
I wish to pay by Switch/Credit card
.... Card Expiry Date ....